Sampling and Statistics Handbook for Research

Sampling and Statistics Handbook for Research

CHESTER H. McCALL, JR.

The Iowa State University Press • **A M E S**

© 1982 The Iowa State University Press. All rights reserved

Printed by The Iowa State University Press, Ames, Iowa 50010

No part of this book may be reproduced in any form, by photostat, microfilm, xerography, or any other means, or incorporated into any information retrieval system, electronic or mechanical, without the written permission of the copyright owner.

First edition, 1982

Library of Congress Cataloging in Publication Data

McCall, Chester H., Jr. (Chester Hayden), 1927–
   Sampling and statistics handbook for research.

   Includes index.
   1. Statistics. 2. Sampling (Statistics) I. Title.
QA276.12.M398   001.4′22   82–15290
ISBN 0–8138–1628–9   AACR2

CONTENTS

Foreword			ix
Preface			xi
Part I	**Introduction, Overview and Concepts**		1
1	Introduction		3
2	**Overview of the Sampling Process**		5
	2.1	The Analysis Unit: Variables and Attributes	5
	2.2	The Population and the Sample	5
	2.3	Parameters and Statistics	6
	2.4	Random and Systematic Sampling	7
	2.5	Stratified and Cluster Sampling	7
	2.6	The Development of Sampling	8
	2.7	The Survey vs. the Experiment	10
3	**Some Basic Data Concepts**		12
	3.1	Scales of Measurement	12
	3.2	Visual Data Presentation	15
Part II	**Descriptive Measures**		25
4	**Measures of Central Tendency**		27
	4.1	The Arithmetic Mean	27
	4.2	The Median	28
	4.3	The Mode	31
	4.4	Further Examples	31
	4.5	Summary	34
5	**Measures of Variation**		35
	5.1	The Range	36
	5.2	Interquartile Range	36
	5.3	Average Deviation	40
	5.4	Standard Deviation	43
	5.5	Further Examples	46
	5.6	Summary	49

6	**Positional Measures**	50
	6.1 Percentiles	50
	6.2 Proportions or Percentages	52
	6.3 Standard Scores	54
7	**Measures of Association**	58
	7.1 Correlation and Regression: The Distinction	58
	7.2 The Linear Case—Two Variables	60
	7.3 The Nonlinear Case—Two Variables	72
	7.4 Some Cautions	78
	7.5 Multiple Variable Relationships	86
	7.6 Rank Order Correlation	88
	7.7 Miscellaneous Measures of Association	92
	7.8 Summary	93
Part III	**Inferential Statistics**	95
8	**Sampling Concepts and Inference**	97
	8.1 Random and Systematic Sampling	97
	8.2 Samples and Populations—Statistics and Parameters	100
	8.3 The Normal Probability Distribution	101
	8.4 Sampling Variation	111
	8.5 Degrees of Freedom	121
9	**Estimation**	123
	9.1 Confidence Intervals	124
	9.2 Finding Confidence Intervals	128
10	**Hypothesis Testing**	141
	10.1 Research Hypotheses vs. Statistical Hypotheses	141
	10.2 Typical Statistical Hypotheses	143
	10.3 Steps in Testing Statistical Hypotheses	144
	10.4 Testing Specific Statistical Hypotheses	146
11	**Multivariate and Nonparametric Techniques**	179
	11.1 Multivariate Techniques	179
	11.2 Nonparametric Techniques	182
Part IV	**Sample Size and Sampling Plans**	185
12	**Sample Size Determination**	187
	12.1 Some Factors Relating to Sample Size	187
	12.2 Estimating Sample Size for Specific Sample Statistics	191
	12.3 Adjusting the Preliminary Sample Size	204

13	**Stratified Sampling Plans**	209
	13.1 Patterns for Allocation of Sample to Strata	209
	13.2 Single Important Variable Approach to Stratification	217
	13.3 "Multi-Important Variable" Approach	219
	13.4 Planning the Survey That Employs a Stratified Simple Random Sample Design	219
	13.5 Total Sample Size and Stratum Allocation	221
	13.6 Estimating Population Parameters and Their Standard Errors	227
	13.7 Formulas for Stratified Simple Random Sampling–Proportional Allocation	229
	13.8 Formulas for Stratified Simple Random Sampling–Disproportional Allocation	233
14	**Cluster Sampling Plans**	235
	14.1 When Cluster Sampling is Appropriate	235
	14.2 Steps in Cluster Random Sampling	237
	14.3 Determining Sample Size	238
	14.4 Estimating Population Parameters and Their Standard Errors	241
	14.5 Definition of Symbols to be Used	243
	14.6 Formulas for a Single-Stage Cluster Sample, with Clusters Varying in Size and Selected with Equal Probability	246
	14.7 Formulas for a Two-Stage Cluster Sample, with Clusters Varying in Size, the First Stage Selected with Equal Probability, and a Constant Second-Stage Sampling Fraction (Self-Weighting)	248
	14.8 Summary	251
15	**Combination Sampling Plans**	253
	15.1 Stratified One-Stage Cluster	253
	15.2 Stratified, Disproportionate Two-Stage Cluster with Equal Sampling Rates in Second Stage	255
	15.3 Stratified, Disproportionate Two-Stage Cluster Sample with Unequal Sampling Rate in Second Stage	255
	15.4 Stratified Three-Stage Cluster	259
	15.5 Comments on Parameter Estimates and Their Standard Errors	261
	15.6 Definitions of Symbols to be Used	261
	15.7 Formulas for Stratified One-Stage Cluster Sample with Clusters Varying in Size and Drawn Disproportionately from Strata	265
	15.8 Formulas for Disproportionate, Stratified Two-Stage Cluster-Random Sample with Clusters Varying in Size and Drawn with Equal Probabilities from Strata in the First Stage, Clusters Sampled at a Constant Self-Weighting Rate within each Stratum in the Second Stage	269
	15.9 Summary	273

APPENDIXES

A	Glossary	275
B	References	279
C	Arithmetic Operations	282
D	Elementary Probability	286
E	Index to Descriptive Formulas	291
F	Appropriate Statistical Methodologies	298
G	Computerized Statistical Programs	301
H	Statistical Tables	303

Index 333

FOREWORD

This HANDBOOK has been designed for researchers who are responsible for studying and solving real world problems. Although the emphasis is on the field of education, its principles have universal applicability. Structured with the consumer in mind, the HANDBOOK provides illustrations which serve as models and ways of thinking about research in a statistically sound framework.

Dr. McCall uses his over twenty-five years of teaching, problem solving and consulting experience in the creation of the HANDBOOK, and the product is a practical research tool. His translation of statistical concepts into comprehensive units for use by the research practitioner is long overdue. In brief, Dr. McCall has tried and succeeded in his effort to demystify the worlds of statistics and educational research. His technical expertise and humanitarian sensitivity as a teacher are manifested in the style, approach and selection of practical illustrations.

During my tenure as Director of Research at the National Education Association it was my pleasure working with Dr. McCall and providing a critique during the development of the HANDBOOK.

Frank W. Kovacs, Ph.D.

PREFACE

This HANDBOOK is intended to serve both as an introduction to basic statistical concepts for research and as a reference document for the researcher. With minor exceptions (primarily in using the formulas in the last three chapters) little is required in the way of algebraic knowledge to use this HANDBOOK.

While the emphasis in this HANDBOOK is on practical problems encountered in educational research, its approach and logic are intended to be equally applicable in other fields.

In 1960, Sam M. Lambert, then Director of the NEA Research Division, established an experimental program called the Sampling Project, the purpose of which was to improve the precision and speed in collecting and reporting on data from nationwide surveys in the field of education. This project was a remarkable success, resulting in sample sizes being reduced by as much as 75%, with response rates on these surveys jumping from the 40% to 50% range to better than 80% for virtually all NEA-supported surveys.

During the early days of this Sampling Project (the objectives of which were revived under the former Director of NEA Research, Dr. Frank Kovacs) descriptive and inferential procedures were catalogued and a preliminary edition, entitled SAMPLING AND STATISTICS HANDBOOK FOR SURVEYS IN EDUCATION, was released in 1965. The successful completion of this HANDBOOK was guided by Dr. Glen Robinson, then Assistant Director of the Research Division. Significant contributions to the project were made by Belinda Fischer Drass, Richard E. Scott, Simeon P. Taylor, III, and Gaye Baber Becker, as well as numerous others providing the vital editorial and production functions.

This HANDBOOK borrows heavily on materials in Chapters 13–15 as well as intermittent materials from other chapters in the 1965 HANDBOOK.

I am personally indebted for critical support to several members of the NEA Research Staff: to Suzanne Gardner for her patient review of the entire manuscript (her suggestions and corrections have materially improved this final document); to Nancy Greenberg for her support in providing an important editorial function as the initial drafts were developed; to Anne Constant who picked up the responsibilities for seeing that the HANDBOOK became a reality; and, finally, to Dr. Frank Kovacs, whose patient prodding and probing over the past two years resulted in this HANDBOOK.

Although I am deeply indebted to the individuals just named, I must accept the responsibility for any shortcomings of this HANDBOOK and invite readers to send their comments, suggestions, or noted deficiencies to me so appropriate changes can be made before subsequent editions are released.

Chester H. McCall, Jr.

I

Introduction, Overview and Concepts

This Part of the HANDBOOK provides an introduction into the style and approach employed throughout the HANDBOOK.

The important ideas of an analysis unit, a population and a sample are reviewed, along with major aspects of the sampling process itself.

And, finally, the concept of scales of measurement and data presentation are discussed.

This Part sets the framework for the somewhat classical approach to applied statistics in Parts II and III.

1

INTRODUCTION

Statistical techniques in general and sampling theory in particular are essential tools to the person performing research in the field of education. This HANDBOOK is designed to provide the researcher with sufficient information to know when and how to use the methodology presented here and, perhaps even more important, when to seek professional assistance.

Modern sampling techniques make possible many studies that could not be done on a comprehensive or census basis. Moreover, sample studies often make data available more quickly, more economically, and sometimes more accurately than do comprehensive studies.

However, if sampling is improperly done and data are carelessly interpreted, the results can be misleading. Stephan & McCarthy (1958, p. 37)[1] state the problem well:

> Samples are like medicine. They can be harmful when they are taken carelessly or without adequate knowledge of their effects. We may use their results with confidence if the applications are made with due restraint. It is foolish to avoid or discard them because someone else has misused them and suffered the predictable consequences of his folly. Every good sample should have a proper label with instructions about its use. This is why many surveys now include rather full descriptions of the methods that were used and the limitations of the results.

It is not expected that this HANDBOOK will be the panacea to all educational researchers' problems. Rather, it is hoped that the HANDBOOK will serve as a useful tool to the researcher seeking a better understanding of statistical methodology as it might be applied to resolve specific problems. Equally important is the development of an ability to know which statistical methods are most appropriate for given situations as well as how to interpret the results in a practical, nonconfusing manner. The book is designed as a ready reference for those concerned with the use of sampling procedures in surveying the opinions, attitudes, and characteristics of various education populations, such as students, teachers, principals, and superintendents, or in collecting factual data pertaining to education.

The balance of Part I provides in Chapter 2 an overview of the sampling process, with particular emphasis on setting the stage for the conceptual understanding of what sampling and inference are all about. Variables or attributes of interest are introduced in terms of populations and samples. The survey sampling approach (as opposed to experimental design) is reviewed. Chapter 3 introduces basic data concepts, including

---

[1] Consult Appendix B for complete reference citations.

an understanding of types of measurement scales. Since much data often need to be assembled and condensed for papers or briefings, selected options for data presentation are developed.

Part II gives a fairly classical presentation of descriptive statistics and discusses measures of central tendency (Chapter 4), measures of variation or dispersion (Chapter 5), positional measures (Chapter 6), and measures of association, such as correlation and regression (Chapter 7). While computational procedures must be introduced, emphasis will be on the interpretation of these measures as they relate to the research objective(s). All formulas in this HANDBOOK are designed for use with raw data only. It is assumed that the reader has access to a small calculator.

Armed with the ability to calculate descriptive measures from a set of basic data, the reader is next exposed to inferential statistics in Part III. Here sampling concepts and a broad overview of estimation and hypothesis testing are introduced (Chapter 8). Estimation procedures (from sample to population) are developed for the arithmetic mean, a total or aggregate, a standard deviation, a proportion (or percentage), and linear regression (Chapter 9). Hypothesis testing techniques are reviewed for seven specific situations, and considerable emphasis is given to the use of chi-square for goodness of fit and analysis of contingency tables (Chapter 10). Although procedures to perform the necessary arithmetic manipulations in multivariate analysis are not described, attention is directed to a discussion of what these techniques are and what they do for the educational researcher. Some cautions in applying available techniques are noted also in Chapter 11.

Part IV pulls together available concepts in sample-size determination and sample selection. A frequent question posed before conducting a survey is, How large a sample do I need? Chapter 12 describes a variety of approaches to this issue. Because so many options are available for designing sampling plans, considerable detail is available on stratified sampling (Chapter 13), cluster sampling (Chapter 14), and combination sampling (Chapter 15).

Extensive appendixes accompany this HANDBOOK. Because statistical terminology varies from text to text, a glossary of terms appears in Appendix A. Appendix B presents complete reference citations as well as references for further reading. Those who need a refresher in the mathematical manipulations associated with calculating some of the summary measures should consult Appendix C.

Although it is not necessary for understanding the material in the main body of this HANDBOOK, a discussion of elementary probability is given in Appendix D for the curious researcher. A descriptive index to the formulas in this HANDBOOK appears in Appendix E. This index is designed to assist the researcher in quickly locating the statistical formula or formulas that apply to a given research problem.

Adapted from an excellent document prepared at the University of Michigan (Andrews & others, 1976), Appendix F serves as a basis for determining what appropriate statistical technique(s) applies to a specific research situation. Appendix G briefly discusses available computerized statistical packages (programs). Appendix H includes the few statistical tables necessary to do the work illustrated in this HANDBOOK. More extensive tables can be found in U.S. Department of Commerce (1966).

2

OVERVIEW OF THE SAMPLING PROCESS

2.1 THE ANALYSIS UNIT: VARIABLES AND ATTRIBUTES

Fundamental to understanding the application of statistical methods is the basic concept of the analysis unit (AU), sometimes referred to as the individual, unit, or basic element. An *analysis unit* is that entity or object about which information is sought. Depending upon the research issue, the AU might be a school system, a senior high school, an individual teacher, or an elementary school student. The AU must be clearly defined if the research process is to be meaningful.

Associated with each AU will be a set of characteristics of interest. Characteristics serve to differentiate among AU's. For example, if the AU is the public school teacher, possible characteristics of interest might be age, sex, salary, years of tenure with the given school system, or level of academic training. Of these characteristics, age, salary, and years of tenure with the given school district are all referred to as *variables*. Sex and level of academic training are referred to as *attributes*. Variables and attributes will be discussed in greater detail in the next chapter. Clearly, *at any point in time, there are associated with each AU possible variables and attributes of interest in a specific research effort.*

2.2 THE POPULATION AND THE SAMPLE

The *population*, or *universe*, is the entire set of AU's of interest in the research. For one study the population might be all public school teachers in the United States. For another study it might be only public school teachers who are members of a specific professional organization. It is important, if not essential, for the population of interest to be clearly defined before a research project is initiated. Too frequently, the population is poorly defined, resulting in an inability to achieve research objectives.

A *sample* is simply part of a population. It is important to stress that the word *sample* in no way connotes "goodness." How the sample is selected is paramount to any successful research effort.

Important considerations when examining a population of interest are its size and the ability of the researcher to identify or locate each and every member of that population. Sometimes lists of population AU's are available, such as a list of teachers in a given school. At other times, and this is quite frequently encountered in research, lists are unavailable. If, for example, a list of all eligible voters in a given congressional district is unavailable, sampling becomes a more complex issue. Such situations are discussed in greater detail later.

Sampling is intended to provide information about the population from which *the sample has been selected in such a way that inferences about the total population can be made.* An inference, in this sense, is the process of generalizing to the population from the sample with the inclusion of some statement as to the "goodness" of the generalization. For example, suppose a sample has been "appropriately" drawn of teachers within a given school district, and it is found that 54% of the teachers in the sample teach in elementary schools. The inference would be to make some statement about all teachers in the given school district. Such inferences are the subject of Part III of this HANDBOOK.

The usefulness of sampling lies not only in reducing the amount of work to be done and the cost of doing it, but often in increasing the accuracy of the data collected and processed. Since errors are inherent in all data collection and tabulating procedures, collecting data from a smaller number of individuals enables the researcher to pay more attention to the accurate processing of the data collected. Moreover, the question of possible nonresponse bias is an ever-present problem in every survey, be it a complete census or a sample. Sampling can give the researcher greater assurance of the accuracy of the data, since it is often easier to obtain a higher proportion of response from a small sample than it is from the total population.

2.3 PARAMETERS AND STATISTICS

Two frequently used terms in the field of statistics are parameter[1] and statistic. A *parameter* is the constant numerical value of any summary measure in a population that is fixed at any instant of time. Examples of summary measures are arithmetic means, medians, modes, average deviations, proportions, and standard deviations. Discussions of those most widely used appear in Parts II, III, and IV. To illustrate, the arithmetic mean salary of all teachers in a given school system for a specific year in a given state is a parameter. Although it may be impossible to determine the value of this or any other parameter, the procedures followed in this HANDBOOK assume that such parameters do exist. Other parameters associated with this same group of AU's might be average age or the percentage favoring a given initiative in a local election.

A *statistic* is the numerical value of any summary measure that is computed from a sample. For example, the arithmetic mean salary of some of the teachers in a given school district is referred to as a statistic.

To illustrate the distinction between parameter and statistic, consider the population of registered voters in a given district. An elected official desires to know the proportion of registered voters who would be favorably influenced on an issue on the ballot if Organization A took a position on this same issue. (Note: This is different from the population of those who actually vote in a given election.) At any fixed moment of time, this proportion for all registered voters is a parameter. In a mail survey of a sample of 200 of these registered voters, the proportion in this sample also indicating they would be favorably influenced by a position taken by Organization A is the sample statistic and is expected to vary from sample to sample.

---

[1]The term *parameter* has a completely different meaning to the statistician than it does to the engineer.

As stated previously, the primary purpose in selecting a sample is to make some inference, based upon sample statistics, about population parameters.

2.4 RANDOM AND SYSTEMATIC SAMPLING

Basic to making inferences from a sample is the assumption that the sample has been drawn randomly from the population of interest. *Simple* or *unrestricted random sampling* is selecting AU's from the population in such a way that each AU has a known probability of being selected. Usually, these probabilities are taken as being equal. In true random sampling, the selection of one AU is in no way tied to or related to the selection of any other AU. Procedures for selecting random samples using the tables in Appendix H are described in Chapter 8.

Obtaining pure random samples from large populations, particularly in sample survey work, is frequently most difficult. *Systematic sampling* is considered in many situations as a reasonable alternative. Systematic sampling is a procedure whereby the individual AU's are taken at fixed intervals—say, every twentieth—from a listing of the population (referred to as the *sampling frame*). An example might be the selection of every tenth teacher from a school system's alphabetical listing of teachers. Such a procedure requires that the first teacher be selected randomly from among the first ten teachers in the listing. If this were teacher number nine, then the sample would also consist of teachers 19, 29, 39, and so forth. Systematic sampling, although possessing different properties from random sampling, is considered by many researchers to be a good approximation, as long as the ordering of the AU's within the sampling frame is in no way related to any of the characteristics to be examined during the research.

2.5 STRATIFIED AND CLUSTER SAMPLING

Frequently, for various reasons the AU's cannot be sampled on a totally random basis since a sampling frame for the entire population may not exist. For example, a large university complex may not maintain one single listing of all faculty but only keep separate listings for each campus. In this case, a natural *stratification* of the AU's (the faculty members) is by campus listing. Sampling can now be accomplished within each campus, and inferences can be made to both individual campuses and the university system as a whole.

In attempting to select a sample of classroom teachers, no simple random sampling is feasible, since no listing exists for all such teachers within the United States. However, teachers can be reached by first *stratifying* school systems by enrollment. Within each stratum, school districts can be considered as a *cluster* of teachers. So, once having selected school districts at random within the various strata, either all teachers within the district or a sample of teachers within the districts can be selected. Situations in which stratified and cluster sampling are appropriate are considered in greater detail in Part IV of this HANDBOOK.

2.6 THE DEVELOPMENT OF SAMPLING

As has been indicated, the objective of sampling is to select part of a population of interest and to draw inferences about that population based upon the sample. Analytic techniques and methods associated with sampling are relatively new (developed within the past 40 years). The development of sampling can be grouped into four rather distinct periods.

2.6.1 Straw Polls

The first attempts at surveying public opinion on a sampling basis were the early straw or trial votes conducted by newspapers to forecast elections. In 1824, straw votes were taken in political elections by newspapers in Wilmington, Delaware, and in Raleigh, North Carolina. By World War I straw polls had become widespread. Often, the purpose was twofold: (1) to estimate the opinion of the public on general social, economic, or political topics and (2) to increase newspaper circulation.

In this early period, straw polls were often conducted by persons quite innocent of the principle of scientific control. A ballot was merely printed in the newspaper, with instructions to fill it out and mail it in. The possible accidental biases are obvious to us today. The opinions of persons who did not or could not purchase a paper were not represented. Moreover, persons were free to buy as many copies of the paper as they wished and mail in an unlimited number of ballots, thus distorting the results (Parten, 1950, pp. 23-24).

2.6.2 Massive Samples

The *Literary Digest* entered the field of opinion sampling in 1916 by conducting a poll that predicted the election of President Woodrow Wilson. From then until 1936 the *Digest* poll reigned supreme because of its great success in predicting election poll outcomes, and the public held it as a monument of accuracy.

The *Digest* did not confine its surveys to political elections but also surveyed public opinion on many social and economic issues. These polls represent what may be termed the period of *massive sample* surveys. Millions of questionnaires were mailed to such persons as telephone subscribers or automobile owners. Typically, replies were received from about one-quarter of those solicited.

Things ran rather smoothly with the polls until 1936; by this time the *Digest*'s record of infallibility caused its sponsors to become overconfident about their ability to predict election outcomes. Before the 1936 presidential election, ballots were mailed to more than ten million persons listed as telephone subscribers. About 2.4 million ballots were returned. The *Digest* forecast received extraordinary publicity because it predicted the defeat of President Roosevelt and ran counter to the estimates of competing, small-scale sample polls. The election results showed that the *Digest* poll had failed miserably. Not only had it failed to predict the winning candidate, but it had missed estimating the popular vote the winning candidate would receive by about 20 percent. Shortly thereafter, both the poll and the magazine passed out of existence (Parten, 1950, pp. 24-25).

Paralleling the *Literary Digest*'s massive-sample approach to surveying public opinion in the early 1930's were the surveys conducted as work relief projects. Thousands of surveys were made during this period under the auspices of government relief agencies, such as the Civil Works Administration (CWA), the Federal Emergency Relief Administration (FERA), and the Works Progress Administration (WPA). Many of these surveys used the massive-sample approach. For example, a national health survey was made through a house-to-house canvass by WPA workers; the study covered 740,000 urban families and 36,000 rural families in 19 states (Parten, 1950, p. 18).

During the Depression years of the 1930's, numerous studies of the characteristics and needs of youth were made (Parten, 1950, p. 22). In 1933 the U.S. Department of Education undertook a massive survey of teacher personnel in the United States. Questionnaires were mailed to nearly a million teachers; about 48 percent returned their questionnaires. The results were reported in a six-volume work (U.S. Department of Interior, 1935).

2.6.3 Quota Sampling

The supremacy of small-scale quota sampling over massive, uncontrolled sampling was vividly demonstrated in the election of 1936. Although the demise of the *Literary Digest* poll sounded the death knell for the massive sampling era, it also signaled the beginning of the period of small-scale quota sampling.

The quota sample had been developed by Cherington, Roper, Gallup, and Crossley, whose sample surveys of opinion have become widely known and respected after their success in predicting the 1936 presidential election. For more than a decade thereafter, quota sampling was the dominant form of sample design (Stephan & McCarthy, 1958, p. 37).

As with other sample designs, the aim of quota sampling is to obtain a small group of individuals who represent the larger group and who have the same characteristics as the larger group. Thus, in a quota sample design, U.S. census data and other information are used to divide the population into many, mutually exclusive subgroups or strata and to estimate the proportion of the population in each of these subgroups. The subgroupings are based on such characteristics as geographic regions, age, sex, economic status, and race. The total sample is then distributed among these subgroupings in proportion to their actual or estimated size. The next step is to allocate the sample among interviewers. The usual procedure is to tell each interviewer the number of persons to be obtained in each of the subgroupings; for example, so many men and so many women, so many persons of high income and so many of low income, and so on for each of the characteristics used to control the selection. With only the requirement to fill the quota in each of the subgroupings, the interviewer is free to choose the respondents (Stephan & McCarthy, 1958, p. 37).

If all interviewers were to select their respondents in a purely random fashion within each "quota control" subgroup, quota sampling could be termed stratified random sampling. But how can one assume that all interviewers will make their selections in a completely random fashion? This lack of control in the interview phase has been recognized as a fundamental weakness of quota sampling by both the proponents and opponents of the method (Stephan & McCarthy, 1958, p. 38).

2.6.4 Probability Sampling

The limitations of the quota method became widely recognized following World War II, and many surveyors began abandoning this technique. The 1948 presidential election can be considered the end of the quota-sampling period and the beginning of the probability-sampling era. The fact that nearly all the major public opinion polls of the time erred in predicting the successful candidate demonstrated to the satisfaction of many researchers that quota sampling was not good enough (Mayer, 1970, p. 190).

In 1946, George Gallup announced that his organization would switch from quota sampling to probability or area sampling methods similar to those used by the U.S. Bureau of the Census. Unfortunately, he did not actually make a major change until 1949 (Parten, 1950, p. 31).

The modern era of nationwide probability sampling was launched by the U.S. Bureau of the Census in 1943 in its sample surveys of congested areas. The technique used, known as "area sampling," employs random and systematic methods of selection that conform to theoretical models from which deductions can be made and the long-run performance of the technique demonstrated (Parten, 1950, p. 239).

In area sampling, maps are used to divide the nation or the geographic regions to be surveyed into primary sampling areas or units; cities, for example. A random sample of these primary units is drawn. Detailed maps of the primary areas are used to draw a random selection of secondary sampling areas; for example, blocks within a city. The third stage is the selection of a random sample of dwelling units within the selected blocks. This design yields a true probability sample that is fully controlled, with the interviewer having no discretion about who is to be interviewed. A fuller description of multistage sample designs is presented in Chapter 15.

The highlights of the history of sample surveying and opinion polling illustrate the struggle of researchers to develop better techniques for achieving the goal of making inferences about the population sampled. In the early part of the century, completely uncontrolled samples called straw polls were widely used. Through stages of massive samples and quota samples, techniques evolved rather rapidly into the recent attempts to employ true probability sampling techniques.

It is important that researchers not consider the sampling designs in use today as final. Rather, today's researchers should view themselves as standing on the threshold of scientific sampling development. As Stephan and McCarthy (1958, p. 16) point out, the *applications* of sampling have stimulated most of the major advances in sampling theory, and new applications should have the same effect in the future.

2.7 THE SURVEY VS. THE EXPERIMENT

The major emphasis in this HANDBOOK is on the survey or the sample survey. In general, a survey design involves identifying the way in which AU's are to be selected from a population so that valid inferences based upon sample data can be made about important characteristics in the population. Usually, more than one characteristic associated with the AU's is of interest.

An experiment, on the other hand, involves assigning AU's in some well-defined manner, usually random, to a control and one or more experimental conditions. These conditions—say, standard teaching methods (the control) vs. several new and innovative methods (the experimental)—are then put into effect, and one or more consequent characteristics are observed (such as differences between pre- and post-tests). The results are then analyzed to assess the possible effect of the various experimental conditions on the output characteristic(s) of interest. The plan for setting up the experiment, conducting the experiment, and analyzing the results is referred to as the "experimental design." For detailed experimental designs in educational research, the reader is referred to Edwards (1968) and Winer (1962).

3

SOME BASIC DATA CONCEPTS

In Chapter 2 the analysis unit (AU) was introduced as the basic entity or individual about whom information is sought. Associated with each AU is usually a set of *characteristics* of interest. If the AU is a school district, possible characteristics might be average daily attendance (ADA), number of elementary and secondary teachers, average salary of teachers within the district, annual expenditures and revenue in dollars, and so forth.

These characteristics were further subdivided into attributes and variables. An *attribute* is a characteristic that is clearly present or clearly absent in an AU. If the AU is the public school teacher, attributes would be sex (male or female), teaching status (retired or active), association membership (NEA, AFT, or neither), or marital status (single, married, divorced, or widowed). Note that an attribute may have more than two categories into which the AU can be placed. On a survey, where the options might be "strongly support," "moderately support," "indifferent," "moderately oppose," or "strongly oppose," the responses to opinion questions would be classified as attributes.

A *variable* is any characteristic or trait that may change with the AU and with which a meaningful numerical value is associated. If the AU is the public school elementary pupil, variables associated with the individual pupil might be age, weight, height, aptitude test score, or time required to run 50 yards. Sometimes, the value of the variable is the result of a measurement (height, weight, age, time); in other cases, the value of the variable is the result of a scoring process, such as an aptitude test score where the numerical value is based upon a particular scoring or grading scheme.

3.1 SCALES OF MEASUREMENT

Attributes and variables are frequently further subdivided into four different scales of measurement: nominal, ordinal, interval, and ratio. These terms are helpful to the researcher in determining appropriate summary measures (Part II) and appropriate procedures for relating sample statistics to population parameters (Parts III and IV). The most basic level of classification of AU's is nominal, while the most refined and versatile is ratio. In addition, the two most refined, the interval and ratio scales, can also be sub-classified into two types: discrete and continuous.

3.1.1 Nominal

Nominal data involve the classification of AU's by names, numbers, or symbols into categories that are clearly mutually exclusive. For example, to distinguish among teachers by categorizing them as male or female would be a nominal classification. Other examples would be teaching level (elementary vs. secondary) and geographic region of the country (Northeast, Southeast, Central, Northwest, or Southwest). Another example might be assigning license plate numbers or letters so that the last two numbers or letters indicate in which county the individual resides. Clearly, an individual would be a resident of only one of the counties.

For an attribute to be nominal, the categories of classification must be mutually exclusive; that is, an AU can be assigned to one—and only one—of the categories (Reynolds, 1977).

3.1.2 Ordinal

Nominal data are easily distinguished from the more refined scales, which require that the categories into which the AU's fall be ordered or ranked according to some criterion. *If AU's can be ordered on a characteristic by either assigning meaningful ranks to the AU's or by tabulating them into categories that are meaningfully ranked, then the characteristic is at least ordinal in its degree of refinement.* Teachers classified by educational degree earned are a good example of tabulating individuals in ordered categories. The researcher would have no difficulty showing that a doctor's degree is a higher order of degree than a master's, which is a higher degree than a bachelor's, which is higher than no degree at all. On the other hand, one could not use the male/female classification as an ordered category, since neither maleness nor femaleness is "better" by any intrinsic criterion.

Another example of an ordinal scale would be a list showing the names of 30 students in a class ranked from high to low (1 through 30) according to the grades made on a test. The list does not show the actual grades. One would know that one person's grade was *higher* than another's, but would not be able to say *how much* higher. Therefore, the data shown on the list would be ordinal in degree of refinement because only *ranks* are shown.

Ordinal data are frequently encountered in opinion surveys. Such surveys often present a statement and ask respondents to check whether they strongly agree, agree, disagree, or strongly disagree with the statement. Since the choices presented have meaningful ranks in terms of strength of agreement, the data are ordinal (Hildebrand, Laing, & Rosenthal, 1977).

Both nominal and ordinal characteristics are considered as attributes.

3.1.3 Interval

If, in addition to possessing the properties of an ordinal characteristic, "distances" between any two values of the characteristic are of known size, the scale of measurement is defined as an *interval*. Such a characteristic must have a numerical value assigned to it. Consider a testing situation in which four individuals (A, B, C, D) are being examined. With this interval scale, the difference between scores for persons A (Score 35) and B (Score 40), is the same as the difference between the scores of persons C (Score 80) and D (Score 85).

It can also be stated that C is nine times the distance from A (80 − 35 = 45) that B is from A (40 − 35 = 5); 45 is nine times five. But, it cannot be said that C's test score indicates that C (80) is twice as good as B (40) in terms of the subject being tested. This is because the scale of measurement for this characteristic starts at an arbitrary, rather than a natural or meaningful, zero point (i.e., a zero on the test does not necessarily mean the absence of what the test is designed to measure).

A common example of a noneducational characteristic measured on an interval scale is temperature as measured in degrees Fahrenheit. The change from 40° F to 60° F is the same amount as the change from 60° F to 80° F, but 80° F is not twice as hot as 40° F. The reason for this is that the meaningful zero point for the absence of heat is not 0° F.

3.1.4 Ratio

A *ratio scale* not only possesses the properties of an interval scale, but also has a meaningful zero point. Data on teachers' salaries are an excellent example. The difference between salaries of $8,000 and $12,000 is not only the same as the difference between $12,000 and $16,000, but $16,000 is also twice as much money as $8,000. Another example of a ratio scale would be years of tenure with a school system. Fifteen years of experience is 75% of 20 years of experience. Still another example would be numbers of students (the characteristic) in an elementary classroom (the AU): 50 students is twice as many as 25. In these examples, the value of each characteristic can be related to a meaningful zero point (the absence of that characteristic).

Both interval and ratio characteristics are considered as variables.

As stated earlier in this chapter, both interval and ratio characteristics can be further subdivided into two categories according to another property associated with measurement. Variables can be classified as discrete or continuous. Characteristics measured in units that are indivisible are termed *discrete*. Characteristics measured in units that can be further divided into smaller units are referred to as *continuous*.

To illustrate, "number of students" is a discrete variable, since it is impossible to speak meaningfully about a half or a quarter of a student. Both age and years of experience are continuous variables; since, in theory, possible fractional values are unlimited. One excellent test in examining a variable is to ask, Between any two adjacent values of the characteristic (say, 15 and 16 years of teaching experience) is there at least one more? If the answer is yes and the process can be repeated indefinitely, the characteristic is a continuous variable. In practice and in this HANDBOOK, little distinction is made between discrete and continuous variables when calculating descriptive statistics and making inferences.

Some variables, such as salaries and test scores, in theory could be classified as continuous but in practice are treated as discrete (i.e., salaries may not be recorded any finer than to the nearest penny and test scores to the nearest score).

The properties of the different scales of measurement are summarized in Exhibit 3.1. An excellent discussion on the mathematical aspects of scales of measurement can be found in Siegel (1956).

EXHIBIT 3.1–PROPERTIES OF DIFFERENT SCALES OF MEASUREMENT

NOMINAL:	Names of categories; mutually exclusive categories.
ORDINAL:	Characteristics of nominal *plus* ordered categories or ranks.
INTERVAL:	Characteristics of ordinal *plus* constant interval size.
Discrete:	Indivisible basic unit of measurement.
Continuous:	Divisible basic unit of measurement.
RATIO:	Characteristics of interval *plus* meaningful zero point.
Discrete:	Indivisible basic unit of measurement.
Continuous:	Divisible basic unit of measurement.

3.2 VISUAL DATA PRESENTATION

Data are the set of characteristics associated with the AU's of interest. Data for public school teachers may consist of a single characteristic, such as salary, or a *set* of characteristics, such as salary, years of experience, highest academic degree, and opinion on a fiscal issue to appear on a ballot in an upcoming election. To this point, the researcher has been given an overview of the sampling process (with greater detail coming later) and an introduction to the scales of measurement associated with characteristics of interest. Numerical aspects of dealing with these data are the subject of the remaining chapters of this HANDBOOK. In this section, possible approaches to presenting data visually for purposes of a briefing or for a report are suggested. These few procedures are by no means exhaustive, but they should make it easier for the reader to review the data. To be covered are tabular and graphic methods.

3.2.1 Tabular Presentation Methods

Clarity in a table summarizing a set of data is essential. The reader (or listener) should not have to probe too deeply to understand what is being presented.

The variable of interest in Exhibit 3.2 is the annual contract salary for public school teachers during the school year 1975-76. Because 1,311 teachers were in the sample, the data have been grouped into eight classes or intervals, with the lowest salary interval being from $5,000 to $6,999. Clearly, from the exhibit, the interval size is $2,000.

EXHIBIT 3.2–ANNUAL CONTRACT SALARY FOR A NATIONWIDE SAMPLE OF PUBLIC SCHOOL TEACHERS FOR SCHOOL YEAR 1975-76*

Annual contract salary	Frequency f	Midpoint X	Limit L	Relative frequency p	Cumulative relative frequency Σp
(1)	(2)	(3)	(4)	(5)	(6)
			20,999.5		1.001
(1) 19,000-20,999	43	19,999.5		0.033	
			18,999.5		0.968
(2) 17,000-18,999	98	17,999.5		0.075	
			16,999.5		0.893
(3) 15,000-16,999	125	15,999.5		0.095	
			14,999.5		0.798
(4) 13,000-14,999	179	13,999.5		0.137	
			12,999.5		0.661
(5) 11,000-12,999	275	11,999.5		0.210	
			10,999.5		0.451
(6) 9,000-10,999	363	9,999.5		0.277	
			8,999.5		0.174
(7) 7,000-8,999	224	7,999.5		0.171	
			6,999.5		0.003
(8) 5,000-6,999	4	5,999.5		0.003	
			4,999.5		. . .
TOTAL	1,311	. . .	. . .	1.001	. . .

*The data are somewhat modified from actual data reported in surveys conducted by NEA Research during these time periods.

Column 2 indicates the *frequency,* or number, of teachers with contract salaries in each of the eight intervals. For example, 98 teachers earned salaries between $17,000 and $18,999 (Row 2). Columns 1 and 2 taken together indicate the frequency with which individual teacher salaries fall within each of the intervals and are referred to as a *frequency distribution.*

Because these data have been grouped, it is impossible to identify where within this interval each of the 98 teachers is located. Two assumptions are usually made in dealing with grouped data.

- The AU's within the interval have values of the variable that average out to the interval midpoint (Column 3).
- The AU's within the interval have values of the variable that are evenly spread out between the lower and higher limits of the interval (Column 4).

Midpoints for the intervals are obtained by averaging the lower and upper value in the interval. (For example, the midpoint of the interval with 275 teachers' salaries is the average of $11,000 and $12,999—Row 5—or $11,999.5). Successive midpoints appear in Column 3.

Limits dividing the successive intervals are halfway between the upper value in one interval and the lower value in the next higher interval. For example, the limit dividing the intervals with 179 and 125 teachers is halfway between $14,999 (Row 4) and $15,000 (Row 3), clearly at $14,999.50. Successive interval limits are given in Column 4.

Frequently, it is of interest to discuss data in terms of percentages or proportion of AU's lying within a given interval, say, between $9,000 and $10,999 (Row 6). The entries in Column 5 are referred to as "relative frequencies or proportions." For example, 0.095, or 9.5%, of the teachers had salaries between $15,000 and $16,999 (Row 3). The entries in Column 5 are obtained by dividing the entries in Column 2 by the *total* of Column 2. The total for Column 5 should equal 1.00, but due to rounding may be off slightly, as it is in this example.

Though not usually presented in a report, the entries in Column 6 are necessary to develop one of the graphic methods presented in the next section. Column 6, most frequently referred to as the "cumulative relative frequency distribution," is obtained by cumulating successively the entries in Column 5, starting with the lowest value and moving toward the highest value of the variable of interest. These successive cumulations are then placed beside the successive limits dividing adjacent intervals. For example, the entry of 0.451 in the last column opposite the entry of $10,999.50 was obtained by adding together 0.003 + 0.171 + 0.277. This quantity, 0.451, is the proportion of teachers in the sample with salaries less than $10,999.50, or 45.1% of the teachers in the sample fall in the first three class intervals.

Columns 1, 2, and 5 are those most frequently encountered in a tabular display of data of this type, namely, a variable. Characteristics that are attributes lend themselves to slightly different tables.

The attribute of interest in Exhibit 3.3 is the highest degree held by public school teachers in the sample during the period from 1973 to 1976. Too frequently, data are presented in this format with only the proportions or percentages displayed. To assist in interpreting the exhibit, arrows (↓) have been placed next to the marginal percentage (%) signs to show that the percentages are read down a column and not across a row. There are times when an initial review of a table such as Exhibit 3.3 does not make this distinction clear.

The entries in the body of the table indicate, for example, that 51.5% of the teachers in the sample in 1974 had a bachelor's degree as their highest degree. In 1976, this percentage had dropped to 49.3%.

EXHIBIT 3.3—DISTRIBUTION OF ACADEMIC LEVELS FOR TEACHERS SAMPLED IN THE NATIONWIDE TEACHER OPINION POLLS, 1973 TO 1976*

Highest degree held (1)		1973 (2)	1974 (3)	1975 (4)	1976 (5)	Totals (6)
Bachelor's	%↓	53.5	51.5	50.9	49.3	51.1
	n	802	772	891	986	3,451
Master's or 6 years	%↓	38.3	45.6	46.2	47.9	44.8
	n	574	684	808	958	3,024
Doctor's	%↓	2.4	2.0	1.5	1.9	1.9
	n	36	30	26	38	130
Others	%↓	5.8	0.9	1.4	0.9	2.1
	n	87	14	24	18	143
TOTALS		1,499	1,500	1,749	2,000	6,748

*The data are somewhat modified from actual data reported in surveys conducted by NEA Research.

Exhibit 3.3, with the proportions removed from the table, is frequently referred to as a "contingency table" or a "four-by-four matrix" (four rows and four columns). This type of table is most frequently encountered when the characteristic of interest is an attribute.

3.2.2 Graphic Presentation Methods

While clarity and lack of ambiguity are also important in using graphs to portray a set of data, they are not quite as critical. The reviewer still needs to understand the words that appear with the graphs, but impressions are perhaps as important as exactness in reviewing graphs. The variable, annual contract salary, presented in Exhibit 3.2, can be graphically presented in a number of ways, the three most common of which are as a frequency polygon (Exhibit 3.4), a frequency histogram (Exhibit 3.5), and a cumulative proportion or relative frequency distribution (Exhibit 3.6).

In Exhibit 3.4 the polygon is obtained by plotting the individual interval frequencies along the vertical axis (referred to as the "Y-axis") against the corresponding interval midpoint along the base axis (referred to as the "X-axis"). Point A, indicated by the large arrow, represents the class interval in Exhibit 3.2 in Row 4 with 179 teachers (on the vertical axis) and a midpoint of $13,999.50 (on the base or horizontal axis). Both the frequency and the salary values are, of necessity, only estimations on the graph. Successive points on the graph are then joined, usually by straight lines, although there is a tendency at times to smooth a curve through these points. The primary value of the frequency polygon is to give the reviewer of the data a feel for how the variable is distributed.

In Exhibit 3.5 the histogram is obtained by plotting the frequency in the interval along the vertical axis between the lower and upper limit of the interval. Line A, indicated by the large arrow, represents the plotting of the frequency of 179 teachers between the lower and upper limits of the class, namely $12,999.50 and $14,999.50. Again, these values have to be estimated on both the vertical and horizontal axes. This graph presents the same information as Exhibit 3.4, the frequency polygon, but in a slightly different form. Both allow for a visual impression of how the data are distributed.

In Exhibit 3.6, the cumulative proportion distribution is obtained by plotting the cumulative relative frequency (proportion) in column 6 along the vertical axis against the corresponding limit separating the two intervals along the base axis. Point A, indicated by the arrow in Exhibit 3.6, represents the plot of the cumulative proportion of 0.451 on the vertical axis against the appropriate limit, which is $10,999.50. Again both values have to be estimated on the graph. This exhibit provides somewhat different information than does the polygon and the histogram. If, for example, a line were drawn from 0.75 on the vertical axis parallel to the base axis until it intersected the curve and then a line were dropped directly to the base axis, an estimate of the annual contract salary corresponding to 0.75 could be obtained. Here, it can be estimated that 0.75, or 75%, of the teachers in the sample have annual contract salaries less than $14,600. This graph is sometimes referred to as an "ogive."

EXHIBIT 3.4—NUMBER OF PUBLIC SCHOOL TEACHERS WITH ANNUAL CONTRACT SALARIES BETWEEN $5,000 AND $21,000 FOR SCHOOL YEAR 1975-76 (A FREQUENCY POLYGON)

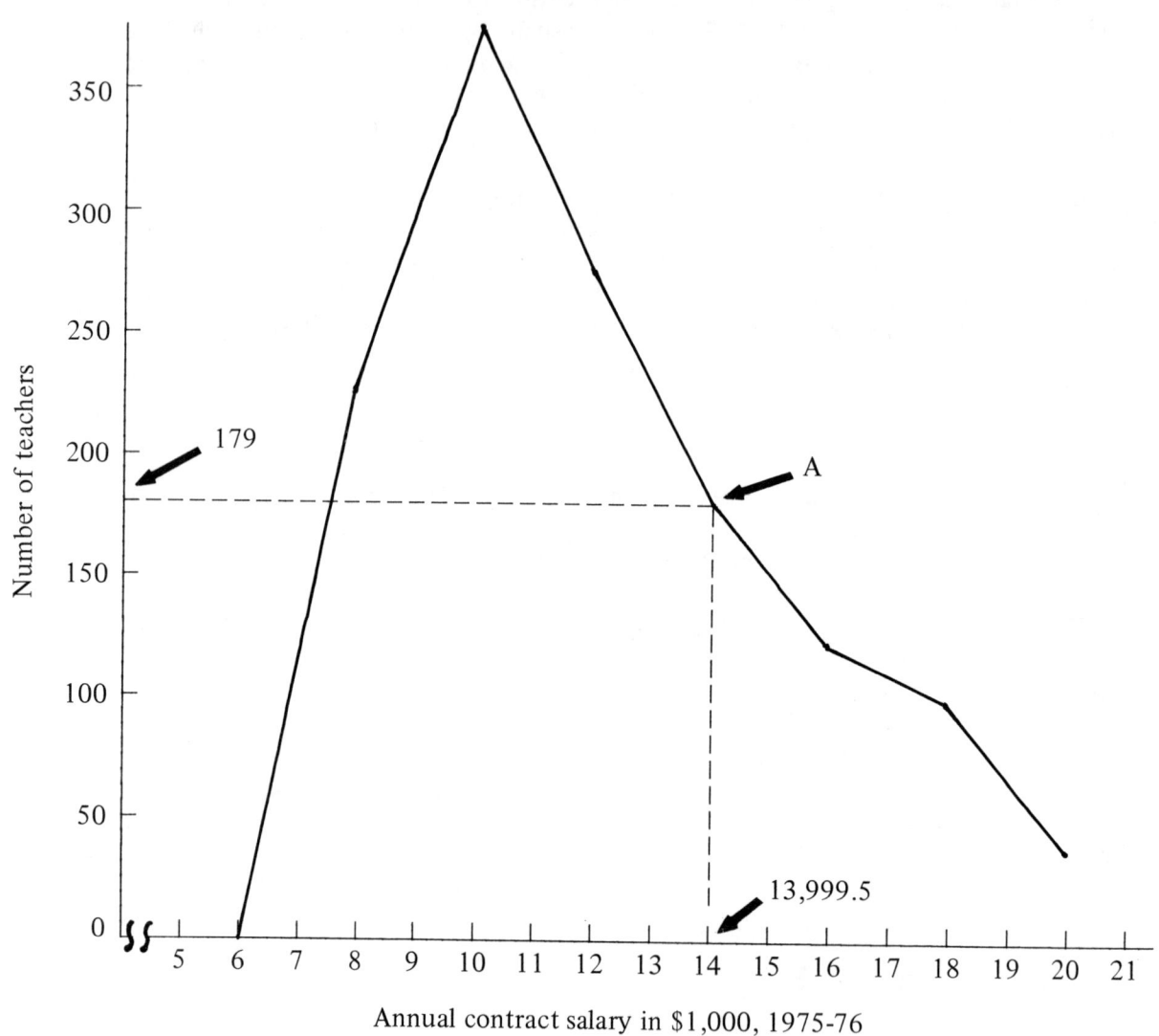

EXHIBIT 3.5–NUMBER OF PUBLIC SCHOOL TEACHERS WITH ANNUAL CONTRACT SALARIES BETWEEN $5,000 AND $21,000 FOR SCHOOL YEAR 1975-76 (A FREQUENCY HISTOGRAM)

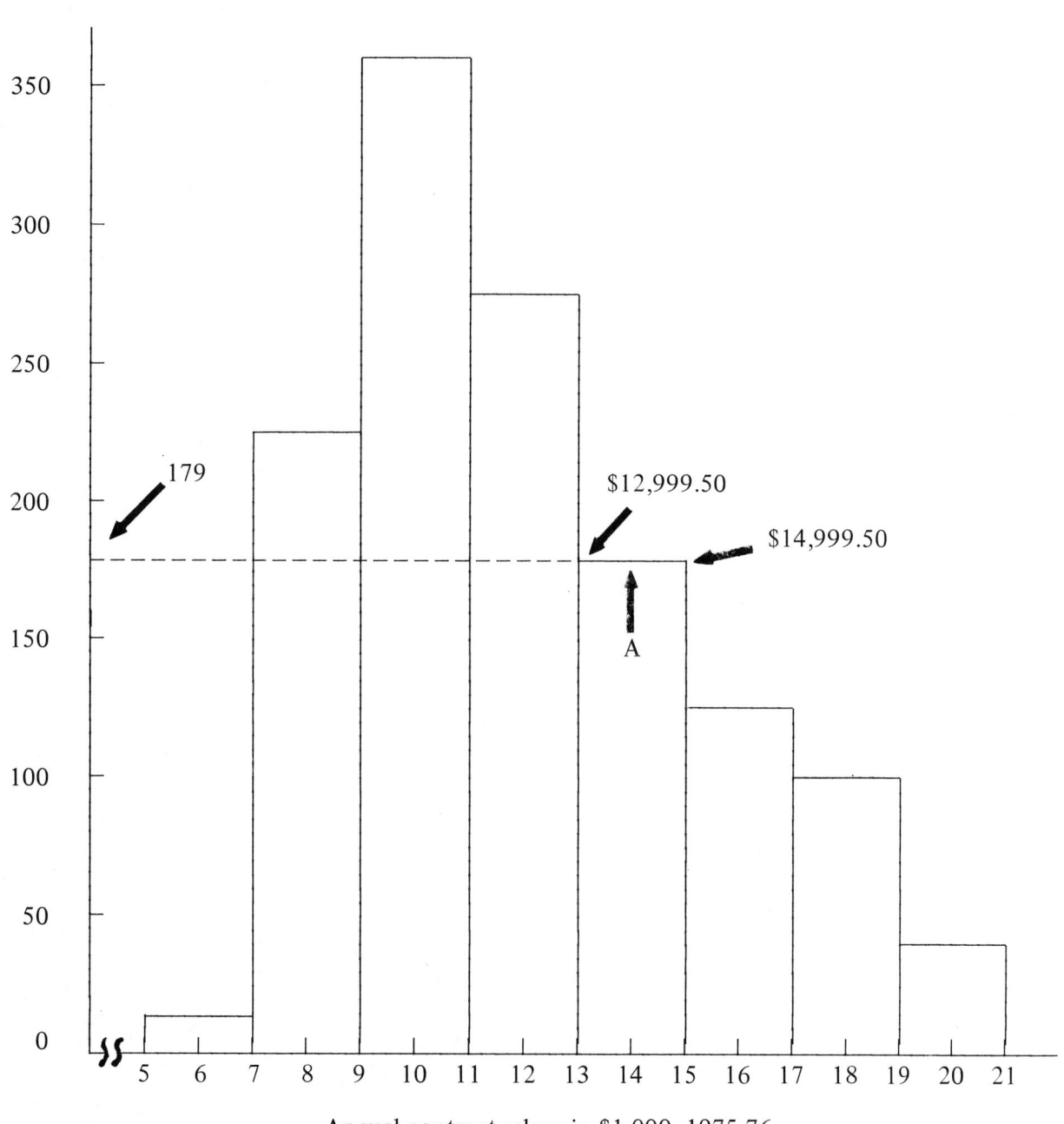

Annual contract salary in $1,000, 1975-76

EXHIBIT 3.6–CUMULATIVE PROPORTION OF TEACHERS EARNING LESS THAN SPECIFIC ANNUAL CONTRACT SALARIES FOR SCHOOL YEAR 1975-76 (A CUMULATIVE PROPORTION DISTRIBUTION)

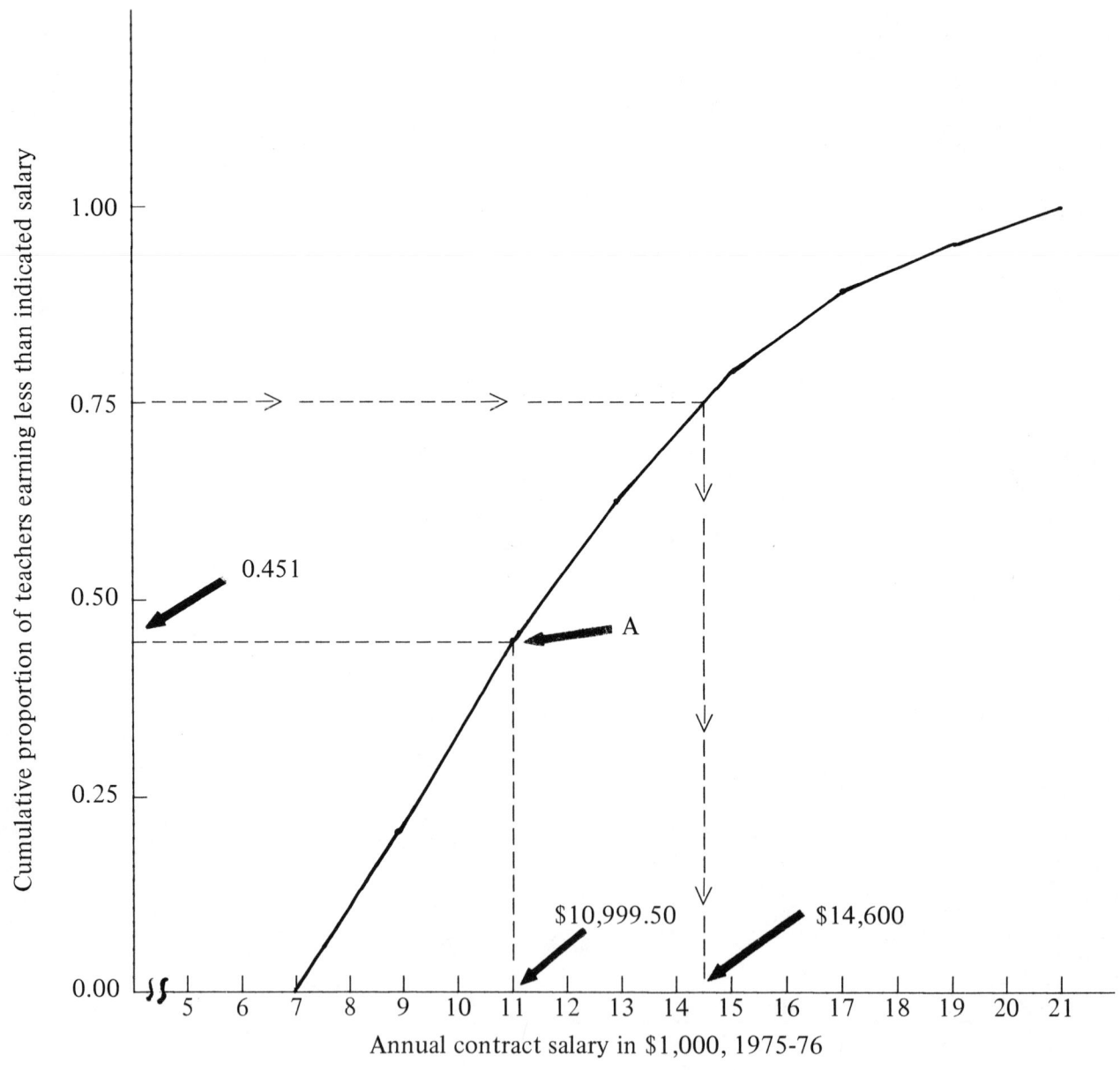

The data on the distribution of academic levels, given in Exhibit 3.3, can be plotted in a number of ways—the two most common of which are bar diagrams and pie charts. Data for only 1973 and 1974 are presented in Exhibits 3.7 and 3.8 for bar charts and pie diagrams. An extension to include all five years should be obvious.

In developing a bar chart, as in Exhibit 3.7, the proportion of the AU's in each category of the attribute is plotted on the vertical scale. The base scale usually represents the populations or samples being compared; in this case, the years 1973 and 1974. Identification of each vertical bar (i.e., bachelor's, master's or 6 years, doctor's, others) is usually either written within the bar or the bars are color-coded, with the code being indicated on the visual. The precise value for the proportions at the top of each bar should be identified, and the sample or population size should be indicated.

In preparing a pie diagram, the size of the slice is determined by multiplying the proportion by 360° (the number of degrees in a circle) and using a protractor to identify the cut points. For example, in 1973 the cut points corresponding to the proportions for the four categories are as follows:

0.535: 192.6°; 0.383: 137.9°; 0.024: 8.6°; 0.058: 20.9°

(Note: 192.6° = 0.535 x 360°.)

For ease in plotting these cut points, the usual procedure is to cumulate the degrees, starting with 0°:

0.535: 0° - 192.6°; 0.383: 192.6° - 330.5°; 0.024: 330.5° - 339.1°;
0.058: 339.1° - 360° (which is the same as 0°)

(Note: 330.5 = 192.6 + 137.9, the values corresponding to 0.535 and 0.383.)

These cut points, dividing the slices of the pie, are indicated for 1973 in Exhibit 3.8. As in the bar chart, identification of each slice can be as indicated in Exhibit 3.8, or each category can be color-coded on the chart. Precise proportions for each category should be identified on the chart, as well as the sample or population size.

The five charts presented in this section are the most commonly used for visually presenting data in educational research. An additional chart is discussed in Chapter 7.

EXHIBIT 3.7–DISTRIBUTION OF ACADEMIC LEVELS FOR TEACHERS SAMPLED IN THE NATIONWIDE TEACHER OPINION POLL, 1973 AND 1974 (A BAR CHART)

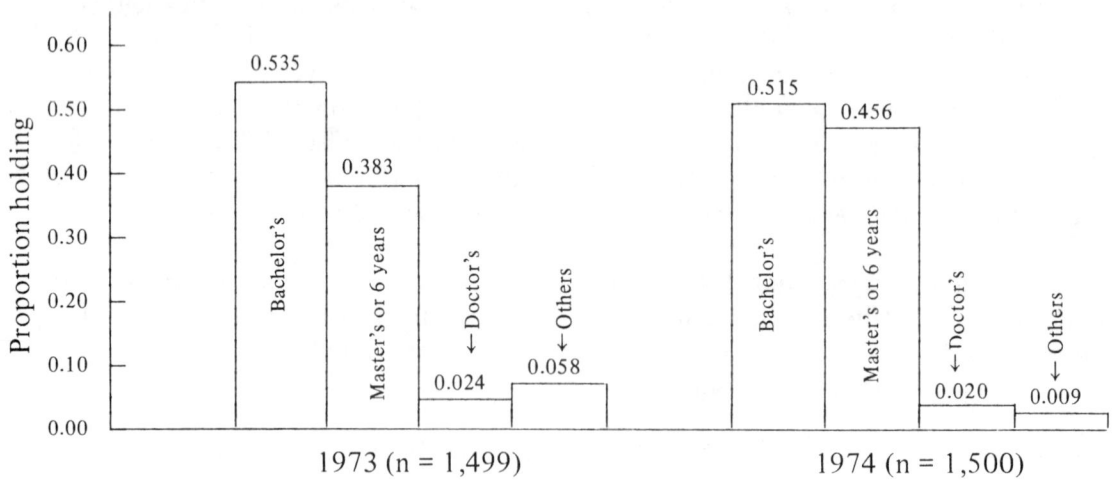

EXHIBIT 3.8–DISTRIBUTION OF ACADEMIC LEVELS FOR TEACHERS SAMPLED IN THE NATIONWIDE TEACHER OPINION POLL, 1973 AND 1974 (A PIE DIAGRAM)

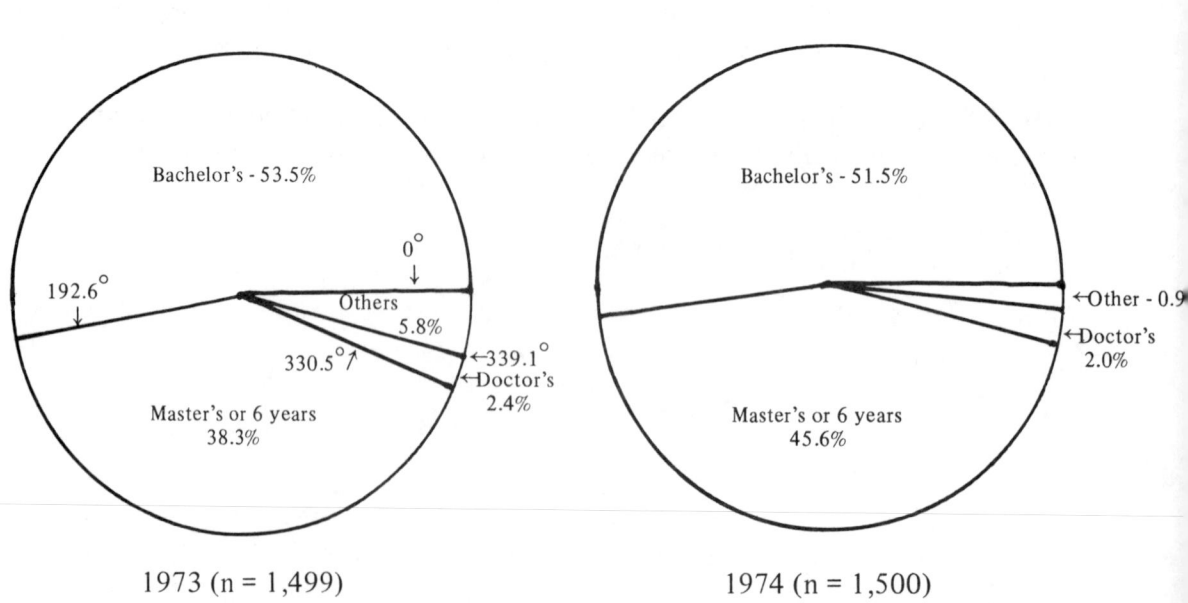

II

Descriptive Measures

The researcher in education is interested in describing the characteristics of the analysis units (AU's) of interest, such as the teacher, the pupil, the school, the school district, or the voter. It is not enough merely to collect data on the AU's and present them in frequency distributions or in contingency tables. The researcher must be able to discuss these data, whether they be related to a sample or a population. Typical of the questions that should be asked are, Are values of the variables associated with the AU's close together or are they widely scattered? Is it possible to describe whether the data are concentrated more at one point than another? What is the shape of the frequency distribution? Is it symmetrical? Are the AU's evenly distributed among possible alternatives for specific attributes? Does any relationship appear to exist among the characteristics?

Descriptive measures are statistics or parameters that the researcher can use to make such assessments and to describe the research findings. Descriptive measures, be they statistics or parameters, provide a basis for summarizing the attributes and variables associated with the AU's of interest. In general, these descriptive measures fall into four categories:

1. How are the characteristics concentrated? (*central tendency*)
2. How are the characteristics scattered or dispersed? (*variation or dispersion*)
3. For a given characteristic, what are the relative positions or locations of individual AU's? (*position*)
4. Are any two or more of the characteristics related to each other? (*association*)

More specifically, *measures of central tendency* identify where the values of the characteristics of interest are concentrated. Three will be discussed in Chapter 4: the arithmetic mean, the median, and the mode.

Measures of variation or *dispersion* indicate how the values of the characteristic are scattered or distributed within the sample or population. Discussed in Chapter 5 are the range, the interquartile range, the average deviation, and the standard deviation (associated with the standard deviation is the variance).

Positional measures indicate the relative position of a particular observation or group of observations within a sample or population for a specific characteristic. Among these measures, discussed in Chapter 6, are percentiles (quartiles and deciles), proportions (percentages), and standard scores (the Z-score, the T-score).

Measures of association indicate the extent to which two or more characteristics are or are not related. Discussed in Chapter 7 are measures of correlation and regression, as well as a miscellaneous group of such measures.

As has been mentioned, descriptive measures can be appropriate to summarize characteristics in a sample or in a population. These descriptive measures are referred to as "statistics" if they relate to a sample and as "parameters" if they relate to a population. Part II defines these descriptive measures, identifies procedures for calculating them from available data (from a sample or a population), provides numerous examples on how the calculations are performed, and discusses the appropriate use of these measures.

Part III, based upon the summary measures developed in Part II, provides a means for making inferences from sample data to a population or populations.

4
MEASURES OF CENTRAL TENDENCY

Measures of central tendency are descriptive measures that tell something about how values of a variable associated with a set of analysis units (AU's) are concentrated. Of the available measures of this type, three are of greatest interest in educational research: the arithmetic mean, the median, and the mode. *Measures of central tendency* are numbers that summarize the concentration of the characteristic associated with the AU's of interest and are computed directly from the observations in the sample or in the population.

Chapters 4, 5, 6, and 7—with minor exceptions—briefly examine computational procedures for raw data only. (Most researchers should have access to some type of small calculator or computer system that can deal with raw data.) *Raw data* are the characteristics of interest as they are obtained from each AU. For example, if the AU is a school district, the raw data might be the number of teachers in the school district, the number of pupils in the school district, or the budgeted dollars for a specific school year. *Grouped data,* which are not discussed computationally in this HANDBOOK, are raw data put into some form of frequency distribution; for example, the annual contract salaries in Exhibit 3.2.

4.1 THE ARITHMETIC MEAN

Perhaps the most widely used measure in summarizing the concentration of a set of observations is the arithmetic mean, or simply the mean. (There are other means, such as the harmonic mean and the quadratic mean, so be certain that the word "mean" refers to the "arithmetic mean.") The *mean* is the simple average of the values of the characteristic of interest. It is obtained by adding up all of the observations for the AU's and dividing by the number of observations. (Appendix C reviews the basic arithmetic operations and symbols.)

The following notation is necessary to identify a formula for the arithmetic mean:

- X the value of an individual observation (characteristic)
- Σ the symbol that means "to add up" or "to sum" what follows the symbol
- ΣX the indication that individual values of the variable are to be added or summed
- n the number of observations or AU's

With this notation, it is seen that a formula for the arithmetic mean is given by:

$$\text{arithmetic mean} = \Sigma X / n \tag{4.1}$$

The symbol for the arithmetic mean varies, depending upon whether it is for a sample or for a population. If for a sample, the symbol is $\overline{X}$ (called "X bar"); and if for a population, the symbol is μ (the Greek letter mu). The formula is the same for both, except that the letter n in (4.1) becomes N when dealing with a population.

Consider the following two examples:

1. Ten students who took a college aptitude test received the following scores:

    143, 139, 125, 119, 110, 108, 106, 99, 95, 89

    The arithmetic mean for this sample of ten students is seen to be:

    $\overline{X} = \Sigma X / n = 1,133 / 10 = 113.3$

2. A sample of ten teachers in a given school system earn the following salaries:

    $8,500; $8,750; $9,500; $9,500; $10,650;
    $11,500; $11,500; $11,500; $14,750; $15,500

    The arithmetic mean for this sample of ten teachers is seen to be:

    $\overline{X} = \Sigma X / n = \$111,650 / 10 = \$11,165$

The arithmetic mean, as a summary measure, may be calculated only for the interval or ratio scales.

The three major advantages of using the arithmetic mean are as follows:

- The mean is generally the most reliable and accurate of the measures of central tendency. For example, if samples of the same size are drawn from the same population, the mean of each sample will fluctuate less widely from sample to sample than either the median or the mode.
- For the above reason, the mean is better suited for making inferences.
- The mean reflects *all* of the observations in the sample or population.

The major disadvantage of the mean is that it tends to be distorted by extreme values of the variable, particularly when the number of AU's is small. Under this condition, other measures may be more appropriate.

4.2   THE MEDIAN

The second measure of central tendency is referred to as the *median,* which is the middle value of the characteristic of interest when the data have been arranged or ranked in either ascending or descending order. If there is no middle value, the median is taken as the average of the two middle observations. If the characteristic cannot be ranked (nominal scale), the median cannot be found.

Consider the two previous examples:

1. On a college aptitude test, a sample of ten students achieved the following scores (ordered from lowest to highest):

    89, 95, 99, 106, 108, 110, 119, 125, 139, 143

    Since there are an even number of scores, the median lies between the two middle scores and is seen to be:

    (108 + 110) / 2 = 109

    The aptitude score of 109 is referred to as the "median score," since half of the scores are below it and half are above it.

2. Ten teachers in a given school system earn the following salaries (ordered from lowest to highest):

    $8,500, $8,750, $9,500, $9,500, $10,650
    $11,500, $11,500, $11,500, $14,750, $15,500

    Since there are an even number of salaries, the median salary lies half way between the two middle salaries and is seen to be:

    ($10,650 + $11,500) / 2 = $11,075

If, in example No. 2 above, the fifth salary from the lowest had been $11,500, instead of $10,650, the median would be identified as $11,500, since the two middle salaries are identical. For this small number of cases, it is clear that half of the salaries would not be above $11,500 and half below $11,500, since four of the ten would be at this figure. This points out that for a small set of AU's the median may be a measure that does not clearly describe the data and should be used with caution.

The median, generally, is the appropriate measure of central tendency to employ when the data have some extreme values that would distort the mean or when the precise values for some of the observations at either end of the scale are unknown. For example, if the top two teachers' salaries were only reported as $12,000 and above, it would be impossible to calculate the arithmetic mean. For the original ten salaries, however, the median would remain at $11,075.

The symbol used in this HANDBOOK for the median in a population is $\tilde{\mu}$ (read as "mu tilde") and in a sample is $\tilde{X}$ (read as "X tilde"). Some authors use the symbol Md to represent the median.

Although no formulas are presented in this HANDBOOK to calculate the median for grouped data, an excellent approximation can be obtained graphically. The cumulative proportion distribution for the data in Exhibit 3.2 is repeated as Exhibit 4.1. Since, by definition, the median is the middle value when the data are ordered, it is the value corresponding to a cumulative proportion of 0.50, indicated by the letter A in Exhibit 4.1.

EXHIBIT 4.1–CUMULATIVE PROPORTION OF TEACHERS EARNING LESS THAN SPECIFIC ANNUAL CONTRACT SALARIES FOR SCHOOL YEAR 1975-76 (A CUMULATIVE PROPORTION DISTRIBUTION)

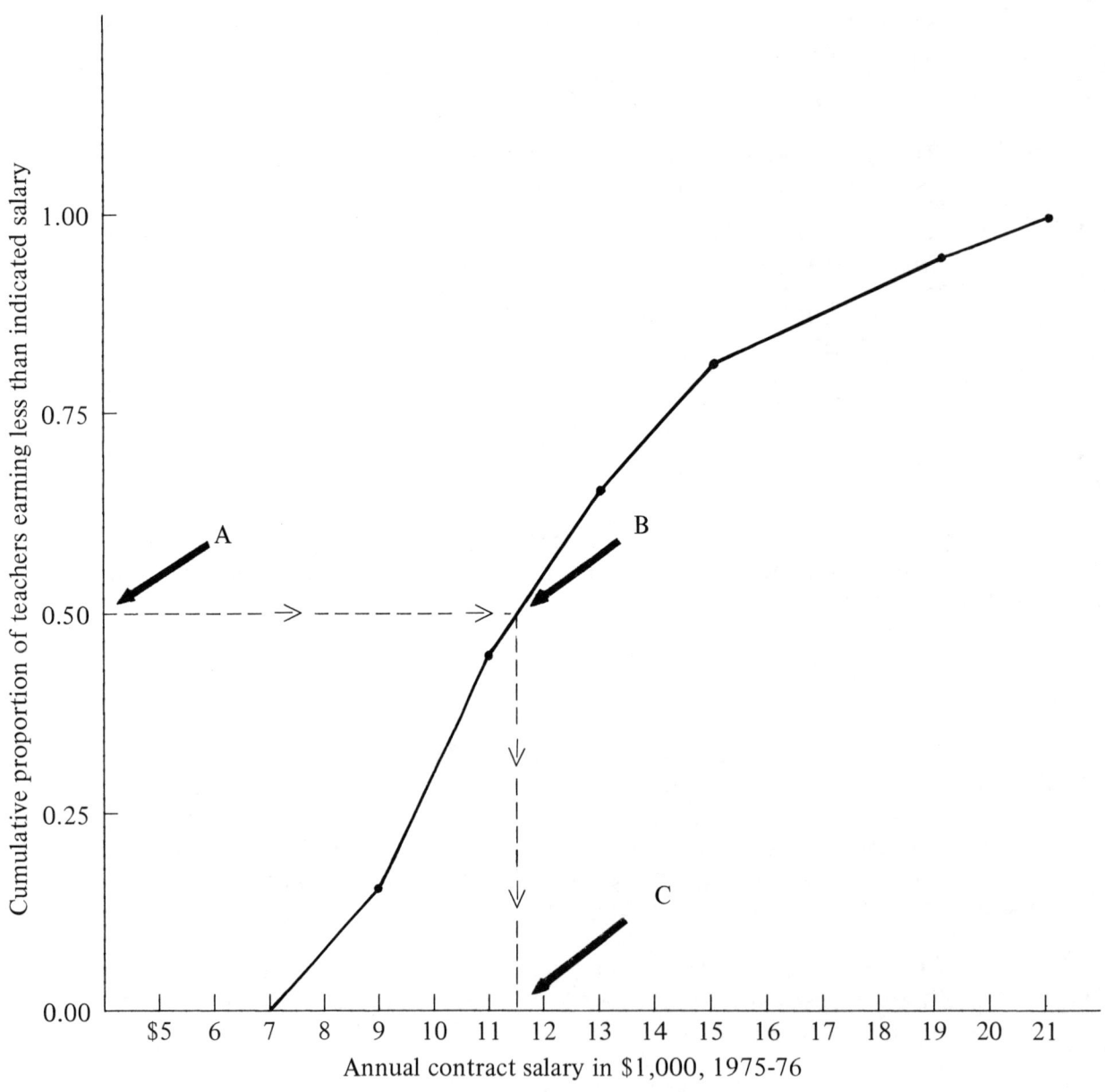

A line is drawn, parallel to the base, until it intersects the cumulative proportion curve at Point B. From this intersection, a perpendicular line is drawn down to the base scale, intersecting it at Point C. The estimated median salary for this group of teachers then becomes approximately $11,500.

4.3 THE MODE

The *mode* is that value in a set of data that occurs more frequently than any other value. A set of data having two modes is said to be "bimodal"; single mode distributions are termed "unimodal." For the ten aptitude tests (Example No. 1) there is no mode, since all scores are different. For the ten teachers' salaries (Example No. 2), the mode is seen to be $11,500, since it occurs more often than any other value.

Generally, the mode is an appropriate measure to use (1) when extreme values of the characteristic might tend to distort the arithmetic mean and (2) in cases where the arithmetic mean does not apply. For example, in an opinion question for which there are five possible responses (ranging from "strongly support" to "strongly oppose") the arithmetic mean cannot be computed but the modal response category can be identified. In addition, if shoe size is the variable associated with the AU's, an arithmetic mean shoe size of 8.89 is not even a possible value of the variable. Here, the modal size of 8-1/2 does exist and does make sense.

The symbol used in this HANDBOOK for the mode in a population is $\overset{\circ}{\mu}$ (read as "mu dot") and in a sample is $\overset{\circ}{X}$ (read as "X dot"). Some authors use the symbol *Mo* to represent the mode.

As in the case of the median, no formulas are presented in this HANDBOOK for calculating the mode for grouped data. An excellent approximation can be made graphically based upon the data in Exhibit 3.2 and the use of the frequency histogram, which is repeated as Exhibit 4.2. The class interval with the largest number of observations is defined as the "modal class." Two lines are drawn, connecting points in the modal class with points in each of the adjacent two class intervals: Point A is connected to Point D and Point B is connected to Point C. Where these two lines intersect (Point E) a line is drawn perpendicular to the base scale, intersecting the base at Point F. The salary at this point is estimated at $10,200, referred to as the mode. (Strictly speaking, of the available techniques for estimating a mode, this is the "delta mode.")

4.4 FURTHER EXAMPLES

To illustrate further the computation of the three measures of central tendency, consider the following two examples:

EXHIBIT 4.2–NUMBER OF PUBLIC SCHOOL TEACHERS WITH ANNUAL CONTRACT SALARIES BETWEEN $5,000 AND $21,000 FOR SCHOOL YEAR 1975-76 (A FREQUENCY HISTOGRAM)

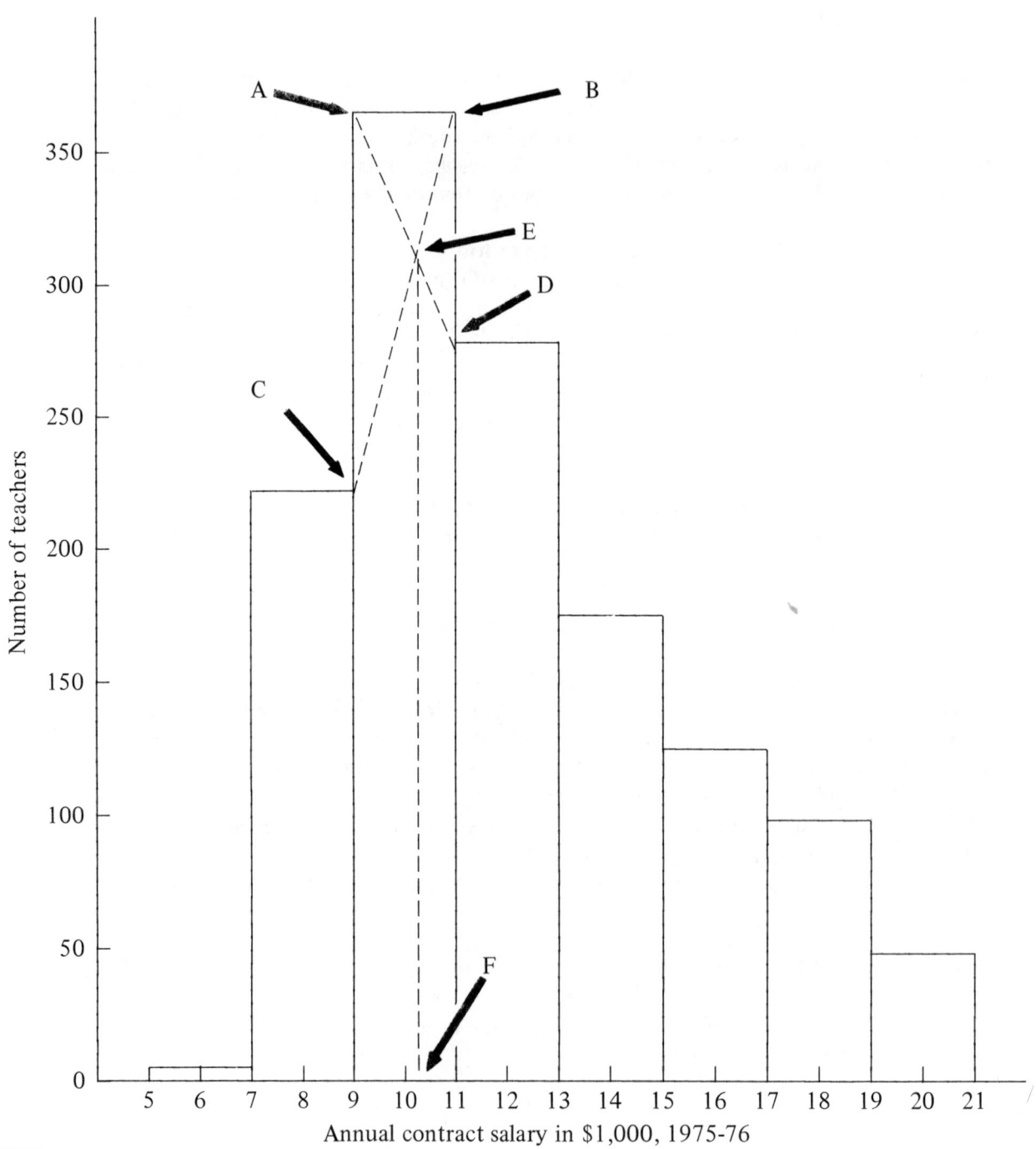

1. In a given school system, a sample of 20 teachers was selected and their number of years of tenure with that system recorded as follows:

2	9	6	9
12	3	3	3
10	14	3	4
5	10	5	12
7	7	11	6

   The data are reordered to look for the median and the mode:

2	4	7	10
3	5	7	11
3	5	9	12
3	6	9	12
3	6	10	14

   The arithmetic mean is seen to be:

   $$\overline{X} = \Sigma X / n = 141 / 20 = 7.05 \text{ years}$$

   The mode can be seen as:

   $$\overset{\circ}{X} = 3 \text{ years}$$

   And, the median is:

   $$\tilde{X} = (6 + 7) / 2 = 6.5 \text{ years}$$

2. In a study of 25 children attending senior high school in a given school district, the family income (in $1,000) was recorded as follows:

$18.1	$22.7	$49.7	$22.5	$34.2
13.6	19.4	31.4	18.9	17.6
24.9	29.6	27.9	30.4	25.6
37.6	33.8	31.3	23.3	25.9
33.5	32.6	35.6	19.8	28.4

   These data are reordered to look for the median and the mode:

$13.6	$19.8	$25.6	$30.4	$33.8
17.6	22.5	25.9	31.3	34.2
18.1	22.7	27.9	31.4	35.6
18.9	23.3	28.4	32.6	37.6
19.4	24.9	29.6	33.5	49.7

   The arithmetic mean is seen to be:

   $$\overline{X} = \Sigma X / n = \$688.3 / 25 = \$27.53 \text{ or } \$27,530$$

Since there are an odd number of observations, the median is found to be

$$\tilde{X} = \$27.9 \text{ or } \$27,900$$

There is no modal family income for this sample of 25 families.

4.5 SUMMARY

Following are indications of appropriate times to use each of the three measures of central tendency:

1. *Arithmetic mean*:

   For characteristics that are on either the interval or ratio scale and:

   - The distribution is reasonably symmetrical with the heavy concentration of values near the middle of the range;
   - The greatest reliability in measuring central tendency is desired;
   - Inferences are to be made to the population from which the sample was selected; and,
   - Further measures, such as variation, are desired.

2. *Median*:

   For characteristics that are on the ordinal scale and have sufficient classes to allow identification of a median; and,

   For characteristics that are on the interval or ratio scale and:

   - The distribution is badly skewed or has some extreme values;
   - There is incomplete information on some values at either extreme;
   - There is a need to know in which half of the group an individual observation falls.

3. *Mode*:

   For characteristics that are on the nominal or ordinal scale; and

   For characteristics that are on either the interval or ratio scale and:

   - Only the typical, or most popular (most frequent) value is desired; and,
   - Only a rough estimate of the central tendency is required. (The mode is usually the easiest of the three to obtain.)

A good rule to follow when reasonable doubt exists about which measure of central tendency is the most appropriate to use is to use more than one.

5

MEASURES OF VARIATION

These descriptive measures tell something about how values of a variable associated with a set of analysis units (AU's) differ from each other or how they vary. These measures of variation are sometimes referred to as "measures of dispersion" or "scatter." To illustrate the importance of such measures, consider the following situation:

> Two teachers are comparing notes after the semester has concluded. They had taught different sections of the same subject and discovered that the average grade (arithmetic mean) for each of the two sections was 81. One teacher thought it had been a wonderful year—all the pupils proceeded at a similar pace. The second teacher, however, indicated that the semester had been difficult because the class had several talented pupils who did extremely well and several slow learning pupils who did comparatively poor work. Obviously, the average grade for the two classes didn't reveal the entire story. In the first case, the pupils were closely grouped around the 81 average—a fairly homogeneous group—with few low and high scores. In the second class, the students had a wide range of abilities, a heterogeneous group, with some scores in the 60's and some in the 90's.

The following is another example of the importance of measures of variation:

> A buyer needs a large quantity of chains of a certain length that will tolerate up to 1,000 pounds of tension without breaking. Two companies submit a sample of chains for testing, and each sample averages 1,050 pounds of tension before the chains break. Is this information sufficient to conclude that both companies produce acceptable chains? Closer examination shows that all ten chains in Company A's sample broke with between 1,025 and 1,075 pounds of tension. However, the ten chains from Company B's sample broke with between 950 and 1,150 pounds of tension. Clearly, the mean provides insufficient information to make a judgment on the distribution of breaking weights for the chains. Some measure of variation is required before a purchase can be made!

These two examples emphasize that measures of central tendency alone are not adequate to describe the distribution of the characteristic of interest. *Measures of variation* are numbers that summarize the degree or extent of scatter of the characteristic associated with the AU's of interest and are computed directly from the observations in the sample or in the population. Of the available measures of this type, the four that are encountered most frequently are discussed in the balance of this chapter.

These are the range, interquartile range, average deviation, and standard deviation. For these measures intuitively to be correct, the more compact or closer together the observations, the smaller should be the calculated value for the measure.

5.1 THE RANGE

The *range,* or total range, is the distance from the lowest to the highest observation in a set of data. Sometimes the range is reported as the difference between the highest and lowest values. In Chapter 4, a sample of ten teachers' salaries was reported as $8,500, $8,750, $9,500, $9,500, $10,650, $11,500, $11,500, $11,500, $14,750, and $15,500. The range is seen to be from $8,500 to $15,500, or $7,000. The range is usually stated in two figures—namely, from $8,500 to $15,500—and requires either an interval or ratio scale of measurement.

Although easy to compute, the range can easily be distorted by extreme observations in the data. For example, if the last salary in the above example was $25,000 and not $15,500, the range would be from $8,500 to $25,000, or $16,500. Contrast this with the $7,000 indicated above.

Of all the measures of variation presented in this chapter, the range is the least reliable because only two observations are used. The remaining observations could all be clustered at either end of the distribution or be fairly evenly scattered without affecting the reported range. The same procedure is used for calculating the range in either a sample or a population.

The range can be extremely useful under some specific conditions; for example, the total range is used in salary surveys when it is important to know the minimum and maximum salaries paid or on a schedule.

5.2 INTERQUARTILE RANGE

The *interquartile range* includes the middle 50 percent of the observations in a set of data. It is usually indicated by two values of the variable under consideration, referred to as the "first and third quartile points." If a set of data (interval or ratio scale) is ranked from lowest to highest, the resultant ordering could be grouped into four equal parts. (This is precisely true only when the number of observations can be evenly divided by four. Otherwise, a slightly more complicated approach is necessary to arrive at the quartile points.) The points, or values of the variable, that divide the data into these four quartiles are referred to as the first, second, and third quartile points. The second quartile point is also the median. The first quartile point, referred to as Q_1, is that point below which 25% of the values fall. In a similar fashion, the second quartile point, Q_2, is that point below which 50% of the values fall; the third quartile point, Q_3, is that point below which 75% of the values fall.

To illustrate, consider the following set of eight salaries:

$10,300, $13,600 Q_1 $13,700, $13,700 Q_2 $13,900, $14,100 Q_3 $14,500, $14,800

Since eight is divisible by four, two salaries will be in each quarter of the data, once the salaries have been ranked. The points dividing these four quarters, as indicated above, are the three quartile points. These quartile points are calculated by taking a value halfway between the upper value in one quarter and the lower value in the next quarter. For this illustration, the three quartile points are seen to be:

Q_1 = (\$13,600 + \$13,700) / 2 = \$13,650

Q_2 = (\$13,700 + \$13,900) / 2 = \$13,800

Q_3 = (\$14,100 + \$14,500) / 2 = \$14,300.

The interquartile range, then, extends from \$13,650 to \$14,300, a range which includes the middle 50% of the salaries for this sample of teachers.

Although no formulas are presented in this HANDBOOK for calculating the interquartile range from grouped data, an excellent approximation can be obtained graphically, similar to that for the median. The cumulative proportion distribution for the data in Exhibit 3.2 (annual contract salaries in \$1,000) is repeated as Exhibit 5.1. Since the interquartile range includes the middle 50% of the observations, estimates for Q_1 and Q_3 can be obtained as follows:

> Q_1 is estimated by starting at 0.25 on the cumulative proportion scale (Point C) and drawing a line parallel to the base scale until it intersects the curve at Point D. A line is then drawn from Point D perpendicular to the base scale until it intersects the base scale. This intersection is approximately at \$9,500 and is Q_1.

> Q_3 is estimated by starting at 0.75 on the cumulative proportion scale (Point A) and drawing a line parallel to the base scale until it intersects the curve at Point B. A line is then drawn from Point B perpendicular to the base scale until it intersects the base scale. This intersection is approximately \$14,500 and is Q_3.

The middle 50% of the contract salaries for this group of teachers lies approximately between \$9,500 and \$14,500. This is the interquartile range.

The three quartile points are also useful in indicating the direction of skewness for the data. *Skewness* is a departure from symmetry. Exhibit 5.2 indicates three examples of symmetry (Figures A, B, C) and positive and negative skewness (Figures D and E, respectively). If a distribution is symmetrical, the distance between the first and second quartile point is the same as the distance between the second and third quartile point. Any difference in the distance between the first quartile point and the median and the median and the third quartile point indicates possible skewness in the direction of the greater distance. Skewness is—

- Positive when $(Q_3 - Q_2)$ is greater than $(Q_2 - Q_1)$
- Negative when $(Q_3 - Q_2)$ is less than $(Q_2 - Q_1)$.

Symmetry implies that $(Q_3 - Q_2) = (Q_2 - Q_1)$. However, it does not follow that the equality of $(Q_3 - Q_2)$ and $(Q_2 - Q_1)$ implies symmetry.

EXHIBIT 5.1–CUMULATIVE PROPORTION OF TEACHERS EARNING LESS THAN SPECIFIC ANNUAL CONTRACT SALARIES FOR SCHOOL YEAR 1975-76 (A CUMULATIVE PROPORTION DISTRIBUTION–OGIVE)

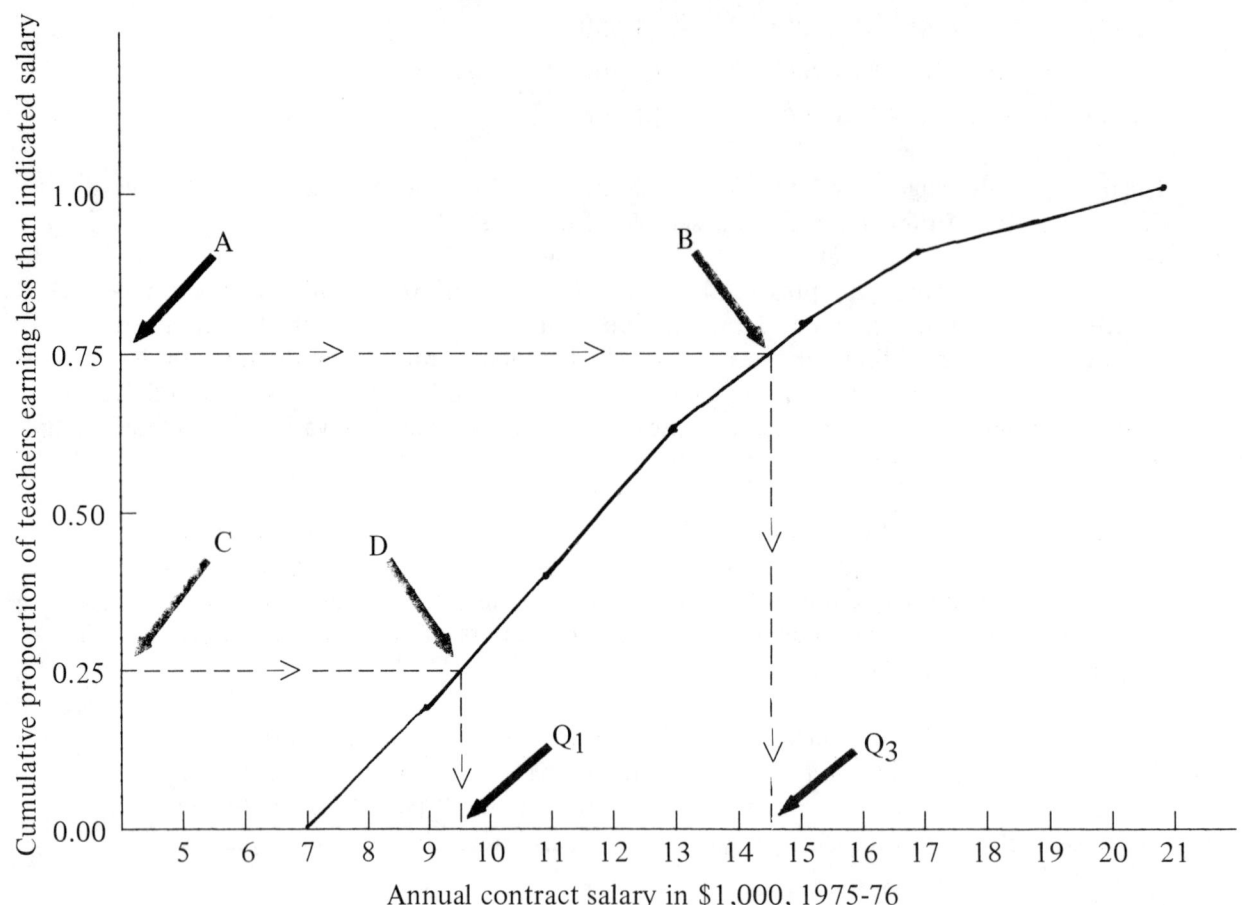

EXHIBIT 5.2—EXAMPLES OF SYMMETRY AND SKEWNESS

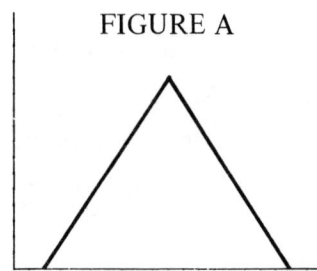
FIGURE A

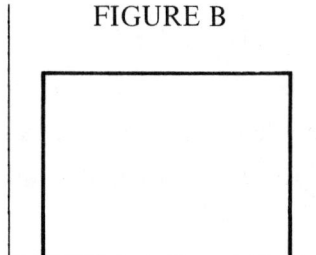
FIGURE B

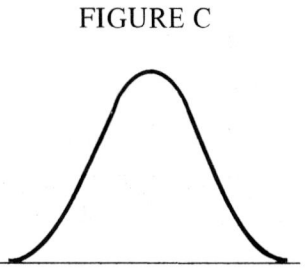
FIGURE C

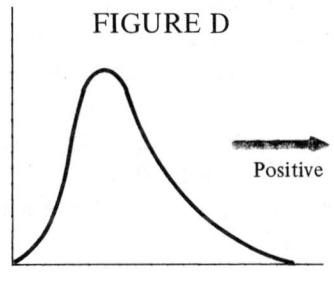
FIGURE D
Positive

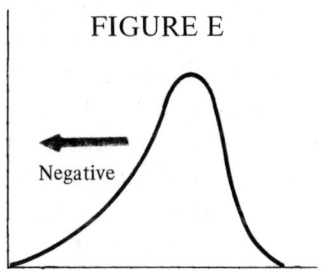
FIGURE E
Negative

Neither the range nor the interquartile range consider the position of each observation in the set of data being examined. Therefore, these measures do not have the characteristics necessary for determination of sample size, which is discussed in Chapter 12.

The interquartile range may be useful as follows:

- When the median is the only summary measure of central tendency reported.
- When the distribution is either truncated or incomplete at either end.
- When there is extreme skewing or there are a few very extreme observations.
- When it is desirable to know the actual limits of the middle 50% of the observations.

5.3 AVERAGE DEVIATION

In analyzing a specific characteristic for a set of AU's (say, salaries associated with teachers in a given school system), nearly every observation will be some distance either above or below the arithmetic mean. The only time an observation does not deviate from the mean is when it coincides with the mean, in which case its deviation is zero. Teachers with salaries above the mean are said to have positive differences from the mean, while teachers with salaries below the mean are said to have negative differences from the mean. If the direction from the mean is ignored and the differences only added up, this result represents the sum of the individual deviations from the mean. If this total is divided by the number of AU's, the resulting measure is *the average of the deviations from the arithmetic mean,* referred to as the "average or mean deviation." An average deviation can also be taken about the median and the mode. Although average deviation usually refers to the variation about the arithmetic mean, it is good practice to be certain that such is the case.

Consider the following sample of eight teachers, where their age is the variable of interest:

Teacher	Age(X)	($X - \bar{X}$)	$|X - \bar{X}|$
	(1)	(2)	(3)
A	34	-6	6
B	37	-3	3
C	38	-2	2
D	39	-1	1
E	40	0	0
F	42	$+2$	2
G	43	$+3$	3
H	47	$+7$	7
	320	-12	24
		$+12$	
		0	

The numbers in Column 1 represent the ages for the eight teachers. The arithmetic mean is 40 years (320 / 8 = 40). In Column 2 the mean is subtracted from each of the individual ages, with some (below the mean) being indicated by a minus sign (−) and some (above the mean) being indicated by a plus sign (+). For this example, one teacher's age is exactly at the mean so that deviation from 40 is shown as 0 (Teacher E). Note that the sum of the minus signs and the sum of the plus signs are both 12. This will always occur, with the exception of possible rounding errors, when the mean is subtracted from each observation. So, Column 2 indicates the amount of the individual teacher's age deviation from the mean, as well as the direction. Column 3 indicates the amount of the deviation from the mean without considering the direction. The symbols surrounding $X - \bar{X}$ in Column 3 are referred to as "absolute value signs" (| |) and effectively say, "Tell me how far from the mean; I don't care about which direction."

Since 24 years is the total of the individual teacher age deviations from the mean, when divided by eight (the number of teachers), the result is the average deviation from the mean, or 3 years (24 / 8 = 3). This summary measure is interpreted as follows: On the average, for this group of teachers, individual ages are three years away from the mean. Some are closer and some are farther away.

Exhibit 5.3 portrays these individual teacher age deviations from the mean.

The appropriate formula for computing the average deviation from the arithmetic mean in this sample is seen to be:

$$\boxed{\begin{aligned} A.D. &= \Sigma|X - \bar{X}| / n \\ &= \Sigma|x| / n \end{aligned}} \qquad (5.1)$$

where n is the sample size and "x" is defined as an individual deviation from the arithmetic mean or $x = (X - \bar{X})$. The same formula applies for a population with $\bar{X}$ being replaced by μ and n by N.

EXHIBIT 5.3–DEVIATIONS OF THE AGES OF EIGHT TEACHERS FROM THE MEAN OF THE GROUP, IN YEARS

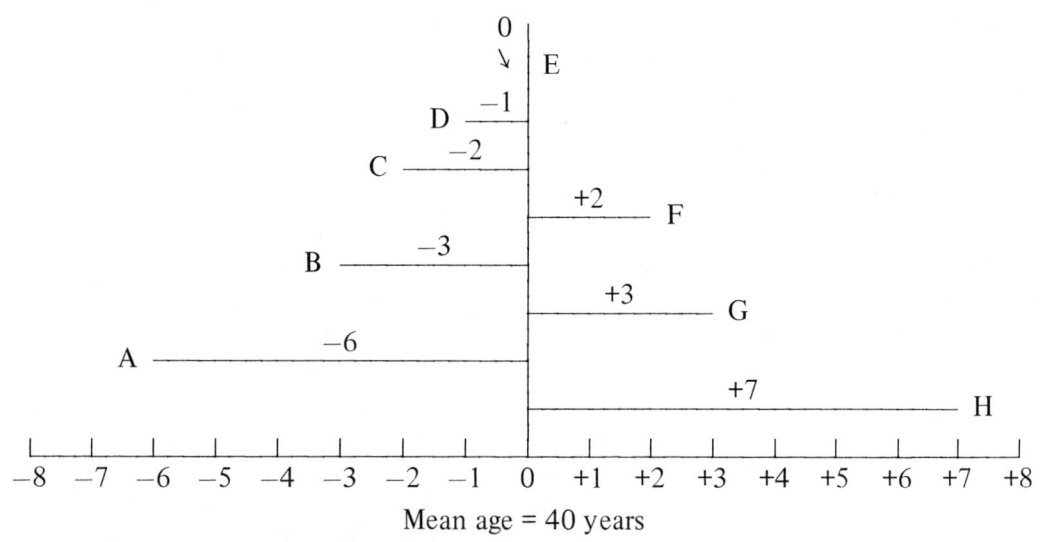

Note: Specific teachers are indicated by the letters A – H.

As an example, a sample of ten teachers has been selected from a school district; their annual contract salary is the variable. These data and the computations necessary to arrive at the average deviation are given below, with salaries being given in $1,000:

Salary (X)	(X − $\bar{X}$)	|X − $\bar{X}$| = |x|
(1)	(2)	(3)
$13.3	−.5	.5
13.6	−.2	.2
13.6	−.2	.2
13.6	−.2	.2
13.7	−.1	.1
13.9	+.1	.1
13.9	+.1	.1
14.0	+.2	.2
14.1	+.3	.3
14.3	+.5	.5
$138.0	−1.2	2.4
	+1.2	
	0	

The arithmetic mean for the group is $138.0 / 10 = $13.8. Remember that this is in $1,000, so the average is really $13,800. Column 2 provides the deviation of each teacher's salary from the average and also indicates the direction. This column (with the pluses and minuses totaled separately) adds to 0, as expected. Column 3 provides the magnitude of each deviation from the mean without giving an indication of direction. The average deviation, then, using formula (5.1) is seen to be:

$$A.D. = \Sigma|X - \bar{X}| / n = 2.4 / 10 = .24$$

or $240. On the average, these ten teachers earn salaries that are $240 away from the mean salary; some are closer to the mean and some are farther away. Column 3 need not really be computed since its sum is the same as the sum of the pluses and minuses in Column 2.

Unlike the range and interquartile range, every observation in the sample, or population, is considered in the computation of the average deviation. The average deviation can be calculated for a characteristic on the interval or ratio scale. When comparing two samples or populations on a single characteristic, the one with the smaller average deviation will have its observations closer together than the one with the larger average deviation. Extremes can, of course, distort the average deviation also.

Although not widely used in describing variation, an understanding of the average deviation is essential in the development and use of the fourth and final measure of variation, the standard deviation.

5.4 STANDARD DEVIATION

The standard deviation and its square, the variance, are by far the most important measures of variation or dispersion, particularly when inferences are to be made from a sample to a population. Although slightly more complicated to calculate, the standard deviation is quite similar to the average deviation. All observations are taken into consideration, and the deviation of each individual characteristic from the arithmetic mean is also computed. It varies less from sample to sample drawn at random from the same population than any other measure of variation. It is more stable; and, therefore, in sampling it yields a more accurate estimate of dispersion in the population.

The standard deviation of a characteristic is the square root of the average of the squared deviations from the arithmetic mean. Like the average deviation, the standard deviation is also an average of deviations from the mean.

The symbol for the standard deviation in a population is σ (the Greek small sigma) and in a sample is S. The standard deviation in a population is defined in Formula (5.2):

$$\sigma = \sqrt{\Sigma(X - \mu)^2 / N}$$
$$= \sqrt{\Sigma x^2 / N} \qquad (5.2)$$

where

- μ is the population arithmetic mean
- N is the population size
- Σ is the summation sign
- $\sqrt{}$ is the square root sign
- x is $(X - \mu)$.

The corresponding definition in a sample simply replaces σ by S, μ by $\overline{X}$, and N by n, the sample size. To be consistent with most statistical references, in this HANDBOOK the formula for the sample standard deviation will be given by (5.3):

$$S = \sqrt{\Sigma(X - \overline{X})^2 / (n - 1)}$$
$$S = \sqrt{\Sigma x^2 / (n - 1)} \qquad (5.3)$$

The assumption is made in using $(n - 1)$ in place of n that the sample is going to be used to make inferences about the population from which the sample was selected. All formulas developed later in this HANDBOOK are based upon Formula (5.3) as the definition of the sample standard deviation. (If no inferences are to be made, the sample may be treated as a population for descriptive purposes. In this case Formula (5.2) is appropriate.)

The sequence of steps involved in Formula (5.3) are as follows:

1. Calculate the arithmetic mean of the sample: $(\overline{X})$
2. Subtract the mean from each of the observations: $(X - \overline{X})$
3. Square each of these individual deviations: $(X - \overline{X})^2$

4. Add all of these squared deviations: $\Sigma(X - \overline{X})^2$
5. Divide the sum just obtained by (n − 1): $\Sigma(X - \overline{X})^2 / (n - 1)$
6. Take the square root of the value obtained in No. 5.

To illustrate the calculation of the standard deviation, the ten annual contract salaries (in $1,000) used in calculating the average deviation are again set forth below:

Salary (X)	$(X - \overline{X}) = x$	$(X - \overline{X})^2 = x^2$
(1)	(2)	(3)
$ 13.3	−0.5	0.25
13.6	−0.2	0.04
13.6	−0.2	0.04
13.6	−0.2	0.04
13.7	−0.1	0.01
13.9	+0.1	0.01
13.9	+0.1	0.01
14.0	+0.2	0.04
14.1	+0.3	0.09
14.3	+0.5	0.25
$138.0	0	0.78

Using Formula (5.3), the sample standard deviation is seen to be:

$$S = \sqrt{\Sigma(X - \overline{X})^2 / (n - 1)}$$

$$= \sqrt{0.78 / (10 - 1)} = (0.0867)^{1/2}$$

$$= 0.29 \text{ or } \$290$$

The symbol "½" following the parenthesis above means the same as a square root sign. The variance for this sample would be S^2 or 0.0867. The variance is important in arriving at more complicated standard deviations because individual variances may be added. This topic is considered in Part IV.

With the advent of the now-obsolete mechanical calculators, it became possible to avoid the numerous subtractions in obtaining the deviations from the mean by using the raw data only. Today, all electronic statistical calculators provide a key for producing the standard deviation directly, with all necessary computations being done internally. A simplified formula (although it looks more complicated) for calculating the sample standard deviation is given by either Formula (5.4) or (5.5), which are slight variations of each other.

$$S = \sqrt{[\Sigma X^2 - (\Sigma X)^2 / n] / (n - 1)} \quad (5.4)$$

$$S = \sqrt{[n\Sigma X^2 - (\Sigma X)^2] / n(n - 1)} \quad (5.5)$$

A corresponding set of formulas for the population standard deviation would be given by (5.6) and (5.7):

$$\sigma = \sqrt{[\Sigma X^2 - (\Sigma X)^2 / N] / N} \qquad (5.6)$$

$$\sigma = \sqrt{[N\Sigma X^2 - (\Sigma X)^2] / N^2} \qquad (5.7)$$

In each of these formulas only a single subtraction is called for. In all four, it is required to calculate only two sums:

ΣX which is the sum of the individual observations

ΣX^2 which is the sum of the individual observations squared.

The use of one of the formulas, (5.4), will suffice to demonstrate how each is used in calculating a sample or population standard deviation. Ages for a sample of eight teachers, used earlier in this chapter, will provide a comparison between the use of Formula (5.3) and Formula (5.4):

Age (X)	X^2	$(X - \overline{X}) = x$	$(X - \overline{X})^2 = x^2$
(1)	(2)	(3)	(4)
34	1,156	−6	36
37	1,369	−3	9
38	1,444	−2	4
39	1,521	−1	1
40	1,600	0	0
42	1,764	+2	4
43	1,849	+3	9
47	2,209	+7	49
320	12,912	0	112

Formula (5.3) yields:

$$S = \sqrt{\Sigma(X - \overline{X})^2 / (n - 1)} = \sqrt{112 / (8 - 1)} = 4 \text{ years}$$

Formula (5.4) yields:

$$S = \sqrt{[\Sigma X^2 - (\Sigma X)^2 / n] / (n - 1)}$$

$$= \sqrt{[12,912 - (320)^2 / 8] / (8 - 1)}$$

$$= \sqrt{112 / 7} = \sqrt{16} = 4 \text{ years}$$

The most common mistake made in using Formulas (5.4) through (5.7) is confusing ΣX^2 with $(\Sigma X)^2$. A review of Appendix C might be helpful at this time.

The standard deviation is an appropriate measure of variation when the characteristic is either on the interval or ratio scale and, as has been stated, is the most important such measure when making inferences from a sample to a population.

5.5 FURTHER EXAMPLES

To illustrate further computations for the average deviation and the standard deviation consider the following two examples:

- For a sample of ten teachers the number of years of tenure for each teacher is recorded. Also recorded are the necessary computations to arrive at the average deviation and the standard deviation.

Years of tenure (X)	X^2	$(X - \bar{X})$	$(X - \bar{X})^2$
(1)	(2)	(3)	(4)
3	9	−8	64
7	49	−4	16
9	81	−2	4
9	81	−2	4
11	121	0	0
11	121	0	0
13	169	+2	4
14	196	+3	9
14	196	+3	9
19	361	+8	64
110	1,384	−16 +16 0	174

The following sums can be seen from the above table:

$\Sigma X = 110 \qquad \Sigma X^2 = 1,384 \qquad \Sigma |X - \bar{X}| = (16 + 16) = 32$

$\Sigma (X - \bar{X})^2 = 174 \qquad n = 10$

The arithmetic mean is seen to be 110 / 10, or 11 years.

The average deviation from the mean for this group of ten teachers is given by Formula (5.1)

$$\text{A.D.} = \Sigma |X - \bar{X}| / n$$
$$= 32 / 10 = 3.2 \text{ years}$$

The standard deviation using Formula (5.3) is:

$$S = \sqrt{\Sigma(X - \overline{X})^2 / (n - 1)}$$

$$= \sqrt{174 / (10 - 1)}$$

$$= \sqrt{19.33} = 4.40 \text{ years}$$

The standard deviation using Formula (5.4) is:

$$S = \sqrt{[\Sigma X^2 - (\Sigma X)^2 / n] / (n - 1)}$$

$$= \sqrt{[1{,}384 - (110)^2 / 10] / (10 - 1)}$$

$$= \sqrt{174 / 9} = 4.40 \text{ years}$$

- In a particular school, students from two sections taking the same subject were given an identical final exam. The results for a sample of ten students from each of the two sections are given below, along with the necessary additional columns to calculate the average and standard deviations:

Section A:

Score (X)	X^2	$(X - \overline{X}) = x$	$(X - \overline{X})^2 = x^2$
(1)	(2)	(3)	(4)
75	5,625	−12	144
79	6,241	− 8	64
83	6,889	− 4	16
85	7,225	− 2	4
87	7,569	0	0
88	7,744	+ 1	1
90	8,100	+ 3	9
92	8,464	+ 5	25
93	8,649	+ 6	36
98	9,604	+11	121
870	76,110	−26	420
		+26	
		0	

Calculations for the arithmetic mean and the average deviation from the mean follow:

$$\overline{X} = \Sigma X / n = 870 / 10 = 87$$

$$\text{A.D.} = \Sigma |X - \overline{X}| / n = (26 + 26) / 10 = 52 / 10 = 5.2$$

Using Formula (5.4), the standard deviation is found to be:

$$S = \sqrt{[\Sigma X^2 - (\Sigma X)^2 / n] / (n - 1)}$$

$$= \sqrt{[76{,}110 - (870)^2 / 10] / (10 - 1)}$$

$$= \sqrt{420 / 9} = 6.83$$

Section B:

Score (X)	X^2	$(X - \bar{X}) = x$	$(X - \bar{X})^2 = x^2$
(1)	(2)	(3)	(4)
79	6,241	− 8	64
80	6,400	− 7	49
80	6,400	− 7	49
84	7,056	− 3	9
86	7,396	− 1	1
88	7,744	+ 1	1
90	8,100	+ 3	9
93	8,649	+ 6	36
95	9,025	+ 8	64
95	9,025	+ 8	64
870	76,036	−26	346
		+26	
		0	

Calculations for the arithmetic mean and the average deviation from the mean follow:

$$\bar{X} = \Sigma X / n = 870 / 10 = 87$$

$$A.D. = \Sigma |X - \bar{X}| / n = (26 + 26) / 10 = 52 / 10 = 5.2$$

Using Formula (5.4), the standard deviation is found to be:

$$S = \sqrt{[\Sigma X^2 - (\Sigma X)^2 / n] / (n - 1)}$$

$$= \sqrt{[76{,}036 - (870)^2 / 10] / (10 - 1)}$$

$$= \sqrt{346 / 9} = 6.20$$

In both instances, the arithmetic means and the average deviations are identical, 87 and 5.2, respectively. Yet, it is clear from examining the data that there is a greater spread among the scores for the sample of ten from Section A than for Section B. This difference is noted in a slightly larger standard deviation for Section A test scores. The mean, average deviation, and standard deviation are all reported in terms of test score units.

5.6 SUMMARY

Although four measures of variation have been presented, the standard deviation is the one most widely used in reporting on sample or population data. In making inferences from a sample to a population it is the essential measure of variation.

The *range* is the simplest to compute and is also appropriate when information about the extremes (such as minimum and maximum salaries) is desired. Its dependence on only the two extreme values makes distortion quite easy if one of these extremes is far removed from the next observation.

The *interquartile range* is easy to interpret and is appropriate when the data are incomplete or truncated at either end (e.g., 25 teachers with salaries of $15,000 or higher). It is easy to estimate graphically.

The *average deviation* from the mean is easy to interpret and does consider all of the observations. It is rarely used in making inferences from a sample to a population.

The *standard deviation* is the most reliable of the four measures, exhibiting the least amount of variation from one sample to another drawn from the same population. It forms the basis for assessing sampling variability when making inferences to a population. As with the average deviation, it is also useful in making statements about variability differences in a given characteristic among different samples or populations.

6

POSITIONAL MEASURES

Although measures of central tendency and variation are perhaps the most frequently used summary measures, two other classes of such measures are also of importance for researchers in education. Positional measures are discussed in this chapter. These measures tend to identify the relative position of an individual observation within the group of interest. For example, just knowing that a test grade is 85 does not indicate where this score lies with respect to other scores in the group.

In this chapter three categories of positional measures are discussed: percentiles, proportions or percentages, and standard scores.

6.1 PERCENTILES

Percentiles and related measures—such as quartiles, deciles, and the median—position an observation within its group in terms of percentages or proportions. To illustrate this concept, Exhibit 3.2 is repeated again as Exhibit 6.1. These data represent annual contract salaries for 1,311 teachers during school year 1975-76. Data in the six columns are as follows:

- *Col. 1:* Class intervals for individual salaries, ranging from the highest set of salaries ($19,000 to $20,999) to the lowest ($5,000 to $6,999). These classes are ordered from highest to lowest.
- *Col. 2:* Class frequency or number of teachers with salaries within the class.
- *Col. 3:* Midpoint of each class, obtained by averaging the upper and lower values of the class interval.
- *Col. 4:* Limit separating one class interval from the adjacent class interval.
- *Col. 5:* Relative frequency within each class; also the proportion of teachers with salaries within each class.
- *Col. 6:* Cumulative relative frequency of teachers with salaries less than each class limit; also the proportion of teachers with salaries less than each class limit.

The plot of the cumulative proportion distribution is also repeated as Exhibit 6.2. Although numerical formulas exist for calculating percentiles, quartiles, and deciles, this HANDBOOK only considers graphic procedures.

EXHIBIT 6.1—ANNUAL CONTRACT SALARY FOR A NATIONWIDE SAMPLE OF PUBLIC SCHOOL TEACHERS FOR SCHOOL YEAR 1975-76*

Annual contract salary	Frequency f	Midpoint X	Limit L	Relative frequency p	Cumulative relative frequency Σp
(1)	(2)	(3)	(4)	(5)	(6)
			20,999.5		1.001
(1) 19,000-20,999	43	19,999.5		0.033	
			18,999.5		0.968
(2) 17,000-18,999	98	17,999.5		0.075	
			16,999.5		0.893
(3) 15,000-16,999	125	15,999.5		0.095	
			14,999.5		0.798
(4) 13,000-14,999	179	13,999.5		0.137	
			12,999.5		0.661
(5) 11,000-12,999	275	11,999.5		0.210	
			10,999.5		0.451
(6) 9,000-10,999	363	9,999.5		0.277	
			8,999.5		0.174
(7) 7,000-8,999	224	7,999.5		0.171	
			6,999.5		0.003
(8) 5,000-6,999	4	5,999.5		0.003	
			4,999.5		...
TOTAL	1,311	...	...	1.001	...

*The data are somewhat modified from actual data reported in surveys conducted by NEA Research during this time period.

When data for a specific variable have been ordered from lowest to highest, as in Exhibit 6.1, the points or values of the variable that divide the group into 100 parts are referred to as percentile points. The median, which has been discussed previously, is certainly the 50th-percentile point because it divides the group in half. The median has also been shown to be the second quartile point, since it divides the variable into the top two and bottom two quarters. Finally, the median is also referred to as the 5th-decile point, since it divides the group into the lowest and highest five-tenths. The median, or 50th-percentile point, is seen in Exhibit 6.1 as being estimated at $11,500. (Some researchers insist that the term for "percentile" should be "centile" because *per* is unnecessary.)

A more general definition for a percentile point is that point on the cumulative proportion distribution (or curve) below which fall a stated percentage or proportion of the observations.

In Exhibit 6.2, estimates for both the 25th-percentile point (also the 1st-quartile point) and the 80th-percentile point (also the 8th-decile point) are indicated. To illustrate the estimation procedure, consider the 80th-percentile point:

- The proportion desired is identified as 0.80 (indicated by Point A in Exhibit 6.2).
- A line is drawn from this point parallel to the base scale until it intersects the cumulative proportion curve at Point B.
- From Point B a line is drawn perpendicular to the base until it intersects the base at Point C. This intersection is then the graphic estimate for the 80th percentile, or the 8th decile, and is seen to be approximately $15,000.

The symbol P_{80} is commonly used to identify the 80th-percentile point. In a similar way the first quartile can be represented as P_{25} and the median as P_{50}.

For a discussion of arithmetic computations for the percentile points, see Edwards (1954).

6.2 PROPORTIONS OR PERCENTAGES

Proportions and percentages are widely used as summary measures, particularly to report survey results. Although not indicators of relative position, strictly speaking, proportions and percentages do indicate the portion of all observations in a group that lie within a specific category (nominal or ordinal scales) or within a specific interval in a frequency distribution (interval or ratio scales). In Exhibit 6.1, the proportion of teachers in each class interval is given in Column 5, also referred to as "relative frequency."

The proportion of observations falling within a given category or class interval is defined as the ratio of the frequency of observations (analysis units) within the category or class to the total number of AU's under consideration (the frequency within a specific category or class interval divided by the total number of observations). For a population this summary measure is found to be given by Formula (6.1):

$$\boxed{\pi = f / N} \tag{6.1}$$

where

- π is the symbol representing the population proportion possessing a specific characteristic
- f is the frequency of analysis units (number of such AU's) possessing the given level of the characteristic
- N the total number of AU's in the population.

A similar formula applies when dealing with a sample, namely,

$$\boxed{p = f / n} \tag{6.2}$$

EXHIBIT 6.2–CUMULATIVE PROPORTION OF TEACHERS EARNING LESS THAN SPECIFIC ANNUAL CONTRACT SALARIES FOR SCHOOL YEAR 1975-76 (A CUMULATIVE PROPORTION DISTRIBUTION)

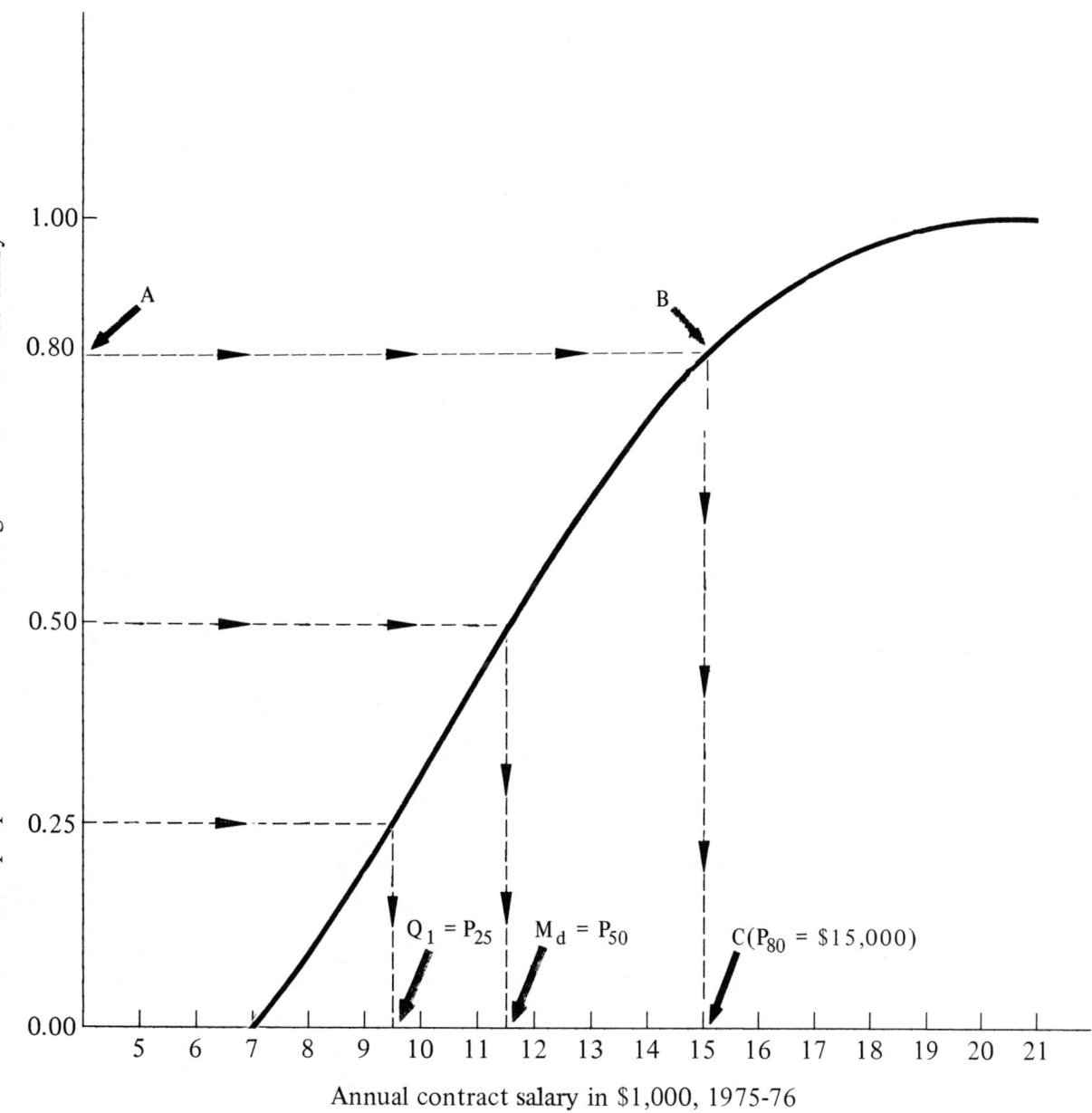

where

    p   is the symbol representing the proportion in a sample possessing a specific characteristic

    f   is the frequency of analysis units possessing the given level of the characteristic

    n   is the sample size.

To convert the indicated proportions (π and p) to percentages, the value is multiplied by 100.

Suppose in a sample of 350 teachers that 250 are in favor of a specific issue and 100 are opposed. Using Equation (6.2), the proportion favoring the issue in the sample is given by:

$$p = f / n = 250 / 350 = 0.71$$

or 71% (0.71 X 100) favor the issue in this sample.

6.3 STANDARD SCORES

Standard scores are a family of summary measures that position an individual observation within the sample or population. In that sense, standard scores are similar to percentiles. Standard scores are widely used in educational and psychological testing and also play an important role in using the normal distribution (to be discussed in Chapter 8) for purpose of statistical inference. Although there are many more such standard scores, only two are presented in this HANDBOOK for illustrative purposes: the Z-score and the T-score. An excellent reference for a more detailed discussion of standard scores is Lyman (1978).

6.3.1 Z-Scores

Suppose that in a given school district in a given year (a population) the average age of all teachers is 41 years and the standard deviation has been calculated at seven years. What can be said about the relative position of a teacher whose age is 48 years? First, this teacher's age is seven years above the average within the district (48 years minus 41 years = 7 years). Being seven years older than the average of all teachers within the district is the same thing as saying that this teacher is one standard deviation above the average.

What can be said, in a similar vein, about a teacher whose age is 27 years? This teacher's age is 14 years below the average for the district (27 years minus 41 years = -14 years; the minus sign indicates below average). Since a standard deviation has been identified as seven years, this teacher is 14 years below average or two standard deviations below the average within this district.

In symbolic form, the relative positioning for each of the teachers above is given by Formula (6.3):

$$Z = (X - \mu) / \sigma \qquad (6.3)$$

where

- X is the individual value of the characteristic (e.g., an individual teacher's age)
- μ is the arithmetic mean for the population (the average age for all teachers within the district)
- σ is the standard deviation within this same population

The symbol Z is used to identify this relative positioning of the individual AU's and is referred to as the "Z-score." The Z value, then, identifies the number of standard deviations an individual AU is above or below the arithmetic mean for the group.

An expression similar to (6.3) for a set of sample data can be seen to be given by:

$$Z = (X - \bar{X}) / S \qquad (6.4)$$

where

- X is the individual value of the characteristic
- $\bar{X}$ is the sample arithmetic mean
- S is the sample standard deviation.

To illustrate, suppose the average number of years of tenure for a sample of 100 teachers within a given school district is 12 with a standard deviation of four years. What can be said about teachers whose tenure is 18 years? How about five years?

The standard Z-score for the teacher with 18 years of tenure [from Formula (6.4)] is seen to be:

$$Z = (X - \bar{X}) / S$$
$$= (18 - 12) / 4$$
$$= 6 / 4 = 1.5$$

This teacher's number of years of tenure is 1.5 standard deviations above average for this group.

The standard Z-score for the teacher whose number of years of tenure is five years is seen to be:

$$Z = (X - \bar{X}) / S$$
$$= (5 - 12) / 4$$
$$= -7 / 4 = -1.75$$

This teacher's number of years of tenure is 1.75 standard deviations below (the minus sign) the average for the group.

This particular standard score will be extremely valuable in introducing the normal distribution in Chapter 8.

6.3.2 T-Scores

By its arithmetic nature, the Z-score will yield numerous negative values within a given set of data. If the data are symmetrical, half of the Z-scores will be negative and half will be positive. To overcome this disadvantage (many individuals are confused by negative numbers), a modification is made to the Z-score to yield a resultant standard score with a mean of 50 and a standard deviation of ten. Clearly preferable! This modified characteristic (from the raw score to the Z-score) is usually referred to as the "T-score" and is also used widely in psychological and educational testing.

Exhibit 6.3 identifies the differences among the scales for the original variable (years of tenure with a given school district) and the corresponding Z-scores and T-scores. As an illustration, if a teacher has been with the system for 8 years, this value of the variable is one standard deviation below average (a Z-score of -1.0) and possesses a T-score of 40 (now one standard deviation—10—below the mean score of 50).

A formula for converting original raw scores in a population into T-scores is given as follows:

$$\boxed{\begin{aligned} T &= 50 + 10\,Z \\ &= 50 + 10\,(X - \mu)\,/\,\sigma \end{aligned}} \qquad (6.5)$$

where

- μ is the population arithmetic mean
- σ is the population standard deviation
- X is the original value, or raw score, for the variable of interest
- T is the new positional measure with its mean of 50 and its standard deviation of ten.

To illustrate the use of Formula (6.5), consider again the example of the teacher whose age is 48 and for which the population mean was 41 and the standard deviation seven years. The corresponding T-score is seen to be:

$$\begin{aligned} T &= 50 + 10\,(X - \mu)\,/\,\sigma \\ &= 50 + 10\,(48 - 41)\,/\,7 \\ &= 50 + 10\,(7\,/\,7) \\ &= 50 + 10 = 60 \end{aligned}$$

Formula (6.5), when dealing with a sample, becomes:

$$\boxed{T = 50 + 10\,(X - \bar{X})\,/\,S} \qquad (6.6)$$

where

- X is the original variable of interest
- $\bar{X}$ is the sample arithmetic mean
- S is the sample standard deviation
- T is the T-score associated with the given value for X.

EXHIBIT 6.3—A COMPARISON AMONG AN ORIGINAL VARIABLE AND THE ASSOCIATED Z-SCORES AND T-SCORES.

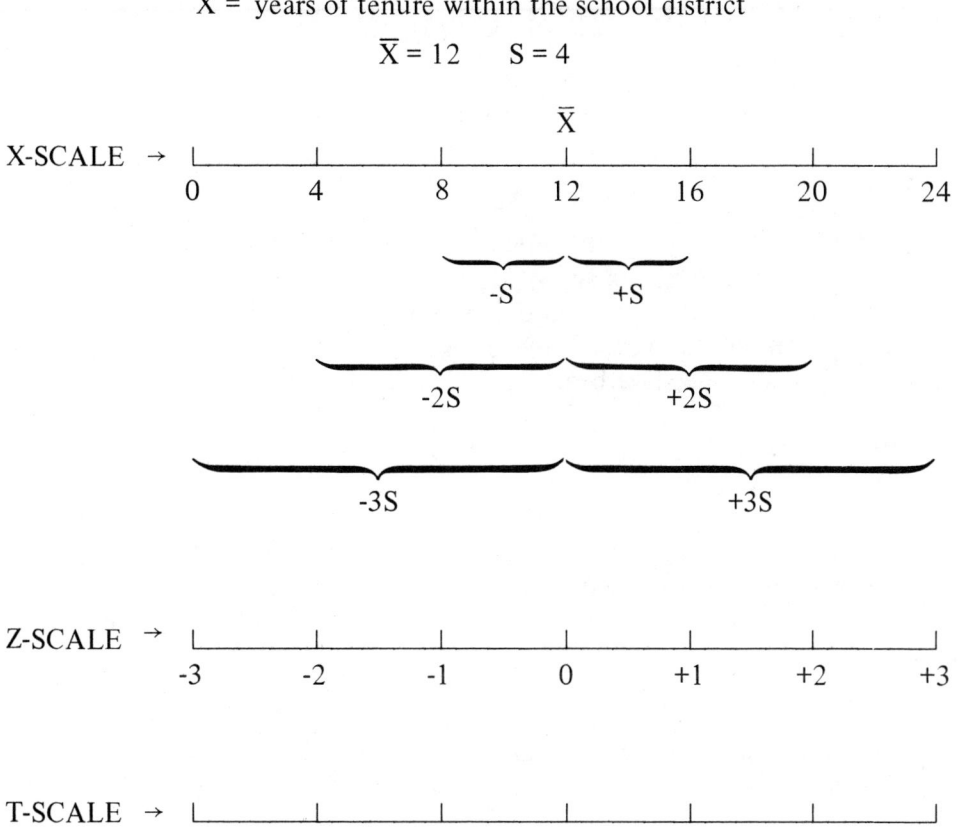

There are times when only T-scores are given and it is desirable to convert the T-score to the raw score, or original variable of interest. For a population of AU's, this can be accomplished through the following formula:

$$X = \mu + \sigma (T - 50) / 10 \tag{6.7}$$

A similar formula applies for sample data by substituting $\bar{X}$ for μ and S for σ.

For the example involving a sample of 100 teachers within a school district it is desired to convert a teacher's T-score of 65 to the corresponding number of years of tenure within the system. Since the sample mean was 12 years and the standard deviation four years, it follows that the original raw score is given as follows:

$$X = \bar{X} + S (T - 50) / 10$$
$$= 12 + 4 (65 - 50) / 10$$
$$= 12 + 4 \times 1.5 = 12 + 6 = 18 \text{ years}$$

The standard T-score of 65 is associated with the original variable value of 18 years of tenure.

7
MEASURES OF ASSOCIATION

The researcher in education is confronted with such statistical problems as measuring how much of a characteristic exists within a sample or a population, how far apart the observations (analysis units) are from one another, and what position an analysis unit (AU) occupies within the distribution. These measures, all of which are concerned with a single characteristic, have been dealt with in the previous three chapters.

Frequently, however, the researcher is concerned with analyzing the relationship or association among two or more characteristics associated with an AU, such as age, years of tenure, and salary of teachers in a specific school district. This chapter considers the bivariate case (two characteristics) in considerable detail. Miscellaneous measures of association are presented and basic concepts associated with more than two characteristics are briefly reviewed in this chapter and discussed in more detail in Chapter 11.

7.1 CORRELATION AND REGRESSION: THE DISTINCTION

In considering AU's from a population or sample of interest, more than one characteristic is usually associated with the unit. For example, if a school district is the unit of interest, characteristics associated with the individual school district might be the average teacher's salary, planned expenditures for the school year, the percentage of males, the pupil/teacher ratio, and the average daily attendance.

Two variables are said to be correlated if there appears to be a fairly consistent pattern to their relationship. Specifically, higher teacher salaries (one variable) tend to be associated with longer tenure (a second variable). Two variables symbolized by X and Y can appear to be related in a linear and in a nonlinear sense. Exhibit (7.1) identifies six situations in which the relationship is linear. The most frequently used measure of linear relationship is referred to as the "Pearson product-moment correlation coefficient" (symbolized in a sample by the letter r and in the population by the Greek letter rho, ρ). Figure A shows a perfect positive relationship between the variables X and Y, with the value for r being +1. Figure B illustrates a perfect negative relationship, with the value for r being -1. In Figure C, although all the points lie on a straight line, the correlation is 0, since for any value of X, the value for Y is the same, namely 5.

Figures D, E, and F indicate departures from a perfect positive correlation, with the values of r being 0.92, 0.91, and 0.54, respectively, with Figure F showing a greater scatter than D or E. Correlations are always between +1 and -1, with values approaching the two extremes indicating a stronger linear relationship. While the correlation coefficient is an index ranging from +1 to −1, a more useful measure is the square of the correlation coefficient (r^2), referred to as the "coefficient of determination." The coefficient of determination can assume a value from 0 to +1 and represents the proportion of the total variation in one variable explained by differences in the other variable.

EXHIBIT 7.1–SOME HYPOTHETICAL DATA PLOTS AND THEIR ASSOCIATED CORRELATIONS

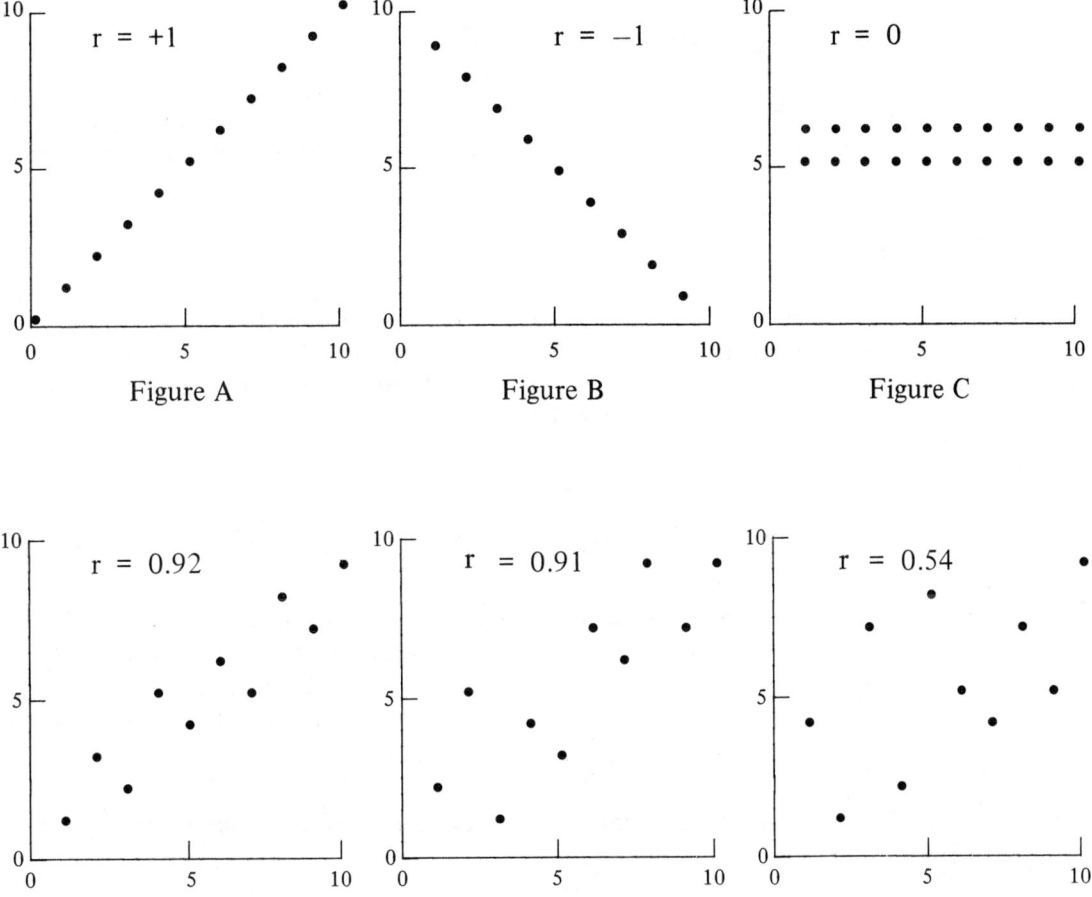

Correlations obviously exist where the relationship is not linear (referred to as "nonlinear"). This topic will be briefly discussed in Section 7.3.

Unlike correlation, which implies association only, regression may imply cause and effect—or the ability to use one variable (referred to as the "independent variable") to predict values for the second variable (referred to as the "dependent variable"). The procedure to accomplish this prediction involves studying the behavior of the two variables (X and Y) simultaneously. The results will be a numerical expression relating specific values of Y to corresponding values of the independent variable, X. This is accomplished through formulas (to be presented in the next section) that provide the "regression line" or prediction equation. Values of X are "plugged" into the regression equation, resulting in a forecast value for Y corresponding to the given X value. To illustrate, suppose that the expression Y = $9,000 + $800X describes the relationship between years of teaching experience (X) and salary. A starting teacher (X = 0; no experience) would get $9,000. For every year of additional teaching experience (an increase in X of one unit), the salary would be expected to increase by $800. Details on calculating such an expression are presented in Section 7.2.

While correlation implies only an apparent association, regression implies the ability to use values of one variable to predict (forecast) values of the second variable.

7.2 THE LINEAR CASE–TWO VARIABLES

In this section, procedures with examples are presented for calculating statistics associated with both correlation and regression, where the relationship between X and Y is assumed to be linear.

7.2.1 Correlation

The measure used to represent the degree of linear correlation is the Pearson product-moment correlation coefficient[1], represented in a sample by the letter r and in the population by the Greek letter rho, ρ. Expressed in terms of measures associated with the variables X and Y, the correlation coefficient is given as:

$$\boxed{r = S_{xy} \div (S_x \cdot S_y)} \tag{7.1}$$

(where the dot, ".", indicates multiplication). S_x and S_y are, respectively, the standard deviations for the X and Y variables. S_{xy} is a new measure and is referred to as the covariance between X and Y. Since the covariance is not calculated directly in this HANDBOOK, no specific formula is presented. If the reader is interested, an excellent discussion can be found in Mendenhall, Ott, & Scheaffer (1971, pp. 11-12).

Computationally, it is easier to calculate r^2 (the coefficient of determination) by using the following formula:

$$\boxed{r^2 = A \div (B \times C)} \tag{7.2}$$

where

$$A = [n\Sigma XY - (\Sigma X)(\Sigma Y)]^2 \tag{7.3}$$

$$B = [n\Sigma X^2 - (\Sigma X)^2] \tag{7.4}$$

$$C = [n\Sigma Y^2 - (\Sigma Y)^2] \tag{7.5}$$

---

[1]The Pearson product-moment correlation coefficient may also be expressed in terms of products of the corresponding X and Y Z scores.

Exhibit 7.2 graphically summarizes the relationship between the average daily attendance in millions of students (X) and the average annual salary of teachers in $1,000 (Y) (for ten states, selected at random from all states). The basic data from which this graph was obtained are the following pairs of X and Y values:

X: 4.28 3.00 2.57 2.07 2.03 1.96 1.92 1.39 1.29 1.12

Y: 15.6 16.3 11.3 11.6 12.6 13.9 15.7 10.5 13.6 11.9

The necessary calculations to arrive at the correlation coefficient follow:

$\Sigma Y^2 = 1,806.58$ $\Sigma X^2 = 54.7077$

$\Sigma Y = 133$ $\Sigma X = 21.63$

$\Sigma XY = 297.154$ $n = 10$

$A = [n\Sigma XY - (\Sigma X)(\Sigma Y)]^2$

$\quad = [10 \times 297.154 - 21.63 \times 133]^2$

$\quad = 8977.5625$

$B = [n\Sigma X^2 - (\Sigma X)^2]$

$\quad = [10 \times 54.7077 - (21.63)^2]$

$\quad = 79.2201$

$C = [n\Sigma Y^2 - (\Sigma Y)^2]$

$\quad = [10 \times 1,806.58 - (133)^2]$

$\quad = 376.8$

$r^2 = A \div (B \times C)$

$\quad = (8977.5625) \div (79.2201)(376.8)$

$\quad = 0.3008$

$r = 0.5484$

The correlation coefficient, 0.5484, is an index on the scale from −1 to +1. The coefficient of determination, 0.3008, indicates the proportion of the variation in Y (Σy^2) that is explained by the variation in X. More details on the interpretation of the of the coefficient of determination will be given in Part III.

EXHIBIT 7.2–A COMPARISON BETWEEN AVERAGE DAILY ATTENDANCE OF STUDENTS IN MILLIONS AND AVERAGE ANNUAL SALARY OF TEACHERS IN $1,000

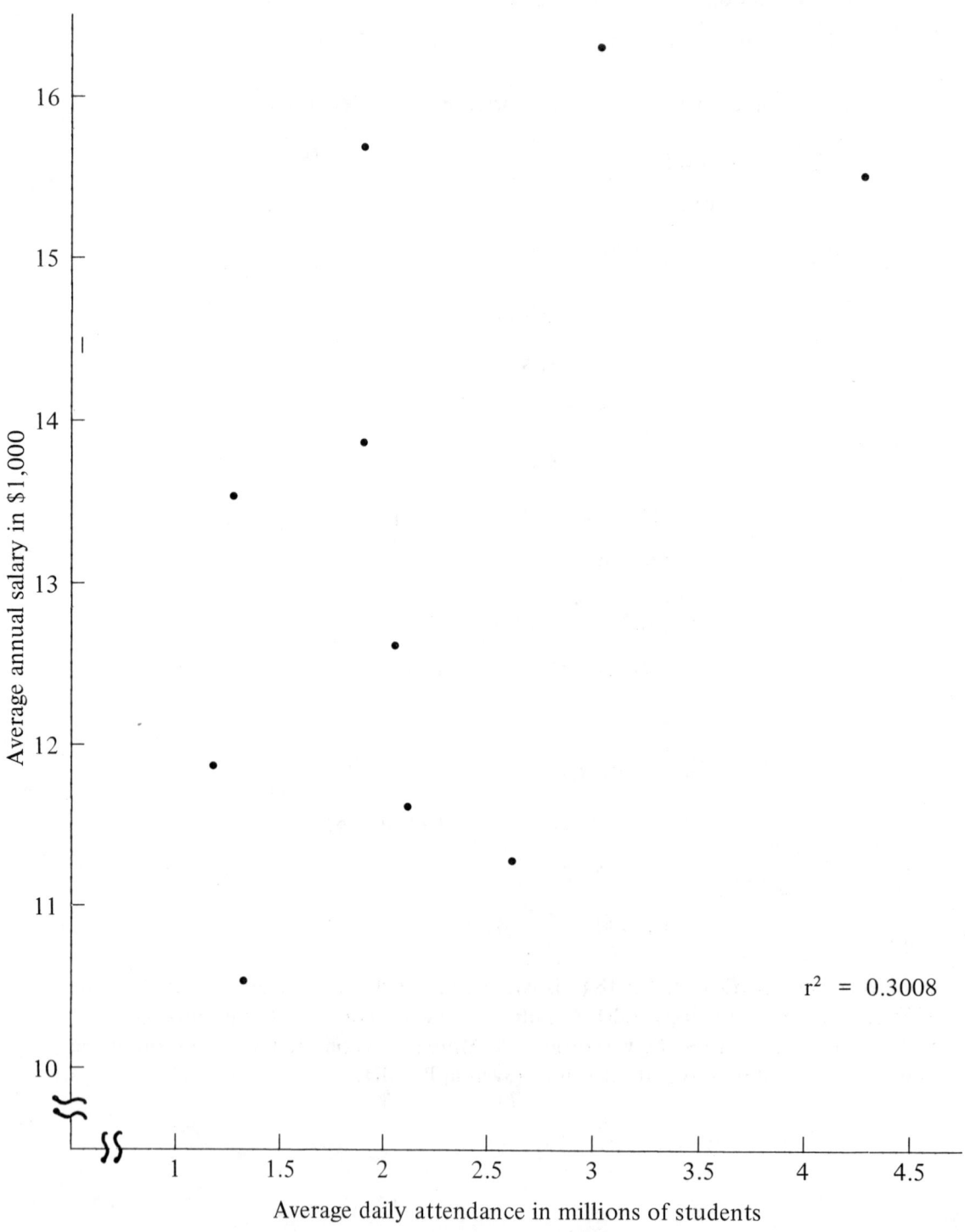

Consider the following second illustration on calculating the correlation coefficient, where X represents a math quality point index (QPI); and Y, the corresponding statistics QPI for ten graduating students:

X: 2.9 2.7 3.1 2.8 2.7 2.4 3.1 3.3 3.4 2.6

Y: 3.0 2.7 3.4 2.7 2.8 2.6 3.2 3.2 3.7 2.8

The necessary calculations follow:

$\Sigma Y^2 = 91.75$ $\quad\quad\quad\quad$ $\Sigma X^2 = 85.02$

$\Sigma Y = 30.1$ $\quad\quad\quad\quad$ $\Sigma X = 29.0$

$\Sigma XY = 88.23$ $\quad\quad\quad\quad$ $n = 10$

$$A = [n\Sigma XY - (\Sigma X)(\Sigma Y)]^2$$
$$= [10 \times 88.23 - 29.0 \times 30.1]^2$$
$$= 9.4^2 = 88.36$$

$$B = [n\Sigma X^2 - (\Sigma X)^2]$$
$$= [10 \times 85.02 - (29.0)^2]$$
$$= 9.2$$

$$C = [n\Sigma Y^2 - (\Sigma Y)^2]$$
$$= [10 \times 91.75 - (30.1)^2]$$
$$= 11.49$$

$$r^2 = A \div (B \times C)$$
$$= 88.36 \div (9.2)(11.49)$$
$$= 0.8359$$

$$r = 0.91$$

Since $r^2 = 0.8359$, it follows that 83.59% of the variation in statistics QPI's for this group of students can be explained by differences in math QPI's. Therefore, only 16.41% of the differences in statistics QPI's remains unexplained by the math QPI's.

7.2.2 Regression: One Variable Subject to Errors in Measurement

Regression involves the prediction of one variable from the value of another variable. Relying on a fit of a line to plotted data by eye alone has two major drawbacks:

1. No two persons will draw the same line.
2. No measure exists this way to indicate how well the data agree with the line.

As a consequence, a well-defined and accepted mathematical procedure is necessary to fit a line (or curve) to the data. Assuming that the relationship is linear, the appropriate model to describe this relationship in the population is:

$$Y = a + \beta X + \epsilon \quad (7.6)$$

where

- β = the amount of change in Y, on the average, for every change of one unit in X (referred to as the "slope of the regression line")

- a = a constant value (the point at which the regression line intersects the Y axis, referred to as the "Y-intercept")

- ϵ = the numerical amount by which an individual Y value, for a given value of X, deviates from the regression line (usually considered as a random variable that is normally distributed, with a mean value of 0 and a variance of σ_ϵ^2, and frequently referred to as the "error").

In the sampling situation, where an estimate of the regression line is desired, the following formulas apply:

$$Y' = a + bX + e \quad (7.7)$$

where

$$b = S_{xy} / S_x^2 \quad (7.8)$$

or $\qquad b = \sqrt{A} \div B$

where A and B are as defined for correlation in Formulas (7.3) and (7.4),

$$a = \overline{Y} - b\overline{X} \quad (7.9)$$

("a" is the point where the line intersects the Y axis.)
and

- e = the amount by which an individual observed value of Y, for a given value of X, deviates from the regression line value, namely, Y′.

Two examples follow on estimating the linear regression equation.

The data in Exhibit 7.3 compare years of teaching experience (the independent variable, X) with contract salary in $1,000 (the dependent variable, Y). These same data are presented graphically in Exhibit 7.4. Plotting data points in the two-variable case is strongly recommended. Reasons for this will become apparent in Section 6. Calculations leading to estimates of both the regression equation and the correlation coefficient are:

$\Sigma Y = 561.6$ $\Sigma Y^2 = 11,230.94$ $\Sigma XY = 6,992.6$
$\Sigma X = 330$ $\Sigma X^2 = 4,620$ $n = 30$
$\overline{X} = 11$ $\overline{Y} = 18.72$ $\Sigma y^2 = 717.79$

$$A = [n\Sigma XY - (\Sigma X)(\Sigma Y)]^2$$
$$= [30 \times 6,992.6 - (330)(561.6)]^2$$
$$= (24,450)^2$$

$$B = [n\Sigma X^2 - (\Sigma X)^2]$$
$$= [30 \times 4,620 - (330)^2]$$
$$= 29,700$$

$$C = [n\Sigma Y^2 - (\Sigma Y)^2]$$
$$= [30 \times 11,230.94 - (561.6)^2]$$
$$= 21,533.64$$

$$b = \sqrt{A} \div B$$
$$= 24,450 \div 29,700$$
$$= 0.823$$

$$a = \overline{Y} - b\overline{X}$$
$$= 18.72 - (0.823)(11)$$
$$= 9.67$$

$$r^2 = A \div (B \times C)$$
$$= (24,450)^2 \div 29,700 \times 21,533.64)$$
$$= 0.9347$$

and

$$Y' = a + bX$$
$$= 9.67 + 0.823X$$

The estimated regression line is plotted in Exhibit 7.4, and forecast values from the regression line are indicated as the column labeled Y′ in Exhibit 7.3 for each of ten values of X. For every increase in one year of teaching experience, on the average, salary increases by 0.823 thousand dollars, or $823. Exhibit 7.4 illustrates that the forecast contract salary for a person with 10 years of teaching experience is $17,900. The difference between $17,900 and $19,400 is the error "e" value for that particular teacher.

EXHIBIT 7.3–YEARS OF TEACHING EXPERIENCE VS. CONTRACT SALARY IN $1,000

Years of teaching experience (X)	Salary in $1,000 (Y)	Y' in $1,000
(1)	(2)	(3)
2	10.2	
2	11.1	11.3
2	11.6	
4	12.2	
4	12.7	13.0
4	13.4	
6	13.4	
6	13.7	14.6
6	14.7	
8	15.1	
8	16.3	16.3
8	17.2	
10	16.4	
10	18.2	<u>17.9</u>
10	<u>19.4</u>	
12	18.8	
12	21.2	19.5
12	22.2	
14	20.7	
14	22.6	21.2
14	24.2	
16	21.7	
16	23.3	22.8
16	24.4	
18	23.3	
18	24.3	24.5
18	25.3	
20	23.8	
20	24.7	26.1
20	25.5	

EXHIBIT 7.4 – A COMPARISON OF YEARS OF TEACHING EXPERIENCE WITH CONTRACT SALARY IN $1,000

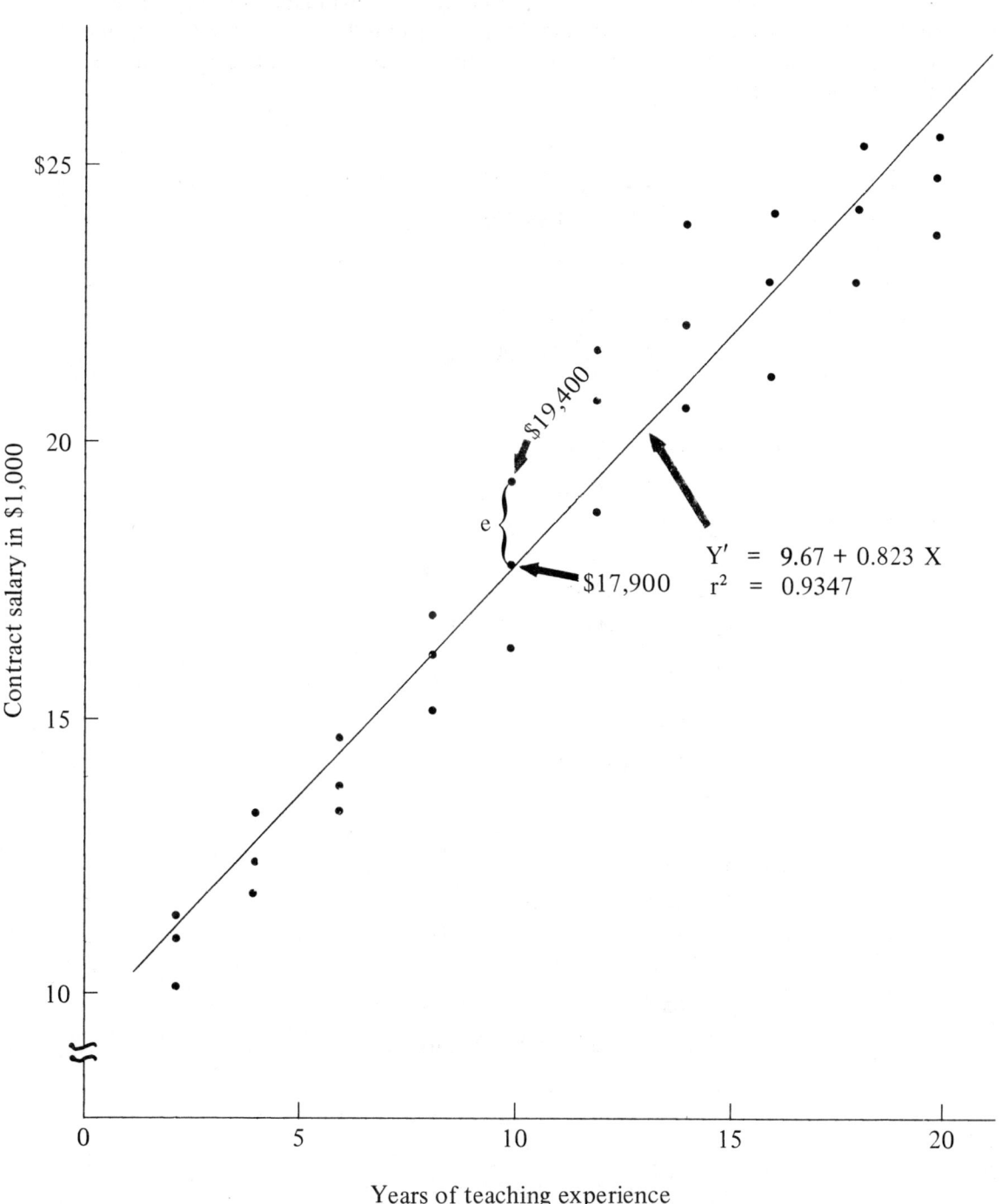

It is clear from both the graphic display and the value for r^2 that 93.47% of the variation in salaries can be attributed to differences in years of teaching experience (certainly not a surprising finding).

Exhibit 7.5 compares aptitude scores for a sample of 27 individuals with corresponding achievement scores. These data are graphically presented in Exhibit 7.6. Calculations for these data, leading to estimates of the correlation coefficient and the regression equation, are:

$\Sigma Y = 2,059 \qquad \Sigma Y^2 = 159,641 \qquad \Sigma XY = 147,435$

$\Sigma X = 1,890 \qquad \Sigma X^2 = 136,800 \qquad n = 27$

$\bar{X} = 70 \qquad \bar{Y} = 76.3 \qquad \Sigma y^2 = 2,623.19$

$$A = [n\Sigma XY - (\Sigma X)(\Sigma Y)]^2$$
$$= [27 \times 147,435 - 1,890 \times 2,059]^2$$
$$= 89,235^2$$

$$B = [n\Sigma X^2 - (\Sigma X)^2]$$
$$= [27 \times 136,800 - (1,890)^2]$$
$$= 121,500$$

$$C = [n\Sigma Y^2 - (\Sigma Y)^2]$$
$$= [27 \times 159,641 - (2,059)^2]$$
$$= 70,826$$

$$b = \sqrt{A} \div B$$
$$= 89,235 \div 121,500$$
$$= 0.734$$

$$a = \bar{Y} - b\bar{X}$$
$$= 76.3 - (0.734)(70)$$
$$= 24.92$$

$$r^2 = A / B \times C$$
$$= 89,235^2 / (121,500)(70,826)$$
$$= 0.9253$$

and

$$Y' = 24.92 + 0.734\ X$$

The estimated regression equation is plotted in Exhibit 7.6, and forecast values from the regression line are indicated as the column labeled Y' in Exhibit 7.5 for each of nine values of X.

EXHIBIT 7.5—APTITUDE TEST SCORES VS. ACHIEVEMENT TEST SCORES

Aptitude score (X)	Achievement score (Y)	Y′
(1)	(2)	(3)
50	59	
50	61	61.6
50	62	
55	63	
55	64	65.2
55	67	
60	67	
60	68	68.9
60	70	
65	70	
65	73	72.6
65	76	
70	74	
70	78	76.3
70	81	
75	77	
75	81	79.9
75	86	
80	82	
80	85	83.6
80	90	
85	84	
85	86	87.3
85	88	
90	87	
90	89	90.9
90	91	

EXHIBIT 7.6—A COMPARISON OF APTITUDE SCORES WITH CORRESPONDING ACHIEVEMENT SCORES

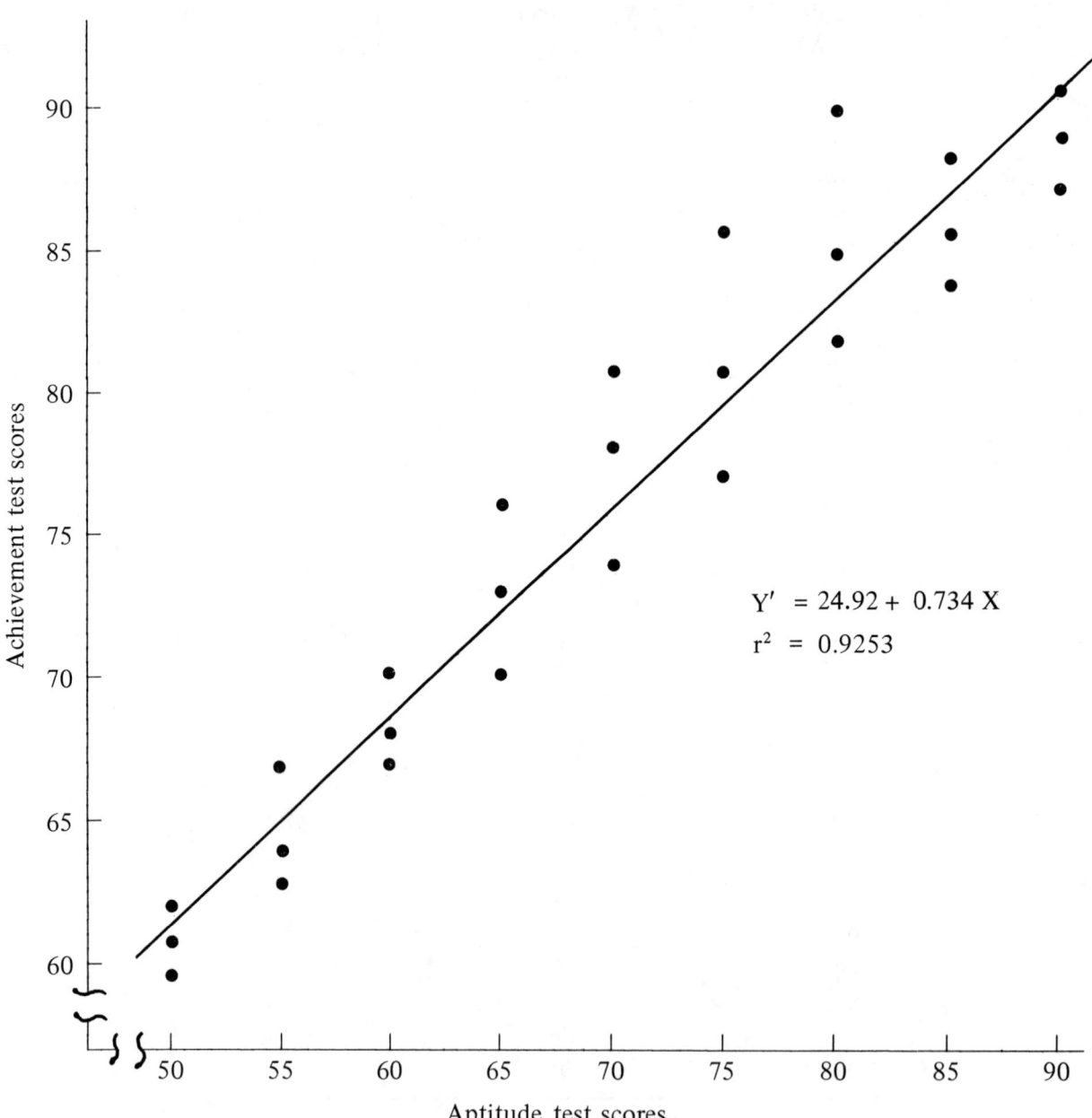

The estimated regression line indicates that, on the average, for each increase of one unit in aptitude test scores, the expected increase in achievement test scores is 0.734.

Once again, as can be seen from the graphic display and the large value for r^2, the linear relationship appears to be quite good, with only 7.47% of the variation in achievement test scores not explained by differences in aptitude test scores (100% − 92.53% = 7.47%).

7.2.3 Regression: Both Variables Subject to Errors in Measurement

The procedures presented in the previous section apply to the two-variable case when values for X are predetermined and a sample is selected to make observations on Y, with Y being subject to measurement error. There is also the situation in which both X and Y may be subject to measurement errors, such as the data in Exhibit 7.5 on aptitude and achievement test scores. A simple procedure for fitting the linear regression function in this situation is given in U.S. Department of Commerce (1966, Chapter 5). The steps for this procedure follow and then an example is given using the data in Exhibit 7.5.

1. The line will pass through the mean of all the X's and the mean of all the Y's, or $(\bar{X}, \bar{Y})$.

2. The slope of the regression line is estimated by dividing the n plotted points into three groups from the lowest to the highest values of X. Each of the extreme groups (call the lowest values of X, Group 1; the highest values, Group 3) should have an equal number of points, as near to n/3 as possible. The estimate for the slope of the line is given as:

$$b = (\bar{Y}_3 - \bar{Y}_1) / (\bar{X}_3 - \bar{X}_1)$$

where

$\bar{Y}_3$ = average Y value for Group 3

$\bar{Y}_1$ = average Y value for Group 1

$\bar{X}_3$ = average X value for Group 3

$\bar{X}_1$ = average X value for Group 1

3. The Y intercept is given by the same formula as previously used:

$$a = \bar{Y} - b\bar{X}$$

To illustrate this process, assume that the data in Exhibits 7.5 and 7.6 represent scores, both of which are subject to measurement error (not too unrealistic). Call the first set of nine pairs in Exhibit 6, Group 1; and the last set of nine pairs in Exhibit 6, Group 3. The corresponding mean values can be seen to be:

$$\bar{Y}_3 = 86.9 \quad \bar{Y}_1 = 64.6 \quad \bar{Y} = 76.3 \quad \bar{X}_3 = 85 \quad \bar{X}_1 = 55 \quad \bar{X} = 70$$

The appropriate estimate for the slope then becomes:

$$\begin{aligned} b &= (\bar{Y}_3 - \bar{Y}_1)/(\bar{X}_3 - \bar{X}_1) \\ &= (86.9 - 64.6)/(85 - 55) \\ &= 0.743 \end{aligned}$$

The Y intercept is seen to be:

$$\begin{aligned} a &= \bar{Y} - b\bar{X} = 76.3 - 0.743 \times 70 \\ &= 24.29 \end{aligned}$$

The resulting regression equation is given as:

$$Y' = 24.29 + 0.743\,X$$

which is not too different from the estimated equation, assuming that the X scores are preselected and the Y values are sampled (note: $Y' = 24.89 + 0.734\,X$).

7.3 THE NONLINEAR CASE—TWO VARIABLES

Since an infinite number of nonlinear relationships between X and Y are possible, the discussion in this section will center around one specific example, the data for which are given in Exhibit 7.7. These same 24 data points are plotted in Exhibit 7.8, along with the estimated linear regression equation. The coefficient of determination is given as 0.7247 (72.47% of the variation in the Y's can be explained by the differences in the X values).

While the straight line seems to do quite well in describing the relationship between X and Y ($r^2 = 0.7247$), some departure from linearity clearly does exist. A possible expression relating X to Y might be:

$$Y' = a + b_1 X + b_2 X^2 + b_3 X^3 + e$$

EXHIBIT 7.7—HYPOTHETICAL DATA TO ILLUSTRATE A NONLINEAR RELATIONSHIP

X	Y
(1)	(2)
2	5
2	6
2	7
7	4
7	5
7	6
12	2
12	3
12	4
17	7
17	8
17	9
22	15
22	16
22	17
27	22
27	23
27	24
32	19
32	20
32	21
37	17
37	18
37	19

EXHIBIT 7.8–A HYPOTHETICAL EXAMPLE OF A SIGNIFICANT DEPARTURE FROM LINEAR REGRESSION

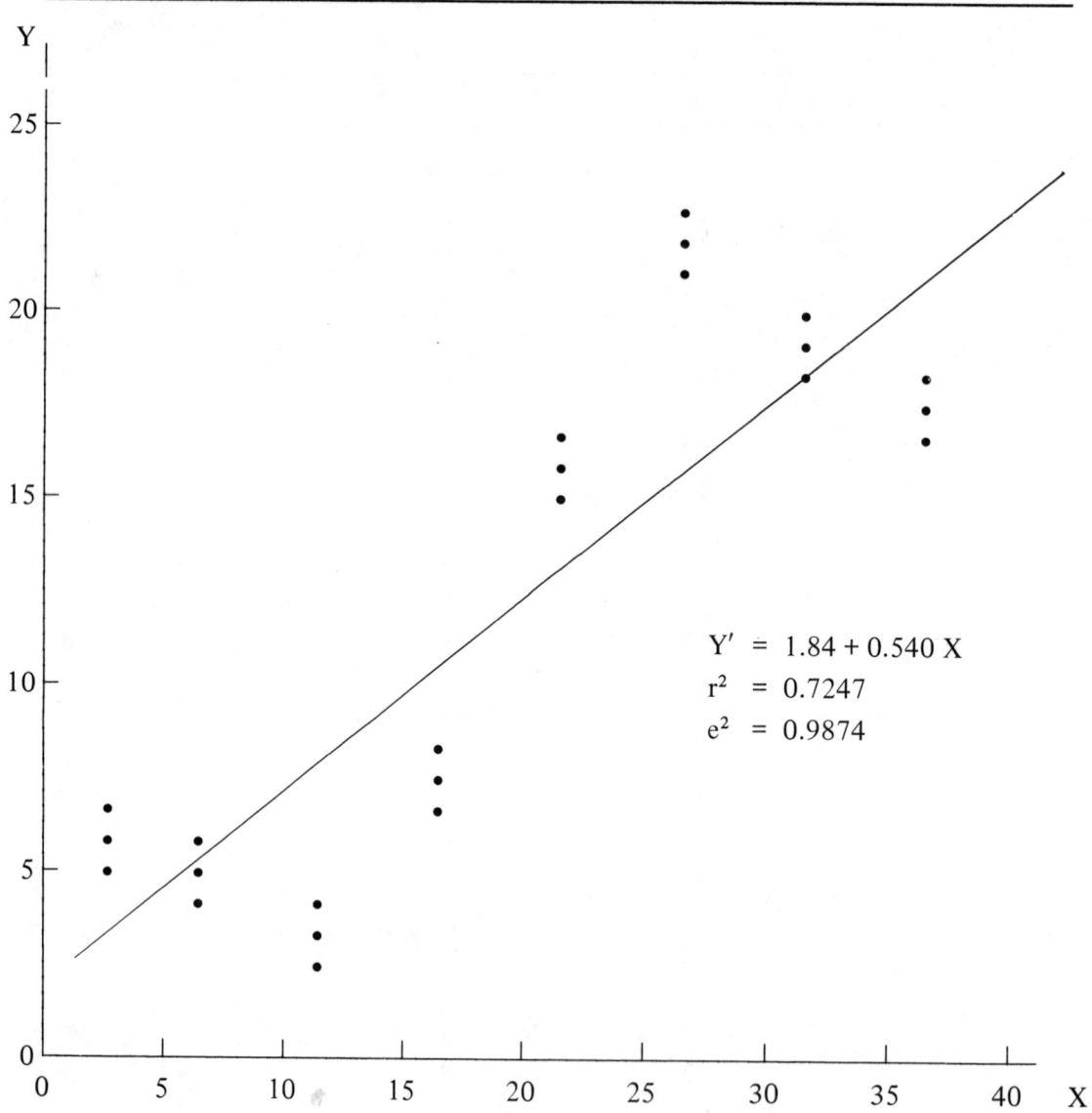

While procedures exist to select an appropriate equation (or possibly several), the intent here is not to provide formulas to estimate such an equation. Instead, a useful procedure is identified for determining whether a significant departure from linearity exists. If there is none, why bother with the arithmetic exercise? If there is, then the search for an appropriate equation can begin.

Testing for the statistical significance of the departure from linearity is discussed in Part III. This section presents a procedure for numerically calculating this departure.

Earlier in this chapter it was pointed out that the coefficient of determination (r^2) identifies the proportion of the variation in Y that can be explained by the linear relationship between X and Y. Or, putting it another way,

$$r^2 = \text{(explained variation)} / \text{(total variation)} \qquad (7.10)$$

In seeking significant nonlinearity some of the unexplained variation must now be explained. Regardless of the form of the nonlinear relationship, an estimate of the maximum amount of variation that can be additionally explained by a nonlinear relationship can be obtained. If the first three points in Exhibit 7.7 are considered, the given value of X = 2 has associated with it three different Y values, namely, 5, 6, and 7. The mean of these Y values—call it $\overline{Y}_x$—is equal to 6. The variation of the three Y values about their mean can be seen to be:

$$\begin{aligned}\Sigma(Y - \overline{Y}_x)^2 &= \Sigma Y^2 - (\Sigma Y)^2 / n \\ &= 110 - 18^2 / 3 \\ &= 110 - 108 = 2\end{aligned}$$

A similar calculation for the variation of the individual Y values about their mean for each given X value can be accomplished. Since the remaining seven sets of three points all have the same scatter, the total of these variations among the Y values for given X's is seen to be 8 x 2 = 16. This represents the total variation in the Y's that cannot be explained by any nonlinear equation, since the best that could be accomplished would be to pass the curve through the eight Y means (the $\overline{Y}_x$s) for the eight distinct values of X. This variation is referred to as the "residual variation."

For the data in Exhibit 7.7, the following calculations can be made using procedures set forth earlier:

$\Sigma Y^2 = 4,945$ $\qquad$ $\Sigma Y = 297$ $\qquad$ $\Sigma XY = 7,494$

$\Sigma X^2 = 12,276$ $\qquad$ $\Sigma X = 468$ $\qquad$ $n = 24$

$\overline{X} = 19.5$ $\qquad$ $\overline{Y} = 12.375$

$$A = [n\Sigma XY - (\Sigma X)(\Sigma Y)]^2$$
$$= [24 \times 7{,}494 - (468)(297)]^2$$
$$= 40{,}860^2$$

$$B = [n\Sigma X^2 - (\Sigma X)^2]$$
$$= [24 \times 12{,}276 - (468)^2]$$
$$= 75{,}600$$

$$C = [n\Sigma Y^2 - (\Sigma Y)^2]$$
$$= [24 \times 4{,}945 - (297)^2]$$
$$= 30{,}471$$

$$b = \sqrt{A} \div B$$
$$= 40{,}860 \div 75{,}600$$
$$= 0.540$$

$$a = \bar{Y} - b\bar{X}$$
$$= 12.375 - (0.540)(19.5)$$
$$= 1.84$$

$$Y' = a + bX = 1.84 + 0.540\,X$$

$$r^2 = A \div (B \times C)$$
$$= (40{,}860)^2 \div (75{,}600)(30{,}471)$$
$$= 0.7247$$

It is further seen that the total variation in Y is given as

$$\text{total variation} = \Sigma(Y - \bar{Y})^2$$
$$= \Sigma Y^2 - (\Sigma Y)^2 / n$$
$$= 4{,}945 - (297)^2 / 24$$
$$= 1{,}269.62$$

Since $r^2 = 0.7247$, the amount of variation explained by the linear relationship clearly is:

$$\text{Explained variation} = (r^2)(\text{total variation in Y})$$
$$= (0.7247)(1{,}269.62)$$
$$= 920.09$$

The residual variation as indicated earlier is given, for this example, as:

$$\Sigma(Y - \bar{Y}_x)^2 = \text{residual variation} = 8 \times 2 = 16$$

Note that this residual is 8 x 2 only because the variation of the Y values for each X is the same.

It then follows that the total variation in Y can be subdivided into three elements—that explained by the linear relationship; the residual variation; and, consequently, the amount of the variation in Y originally unexplained by the linear relationship but now explained by the increment due to the best possible nonlinear relationship.

Since the variation in Y that cannot be explained by the best nonlinear relationship is 16, the increment over the variation unexplained by the linear relationship is seen to be:

Total variation = variation due to linear relationship + variation incrementally due to the best nonlinear relationship + the residual.

Substituting the known quantities in the above equation yields:

1,269.62 = 920.09 + incremental variation due to best nonlinear relationship + 16.

Hence, the incremental variation explained by the nonlinear over the linear relationship is found to be:

Incremental variation due to best nonlinear relationship
= 1,269.62 − 920.09 − 16 = 333.53.

Summarizing the four terms obtained thus far, yields:

1,269.62 = total variation in Y = $\Sigma(Y - \bar{Y})^2$
 920.09 = variation in Y explained by the linear regression
  16.00 = variation in Y unexplained by the best nonlinear relationship
 333.53 = incremental variation in Y explained by the best nonlinear relationship over the linear relationship

The issue is whether this incremental explained variation is statistically significant, thereby warranting possible search for such a relationship. Procedures for examining this possible significance are given in Part III.

Some excellent examples of specific fitting procedures for the nonlinear case can be found in U.S. Department of Commerce (1966, Chapters 5 and 6).

One final point: The proportion of the total variation in Y that can be explained by a curve passing through the individual Y means is referred to as the "correlation ratio" and, in this case, is given by:

$$e^2 = (\text{total variation} - \text{residual}) / (\text{total variation})$$
$$= (1269.62 - 16) / (1{,}269.62)$$
$$= 0.9874.$$

The Greek letter eta-squared (η^2) represents this value in the population from which the sample has been selected.

7.4 SOME CAUTIONS

Blind use of the correlation and regression formulas can be dangerous. All available data points (X, Y) should be plotted to allow for a *visual* review of the apparent relationship between X and Y. This section indicates three situations in which calculating the correlation coefficient *without* plotting the data can give misleading conclusions.

7.4.1 Extremes

In Exhibit 7.9 consider the first four data points. (Using such a small sample is done *only* to illustrate the point; it is not recommended as good sampling practice.) These points are plotted in the lower lefthand corner of Exhibit 7.10. It is clear from the plot, as well as from the calculated correlation coefficient (r = −1.00), that a perfect negative correlation exists.

Assume now that a fifth pair of values (5, 5) is added to the initial four points, as seen in Exhibit 7.10. The numerical value of the correlation coefficient is now r = 0.00. Hence, a single new pair of values has mathematically changed a perfect negative correlation into a zero correlation.

If a sixth pair of values (15, 15) is now added to the first five, the numerical value of the correlation coefficient becomes r = 0.923, indicating once again how the addition of a single new value can dramatically alter the value of the correlation coefficient.

If a seventh point (25, 30) is added to the first six, the value of the correlation coefficient becomes 0.978. Note that if only the first four points and the seventh point are included, the numerical value for the correlation coefficient becomes r = 0.980. In the latter case an extreme point has had a major influence on the overall value of the correlation coefficient.

EXHIBIT 7.9–HYPOTHETICAL DATA POINTS ON EXTREME VALUES IN CORRELATION

Item	X	Y	r
(1)	(2)	(3)	(4)
1	1	4	
2	2	3	
3	3	2	
4	4	1	−1
5	5	5	0
6	15	15	0.923
7	25	30	0.978

EXHIBIT 7.10 – A HYPOTHETICAL EXAMPLE ON HOW EXTREME VALUES CAN ALTER THE CORRELATION COEFFICIENT

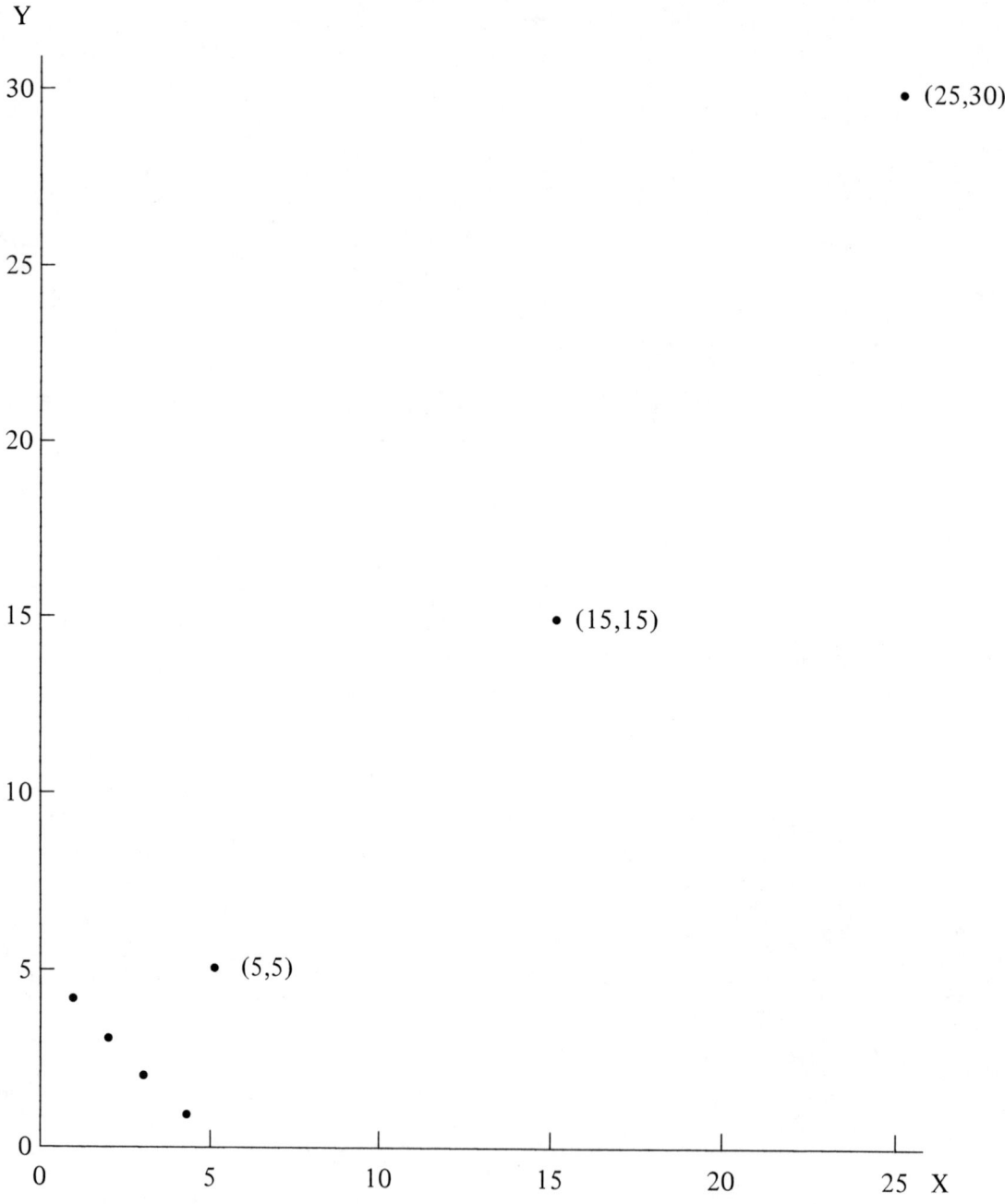

The message here is that extreme values (or single points) may distort or mask the true correlation.

7.4.2 Curvilinearity

Twenty-one data points (see Exhibit 7.11) are plotted in Exhibit 7.12. If one were not to plot the data, but only to calculate the correlation coefficient, the numerical value would be r = 0.00. Obviously, an examination of the data suggests a curve or possibly a pair of regressions.

If only the first 12 data points are considered, the linear correlation coefficient is r = −0.9837, with the regression equation given as Y' = 18.6 − 0.8 X (see Exhibit 7.12). On the other hand, if the last 12 data points are considered, the linear correlation coefficient will be r = +0.9837, with the regression equation given as Y' = −8.6 + 0.8 X (see Exhibit 7.12).

Thus, two or more linear regressions or a nonlinear regression may not surface when a single linear regression is calculated. This again emphasizes that visual examination of the data is essential.

7.4.3 A Family of Regressions

The relationship between X and Y sometimes varies, depending on the level of another variable or factor. The data in Exhibit 7.13 are plotted in Exhibit 7.14. The overall correlation for the 20 pairs of data is r = 0.9140, with the linear regression line being Y' = 3.1 + 0.617 (see Exhibit 7.14). If the first four data points are considered separately, however, the correlation coefficient is r = −0.8944, with the associated regression equation being Y' = 8.2 − 0.8 X.

As a matter of fact, if each successive set of four data points is treated independently of every other set of four, the calculated value of the correlation coefficient is identical, namely, r = −0.8944. If the successive sets of four data points can be considered as differing due to a third variable or factor (say, size of school district), then a simple linear regression, based on all data points, is clearly misleading.

This emphasizes the point that a third variable or factor may significantly influence what appears to be the relationship in a linear sense between two variables.

* * * * * * *

NEVER RELY ON CALCULATED VALUES IN LINEAR REGRESSION AND CORRELATION SITUATIONS WITHOUT PLOTTING THE BASIC DATA! JUDGMENT AND EXPECTATIONS OF RELATIONSHIPS BASED UPON YOUR KNOWLEDGE OF THE SUBJECT MATTER SHOULD BE CONSIDERED.

EXHIBIT 7.11–HYPOTHETICAL DATA POINTS FOR NONLINEAR CORRELATION

Item	X	Y
(1)	(2)	(3)
1	2	16
2	2	17
3	2	18
4	7	12
5	7	13
6	7	14
7	12	8
8	12	9
9	12	10
10	17	4
11	17	5
12	17	6
13	22	8
14	22	9
15	22	10
16	27	12
17	27	13
18	27	14
19	32	16
20	32	17
21	32	18

EXHIBIT 7.12 – A HYPOTHETICAL EXAMPLE OF A NONLINEAR REGRESSION YIELDING A LINEAR CORRELATION COEFFICIENT, r = 0.

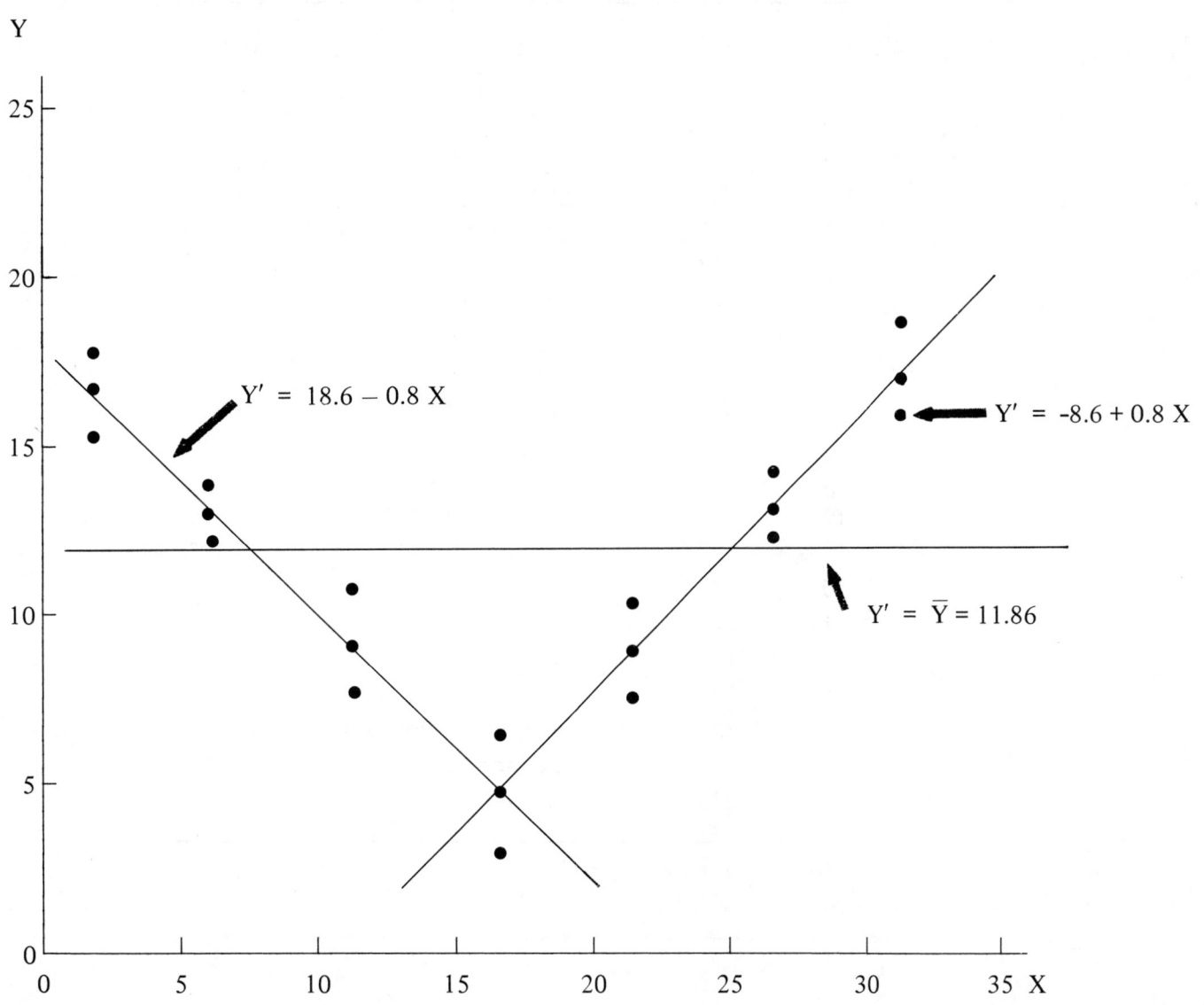

EXHIBIT 7.13—SOME HYPOTHETICAL DATA ILLUSTRATING A FAMILY OF REGRESSIONS YIELDING AN ERRONEOUS OVERALL REGRESSION LINE

X	Y	First 4		All 20
(1)		(2)		(3)
2	7	ΣY^2 =	108	4,060
3	5	ΣY =	20	260
5	5	ΣXY =	72	5,080
6	3	ΣX^2 =	74	6,610
8	11	ΣX =	16	320
9	9	n =	4	20
11	9			
12	7	$\bar{X}$ =	4.0	16.0
14	15	$\bar{Y}$ =	5.0	13.0
15	13			
17	13	r =	-0.8944	0.9140
18	11	r^2 =	0.8000	0.8354
20	19			
21	17			
23	17			
24	15			
26	23	Unexplained variation	1.6	111.95
27	21	Explained variation	6.4	568.05
29	21	Total variation	8	680
30	19			

First 4 $Y' = 8.2 - 0.8X$
All 20 $Y' = 3.1 + 0.617 X$

EXHIBIT 7.14–A HYPOTHETICAL EXAMPLE OF A FAMILY OF REGRESSIONS YIELDING AN ERRONEOUS OVERALL REGRESSION LINE

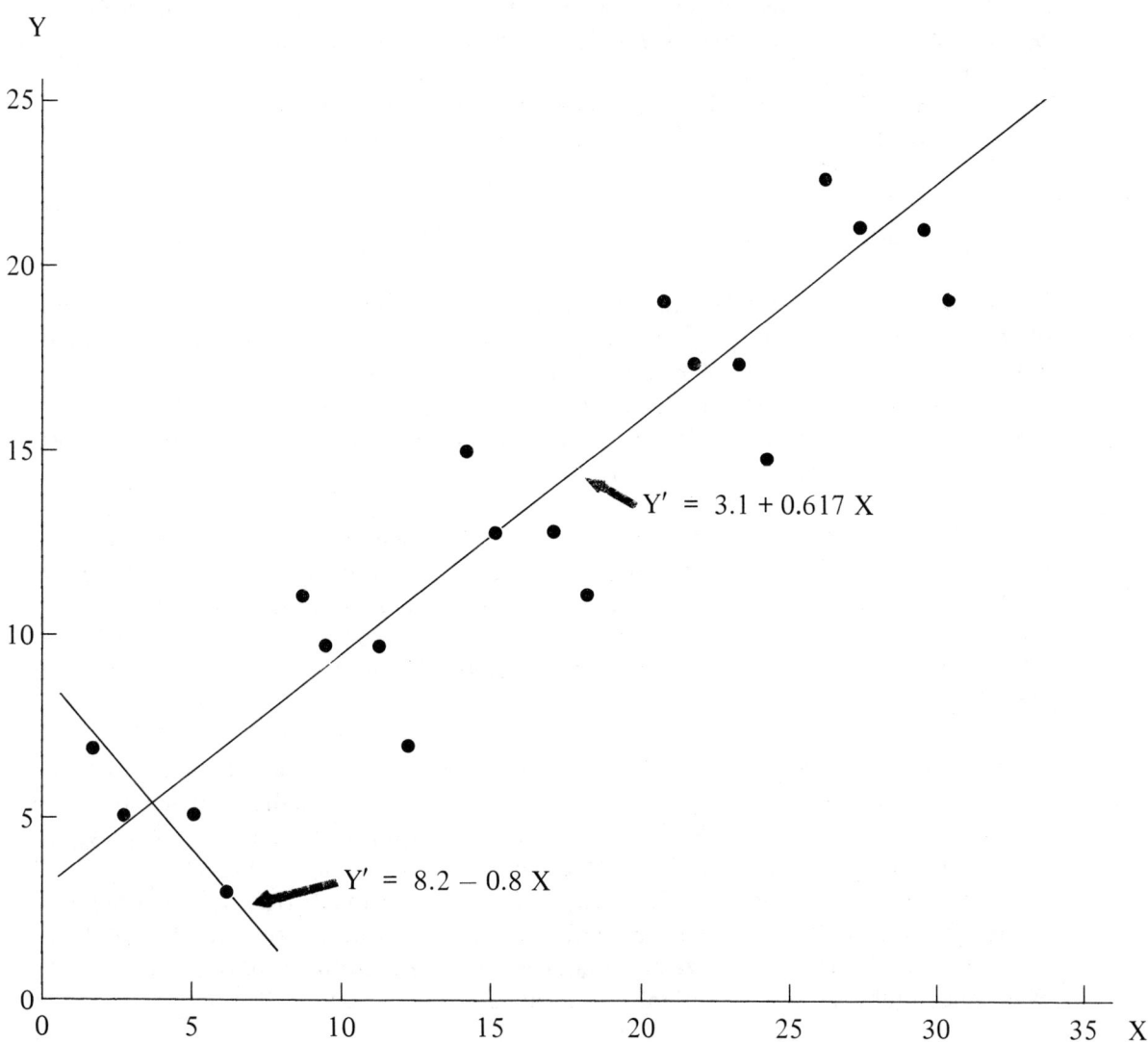

7.5 MULTIPLE VARIABLE RELATIONSHIPS

In many research situations, the analyst is interested in the extent to which more than two characteristics associated with the AU's are related. Statistical techniques appropriate to these situations are classified under multivariable or multivariate analysis and can be separated into multiple correlation, partial correlation, and multiple regression. More detailed information on these three multivariate techniques may be found in Bennett & Bowers (1976) and U.S. Department of Commerce (1966). Additional multivariate analysis techniques are the special topics of Chapter 11.

7.5.1 Multiple Correlation

In a *multiple correlation* problem, the researcher is interested in measuring the extent of the simultaneous relationship between one variable and two or more other variables. A low correlation between salaries and experience in a nationwide sample of teachers might be higher if the average salaries of the school systems where the teachers are employed were also considered. In this situation the introduction of the third variable might improve the apparent relationship.

The multiple correlation coefficient is a measure of the strength of the relationship between one variable and two or more other variables taken *together*. It is not merely the sum of the correlation coefficients of the variables taken separately; if it were, the value of the coefficient could be more than 1.00. Since the variables may tend to be intercorrelated, the multiple correlation coefficient takes this intercorrelation into consideration.

When working with sample data, the multiple correlation coefficient is symbolized by the capital letter R, which is subscripted with the symbols of the variables that are being correlated. For example, the multiple correlation coefficient in the previous illustration would be symbolized as: $R_{y.xz}$, where Y is the salary of the teachers, X is the years of experience, and Z is the average salary level of the district in which the person teaches. The multiple correlation coefficient assumes values only between 0 and +1. In some texts the multiple correlation coefficient might also be symbolized by $R_{1.23}$, where the numbers stand for variables 1, 2, and 3.

There is also a coefficient of multiple determination (R^2), which bears the same relationship to R that the coefficient of determination (r^2) bears to the coefficient of correlation. R^2 is a proportion just as in r^2 and is interpreted in a similar manner.

7.5.2 Partial Correlation

In addition to the measures of multiple correlation that consider the importance of all or several independent variables combined, it is sometimes desirable to measure the importance of each of the individual variables while holding constant the effects of other variables. The *coefficient of partial correlation* measures the correlation between the dependent variable and each of several independent variables, while holding all other variables in the analysis constant.

For example, a part of the relationship between teachers' salaries and teaching experience may be obscured by the wide variation in the average salary levels of the districts in which teachers are employed. By using a coefficient of partial correlation, the correlation between salaries and experience can be measured while holding constant the effect of the differences in average salary levels of the districts. Two or more factors could be held constant at the same time, such as the average salary level of the district and number of years of college preparation of the teachers.

First-order partial correlations occur when the researcher holds one variable constant while measuring the relationship between two other variables.

Second-order partial correlations occur when the researcher holds two variables constant simultaneously while measuring the relationship between two other variables.

The small Roman letter r, subscripted as follows, $r_{xy.z}$, is used to symbolize the coefficient of partial correlation between variables X and Y when Z is held constant. Also used to symbolize this partial correlation would be $r_{12.3}$.

7.5.3 Multiple Regression

This multivariate technique is analogous to bivariate regression, except that two or more independent variables are used to predict or forecast a single dependent variable. To illustrate, consider the following set of variables where the AU is a public school teacher:

$$Y = \text{annual contract salary in } \$1,000$$
$$X_1 = \text{years of tenure}$$
$$X_2 = \text{semester credits in college}$$
$$X_3 = \text{average schedule contract salary in the teacher's school district}$$

A multiple regression equation using X_1, X_2, and X_3 to predict Y might be:

$$Y' = a + b_1 X_1 + b_2 X_2 + b_3 X_3 \tag{7.11}$$

where the values for a, b_1, b_2, and b_3 would be estimated from the sample. If b_1 is associated with years of tenure, it would indicate the change in annual contract salary in $1,000 for a one-year change in tenure when X_2 and X_3 are held constant at their average values.

Another possible multiple regression (this time nonlinear), relating these four variables, might be:

$$Y' = a + b_1 X_1 + b_2 X_2 X_3 + b_3 X_3^2 \tag{7.12}$$

The researcher is referred to U.S. Department of Commerce (1966) for greater details on procedures for estimating the coefficients in (7.11) and (7.12).

7.6 RANK ORDER CORRELATION

Techniques exist to examine the possible relationships between two or more characteristics when the characteristics of interest are ranked (i.e., are of at least the ordinal scale). Two procedures follow.

7.6.1 Two Classifications (Spearman's Rho)

Often in educational research the investigator encounters conditions in which either one or both of the characteristics cannot be measured or scored satisfactorily, but the observations can be placed in rank order. Under these conditions, in which data are in ordinal scale form, it is possible to say that any one observation is higher than another, but it is impossible to say how much higher. In such a distribution, after all the AU's have been arranged in order, they are assigned a number indicating their rank, i.e., 1, 2, 3, etc. Where ties occur, the average of the ranks is assigned to each AU. (To illustrate, if a tie occurs for what would ordinarily be the fourth, fifth, and sixth ranking, the average of these ranks, namely 5, is assigned to each AU.)

The *Spearman rank correlation coefficient* (Spearman rho) is appropriate for measuring the relationship between two sets of ranked characteristics. This measure is an adaptation of the Pearson coefficient and has the same interpretative values, i.e., -1 to $+1$. The Spearman rho—sometimes symbolized by r', by r_s, and by R—was designed primarily to be used where it is possible to work only with ranked or ordinal data; however, the rank correlation coefficient can also be helpful when the variables can be measured on an interval or ratio scale but instead are recorded as ranks on an ordinal scale. The Spearman rank-difference method is often applied in the place of the Pearson product-moment method when samples are small because of the ease of computation.

Since the Spearman rank correlation coefficient is widely used in educational research, an example of its computation is included here.

A teacher in a special section for gifted children has given these ten pupils their semester averages. In addition, the ten pupils have been ranked according to their cooperativeness, with a rank of 1 being "most cooperative" and a rank of 10 being "least cooperative." Results for these ten students appear in Exhibit 7.15. Entries in each of the five numbered columns are:

        Col. 1: Individual semester averages

        Col. 2: Cooperativeness rankings (R_1)

        Col. 3: Rankings of the semester averages (R_2)

        Col. 4: The difference between the rankings in Column 2 and Column 3 ($d = R_1 - R_2$)

        Col. 5: The square of the value in Column 4; note that all entries are positive.

Since Students B and F both had the same semester average, namely 83, their ranks become the average of their two successive ranks, namely $(5 + 6) / 2 = 5.5$. The total of the positive entries in Column 4 must equal the total of the negative entries in Column 4.

The appropriate formula for calculating the Spearman rank order correlation coefficient is given in Formula (7.13):

$$\boxed{r_S = 1 - 6(\Sigma d^2) / n(n^2 - 1)} \tag{7.13}$$

For this particular situation, it is seen that:

$$\Sigma d^2 = 31.5 \quad \text{and} \quad n = 10.$$

Substituting these values in (7.13) leads to the Spearman rank order correlation coefficient:

$$\begin{aligned} r_S &= 1 - 6(31.5) / 10(10^2 - 1) \\ &= 1 - 189 / 990 \\ &= 1 - 0.1909 \\ &= 0.8091 \end{aligned}$$

This calculated value for r_S of 0.8091 is interpreted exactly as the Pearson correlation coefficient. See Siegel (1956) for a fuller discussion of this rank-difference correlation coefficient, including the treatment of cases in which there are a large proportion of ties in either characteristic. In such cases, a correction is necessary, although the difference is usually not very large. The Kendall tau coefficient provides an alternative method for assessing the relationship between two sets of ranked characteristics. See Siegel (1956, pp. 213-23).

7.6.2 More Than Two Classifications (Coefficient of Concordance)

Frequently, it may be of interest to establish the extent of agreement among a number of classifications on which a set of AU's is being ranked. One such situation can be seen in Exhibit 7.16, in which three interviewers have ranked eight applicants for a specific position. Entries in Columns 1, 2, and 3 represent the rankings for the eight applicants by each of the interviewers. The entries in Column 4 represent the sum of the individual applicant's rankings by the three interviewers. If the interviewers were in complete agreement, Applicant A would have all 1's (summing to 3) and Applicant H would have all 8's (summing to 24). As the judges tend to be in greater disagreement, the sums of the rankings will tend to become similar to each other. Thus the variability of the R_j values is directly tied to the agreement or disagreement among the interviewers. This fact is taken into consideration in calculating Kendall's coefficient of concordance, symbolized by W. The formula for calculating this coefficient is given as Formula (7.14):

$$W = 12s / k^2 n(n^2 - 1) \qquad (7.14)$$

where:

$$s = \Sigma R_j^2 - (\Sigma R_j)^2 / n$$

k = the number of classifications (in this case, interviewers)

n = the number of AU's (in this case, applicants)

Sums for calculating the value for s can be found in Columns 4 and 5 of Exhibit 7.16. Substitution of data from Exhibit 7.16 into Formula (7.14) yields:

$$s = 1768 - (108)^2 / 8$$
$$= 1768 - 1458 = 310$$
$$k = 3$$
$$n = 8$$

Therefore,

$$W = 12 \times 310 / 3^2 \times 8(8^2 - 1)$$
$$= 3720 / 4536 = 0.8201$$

This value for W = 0.8201 is descriptive of the extent of agreement among the judges. W lies on a scale from 0 (disagreement) to 1.0 (complete agreement). A procedure for determining whether the sample value for W is significantly different from 0 is discussed in Siegel (1956, pp. 235-238).

EXHIBIT 7.15 – SEMESTER AVERAGES AND COOPERATIVENESS RANKS FOR TEN PUPILS IN A CLASS OF GIFTED STUDENTS

Pupil	Semester average	Cooperativeness rank (R_1)	Semester average rank (R_2)	d	d^2
	(1)	(2)	(3)	(4)	(5)
A	75	8	9	−1	1
B	83	3	5.5	−2.5	6.25
C	96	2	1	+1	1
D	72	9	10	−1	1
E	94	4	2	+2	4
F	83	7	5.5	+1.5	2.25
G	88	6	4	+2	4
H	81	5	7	−2	4
I	79	10	8	+2	4
J	93	1	3	−2	4
				−8.5	31.5
				+8.5	
				0	

EXHIBIT 7.16 – RANKINGS OF EIGHT JOB APPLICANTS BY THREE INTERVIEWERS

Applicant	Interviewer 1	2	3	R_j	R_j^2
	(1)	(2)	(3)	(4)	(5)
A	1	2	1	4	16
B	4	1	2	7	49
C	2	3	4	9	81
D	3	5	3	11	121
E	5	4	7	16	256
F	7	7	8	22	484
G	6	8	5	19	361
H	8	6	6	20	400
				108	1,768

7.7 MISCELLANEOUS MEASURES OF ASSOCIATION

As has been pointed out previously, the Pearson product-moment correlation is the most widely used measure of the closeness of the relationship between two characteristics. However, it cannot be used appropriately unless data for *both* variables are at least of the interval scale. There are times when an investigator is faced with the problem of wanting to examine the relationship between two characteristics and the data for one or both are not at least of the interval scale. Such conditions occur rather frequently in educational research. When this happens, there are special coefficients similar to or approximating the Pearson coefficient that are appropriate.

In this HANDBOOK the researcher is presented with some of these special correlation measures, so that they can be investigated by consulting some of the references. Excellent references are Siegel (1956) and Edwards (1954). To assist the researcher in making an initial decision about the special measures that may be appropriate, a brief discussion of the major alternative measures and their possible uses are presented here.

7.7.1 One Dichotomous Characteristic

Suppose the investigator wishes to find the relationship between two characteristics, one of which is an attribute and can be expressed in only two categories, such as "yes" and "no." An attribute with only two categories or two choices is termed *dichotomous*. Since the other of the two characteristics is tabulated or scored on at least an interval scale, the resulting correlation is termed a *biserial* correlation. Biserial coefficients of correlation are frequently used in educational research.

The following is an example of a biserial correlation. Suppose a sample of teachers is asked the question: If you could go back and choose your life's occupation again, would you choose teaching? ____ Yes; ____ No. Also, suppose a measure of the extent to which willingness to teach again may be either positively or negatively correlated with the age of teachers in this sample is needed. One characteristic—the willingness to teach again—is an attribute and is dichotomous; the other, age, is on the ratio scale. Hence, a biserial correlation is an appropriate methodology.

Two biserial correlation coefficients are available for use in such problems. One is the *biserial coefficient* and the other is the *point biserial coefficient*. Of these two alternatives, the point biserial coefficient is usually the preferred one. See Edwards (1954, Chapter 10) for a discussion of the appropriate use of the biserial coefficients and their method of computation.

7.7.2 Two Dichotomous Characteristics

In some situations both characteristics of interest are classified as dichotomous; for example, two yes/no questions on an opinion survey. The research question of interest on the opinion survey might relate to the extent of agreement among the respondents in their answers to two of the yes/no questions. Other situations in which a characteristic might be classified as dichotomous are:

- Male vs. female responses to a yes/no question.
- Responses to a yes/no question, comparing teachers with less than ten years of tenure with teachers having ten or more years of tenure.
- Relationship between years of tenure (teachers with less than ten years vs. those with ten years or more) and salary (teachers earning less than $18,000 vs. those earning $18,000 or more).

When data associated with each of the above examples are presented in tabular form, there will be two columns and two rows: male/female vs. yes/no; less than ten years of tenure/ten years or more tenure vs. yes/no; less than ten years tenure/ten years or more tenure vs. less than $18,000 salary/$18,000 or more salary. Each of these tabular displays is referred to as a "2 x 2 (two-by-two) or four-fold table." Sometimes these tables are referred to as "2 x 2 contingency tables." A number of possible alternatives for measuring association of two dichotomous characteristics exist:

- *Phi coefficient*: An appropriate measure when both characteristics are truly dichotomous, such as yes/no responses to a question or classification as male/female.
- *Tetrachoric correlation coefficient*: May be used when both characteristics have been artificially compressed into two categories and the underlying variables are normally distributed. The example above on years of tenure and salary might fall into this category.
- *Contingency coefficient*: This measure applies to the two-by-two table as well as tables with more than two categories for the characteristics of interest. Unlike the phi coefficient and the tetrachoric r, this measure is not interpretable as a correlation coefficient, since its limits do not range between -1 and $+1$. It is related to a procedure (described in Part III) referred to as "chi-square" and will be discussed briefly at that point.

7.8 SUMMARY

Exhibit 7.17 provides a guide for selecting the appropriate measure of association for given levels of scale for the characteristics of interest in the bivariate case. For example, if both characteristics are ordinal (i.e., the data have been ranked from highest to lowest or from best to worst), Spearman's rho and Kendall's tau are appropriate. On the other hand, if both characteristics are either nominal or ordinal and each possesses two or more categories, then the appropriate measure is the contingency coefficient.

The scale level of the characteristics indicated in Exhibit 7.17 is the level being used in the analysis and not necessarily the originally recorded level. For example, scores may have originally been reported on a test (probably an interval scale), yet the analysis places these scores in rank order (now on the ordinal scale).

If the measure of association is based upon a sample, then procedures given in Part III will be appropriate for drawing inferences about the population from which the sample has been drawn.

EXHIBIT 7.17–GUIDE FOR CHOICE OF MEASURES OF ASSOCIATION, TWO CHARACTERISTICS[a]

Characteristics	Measures of association
Both interval or ratio	Pearson's r Correlation ratio
Both ordinal	Spearman's rho Kendall's tau[c]
One nominal or ordinal and dichotomous; one interval or ratio	Biserial coefficient[b] Point biserial coefficient[b]
Both nominal and/or ordinal and both dichotomous	Phi coefficient[c] Tetrachoric correlation coefficient[c] Contingency coefficient[c]
Both nominal and/or ordinal and two or more categories	Contingency coefficient[c]

[a] If no reference is cited, methodology and calculations are presented in this HANDBOOK.
[b] Edwards (1954)
[c] Siegel (1956)

III

Inferential Statistics

A major interest of a researcher is to explore a population of analysis units by some sampling procedure to gain a keener insight into the behavior of the characteristics of interest. In addition, researchers may be interested in confirming some belief or hypothesis relative to characteristics within a population. In either situation, a sample (or samples) is to be selected from the population of interest and some inference made, based upon the sample data, about the population characteristic(s). For example, an analyst may believe that the more crowded the classroom conditions, the more likely it will be that student achievement levels decline, all other influencing factors being held constant. Clearly, the researcher will be forced to take a sample or samples and, based upon the sample results, make some generalization or inference to the population from which the samples were selected. This process is referred to as *statistical inference* and is the subject of the next four chapters in this HANDBOOK.

Associated with estimates based upon sample data will be errors that are not controllable by the researcher, namely, sampling errors. The researcher who believes data are sufficiently important to merit reporting is obligated to inform the users of the possible errors, especially if the researcher has reason to think the data are subject to wide error. But even if the possible errors are relatively small, the researcher should report this fact. Should this not be done, the reader will be unable to use the data with the amount of confidence the data deserve.

Most persons are aware that the possibility of error lurks in every estimate they are called upon to make. Therefore, even in everyday life one consciously or unconsciously tries to increase the probability of estimates being correct by stating them as a *range* of values rather than as a single value.

To illustrate: After a teachers association meeting in a certain school district, the question arose as to how many persons attended the meeting. One person present estimated 300. Another was more cautious and said *around* 300; another said between 275 and 325. A fourth person, still more conservative, estimated between 250 and 350. Each estimator increased the possibility of being correct by broadening the *range* of values that could include the true number. Thus, by increasing the range of possible values, the probability of the estimate being correct is increased. Of course, the range can be increased so much that the estimate becomes useless.

In reporting research findings consideration must be given to this expected error or variability. In probability sampling, descriptive summary measures almost always vary from the population parameters that they are to estimate.

If the sample is properly selected according to a probability design, around the estimate of the population parameter a range of values may be specified that can be expected to include the true value of the parameter with a stated probability.

Standard errors are the measures used by researchers to determine the probable extent of the sampling error associated with the descriptive statistics obtained from sample data. Thus, *standard errors* are the measures of probable sampling error when statistical inferences are made about population parameters using sample data.

Standard errors of descriptive statistics derived from sample observations are used in connection with a specific probability (e.g., 0.90, 0.95, 0.99) to obtain the *confidence interval* within which the true population parameter can be expected to fall. The confidence interval of a mean, for example, represents a range of values above and below the sample mean within which the true mean can be expected to fall with a stated level of probability, or confidence.

Suppose the mean of the salaries reported by a sample of teachers was $10,500, and the confidence interval is plus or minus $100 at the 0.95 level of confidence. This would indicate that the chances are 95 in 100 that the confidence interval of $10,400 to $10,600 computed from this sample will include the true mean of the population.

An understanding of the expected variability in sample statistics as estimates of population parameters is essential for comprehending statistical inference. This concept is emphasized throughout the next four chapters.

Sampling concepts are developed in Chapter 8 through several simple examples. The concepts of statistics/parameters, and sample/population are reviewed; and the normal distribution (sometimes referred to as "Gaussian") is introduced and its role in statistical inference emphasized through numerous illustrations. The effects of sampling variation on inferences are presented. The chapter is closed out with a brief discussion of degrees of freedom.

In Chapter 9 estimation concepts are developed for five situations: arithmetic mean, a total or aggregate, a proportion or percentage, linear bivariate regression, and variance (standard deviation).

The topic of hypothesis testing is introduced in Chapter 10 for the following cases: a single arithmetic mean, a single proportion, two arithmetic means, two proportions, and two variances. In addition, a considerably detailed discussion is presented for situations in which frequencies (really proportions) are compared for a variety of cases. This latter situation is referred to as "goodness of fit" or "contingency table" analysis.

The final chapter in Part III reviews, primarily from a conceptual viewpoint, various approaches to analyzing data when there are more than two variables associated with AU's, as well as nonparametric techniques.

8
SAMPLING CONCEPTS AND INFERENCE

8.1 RANDOM AND SYSTEMATIC SAMPLING

Properly applied, sampling concepts serve as a valuable tool for the researcher. Fundamental to statistical inference is the acceptance of probability theory and its effect on sampling. Random sampling is a procedure by means of which sample analysis units (AU's) are selected from a population of interest in such a way that each AU has a known and fixed probability of being in the sample. In most instances, these probabilities are taken as being equal. For example, for a population of 10,000 teachers, random sampling would be such that the probability of a teacher's being selected is 1 in 10,000 or 0.0001.

The phrase *"simple random sample"* or *"unrestricted random sample"* means that a sample has been selected in such a way that each such sample of, say, n AU's has the same likelihood or probability of being selected. Simple random sampling is not always possible; however, because of its fundamental importance in sampling theory and its close relationship to sample designs actually used in practice, it will be the primary sampling procedure assumed in the chapters that follow.

8.1.1 Selecting a Simple Random Sample

Two criteria must be met in selecting from a population the AU's to be included in a simple random sample:

1. Each combination of a specific number of AU's has the same probability of being selected.
2. The selection of any one AU is in no way tied to the selection of any other.

These two criteria are illustrated by a lottery, by the drawing of numbers in the selective-service draft, and by other operations in which the "laws of chance" are allowed to operate freely. Two procedures that allow the laws of chance to operate freely are the lottery and the random number method, explained below.

Suppose the population is a school system with 3,000 teachers and a random sample of 25 teachers from among these 3,000 teachers is desired. This could be accomplished by numbering every teacher from 0001 to 3000, associating with each teacher a four-digit number. Assume 3,000 small slips of paper are numbered from 0001 to 3000, placed in a box, and shaken thoroughly. From this box, 25 slips are selected with the following numbers on them:

2637	2876	1747	2457	0893	0606	0068	1277	0637	2913
2280	0978	0802	1204	2696	0474	0760	2485	1998	2631
1128	2401	0833	1463	2580					

These slips indicate which of the 3,000 teachers would be selected as the 25 for this sample. Thus, an unrestricted random sample of size 25 would have been selected from this population of 3,000 teachers.

As the population increases in size, it becomes more and more difficult to obtain an unrestricted random sample by the lottery method. The problem of selecting a random sample from the 2.1 million public school teachers in the United States, even if a listing of all the teachers were available, would be overwhelming.

To make it feasible to sample randomly from large populations, tables of random numbers (digits) are available. In Appendix H is a table of 20,000 random digits generated by NEA Research. The use of the entries in these tables of random numbers eliminates the necessity of numbering slips of paper when one is sampling randomly. The selection of numbers from these tables constitutes the equivalent of drawing numbered slips of paper from a box.

Exhibit 8.1 is a set of 250 random digits. The grouping of the digits by fives is for convenience in reading rather than for any reason associated with either the compilation or the use of the digits.

To illustrate the use of the random numbers in Exhibit 8.1 in selecting a sample of five teachers from the population of 3,000 teachers mentioned previously, the following procedure is one of many that could be used. A starting point would be selected arbitrarily, as would the direction in reading from the table. The first five numbers under 3001 would constitute the sample of five teachers.

EXHIBIT 8.1—A SET OF 250 RANDOM DIGITS

	(1)	(2)	(3)	(4)	(5)
1	40268	43753	35372	43232	20911
2	11529	90075	37849	45666	97768
3	77642	→ 47237	30683	36674	90467
4	15949	04609	97348	87335	43810
5	01530	23682	92048	44667	56734
6	69785	68322	82814	50347	54580
7	62714	87825	67156	01214 ←	30284
8	51543	41061	28475	20513	18131
9	34417	29268	15669	18811	74261
10	76840	62974	63360	87537	16711

Suppose Column 2, Row 3, is selected as a starting point. (See arrow in Exhibit 8.1.) The digits at this point are 47237; the first set of four of these digits (4723) is greater than 3000; therefore, it is ignored. The search procedure moves down the column and then to the next column on the right. The next set of digits is 04609; the first four digits are less than 3001; therefore, number 0460 is in the sample. Continuing in this manner, the following five numbers for teachers to be in the sample are found:

    0460   2368   2926   2847   1566

In using a table of random numbers, it does not matter whether the first or the last four digits are taken in each set of five. The start may be at any point and go in any direction—up, down, sideways, or diagonally—until the desired quantity of numbers needed to meet the specific sample size is obtained, as long as the procedure is consistent and no numbers that are within the population size are skipped.

8.1.2 Selecting a Systematic Sample

In some sampling problems it is impossible, if not impractical, to number all the individuals in the listing of the population or frame to be sampled. Frequently, however, the frame from which the sample is to be selected is arranged in some order (e.g., an alphabetical listing of 3,000 teachers in a school system). Rather than number all 3,000 teachers on the list, it is much simpler to select a sample of 25 teachers by picking every 120th teacher (3,000 divided by 25). Such a procedure is referred to as "systematic sampling."

To use systematic sampling introduces a condition about the ordering of the list from which the sample is selected. The arrangement of the AU's must in no way be related to the characteristics being measured in the survey. Where this condition exists or can be achieved, systematic sampling is frequently used as a substitute for simple random sampling.

To illustrate how a systematic sample could be selected, consider again the school system with 3,000 teachers. The problem is to obtain a sample of 25 by using a systematic procedure. This implies that the first teacher must be selected from among the first 120 in the list. To ascertain which teacher is to be first chosen requires selecting a random number between 001 and 120. Entering Exhibit 8.1, for example, in Column 4 and moving down the column, the first three digits that fall between 001 and 120 are 012 in Row 7. (See arrow in Exhibit 8.1.) Thus, teacher number 12 will be the first selected. The remaining 24 teachers will be every 120th teacher from teacher 12, or teachers numbered 132, 252, 372, 492, 612, 732, 852, 972, 1092, 1212, 1332, 1452, 1572, 1692, 1812, 1932, 2052, 2172, 2292, 2412, 2532, 2652, 2772, 2892. The resultant sample of 25 teachers is technically referred to as a "systematic sample with a random start."

In using this plan each teacher does not need to be assigned a number because the sample is selected by counting down the first 12 names on the alphabetical list of teachers and underscoring the twelfth name; counting the next 120 names on the list, underscoring name 132; counting 120 more names, underscoring name 252; and so on through the list.

If the population is unusually large with names on individual cards arranged alphabetically, it is sometimes simpler to use a measuring procedure in selecting the sample. To do this, the linear space occupied by the number of cards equal to the total sample size, say 1.25 inches for 120 cards, must be carefully measured. A first card is picked at random, as described previously. The second card is 1.25 inches from the first card, and so on through the card deck. The researcher should resort to the card measuring procedure only when there is a tremendous frame to be sampled, and there is no alternative.

Either method employed in the systematic sampling plan for 25 teachers from a population of 3,000 yields only 120 possible different samples of teachers, whereas an unrestricted random sample yields an extremely large number of different possible samples. The magnitude of the difference between the possible sample results suggests that caution should be taken in replacing unrestricted random sampling procedures by systematic sampling procedures.

The relationship of estimates made from samples drawn by systematic sampling compared with those made from samples drawn in a simple random manner depends upon the peculiar properties of the population. For some populations, surprisingly enough, systematic sampling is more precise than simple random sampling; for other populations, it is less precise. This makes it difficult to give blanket advice about when systematic sampling should be used. Certainly, knowledge of the structure of the population and the sampling frame is necessary for its proper use. Generally speaking, if the order of the sampling units in the population frame to be sampled can be regarded as arranged at random in regard to characteristics to be estimated, *on the average* systematic sampling should be equivalent to simple random sampling. Because systematic sampling is administratively much simpler and much less time-consuming than unrestricted random sampling in most sampling operations, it is widely used in selecting samples for surveys.

8.2 SAMPLES AND POPULATIONS–STATISTICS AND PARAMETERS

As indicated previously, a sample is a part of a population. Having a sample does not necessarily mean "goodness." It is important to know how the sample has been selected before inferences can be made to the population from which the sample has been selected. When unrestricted random sampling has been employed (or, in some cases, systematic sampling with a random start), procedures exist for making such inferences. These procedures are discussed in the chapters which follow.

In general, the researcher is interested in selecting a sample; calculating a summary measure, such as the arithmetic mean; and making some statement about the population arithmetic mean. The summary measure in the sample is referred to as a "statistic"; and the corresponding summary measure in the population, as a "parameter." At any moment in time a parameter has a fixed value, while the corresponding value of a statistic can be expected to vary from sample to sample.

Exhibit 8.2 summarizes the major summary measures presented in this HANDBOOK and identifies the symbols used for these measures in both a sample and a population. Symbols for the parameters are Greek letters. The third column, labeled "estimate of parameter," will be the same as the final column for material presented in this HANDBOOK. Sometimes, a sample statistic has to be slightly modified to provide an acceptable estimate for the corresponding population parameter. Such cases are beyond the scope of the discussions which follow.

EXHIBIT 8.2—POPULATION AND SAMPLE SYMBOLS

Term	Population parameter		Estimate of parameter		Sample statistic	
Arithmetic mean	μ	(pronounced mu)	$\hat{\mu}$	(mu hat)	$\bar{X}$	(X bar)
Median	$\tilde{\mu}$	(mu tilde)	$\hat{\tilde{\mu}}$	(mu tilde hat)	$\tilde{X}$	(X tilde)
Mode	$\dot{\mu}$	(mu oh)	$\hat{\dot{\mu}}$	(mu oh hat)	$\dot{X}$	(X oh)
Standard deviation	σ	(sigma)	$\hat{\sigma}$	(sigma hat)	S	
Variance	σ^2	(sigma squared)	$\hat{\sigma}^2$	(sigma hat squared)	S^2	
Covariance	σ_{xy}	(sigma sub-XY)	$\hat{\sigma}_{xy}$	(sigma hat sub-XY)	S_{xy}	
Proportion	π	(pi)	$\hat{\pi}$	(pi hat)	p	
Correlation coefficient	ρ	(rho)	$\hat{\rho}$	(rho hat)	r	

8.3 THE NORMAL PROBABILITY DISTRIBUTION

The concept of what is commonly referred to as the "normal probability distribution" and its theoretical graphic representation, the normal probability curve, is basic to probability sampling. The curve of the normal distribution (sometimes called the Gaussian curve or the DeMoivre-LaPlace distribution) with its characteristic bell shape is well-known to every student of elementary statistics. Other properties of the normal distribution are:

1. The curve is symmetrical about its central axis.
2. The values of the mean, median, and mode are equal.
3. The curve represents a specified probability distribution, i.e., the area under the curve is considered equal to one, or 100%.

The first two properties are clearly shown in the bell-shaped graph of a normal distribution in Exhibit 8.3.

The third property enables the researcher to make certain statements regarding the distribution of the characteristic represented by the curve. The following illustrate the types of statements that can be made by using the table of normal areas in Appendix H:

1. Approximately 68% of the AU's fall within plus and minus one standard deviation of the mean (± σ)
2. Approximately 95% of the AU's will fall within plus and minus two standard deviations of the mean (± 2σ).
3. More than 99% of the AU's fall within plus and minus three standard deviations of the mean (± 3σ).

EXHIBIT 8.3–NORMAL PROBABILITY CURVE

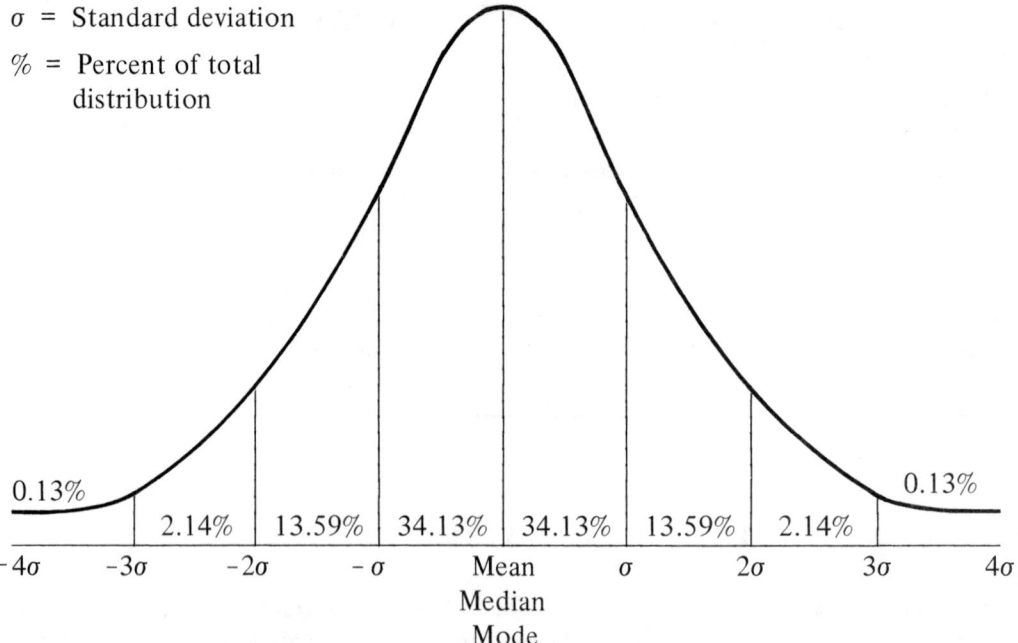

The relationship between the *standard deviation* and the percent of the observation falling within specific distances from the mean for a normally distributed characteristic is most important to understanding inference. So standard are these relationships that nearly every statistical text contains a table relating fractions or multiples of standard deviations to the proportion of a normal distribution found within those distances of the mean. Table H.2 in Appendix H shows these relationships. Exhibit 8.4 presents excerpts from this Appendix H table and is included here for convenience. Examination of Exhibit 8.4 reveals that it is set up in terms of Z-units, or standard scores, discussed in Chapter 6.

To illustrate the use of the table, recall that the raw value of a specific observation in a distribution can be transformed into a Z-score by using Formula (6.3), which is:

$$Z = \frac{X - \mu}{\sigma}$$

where:

    Z   is the relative deviation of an observation from the mean of all the observations of one characteristic.

    X   is the particular observation of the characteristic for which Z is desired.

    X − μ   is the deviation of the observation from the mean of all observations in the distribution.

    σ   is the standard deviation of the characteristic in the population.

EXHIBIT 8.4–EXCERPTS FROM APPENDIX TABLE H.2, WHICH SHOWS THE PROPORTION OF OBSERVATIONS IN A NORMAL DISTRIBUTION THAT FALL BETWEEN THE MEAN AND SPECIFIC NUMBERS OF STANDARD DEVIATIONS FROM THE MEAN

Z	0.00	0.01	0.02	0.03	0.04	0.05	0.06	
(1)	(2)	(3)	(4)	(5)	(6)	(7)	(8)	
.	.	.	.	.	.	.	.	.
.	.	.	.	.	.	.	.	.
.	.	.	.	.	.	.	.	.
1.5	0.4332	0.4345	0.4357	0.4370	0.4382	0.4394	0.4406	.
1.6	0.4452	0.4463	0.4474	0.4485	0.4495	0.4505	0.4515	.
1.7	0.4554	0.4564	0.4573	0.4582	0.4591	0.4599	0.4608	.
→ 1.8	0.4641	0.4649	0.4656	0.4664	0.4671	0.4678	0.4686	.
1.9	0.4713	0.4719	0.4726	0.4732	0.4738	0.4744	0.4750	.
.	.	.	.	.	.	.	.	.
.	.	.	.	.	.	.	.	.
.	.	.	.	.	.	.	.	.

Suppose in a given school system the number of years of teaching experience among the instructional faculty is normally distributed. The mean number of years of experience (μ) of the faculty is 15 years, and the standard deviation (σ) is 5 years. If a teacher had 24 years of teaching experience, the standard score would be:

$$Z = \frac{X - \mu}{\sigma}$$

$$= \frac{24 - 15}{5}$$

$$= \frac{9}{5}$$

$$= 1.80$$

This means that the teacher's 24 years of experience is 1.80 standard deviations above the mean of the population. Three questions about this teacher's experience might be of interest:

1. What percent of the teachers in this school system are as close or closer to the mean years of experience of teachers as this teacher is?
2. What percent of the teachers have the *same* or *less* than the 24 years of experience this teacher has?
3. What percent of the teachers have *more* than the 24 years of experience this teacher has?

All three questions can easily be answered by consulting Exhibit 8.4. Column 1 of the table is headed "Z." In this column is seen 1.8, indicated by an arrow. In this row in the column headed 0.00 can be read 0.4641. This is the proportion of the distribution between the mean of the group and 1.8 Z-units, or standard deviations, above the mean. The corresponding percentage is seen to be 46.41% (0.4641 x 100):

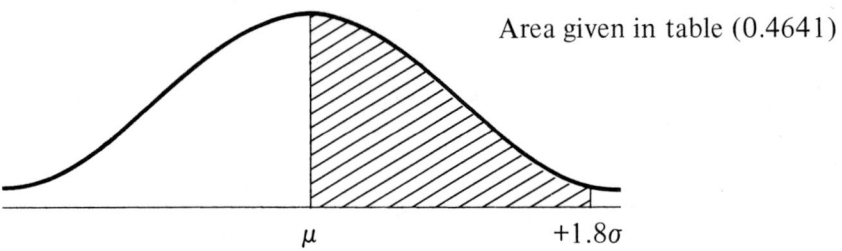

With this information the three questions can be answered. The first question, reworded, was, What percent of the teachers in the school system are within plus or minus 1.80 standard deviations of the mean? The statisticians refer to this as a "two-sided" or "two-tailed" situation because the researcher wishes to know the percentage of the distribution falling on *both* sides of the mean. It is a good idea to draw a simple diagram of the situation, as follows:

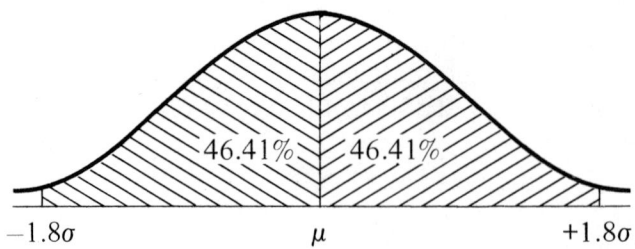

Since the percent of the distribution above and below the mean is desired, the two percentages are added to get 92.82% for the answer. In other words, 92.82% of the teachers in this school system were within ±1.8 standard deviations of the mean number of years of teaching experience. (Note that the percent desired is shaded.)

The second question was, What percent of the teachers have the *same* as or *less* than 24 years of experience. The statisticians term this a "one-sided" or "one-tailed" situation since it involves only the portion of the distribution falling *at* or *below* a certain point in the distribution. Again, drawing a simple diagram of the situation and shading the percent desired is recommended.

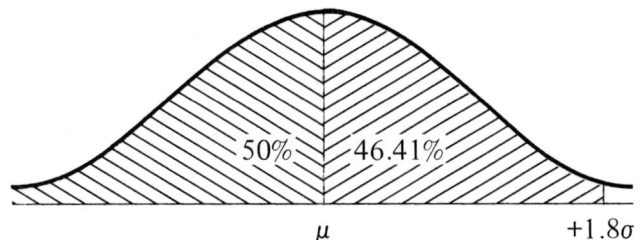

By substituting in Formula (6.3) it is calculated that 24 years of experience in this school system has a standard score of Z = 1.80. From Exhibit 8.4, it was found that 46.41% of a normal distribution falls between the mean and +1.80 standard deviations. Because the mean and the median are identical in a normal distribution, 50% of the AU's fall below the mean. The 50% below the mean is added to the 46.41% above the mean, indicating that 96.41% of the teachers in this population have 24 years of teaching experience or less.

The third question was, What percent of the teachers have *more* than 24 years of experience? This is also termed a "one-sided" or "one-tailed" situation because it involves only the portion of the distribution falling *above* a certain point. The shaded portion in the diagram below is the percent desired:

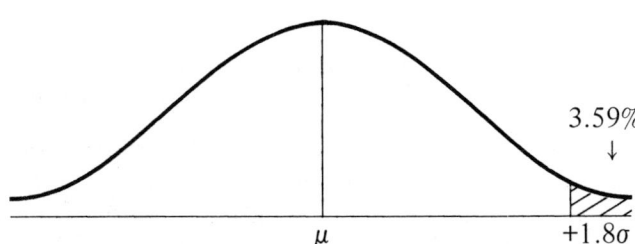

The same logic used in answering Question 2 applies here, but now only the percentage of the distribution falling *above* +1.80 standard deviations is desired. In Question 2 it was found that 96.41% falls below +1.80 standard deviations; therefore subtracting 96.41 from 100.00 yields 3.59% above the +1.80 standard deviation, leading to the conclusion that only 3.59% of the population have more than 24 years of teaching experience.

It is possible to start with a percentage of area under the normal curve and then determine the corresponding Z-value, which in turn can be converted to a value of the characteristic of interest. For example, suppose the range that includes the middle 90% of teachers in the population is sought. The diagram for this situation is:

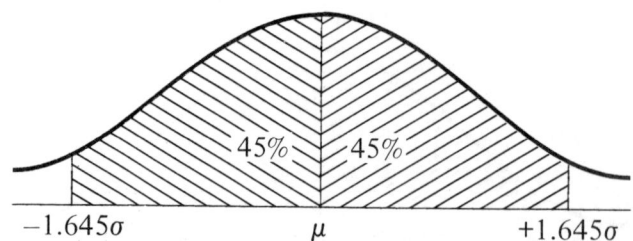

This is a "two-tailed" situation, since the percent of teachers falling on *both* sides of the mean is desired. Therefore, the 90% is divided by 2, yielding 45%, which is the percent falling above and below the mean. This is converted to a proportion by dividing by 100, obtaining 0.4500.

In the *body* of Exhibit 8.4 the proportion 0.4500 is half way between 0.4495 and 0.4505. Therefore, the Z-value is found to be between 1.64 and 1.65; or, by interpolation, 1.645.

This Z-value is substituted in Formula (8.1), which can be derived from Formula (6.3):

$$X = \mu \pm Z\sigma \qquad (8.1)$$

where:

- X is the desired value of a characteristic in a population.
- Z is the standard score associated with the desired value. It is found by using Table H.2 in the Appendix.
- σ is the standard deviation of a characteristic in a population.
- μ is the arithmetic mean of the observations of a characteristic in a population.

Substituting in Formula (8.1) the upper limit of experience of the desired range (the middle 90%) is found to be:

$$\begin{aligned} X &= \mu + Z\sigma \\ &= 15 + 1.645\,(5) \\ &= 23.2 \text{ years} \end{aligned}$$

Again, substituting in Formula (8.1), the lower limit of experience of the desired range is seen to be:

$$X = \mu - Z\sigma$$
$$= 15 - 1.645\,(5)$$
$$= 6.8 \text{ years}$$

Therefore, the teaching experience range that includes the middle 90% of the teachers in this population is between 6.8 years and 23.2 years.

The procedures for determining the area under a normal curve when using sample data are similar to those described here when using population data. The only difference is that the symbols used in the formulas are changed so that Formula (6.4) is used in place of (6.3) and Formula (8.1) becomes (8.2) for the *raw value based on sample observations,* as follows:

$$X = \bar{X} \pm (Z \cdot S) \qquad (8.2)$$

where:

    X is the desired value of a characteristic in a sample.

    Z is the standard score associated with the desired value. It is found by using Appendix Table H.2.

    S is the standard deviation of a characteristic based on a sample.

    $\bar{X}$ is the arithmetic mean of the observations of a characteristic based on a sample.

Consider the following series of questions based upon a sample of 500 teachers, whose mean salary is $10,500 and standard deviation is $3,000:

1. What percentage of the teachers had salaries between $9,000 and $12,000.
2. What percentage of the teachers had salaries under $8,000?
3. How many teachers would be expected to have salaries over $7,250?
4. What is the interquartile range (middle 50%) for these 500 teachers?
5. What is the 80th percentile salary?

For each of these situations a diagram is drawn first to identify the desired area under the normal curve. For the first question, the diagram is:

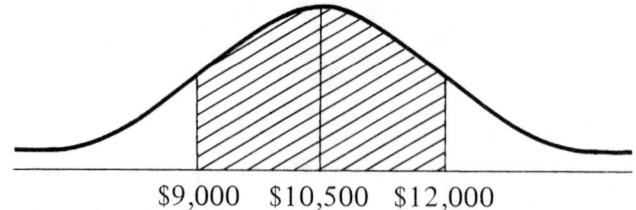

The two salaries should be converted to standard scores, and then the proportions associated with these standard scores should be identified from Table H.2 in the Appendix.

$$Z = (X - \bar{X}) / S$$
$$= (\$9,000 - \$10,500) / \$3,000$$
$$= -\$1,500 / \$3,000 = -0.50$$

and:

$$Z = (\$12,000 - \$10,500) / \$3,000$$
$$= +\$1,500 / \$3,000 = +0.50$$

Since both standard scores are 0.50, the corresponding areas are the same; namely, 0.19146. The areas corresponding to the two standard scores of −0.50 and +0.50 are added, yielding 0.38292; or 38.29% of the teachers have salaries between $9,000 and $12,000.

For the second question, the diagram is:

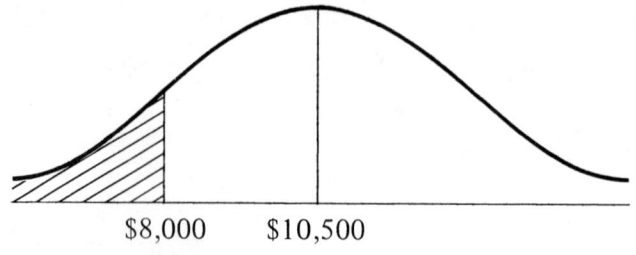

In this situation, the standard score for the salary of $8,000 is found to be:

$$Z = (X - \bar{X}) / Z$$
$$= (\$8,000 - \$10,500) / \$3,000$$
$$= -\$2,500 / \$3,000 = -0.83$$

The area between this standard score and the mean is obtained from Table H.2 in Appendix H; namely, 0.29673. Recall that this is the proportion of AU's between the mean and this standard score. Since the proportion less than this standard score is desired, the proportion 0.29673 must be subtracted from 0.50000, yielding 0.20327. For this question, 20.327% (or 20.33%) of the teachers in this sample had salaries under $8,000.

For the third question, the diagram is:

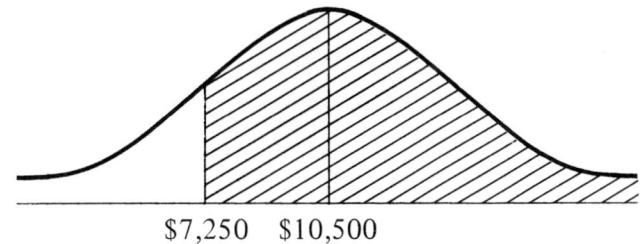

$7,250 $10,500

The necessary standard score corresponding to a salary of $7,250 is seen to be:

$$Z = (X - \bar{X}) / S$$
$$= (\$7,250 - \$10,500) / \$3,000$$
$$= -\$3,250 / \$3,000 = -1.08$$

The area between this standard score and the mean is obtained from Table H.2 in the Appendix and is seen to be 0.35993. Since the desired number is for those cases greater than $7,250, this proportion must be added to 0.50000 (the proportion greater than the mean) to obtain the proportion greater than $7,250. This figure is 0.85993, or 85.993% of the teachers in this sample have salaries greater than $7,250. This results in approximately 430 teachers (0.85993 x 500).

Question 4 is somewhat different from the first three in that the salaries associated with a proportion are sought. The diagram for this situation is:

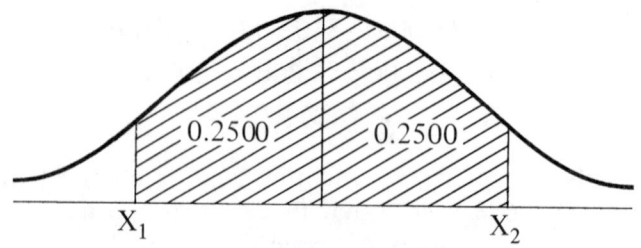

Since the middle 50% of the cases are to be included, 25% will be on each side of the mean. Table H.3 in the Appendix identifies standard scores corresponding to specific proportions between the mean and the given standard score. In this case, the desired proportion of 0.25 yields standard scores of −0.6745 and +0.6745. Substitution in Formula (8.2) yields the following salaries:

$$X_1 = \bar{X} - (Z \times S) = \$10,500 - (0.6745 \times \$3,000)$$
$$= \$10,500 - \$2,023.50$$
$$= \$8,476.50$$

and:

$$X_2 = \bar{X} + (Z \times S) = \$10,500 + (0.6745 \times \$3,000)$$
$$= \$10,500 + \$2,023.50$$
$$= \$12,523.50$$

or the middle 50% of the teachers in this sample have salaries between $8,476.50 and $12,523.50.

The final question requires recalling the definition of the 80th percentile; namely, the salary that has 80% of the salaries less than it. The diagram for this situation is:

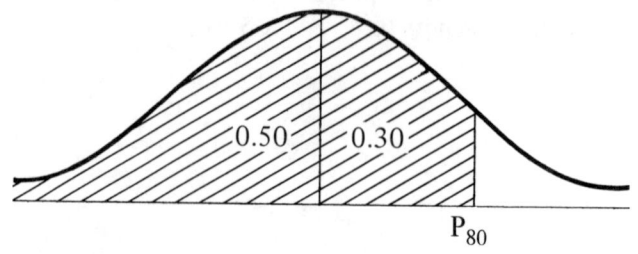

Since 80% of the AU's are to be less than the specific salary, 30% must lie between this salary and the mean. Hence, from Table H.3 in the Appendix the required salary is obtained from Formula (8.2):

$$P_{80} = \bar{X} + (Z \times S) = \$10,500 + (0.842 \times \$3,000)$$
$$= \$10,500 + \$2,526$$
$$= \$13,026$$

For this sample, 80% of the teachers have salaries less than \$13,026. It can also be stated that 20% of the teachers have salaries greater than \$13,026.

The previous analysis on the sample of 500 teachers is based upon an assumption that the data are normally distributed. If the data depart from a normal distribution, the conclusions drawn above would not follow.

8.4 SAMPLING VARIATION

Suppose a population consists of 500 teachers in a given school system. If five separate samples (with replacement) of five teachers each are selected and the mean age of teachers in each sample computed, each of the five sample means would probably be different. The difference in the means or other descriptive statistics obtained from random samples of the same size drawn from the same population is termed *"sampling variation."*

8.4.1 Sampling Distribution and the Standard Error

If the means of samples of the same size (n) drawn from a population of size N are arranged in a frequency distribution, the result is termed a *"sampling distribution of the means"* of samples with size n. This sampling distribution can be treated as any other frequency distribution, and its standard deviation can be computed. If this is done for the distribution of all possible samples of a given size, the resulting standard deviation is also called the *"standard error of the mean."*

The "standard error" is not actually an "error" or a computational mistake. Rather, it is a measure of the scatter of the means, or other statistics, computed from all samples of the same size drawn from a given population.

To illustrate the concepts involved, consider a small school system having a total of only four teachers. The ages of the four teachers who make up this tiny population, or universe, are shown in Exhibit 8.5. The exhibit also shows that the parameters of this population of four are as follows:

Mean μ = 45 years
Variance σ^2 = 125
Standard deviation σ = 11.2 years

EXHIBIT 8.5 – THE AGES FOR AN ARTIFICIAL POPULATION OF FOUR TEACHERS

Teacher	Age in years (X)	$X - \mu$	$(X - \mu)^2$
(1)	(2)	(3)	(4)
A	30	−15	225
B	40	− 5	25
C	50	+ 5	25
D	60	+15	225
Total	180	0	500

$\mu = 45$

$\sigma^2 = 125$
$\sigma = 11.2$

Suppose, in sampling with replacement, that all possible samples of size two (n = 2) are selected; and, the arithmetic mean of each sample calculated. There are 16 such samples possible when the order of selection is taken into consideration; each possible sample along with its mean is shown in Exhibit 8.6. Each sample mean can be treated as though it were an observation in a distribution of 16 observations. The mean of the 16 possible sample means ($\mu_{\bar{X}}$, mean of the means) is 45 years. The variance of the means is $\sigma^2_{\bar{X}} = 62.5$ (see Column 5). The standard deviation of the means, which is the square root of the variance, is $\sigma_{\bar{X}} = 7.9$ years. This standard deviation of the means is also the "standard error of the mean" for all the possible samples of two teachers from this population of four teachers.

The symbol used to designate the standard error of the mean is $\sigma_{\bar{x}}$. Some authors of statistical texts use the terms "standard error" and "standard deviation of the sampling distribution" interchangeably.

There would be a different standard error of the mean for all the samples of size 3 from this population. Of course, a sample of size 4 would be the total population and thus yield no sampling variation.

Statistical inference would be severely limited if it were not for one important principle relating to the distribution of means and certain other statistics of samples. This principle is *regardless of whether or not the characteristics are normally distributed in the population, the means of samples of a given size drawn from that population will tend to be normally distributed.* As the size of the sample is increased, the more the distribution of the sample means will approach normality. This mathematical principle is referred to as the "central-limit theorem."

Conversely, the smaller the sample size, the more the form of the distribution of the population affects the form of the sampling distribution of the means. The extreme case would be samples with only one individual each; in this event the distribution of means (if means of samples of one have any real meaning) would be in the same form as that of the population.

EXHIBIT 8.6 – ALL POSSIBLE SAMPLES OF SIZE TWO THAT CAN BE DRAWN WITH REPLACEMENT FROM THE POPULATION OF FOUR TEACHERS GIVEN IN EXHIBIT 8.5

Sample pair (1)	Ages of sample pair (2)	Sample mean ($\bar{X}$) (3)	($\bar{X} - \mu_{\bar{X}}$) (4)	($\bar{X} - \mu_{\bar{X}}$)^2 (5)	$\Sigma(X - \mu_{\bar{X}})^2$ of each sample (6)
A-A*	30-30	30	−15	225	0
A-B	30-40	35	−10	100	50
A-C	30-50	40	− 5	25	200
A-D	30-60	45	0	0	450
B-A	40-30	35	−10	100	50
B-B*	40-40	40	− 5	25	0
B-C	40-50	45	0	0	50
B-D	40-60	50	+ 5	25	200
C-A	50-30	40	− 5	25	200
C-B	50-40	45	0	0	50
C-C*	50-50	50	+ 5	25	0
C-D	50-60	55	+10	100	50
D-A	60-30	45	0	0	450
D-B	60-40	50	+ 5	25	200
D-C	60-50	55	+10	100	50
D-D*	60-60	60	+15	225	0
Total		720		1,000	2,000
		$\mu_{\bar{X}} = 45$		$\sigma_{\bar{X}}^2 = 62.5$	

*These samples would be possible when sampling *with* replacement. They would not be possible when sampling *without* replacement.

Exhibit 8.7 compares the frequency distribution of the ages of the population of four teachers shown in Exhibit 8.5 with the sampling distribution of the means of all samples of size two that it is possible to draw from this population of four shown in Exhibit 8.6.

Notice that even with this small population, which is certainly not normally distributed but is referred to as "rectangular," the distribution of the means of samples of size two is symmetrical and approaches a normal distribution. The relationships between the population frequency distribution and the sampling distribution are shown graphically in Exhibits 8.8 and 8.9.

This strong tendency of the distribution of the means of samples of the same size to be normally distributed regardless of the shape of the population sampled is important because it permits defensible statistical inferences from many sample statistics of characteristics that are not normally distributed in the population. Thus, with reasonable precautions, conclusions can be drawn about population parameters, such as the mean, based upon the use of normal probability distribution formulas and tables.

EXHIBIT 8.7—FREQUENCY DISTRIBUTION OF AGES OF THE POPULATION OF FOUR TEACHERS SHOWN IN EXHIBIT 8.5, AND THE SAMPLING DISTRIBUTION OF THE MEAN AGE FOR ALL THE SAMPLES OF TWO TEACHERS EACH THAT IT IS POSSIBLE TO DRAW FROM THIS POPULATION

Age in years	Distribution of teachers in sample (n = 1)	Distribution of mean age of samples of two teachers each (n = 2)
(1)	(2)	(3)
30	1	1
35	0	2
40	1	3
45	0	4
50	1	3
55	0	2
60	1	1
Total	4	16

8.4.2 Standard Error of a Sample Mean in Relation to a Population Mean

In the repeated random sampling of a given population with samples of a specific size, not only do the means of the samples vary from one another but they also vary from the true value of the population mean. The average of the sampling distribution of all sample means is the population mean. An important principle in statistical inference is that *the mean of the means of all possible random samples of a given size n drawn with replacement or from an infinite population equals the mean of the population (i.e., $\mu_{\bar{X}} = \mu$)*. The average of the estimates over all possible estimates is referred to as the "expected value" of the sample estimate. For example, the expected value, or the average of the 16 possible samples of two shown in Exhibit 8.6, is 45 years, which equals the actual mean age of the population of four teachers.

Since the average of the means of all the possible samples of the same size is identical with the population mean, the standard error becomes a measure of the difference between the sample mean and the true mean of the population *on the average*. This relationship is more readily seen when it is noted that to arrive at the standard deviation (standard error) of the distribution of means of samples of a given size, the deviation of each sample mean from the average of all the means is obtained. This is the same as taking deviations from the population mean.

EXHIBIT 8.8–FREQUENCY DISTRIBUTION OF THE AGES OF THE POPULATION OF FOUR TEACHERS SHOWN IN EXHIBIT 8.5.

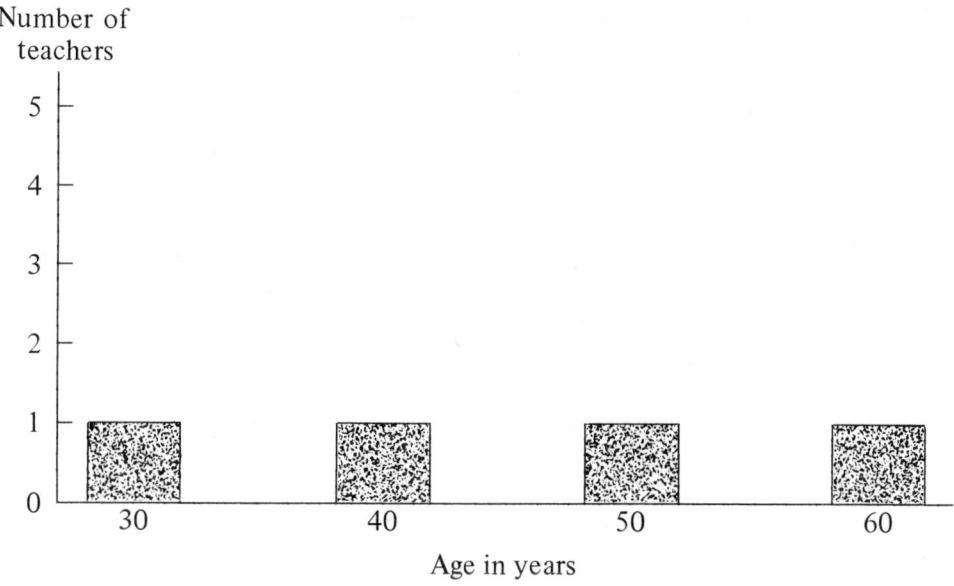

EXHIBIT 8.9–SAMPLING DISTRIBUTION OF THE MEAN AGE OF ALL SAMPLES OF TWO TEACHERS EACH THAT IT IS POSSIBLE TO DRAW (WITH REPLACEMENT) FROM THE POPULATION OF FOUR TEACHERS SHOWN IN EXHIBIT 8.7.

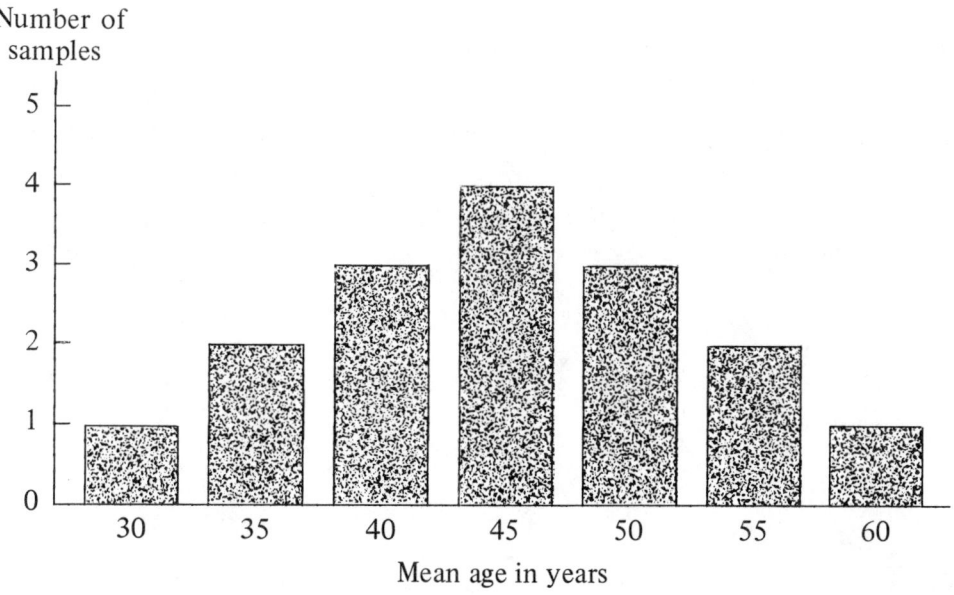

If the sampling procedure is completely random, the average of the means of all possible samples of size n will always equal the population mean. There are times, however, when the average of the means of all the samples of size n that it is possible to draw from a population would not equal the true value of the population mean. The amount by which the average of the means of all samples that it is possible to draw by the same procedure from a population differs from the true mean of the population is called the "bias" of the mean of the samples selected in that manner.[1] Whenever the average of the sample means of all samples of a given size that it is possible to draw by the same procedure from a population is identical to the true mean of the population, the sampling procedure is said to yield an "unbiased" estimate of the population mean.

It does not follow, however, that an estimate that is unbiased is without sampling error. For example, the sample A-B drawn at random from the population of four teachers in Exhibit 8.5 has a mean of 35 years, which is ten years less than the true mean age of the population of four teachers. Strange as it may seem, the mean of 35 years obtained from sample A-B is said to be an "unbiased estimate" of the population mean. The reason is that the *procedure* used to select this sample was completely random and the formula used to obtain the estimate is unbiased. Therefore, the average of the means for *all* the 16 possible samples drawn in *this random manner* equals the true mean value of 45 years for the population.

Perhaps no one word has created as much confusion between the statistician and the layperson as has the word *bias*. The confusion arises from the derogatory meaning of the word as it is commonly used. A person who is prejudiced and who refuses to look objectively at both sides of an issue is said to be biased. No such derogatory meaning is implied when the term is used technically in statistics. Indeed, it is sometimes considered better in sample surveys to have a small consistent bias inherent in a sampling procedure than to have a large random error. More will be said about this point in the discussion on stratified sampling in Chapter 13.

8.4.3 Standard Error of a Sample Mean in Relation to a Population Standard Deviation

Another important relationship of the sampling distribution of means should be discussed. Stated as a mathematical principle it is that *when sampling from a population of infinite size or when sampling with replacement, the standard error of the sampling distribution of means of samples of a given size, n, is given by the following formula:*

$$\sigma_{\bar{X}} = \frac{\sigma}{\sqrt{n}} \tag{8.3}$$

---

[1] For certain types of restrictions on randomness, such as stratification, formulas for computing unbiased estimates of population parameters are available. These formulas mathematically compensate for the bias of the sampling procedure.

where:

$\sigma_{\bar{X}}$ is the standard error of the sampling distribution of the means for a characteristic of all possible samples of size n from a given population.

σ is the standard deviation of a characteristic in the population.

n is the number of individuals in the sample.

There are two ways of thinking about this relationship:

1. In a given population with standard deviation, σ, the *larger* the size of the sample, n, the *smaller* the standard error of the mean (the standard deviation of the sampling distribution of the means).

2. With a given sample size, n, the *larger* the standard deviation of a characteristic in the population sample, the *larger* the standard error of the mean (the standard deviation of the sampling distribution of the means).

These relationships are exceedingly useful tools in determining the appropriate sizes of samples to use in surveys. Usually laypersons tend to judge the dependability of a sample in terms of the *proportion* or percentage of the population in the sample, but the preceding relationships reveal that the dependability of a sample mean is primarily a function of other factors. The relationships indicate that, at least in infinite or extremely large populations, the standard error of the sample means is directly related to the standard deviation of the population and inversely related to the square root of the number of individuals in the sample. The application of these principles will be discussed in following chapters.

The variance and standard deviation of the ages of the population of four teachers shown in Exhibit 8.5 illustrate the relationships between the population standard deviation and the standard error. The population mean is 45 years, and the standard deviation of the four ages from the population mean is 11.2 years. According to Formula (8.3), the standard error of the sampling distribution of the means of all possible samples of size two should be:

$$\sigma_{\bar{X}} = \frac{\sigma}{\sqrt{n}}$$

$$= \frac{11.2}{\sqrt{2}}$$

$$= \frac{11.2}{1.414}$$

$$= 7.9 \text{ years}$$

This value agrees with the value $\sigma_{\bar{X}}$ = 7.9 years, computed from Exhibit 8.6.

8.4.4 Standard Error of the Mean When Sampling Without Replacement

For random samples selected from an infinite or very large population, the standard error of the sampling distribution of the means is $\sigma_{\bar{X}}$. This same relationship also holds for random sampling *with* replacement from small populations, as demonstrated in the illustration of the population of four teachers. However, a problem arises when a small population is sampled *without* replacement. Under such conditions, the previous formula ($\sigma_{\bar{X}} = \sigma / \sqrt{n}$) tends to overestimate the standard deviation of the sampling distribution.

For example, in Exhibit 8.6 the standard error of the 16 means of all samples of two that were possible *with* replacement was $\sigma_{\bar{X}} = 7.9$. But now consider *only* those 12 samples of two that are possible *without* replacement. Notice that it would not be possible to draw the four samples A-A, B-B, C-C, D-D when sampling *without* replacement. The standard error for the sampling distribution of the means of only these 12 samples is calculated as $\sigma_{\bar{X}} = 6.5$, which is less than the standard error of $\sigma_{\bar{X}} = 7.9$ for samples of two, assuming replacement. A *finite population correction* factor can be applied to Formula (8.3) to obtain the corrected value. The factor for this formula is $\sqrt{(N-n)/(N-1)}$. Some authors call this a "finite multiplier"; others refer to it as the "finite correction" factor. Theoretically, this factor should be applied to the standard error of a mean whenever sampling from a finite population; however, when the sampling ratio (n / N) is small, the effect of the multiplier is negligible.

If Formula (8.3) is modified to include the finite population correction, the formula for the *standard error of the mean of finite samples* becomes:

$$\sigma_{\bar{X}} = \sigma \sqrt{\frac{N-n}{n(N-1)}} \qquad (8.4)$$

where:

$\sigma_{\bar{X}}$ is the standard error of the sample mean, i.e., the standard deviation of the distribution of sample means of all possible samples of size n from a given population.

σ is the standard deviation of a characteristic in a population.

N is the number of AU's in the population.

n is the number of AU's in the sample.

Applying this finite population correction for the example population of four yields:

$$\sigma_{\bar{X}} = \sigma \sqrt{\frac{N-n}{n(N-1)}}$$

$$= 11.2 \sqrt{\frac{4-2}{2(4-1)}}$$

$$= 6.5 \text{ years}$$

8.4.5 Standard Errors of Statistics When Sampling Without Replacement

The illustration of the application of the finite population multiplier to the standard error of the mean may be generalized to cases of the standard errors of other statistics and estimates of the various standard errors. However, the finite population correction or finite multiplier, as it is sometimes called, can be confusing because it appears in different forms in formulas for various parameters and statistics. No matter what the form, the multiplier is always less than one and, therefore, reduces the size of the standard error. It takes into account the size of the sample *in relation to* the size of the population and reduces the standard error accordingly as the sample size approaches the full population size. The essential base of the finite multiplier is $1 - n/N$, where N is the population size and n is the sample size. The fraction n/N is the proportion of the population included in the sample and is called the "sample, or sampling, fraction"; it is often designated by f. For the sake of simplicity the finite correction factor is often expressed as $(1 - f)$. An algebraically equivalent way of writing $1 - n/N$ is $(N - n)/N$. When $(N - 1)$ is used in the denominator rather than N, the finite multiplier becomes $(N - n)/(N - 1)$. For large populations the difference between N and $(N - 1)$ is insignificant.

Until a researcher gains experience with the effect of including the finite multiplier, the following rule of thumb should be followed: It is *never* wrong to use the finite correction factor (when working with a finite population), but it may be wrong to leave it out.

8.4.6 Estimating the Standard Error of the Mean from a Sample

The preceding sections define and illustrate the standard error of the mean, which was found to be the same as the standard deviation of the distribution of sample means. Certain relationships between the distribution of means of all samples of the same size that can be drawn from a population and the actual or true mean of the population were demonstrated. It was further shown that if the standard deviation of a population is *known,* the standard deviation (standard error) of the means of samples drawn from that population can be determined accurately. But such procedures are applicable *only* when the true standard deviation of the characteristic in the population is known. And most of the time it is *not* known.

Thus, in most sample surveys, there is no choice but to substitute the observed sample standard deviation, S, for the population standard deviation, σ. When this substitution is made, Formula (8.4) becomes Formula (8.5) and provides an *estimate of the standard deviation (standard error) of the distribution of all possible samples of size n from a given population when S is used as a substitute for the unknown σ, when the finite population correction is needed.*

Algebraic simplification of Formula (8.5) yields Formula (8.6):

$$\hat{\sigma}_{\bar{X}} = S_{\bar{X}} = \sqrt{\frac{S^2}{n}(1 - n/N)} \quad (8.5)$$

$$\hat{\sigma}_{\bar{X}} = S_{\bar{X}} = S\sqrt{n^{-1} - N^{-1}} \quad (8.6)$$

(n^{-1} is referred to as the reciprocal of n and is nothing more than 1 divided by n.)

where:

$\hat{\sigma}_{\bar{X}}$ is an estimate of the standard error of the sample mean, i.e., standard deviation of the distribution of means of all possible samples of size n from a given population.

$S_{\bar{X}}$ is the standard error of the mean (i.e., standard deviation of the distribution of means of all possible samples of size n) when S is used as a substitute for σ.

S is the standard deviation of the characteristic based on sample observations.

n is the number of AU's in the sample.

N is the number of AU's in the population.

Appropriate substitution in Formula (8.3) would give a formula for *estimating the standard error of the mean from sample data when the population size is infinite or when the sampling is done with replacement.*

To return once again to the population of four teachers: Suppose the sample A-C (ages 30 and 50 years) had been randomly selected. The mean of this sample of two is 40 years, and the sum of the squared deviations is 200 (Column 6), which was found by the following method: $(30 - 40)^2 + (50 - 40)^2$. Substituting in Formula (5.3) yields the standard deviation of the sample:

$$S = \sqrt{\frac{\Sigma x^2}{n-1}}$$

$$= \sqrt{\frac{200}{2-1}}$$

$$= 14.1 \text{ years}$$

The sample standard deviation (S) can now be substituted in Formula (8.6) to obtain an estimate of the standard error of the distribution of the means of all samples of size two that it is possible to draw from the population without replacement:

$$\hat{\sigma}_{\bar{X}} = S\sqrt{n^{-1} - N^{-1}}$$

$$= 14.1\sqrt{2^{-1} - 4^{-1}}$$

$$= 7.1 \text{ years}$$

This value, $\hat{\sigma}_{\bar{X}} = 7.1$ years, is an estimate of the standard error of the mean obtained from *this single* random sample. Had the random selection process given a different sample, the estimate would have been different.

Thus, from the single sample A-C, two estimates have been determined: (a) an estimate of the population mean, $\hat{\mu}$ and (b) an estimate of the standard error of the mean of samples of this size ($\hat{\sigma}_{\bar{X}}$). In other words, the data have yielded both an estimate of the population mean ($\hat{\mu}$ = 40 years) and an estimate ($\hat{\sigma}_{\bar{X}}$ = 7.1 years) of how far this estimated mean might be expected to vary from the true mean of the population because of sampling variation. The latter estimate, the standard error of the mean, is the basic yardstick used to measure the precision of the estimated mean. This precision, associated with the *confidence interval*, will be discussed in Chapter 9.

8.5 DEGREES OF FREEDOM

Closely related to the concept of statistical bias is the concept of "degrees of freedom." This phrase occurs again and again in a great variety of statistical problems and in the use of statistical tables.

Suppose one is asked to write down any three numbers. Clearly, the possible combinations are unlimited. If, however, the selection of these three numbers is constrained by having them add to 30, only two of the three numbers can be selected freely. Once the first two have been selected, the third number is automatically determined by the fact that the three numbers must add to 30. The choices are governed by the relationship:

$$X_1 + X_2 + X_3 = 30.$$

Thus, only two degrees of freedom are available in selecting the values for the three X's. In this situation there are three variables with one restriction on them; therefore, the number of independent variables, or "free" choices, is given as $3 - 1 = 2$.

If, as another example, one must name five numbers with a sum of 40 and with the first two adding to 15, there is no freedom to select all five numbers. In fact, selecting one of the first two automatically determines the other value. The restrictions on the selection of the five variables are given by the following two equations:

$$X_1 + X_2 = 15$$
$$X_1 + X_2 + X_3 + X_4 + X_5 = 40$$

Having selected X_1 (say, 3) automatically determines X_2, as $3 + X_2 = 15$, or $X_2 = 12$.

Since $X_1 + X_2 = 15$, it is seen that:

$$15 + X_3 + X_4 + X_5 = 40$$

Since $X_3 + X_4 + X_5 = (40 - 15) = 25$, only two of the three remaining variables can be freely chosen. Thus, there is freedom to select only one of the first two numbers and only two of the last three numbers, making a total of three degrees of freedom. It follows that the degrees of freedom are equal to the number of free variables minus the number of independent restrictions upon these free variables or, in this case, degrees of freedom (d.f.) = 5 − 2 = 3.

The application of the concept of the degrees of freedom in relation to problems of statistical bias will be evident in formulas containing denominators of (n − 1). In many problems involving statistical bias and statistical inferences, the number of degrees of freedom a sample statistic has in a sample of size n is (n − 1). Division by (n − 1) rather than n in formulas for computing the sample variance, S^2—such as Formula (5.3), when it is squared—yields a mathematically *unbiased* estimate of the population variance, σ^2. However, although division by (n − 1) rather than n in formulas for computing the variance—such as Formula (5.3), when squared—will yield an *unbiased* estimate of the population variance, the square root of that variance—or the standard deviation, S—is *not* an unbiased estimate of the standard deviation of the population, σ.

Some statistical texts, such as Dixon & Massey (1951) give tables of sample sizes and appropriate factors by which S, when computed from a sample of specific size, can be multiplied to obtain an unbiased estimate of the standard deviation of the population, $\hat{\sigma}$. For samples larger than 25, an approximate value of this multiplier is given by the expression:

$$\frac{\sqrt{n(n-1)}}{\sqrt{n(n-1)-1}}$$

For example, for n = 25 this multiplier is 1.00083. Thus, *for all practical purposes* an *unbiased* estimate of the standard deviation of a population (σ) is obtained from computation of the sample standard deviation by formulas—such as (5.3), (5.4) and (5.5)—that contain division by (n − 1) rather than by n.

9
ESTIMATION

Chapter 8 introduced the concept of *standard error of a statistic* or standard deviation of the distribution of all possible values for a sample statistic for samples of the same size drawn from an infinite (extremely large) population. For illustrative purposes, the sample mean was selected as the sample statistic. The magnitude of the standard error of the sample mean was shown to depend upon three factors: the variability in the population from which the sample was drawn (σ), the sample size (n), and, when sampling without replacement from finite populations, the population size (N). More specifically, when only sample data were available, the estimate for the standard error of the mean was given as:

$$\hat{\sigma}_{\overline{X}} = S\sqrt{n^{-1} - N^{-1}} \qquad (9.1)$$

This number provides a basis for judging the extent of the sampling variability in the sample arithmetic mean as an estimate for the population mean. Similar standard errors are available for other statistics as estimates of parameters, such as proportions and totals or aggregates.

An important goal of a researcher is to confine errors in a survey or an experiment to sampling errors, errors associated with the expected variability in a sample statistic due to the randomness of the sampling process only. Probability sampling theory is based on the assumption that sampling errors will occur but that their size and distribution will be random. To the extent that the sampling errors of probability samples are actually random, the standard error of a statistic obtained from a sample becomes a measure of the precision of the statistic.

In practice, it is usually impossible for the researcher to know how far a particular sample value lies from the true value in the population. But an estimate of the standard error of the statistic enables the researcher to establish a range of values around the the estimated sample value within which there is specific likelihood that the true value falls in the population. Such a range or band of values is termed the *confidence interval*. The upper and lower values of this interval are termed the *confidence limits*.

In practice, a single sample is usually selected and a sample arithmetic mean calculated. This sample mean is referred to as a "point estimate" of the population mean. Since point estimates will vary from sample to sample, the confidence interval provides a more meaningful way by which to estimate the population mean, yielding a range within which the population mean is expected to fall with an associated confidence. For example, in selecting a sample of teachers from within a large school district, the average number of years of teaching within the district is found to be 7.9. It cannot be concluded that 7.9 is the average for all teachers within this district; rather, the true mean value probably lies somewhere within a range on either side of 7.9 years.

In addition to dependence upon variability in the population, sample size, and population size, the confidence limits will also depend upon the degree of confidence (confidence level) desired in these limits.

9.1 CONFIDENCE INTERVALS

The concept of confidence intervals for parameters is based upon two principles discussed in Chapter 8. These are as follows:

- The central limit theorem states that regardless of the shape of the distribution of a characteristic in a population, the distribution of certain sample statistics pertaining to that characteristic will tend to be normally distributed.
- The standard deviation of a normally distributed sample statistic (e.g., mean)—termed the "standard error"—is a measure of the dispersion or scatter of similar statistics obtained from all possible samples of a specific size.

When the researcher uses the standard error, properties of the normal distribution make it possible to discuss expected variability in sample statistics, such as the arithmetic mean. For example, within one standard deviation on either side of the population mean will lie approximately 68% of the sample means for samples drawn randomly and of the same size.

9.1.1 Application to a Sample Mean

To illustrate how this property of the normal distribution can be applied, consider the following example.

From a sample of 1,000 teachers the mean salary is found to be $12,500, with a standard deviation of $2,000. Symbolically, these would be written

$$\bar{X} = \$12{,}500 \qquad S = \$2{,}000$$

Since the population is very large, the finite correction factor is not considered. An estimate for the standard error of the mean, rounded to the nearest dollar, based upon the sample data, is seen to be:

$$\boxed{S_{\bar{X}} = S/\sqrt{n}} \tag{9.2}$$

$$= \$2{,}000 / \sqrt{1{,}000}$$

$$= \$63$$

In theory, if the population mean were known, this estimate of the standard error of the mean could be used to establish limits around the population mean within which selected percentages (or proportions) of sample means of the same size would be expected to fall. For example, within ± 1.96 $S_{\bar{X}}$ would be expected to lie 95% of the sample means for samples of the same size drawn randomly from the same population.

In this case, these limits would be ± 1.96 × $63 = ± $123. Since the population mean is not known, but is to be estimated based upon the sample of 1,000, applying these same limits around the sample mean of $12,500 should yield limits (actually, confidence limits) with associated odds of 95 to 5 that the true population mean falls within these limits. Putting it another way, if 95% of the sample means would be expected to fall within ± 1.96 $S_{\bar{X}}$ then 95% of the limits around sample means would be expected to include the true population mean.

For this situation, in which both the sample and the population are large, the 95% confidence limits for the population mean, based upon sample statistics only, would be:

$$\boxed{\bar{X} - 1.96\, S_{\bar{X}} < \mu < \bar{X} + 1.96\, S_{\bar{X}}} \quad (9.3)$$

$$\$12{,}500 - 1.96 \times \$63 < \mu < \$12{,}500 + 1.96 \times \$63$$

$$\$12{,}500 - \$123 < \mu < \$12{,}500 + \$123$$

$$\$12{,}377 < \mu < \$12{,}623$$

The odds that the true population mean has been located are 95%, or 95 to 5, or 19 to 1. These are the 95% confidence limits. The last expression ($12,377 < μ < $12,623) is read: μ is greater than $12,377 but less than $12,623.

9.1.2 Different Confidence Levels for the Same Sample Size

The confidence level selected to establish the limits around the sample statistic is a decision that depends upon the judgment of the researcher. The desired precision of the sample statistic as an estimate of the population parameter is the primary factor in selecting the confidence level. As a rule, these decisions are made at the *beginning* of a study and are of fundamental importance in determining the optimum size of the sample. These problems will be discussed in Chapter 12.

Consider the sample of 1,000 teachers with the associated sample mean ($12,500) and standard error ($63). From the properties of the normal distribution, the following relationships exist between the standard deviation of the normal distribution and the proportion of cases falling within stated ranges of values from the mean:

- 90% of the cases fall within ± 1.654σ of the population mean
- 95% of the cases fall within ± 1.96σ of the population mean
- 99% of the cases fall within ± 2.576σ of the population mean.

The three levels of confidence above are commonly used in research. To find the confidence interval from the sample of 1,000 teachers at each of these three levels, the standard error of the mean, ($S_{\bar{X}}$ = $63) is multiplied by the number of standard error units corresponding to the confidence level desired, then added to and subtracted from the sample mean. The interval limits for the three levels of confidence are as follows:

90%: $\bar{X} \pm 1.645 S_{\bar{X}}$	95%: $\bar{X} \pm 1.96 S_{\bar{X}}$	99%: $\bar{X} \pm 2.576 S_{\bar{X}}$
$12,500 ± 1.645 × $63	$12,500 ± 1.96 × $63	$12,500 ± 2.576 × $63
$12,500 ± $104	$12,500 ± $123	$12,500 ± $162
$12,396 to $12,604	$12,377 to $12,623	$12,338 to $12,662

Thus, with a sample of a *given size* (which in this example is 1,000), to be *90%* sure that the population mean lies within the confidence interval, the interval is 1.645 standard error units on both sides of the sample mean. For the same sample, to be *95%* sure that the confidence interval includes the population mean, the interval is 1.96 standard error units on either side of the sample mean. For *99%* assurance the interval must be plus and minus 2.576 standard error units from the sample mean. An examination of the above confidence limits indicate that, as the level of confidence gets larger (from 90% to 95% to 99%), the limits get further apart and, consequently, the precision associated with the sample estimate deteriorates, going from ± $104 to ± $123 to ± $162.

Although the 90%, 95%, and 99% levels of confidence are those most frequently encountered, the researcher is free to select any level deemed acceptable for the particular situation. While the normal distribution has been used in this section to illustrate the concept, other distributions will be introduced later in Chapter 9 to account for small samples and for sampling distributions that are not normal.

9.1.3 A Graphic Look at Confidence Intervals

The normal theory (central limit theorem) works very well, even when samples are quite small. Assume that 20 samples of size 5 (n = 5) are drawn from a large population of teachers. The characteristic of interest is years of tenure within a given school district. The population mean is known to be 7.6 years; and the standard deviation, 2 years.

Exhibit 9.1 summarizes the raw data (Column 4) and certain derivative information. The arithmetic mean for each sample is given in Column 1; and the standard deviation, in Column 2. Assuming that the sample standard errors can be used to approximate the population standard error, 95% confidence limits (± $1.96 S_{\bar{x}}$) have been constructed (see Column 3). These limits vary in size because the sample standard deviations vary in size.

On the lefthand side of Exhibit 9.1, the individual confidence intervals are plotted on a scale of from 4 to 11 years of tenure (see bottom of exhibit). A vertical line has been drawn at the population mean of 7.6.

In repeated sampling from a normal distribution, one would expect to find that 95% of the confidence intervals about the sample means would include the population mean and 5% would not. For this example, in which the population form is unknown and the samples are quite small, use of normal theory gives results consistent with what one might expect in repeated sampling. In fact, 17 out of 20 of the confidence intervals do include the population mean of 7.6 years of tenure.

In three cases, samples 1, 15 and 16, the confidence interval does not include the population mean. The risk in using the 95% confidence level is 5%; that is, there is a 5% chance that the limits based upon a sample do not include the population parameter being estimated. If this risk is too great, it can be reduced by choosing the 99% confidence level. The limits are now wider (poorer precision in the estimate), but the risk of being wrong has decreased to 1%.

EXHIBIT 9.1–CONFIDENCE LIMITS BASED UPON 20 SAMPLES OF 5 TEACHERS EACH, DRAWN FROM THE SAME LARGE SCHOOL DISTRICT

Sample	Confidence intervals μ	$\overline{X}$ (1)	S (2)	95% limits (3)	Raw data (4)
1		9.00	0.71	8.38 – 9.62	10, 9, 9, 9, 8
2		8.00	2.83	5.52 – 10.48	10, 10, 10, 6, 4
3		7.00	2.00	5.25 – 8.75	9, 8, 8, 6, 4
4		7.00	2.24	5.04 – 8.96	10, 8, 7, 6, 4
5		7.60	2.07	5.78 – 9.42	10, 9, 8, 6, 5
6		6.40	2.30	4.38 – 8.42	9, 8, 7, 4, 4
7		6.60	2.30	4.58 – 8.62	9, 9, 6, 5, 4
8		8.00	1.87	6.36 – 9.64	10, 9, 8, 8, 5
9		6.20	2.28	4.20 – 8.20	10, 6, 6, 5, 4
10		6.80	1.64	5.36 – 8.24	8, 8, 7, 7, 4
11		8.60	2.61	6.31 – 10.89	10, 10, 10, 9, 4
12		6.60	1.14	5.60 – 7.60	8, 7, 7, 6, 5
13		8.60	1.67	7.13 – 10.07	10, 10, 9, 8, 6
14		7.20	1.92	5.51 – 8.89	10, 8, 7, 6, 5
15		9.40	0.89	8.62 – 10.18	10, 10, 10, 9, 8
16		6.00	1.58	4.61 – 7.39	8, 7, 6, 5, 4
17		8.00	1.58	6.61 – 9.39	10, 9, 8, 7, 6
18		8.20	2.49	6.02 – 10.38	10, 10, 9, 8, 4
19		7.00	2.74	4.60 – 9.40	10, 10, 5, 5, 5
20		7.00	2.24	5.04 – 8.96	10, 8, 7, 6, 4

4 5 6 7 8 9 10 11
Years of Tenure

9.2 FINDING CONFIDENCE INTERVALS

In most situations the determination of confidence limits based upon a sample only requires a series of consistent steps. In this section these steps will be applied to developing confidence limits for the arithmetic mean, a total or aggregate, a proportion, and predictions from a linear bivariate regression. In establishing confidence limits for a variance (or a standard deviation), the approach is somewhat different and will be described as the final topic in this section.

To establish a confidence interval, based upon sample data only, involves the following steps:

1. Specify the parameter to be estimated (e.g., the arithmetic mean).
2. Establish the desired level of confidence (e.g., 95%).
3. Determine the standard error for the given sample statistic.
4. Identify the appropriate sampling distribution for the specific sample statistic (up to this point the only distribution that has been used is the normal; others will now be introduced).
5. Associate with the given sample the appropriate degrees of freedom (up to this point degrees of freedom have not entered into the analyses; degrees of freedom, essentially, take the sample size into consideration).
6. Use the sample data and the above information to calculate the desired confidence limits.

9.2.1 For an Arithmetic Mean

The arithmetic mean has been used earlier in the HANDBOOK to develop the concept of sampling distributions and standard errors. In this section two examples are presented using the appropriate sampling distribution for large and small populations.

Assume that a sample of 25 retired teachers has been selected from all retired teachers within a given state. The total number of retired teachers in the state is quite large. The average take-home retirement benefit for these 25 teachers is $700, with a standard deviation in the sample of $200. Estimate with 90% confidence the limits for the mean take-home pay for all retired teachers within the state. The standard error of the mean is given by Formula (9.2) and is seen to be:

$$S_{\bar{X}} = S/\sqrt{n}$$
$$= \$200/\sqrt{25}$$
$$= \$40$$

The appropriate sampling distribution for this estimation situation is referred to as "Student's 't' distribution" and appears as Table H.4 in Appendix H. Across the top of the table are the risks associated with the various confidence levels. For example, in this situation the confidence level is 90%; therefore, the associated risk in making a wrong interval estimate is 10%. Along the lefthand column of Table H.4 are the degrees of freedom. For this example the *degrees of freedom are the sample size minus one or (n − 1)*. In examining this table note that as the degrees of freedom (and hence the sample size) get larger, the value in Table H.4 is getting smaller and for 1,000 degrees of freedom is effectively equivalent to the normal standard score, which includes the indicated proportion of the cases. For example, the value within the table, usually referred to as $t_{\alpha/2}$, for the 95% confidence level starts at 12.706 for a sample of two and decreases rapidly as the sample size increases. For 100 degrees of freedom (a sample of 101), the tabular value corresponds almost exactly with that for the normal distribution, namely, 1.984. The values within Student's "t" table provide larger multipliers than normal for small samples, thereby taking into consideration the greater variability expected with small samples. (The greek letter alpha corresponds to the risk being taken, and $1 - \alpha$ corresponds to the confidence level.)

The confidence limits for the population mean are given by Formula (9.4), namely:

$$\boxed{\overline{X} - t_{\alpha/2}\, S_{\overline{X}} < \mu < \overline{X} + t_{\alpha/2}\, S_{\overline{X}}} \tag{9.4}$$

which is seen to be analogous to Formula (9.3), with the appropriate value for the "t" distribution replacing the normal standard score.

From Table H.4 the appropriate "t" value for 90% confidence and 24 degrees of freedom ($25 - 1 = 24$) is 1.711. Substituting values in (9.4) yields:

$$\$700 - 1.711 \times \$40 < \mu < \$700 + 1.711 \times \$40$$
$$\$700 - \$68 < \mu < \$700 + \$68$$
$$\$632 < \mu < \$768.$$

Based upon the sample of 25 retired teachers, there is 90% confidence that the limits indicated above include the true population mean for all retired teachers within the state.

As a second example, consider a sample of 50 seniors in a high school in which 200 seniors will be attending college. These 50 seniors, randomly selected from among the 200 seniors, were given an aptitude test and achieved an average score of 600, with a standard deviation of 75 units. The average value for all 200 seniors is to be estimated with 95% confidence.

The first step is to calculate the *standard error of the mean with the appropriate finite correction factor,* as given in Formula (9.5):

$$\boxed{S_{\overline{X}} = S\sqrt{n^{-1} - N^{-1}}} \tag{9.5}$$

$$= 75\sqrt{50^{-1} - 200^{-1}}$$
$$= 75\sqrt{0.015}$$
$$= 75 \times 0.1225$$
$$= 9.2$$

With 49 degrees of freedom (50 − 1 = 49) at 95% confidence, the appropriate "t" value is seen to be approximately 2.009. These values are now substituted in Formula (9.4):

$$\bar{X} - t_{\alpha/2} S_{\bar{X}} < \mu < \bar{X} + t_{\alpha/2} S_{\bar{X}}$$

$$600 - 2.009 \times 9.2 < \mu < 600 + 2.009 \times 9.2$$

$$600 - 18.5 < \mu' < 600 + 18.5$$

$$581.5 < \mu < 618.5$$

The odds are 19 to 1 (95%) that the above confidence limits contain the true mean aptitude test score for the entire group of 200 seniors. *These are the 95% confidence limits.*

9.2.2 For a Total or Aggregate

The dean of students at a college wishes to know the total amount of money spent monthly within the community by students enrolled in the summer school program. These would be other than campus-related expenditures. The intent of the study is to indicate how much college students contribute to the local economy during the summer months.

The parameter being estimated is a total or an aggregate and is represented by the Greek letter tau (τ) in the population. The sample estimate is denoted by tau-hat ($\hat{\tau}$) or T.

From the summer school roster of 3,000 a sample of 250 students is selected. A short questionnaire, asking for amounts spent in different categories of expenditures, was distributed to each person in the sample. The average monthly expenditure was found to be $225, with a standard deviation of $35. The dean wanted 95% confidence associated with the interval estimate.

The estimate for the total amount spent by all 3,000 students can be obtained from Formula (9.6), namely:

$$\boxed{\hat{\tau} = T = N \Sigma X / n = N \bar{X}} \qquad (9.6)$$

$$= 3{,}000 \times \$225$$

$$= \$675{,}000 \text{ per month}$$

The standard error for this estimate is given by Formula (9.7):

$$\boxed{S_T = S\sqrt{N(N-n)n^{-1}}} \qquad (9.7)$$

$$= \$35 \sqrt{3{,}000 \times (3{,}000 - 250) \times 250^{-1}}$$

$$= \$35 \sqrt{33{,}000}$$

$$= \$35 \times 181.66$$

$$= \$6{,}358$$

Following the same pattern as used in estimating confidence limits for the arithmetic mean, the confidence limits for a total are given by Formula (9.8):

$$\boxed{T - t_{\alpha/2}\, S_T < \tau < T + t_{\alpha/2}\, S_T} \qquad (9.8)$$

Since the sample size is large, the appropriate "t" values for 95% confidence limits corresponds exactly with the normal standard score, namely 1.96. Substitution of the above values in (9.8) yields the following:

$$\$675{,}000 - 1.96 \times \$6{,}358 < \tau < \$675{,}000 + 1.96 \times \$6{,}358$$

$$\$675{,}000 - \$12{,}462 < \tau < \$675{,}000 + \$12{,}462$$

$$\$662{,}538 < \tau < \$687{,}462$$

The dean can have 95% confidence associated with the statement that the total true average monthly expenditures for all 3,000 summer school students lies between $662,540 and $687,460. The risk that this statement is wrong is 5%.

As a second example, consider a large school system that is planning to buy systemwide insurance to cover money in all school petty cash funds. Since the amount of the insurance premium depends upon the total monies in these funds, on the average, an estimate is needed of this total. From a sample of 25 schools within the district, an average of $425 is noted in the 25 petty cash funds. The standard deviation is $65. There are 125 schools within the district. The insurance firm requires that 99% confidence limits be calculated for the total dollars within the petty cash funds.

The estimate for the total petty cash dollars, from Formula (9.6), is seen to be:

$$T = N\bar{X} = 125 \times \$425 = \$53{,}125$$

and the associated standard error of the total becomes, from Formula (9.7):

$$\begin{aligned}
S_T &= S\sqrt{N(N-n)\,n^{-1}} \\
&= \$65\sqrt{125(125-25)\,25^{-1}} \\
&= \$65\sqrt{500} \\
&= \$65 \times 22.36 \\
&= \$1{,}453
\end{aligned}$$

The appropriate tabular value from the "t" table (Table H.4) is approximately 2.62 (124 degrees of freedom and 99% confidence). Substitution of the above values in Formula (9.8) yields the desired confidence limits:

$$T - t_{\alpha/2}\, S_T < \tau < T + t_{\alpha/2}\, S_T$$
$$\$53{,}125 - 2.62 \times \$1{,}453 < \tau < \$53{,}125 + 2.62 \times \$1{,}453$$
$$\$53{,}125 - \$3{,}807 < \tau < \$53{,}125 + \$3{,}807$$
$$\$49{,}318 < \tau < \$56{,}932$$

The insurance firm has 99% confidence that the true total, on the average, ranges between the above limits. Not much variation in the day-to-day systemwide total is assumed. If great day-to-day variation in this total is expected, a different sampling procedure should be used.

9.2.3 For a Proportion or a Percentage

A school board is interested in determining teachers' opinions about a merit pay proposal. Within the system are 2,000 teachers. A sample of 200 is selected randomly; and opinions on a number of issues, including merit pay, are solicited. In this sample, 115 are opposed to the merit pay proposal being considered by the board. The board desires to establish 90% confidence limits around the sample proportion. (Since a percentage is 100 times a proportion, the procedures that follow can be applied to proportions and then multiplied by 100 to arrive at equivalent percentage statements.)

The estimate of the population proportion (π) is given by Formula (9.9):

$$p = f / n \qquad (9.9)$$

where: f is the number in the category of interest
        n is the total sample size

The proportion opposed to the merit pay proposal is:

$$p = 115 / 200 = 0.575$$

The standard error of a sample proportion, including the finite correction factor, is indicated in Formula (9.10):

$$S_p = \sqrt{\frac{p(1-p)}{(n-1)}\left[1 - \frac{n}{N}\right]} \qquad (9.10)$$
$$ = \sqrt{p \times q\,(n-1)^{-1}\,N^{-1}\,(N-n)}$$

where: $q = 1 - p$

Either expression will yield the standard error of the sample proportion, based upon sample data only.

The standard error of the sample proportion is estimated from (9.10) as:

$$S_p = \sqrt{\frac{0.575(1-0.575)}{(200-1)}\left[1 - \frac{200}{2,000}\right]}$$

$$= \sqrt{\frac{0.575 \times 0.425 \times 0.90}{199}}$$

$$= \sqrt{0.001105}$$

$$= 0.033$$

The confidence limits for the population proportion based upon a sample are given by Formula (9.11):

$$\boxed{p - t_{\alpha/2}\, S_p < \pi < p + t_{\alpha/2}\, S_p} \qquad (9.11)$$

For this sample size, the appropriate "t" value from Table H.4 is approximately 1.66 (90% confidence and 199 degrees of freedom). Substitution in Formula (9.11) yields:

$$0.575 - 1.66 \times 0.033 < \pi < 0.575 + 1.66 \times 0.033$$

$$0.575 - 0.055 < \pi < 0.575 + 0.055$$

$$0.52 < \pi < 0.63$$

It is clear from these 90% confidence limits that a majority of the teachers do not favor the merit pay proposal. Note that 50% is not included within these limits.

Consider a slightly different example. A sample of 150 students within a school district has been selected from among graduating seniors. Ninety of these seniors plan to attend college and pursue graduate studies after completion of their undergraduate programs. With 95% confidence, estimate the proportion among all graduating seniors (there are 1,750 of them) who expect to pursue graduate studies.

The sample proportion planning to pursue graduate studies is obtained from Formula (9.9) and is seen to be:

$$p = f / n = 90 / 150 = 0.60$$

Based upon the second equation in (9.10), the standard error of this sample proportion is:

$$S_p = \sqrt{p \times q (n-1)^{-1} (N-n) N^{-1}}$$

$$= \sqrt{0.60 \times 0.40 \times 149^{-1} (1{,}750 - 150) \, 1{,}750^{-1}}$$

$$= \sqrt{0.001473}$$

$$= 0.038$$

The degrees of freedom are 149 (150 − 1), yielding the appropriate tabular "t" value as 1.98 (from Table H.4) for 95% confidence. The desired confidence limits, then, are given by Formula (9.11):

$$p - t_{\alpha/2} S_p < \pi < p + t_{\alpha/2} S_p$$
$$0.60 - 1.98 \times 0.038 < \pi < 0.060 + 1.98 \times 0.038$$
$$0.60 - 0.075 < \pi < 0.60 + 0.075$$
$$0.525 < \pi < 0.675$$

There is 95% confidence that the proportion of those graduating seniors who plan to pursue graduate programs in college lies somewhere between 0.525 and 0.675, or between 52.5% and 67.5%. This set of confidence limits could be converted to numbers of graduating seniors by multiplying the two limit proportions by 1,750, giving an interval of from 919 to 1,181 persons.

For very small samples (say, under 50) these confidence interval procedures are not accurate and should be replaced by other techniques, such as those given in U.S. Department of Commerce (1966).

9.2.4 In Bivariate Linear Regression

Chapter 7 presented procedures for estimating a regression line in the bivariate linear situation (i.e., a line and not a curve). The regression line between years of teaching experience and contract salary in $1,000 was calculated as:

$$Y' = 9.67 + 0.823 X$$

where X ranges between 2 and 20 years of teaching experience and Y' is the predicted contract salary in $1,000. Observed contract salaries for the 30 teachers in the sample were between $10,200 (Y = 10.2) and $25,500 (Y = 25.5). Assuming that this sample was drawn from a large population of teachers, two questions might be asked:

1. For all teachers with the same number of years of teaching experience, what are the confidence limits for the average contract salary for all such teachers?
2. For all teachers with the same number of years of teaching experience, what are the limits within which a certain proportion of individual salaries might be expected to fall?

The first question calls for confidence limits on an average value based upon the regression equation; the second, for limits on individual Y values. The second set of limits should, logically, be larger than the first set. Although related, the two cases are dealt with separately.

Case No. 1

The predicted average contract salary for a given value of X (years of teaching experience) is given by the regression equation in (9.12). Assume that the desired confidence limits are for teachers in the population with ten years of teaching experience. Substitution in the regression equation yields:

$$Y' = 9.67 + 0.823\ X$$
$$= 9.67 + 0.823\ (10)$$
$$= 17.9 \qquad (\$17{,}900)$$

The standard error for the mean predicted Y value is given by Formula (9.12):

$$\boxed{S_{\bar{y}'} = \sqrt{\frac{(1-r^2)\ \Sigma\ (Y-\bar{Y})^2}{(n-2)} \times \left[\frac{1}{n} + \frac{(X-\bar{X})^2}{\Sigma\ (X-\bar{X})^2}\right]}} \qquad (9.12)$$

Values to be inserted in Formula (9.12) are repeated below from Chapter 7 and from the conditions of the situation[1]:

$$X = 10 \text{ years} \qquad\qquad n = 30 \text{ teachers}$$
$$\Sigma\ (Y-\bar{Y})^2 = 717.79 \qquad \Sigma\ (X-\bar{X})^2 = B/30 = 29{,}700/30$$
$$r^2 = 0.9347 \qquad\qquad\qquad\qquad = 990$$
$$\bar{X} = 11 \text{ years}$$

---

[1] The (n - 2) in Formula (9.12) is analogous to the (n - 1) used when only a single variable, say X, is under consideration.

Substituting these values in the above equation for $S_{\bar{y}'}$ yields:

$$S_{\bar{y}'} = \sqrt{\frac{(1 - 0.9347) \times 717.79}{(30 - 2)} \times \left[\frac{1}{30} + \frac{(10 - 11)^2}{990}\right]}$$

$$= \sqrt{\frac{0.0653 \times 717.79}{28} \times \left[\frac{1}{30} + \frac{1}{990}\right]}$$

$$= \sqrt{1.674 \times 0.0343}$$

$$= \sqrt{0.0574}$$

$$= 0.24$$

The appropriate confidence limits for the average Y value, designated here as the parameter $\mu_{\bar{y}.x}$, for the given X value are given in Formula (9.13):

$$\boxed{Y' - t_{\alpha/2}\, S_{\bar{y}'} < \mu_{\bar{y}.x} < Y' + t_{\alpha/2}\, S_{\bar{y}'}} \qquad (9.13)$$

For the confidence level of 95% and (n − 2) degrees of freedom, 30 − 2 = 28, the appropriate tabular "t" value from Table H.4 is 2.048. (The degrees of freedom for this set of confidence limits are n − 2 and not n − 1.)

Substitution of appropriate values in Formula (9.13) yields:

$$17.90 - 2.048 \times 0.24 < \mu_{\bar{y}.x} < 17.90 + 2.048 \times 0.24$$

$$17.89 - 0.49 < \mu_{\bar{y}.x} < 17.89 + 0.49$$

$$17.41 < \mu_{\bar{y}.x} < 18.39$$

or the 95% confidence limits for the average contract salary for all teachers in the population with ten years of experience is between $17,400 and $18,380.

Case No. 2

For the second case the approach is identical for predicting limits for individual teacher contract salaries for a given number of years of teaching experience, except that the appropriate standard error is given by the following expression:

$$\boxed{S_{y'} = \sqrt{\frac{(1 - r^2) \sum (Y - \bar{Y})^2}{(n - 2)} \times \left[1 + \frac{1}{n} + \frac{(X - \bar{X})^2}{\sum (X - \bar{X})^2}\right]}} \qquad (9.14)$$

Substituting the same data on the sample of 30 years in Formula (9.14) gives the following standard error for individual contract salaries:

$$S_{y'} = \sqrt{\frac{(1-0.9347) \times 717.79}{(30-2)} \times \left[1 + \frac{1}{30} + \frac{(10-11)^2}{990}\right]}$$

$$= \sqrt{\frac{0.0653 \times 717.79}{28} \times \left[1 + \frac{1}{30} + \frac{1}{990}\right]}$$

$$= \sqrt{1.674 \times 1.0343}$$

$$= \sqrt{1.73}$$

$$= 1.32$$

The appropriate confidence limits for individual Y values, designated here as Y_X, for a given X value are given in Formula (9.15):

$$\boxed{Y' - t_{\alpha/2} S_{y'} < Y_X < Y' + t_{\alpha/2} S_{y'}} \qquad (9.15)$$

Since the degrees of freedom remain the same at $(n-2)$, the appropriate tabular "t" value is still 2.048. Because all teachers with ten years of teaching experience are again the group of interest, the predicted value based upon the regression equation given on page 152 remains the same; namely, 17.89 ($17,890). Substituting in Formula (9.15) yields:

$$17.89 - 2.048 \times 1.32 < Y_X < 17.89 + 2.048 \times 1.32$$

$$17.89 - 2.70 < Y_X < 17.89 + 2.70$$

$$15.19 < Y_X < 20.59$$

or the 95% confidence limits for individual contract salaries for all teachers with ten years of teaching experience in the school district range from $15,190 to $20,590. That these limits are quite large is due primarily to the small sample size.

A comparison of Formulas (9.12) and (9.14) shows them to be identical, except for the extra " 1 + " in the second formula, a term that enlarges the confidence limits, as would be expected when dealing with individual rather than average salaries.

9.2.5 For a Variance or a Standard Deviation

Although not frequently used in educational research, one final set of confidence limits for a population variance or standard deviation is given in this section. For samples of less than 100 from large populations approximately normally distributed, the following series of steps should be followed:

1. Establish the desired level of confidence, as in the previous situations.
2. Calculate the sum of the squared deviations from the mean:

$$\Sigma(X - \overline{X})^2 = (n-1)S^2 = \Sigma X^2 - (\Sigma X)^2 / n$$

3. Use (n − 1) degrees of freedom.

4. Use the appropriate distribution for selecting the tabular values to construct the confidence limits—the chi-square distribution. The chi-square (χ^2) distribution is not a single distribution but is a family of curves; the area and shape of each are determined by the number of degrees of freedom. For small numbers of degrees of freedom the chi-square curves are highly skewed. As the degrees of freedom increase, the χ^2 curves become more symmetrical. Exhibit 9.2 shows the relationships among the χ^2 curves for 3, 4, 6, 8, and 10 degrees of freedom. Tabular chi-square values from 1 to 100 degrees of freedom are given in Table H.5 in Appendix H. To read the table, look at the row indicated as 10 df (degrees of freedom). Go across that row to the column headed 0.050, and read the tabular chi-square: 3.94. In Exhibit 9.2 the area from 0 to 3.94 is shaded on the chi-square curve with 10 degrees of freedom. The shaded area corresponds to 0.05 or 5% of the area under the curve for 10 degrees of freedom. The analogous percentile at the other end of the distribution (i.e., excluding 5% at the upper end of the curve) would be read in the same row but under the column headed 0.950; namely, 18.31. These two tabular chi-square values exclude 10% of the area under the curve and 5% at either tail of the distribution. These two values would correspond to a 90% confidence region.

5. The appropriate confidence limits for the population variance would be given by the following:

$$\frac{\Sigma (X - \bar{X})^2}{\chi^2_{1-\alpha/2}} < \sigma^2 < \frac{\Sigma (X - \bar{X})^2}{\chi^2_{\alpha/2}} \qquad (9.16)$$

where the two chi-square values are read from the chi-square table for (n − 1) degrees of freedom and at the appropriate confidence levels.

Consider a sample of 50 high school seniors, selected from a much larger group who have taken a college entrance examination. The standard deviation of this sample set of results is 45 score units. It is desired to establish a confidence interval at the 90% confidence level for the standard deviation in the population from which this sample was selected. From the sample data, necessary sum of squared deviations from the arithmetic mean can be computed:

$$\begin{aligned}\Sigma (X - \bar{X})^2 &= (n - 1) S^2 \\ &= (50 - 1) \times (45)^2 \\ &= 49 \times 2{,}025 \\ &= 99{,}225\end{aligned}$$

Since the degrees of freedom are (n − 1) and, therefore, 50 − 1 = 49, this is the appropriate row to enter into the chi-square table. Since 90% confidence is desired, the appropriate tabular entries to be used for the confidence limits are in the columns headed 0.050 and 0.950; namely, 33.93 and 66.34. These values, plus the sum of squared deviations from the mean, are substituted in Formula (9.16), yielding:

EXHIBIT 9.2–CHI-SQUARE CURVES FOR 3, 4, 6, 8, AND 10 DEGREES OF FREEDOM

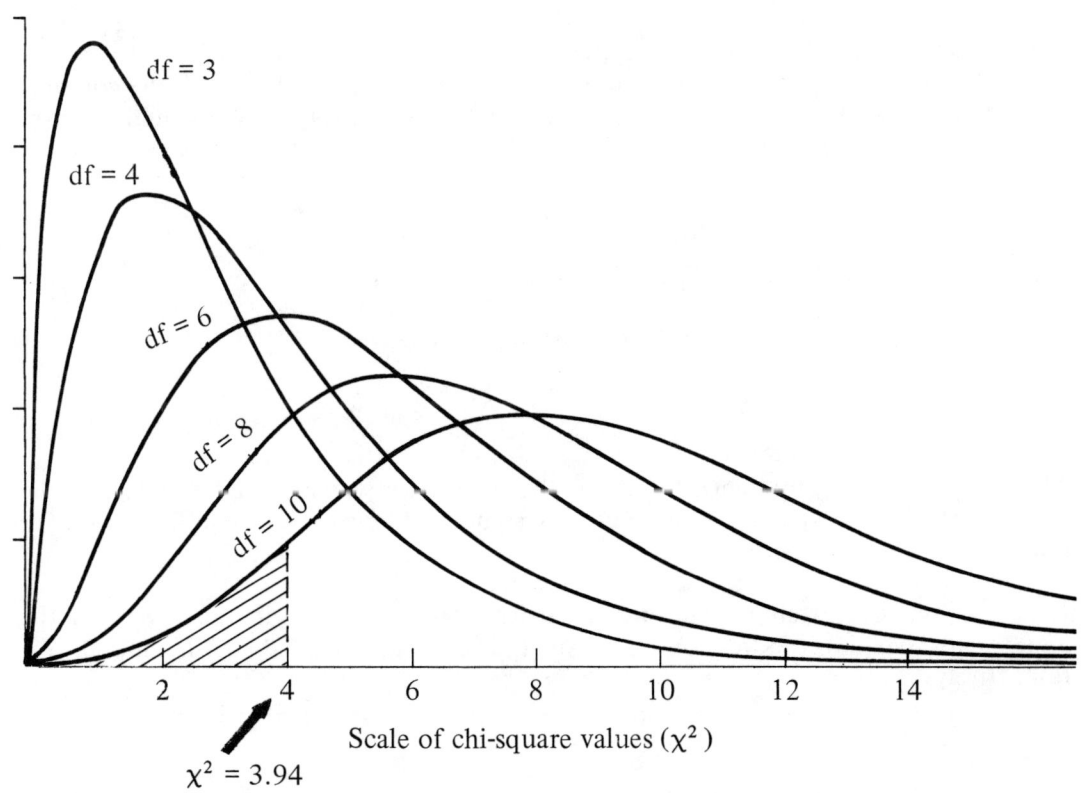

$$\frac{\Sigma (X - \bar{X})^2}{\chi^2_{1-\alpha/2}} < \sigma^2 < \frac{\Sigma (X - \bar{X})^2}{\chi^2_{\alpha/2}}$$

$$\frac{99{,}225}{66.34} < \sigma^2 < \frac{99{,}225}{33.93}$$

$$1{,}495.70 < \sigma^2 < 2{,}924.40$$

$$38.7 < \sigma < 54.1$$

Above are the 90%-confidence limits for both the variance and the standard deviation in the population of graduating seniors completing the specific college entrance examination.

If the desired limits had been associated with 95% confidence instead of 90% confidence, the appropriate tabular chi-square values would be associated with the columns headed 0.025 and 0.975; namely, 31.56 and 70.22, respectively. These would result in the following confidence limits:

$$\frac{99{,}225}{70.22} < \sigma^2 < \frac{99{,}225}{31.56}$$

$$1{,}413.06 < \sigma^2 < 3{,}144.01$$

$$37.6 < \sigma < 56.1$$

Above are the 95% confidence limits for the population variance and standard deviations. As should be expected, these limits are somewhat larger than the 90%-confidence limits.

For 99% limits, the tabular chi-square entries would be taken in the row with the appropriate degrees of freedom and in the columns headed 0.005 and 0.995, respectively.

10
HYPOTHESIS TESTING

Just what is an hypothesis? It is a belief or a statement that may be made in order to test the validity of some situation. It may be termed a tentative assumption about an aspect of the world around us. In educational research an example of a *research hypothesis* might be that "reduction in class size has an effect on the achievement of students." To test this hypothesis requires collecting data under controlled conditions by establishing an appropriate *experimental design*. [This HANDBOOK will not dwell on experimental design concepts, except for a few basic situations. The reader is referred to Winer (1962) and Iversen and Norpoth (1977) for more details.] Another research hypothesis that might require an experimental design would be that "teachers become more effective with training and experience."

Still another hypothesis might be that "younger teachers have different opinions from teachers with longer tenure on a number of issues affecting the teaching profession." This research hypothesis could be assessed by designing a *survey sampling plan* and would require identifying the population of teachers of interest and then following through with the development of a survey instrument and the actual sampling of teachers. This research approach is discussed in great detail in Chapters 13, 14, and 15.

10.1 RESEARCH HYPOTHESES VS. STATISTICAL HYPOTHESES

In theory, once an hypothesis has been established, the researcher will begin to collect the data that will lead to the acceptance or the rejection of the hypothesis. In practice, however, the research hypothesis usually does not lend itself to an easy hypothesis for testing. This is illustrated by the following three examples of research hypotheses:

- *Reduction in class size has an effect on the achievement of students.*

    To test such an hypothesis requires setting bounds on the statement. Some of the issues to be resolved before any testing can occur are, How will achievement be measured? What class size ranges will be included? What levels in school will be considered? What about the impact of teaching methods and individual teachers? What is meant by "has an effect on achievement"? To test the hypothesis as it is now worded requires answering all of the above questions and perhaps many others. Since the phrase "has an effect on achievement" may mean different things to different researchers, it may be more appropriate to reword the research hypothesis as follows: "Reduction in class size has no effect on achievement of students." The new hypothesis is referred to as the "statistical hypothesis" and, in this case, also as the "null hypothesis" (no effect exists).

- *Teachers become more effective with training and experience.*

   The statement is too broad and needs to be delimited: Which teachers? Elementary? Secondary? Both? How will effectiveness be measured? What kind of training is included? What constitutes experience? What is meant by "becomes more effective"? To test the research hypothesis requires answering each of these questions plus many more. The phrase "becomes more effective" is also open to interpretation. Therefore, a more appropriate wording of the research hypothesis might be: "Teachers do not become more effective with training and experience." The new hypothesis is also referred to as the "statistical hypothesis" and as the "null hypothesis."

- *Younger teachers have different opinions from teachers with longer tenure on a number of issues affecting the teaching profession.*

   The statement is somewhat broad and should be qualified before data collection can begin. Some of the questions that must be answered before an appropriate survey sampling plan can be developed are, What are the issues of importance? How are "younger teachers" defined? By age? By years of teaching experience? What is meant by "longer tenure"? What part of the teaching profession is of interest? Specifically, what is meant by "have different opinions"? The phrase "have different opinions" can be interpreted differently by different researchers: to be different, opinions must disagree by 5%? by 10%? by 25%? To avoid this requirement, the above hypothesis might be reworded as follows: "Younger teachers do not have different opinions from teachers with longer tenure on a number of issues affecting the teaching profession." Once again a statistical hypothesis (and also a null hypothesis) has been developed.

An examination of the above three statistical hypotheses should lead to a common observation—the researcher is stating that there is no difference or no effect:

1. "Reduction in class size has no effect ....."
2. "Teachers do not become more effective ....."
3. "Younger teachers do not have different opinions ....."

The research hypothesis has been converted into an hypothesis that effectively states that whatever it is that is being studied has no effect or impact. In other words, a null hypothesis.

By establishing the statistical hypothesis, the researcher is indicating that the hypothesis will be rejected if enough differences are observed in the sample(s) for the hypothesis to be false and for some alternative to be true. Hypothesis testing involves *tests of significance* in which the difference between two or more measures is compared to determine whether the difference happened by chance alone in simple random sampling or if something other than chance influenced the magnitude of the difference. If the observed difference(s) is larger than expected by chance alone when sampling under the assumption that the hypothesis is true, the hypothesis is rejected; and the results are said to be significant at some level of probability, most frequently taken in educational research as 0.10, 0.05, or 0.01.

To illustrate this concept, consider the third hypothesis above on teacher opinions. Suppose all necessary questions have been resolved and a sample of 200 teachers has been randomly selected from the population of interest in each of two tenure categories. Responses for these 400 on one of the issues disagree by 0.05 (for example, the younger teachers favor the issue by 0.55 and the other teachers by 0.60). Is this difference of 0.05 large enough to conclude that there is a difference on this issue within the population from which the samples were selected? What if the difference were 0.10? 0.02? Certainly, the larger the difference, the more likely the hypothesis is wrong; but how large does this difference have to be? Since sample statistics vary from sample to sample, the basic issue is, if the hypothesis is true, how much variation can be allowed by chance alone before the hypothesis can be rejected? Suppose further that the researcher will allow sampling variation between two sample means to fall within the 90% range of expected variation when the hypothesis is true. If the difference between the two sample means—using the appropriate test statistic (discussed in detail in a moment) —exceeds this 90% range, then the researcher might conclude that it is unlikely that the hypothesis is true; therefore, it is rejected, with the analyst knowing full well that there is a 10% chance that the differences might be due to chance alone. If that 10% risk is too great, a 5% region, or even a 1% region, might be selected before the hypothesis is rejected. These concepts are related directly to those presented in the discussion on estimation and sampling distributions given in the previous chapter.

It is seen, then, that the analyst must specify the acceptable risk in rejecting the hypothesis when it is true. This risk is referred to as the "level of significance" and is usually represented by the Greek letter alpha (α). When the results of a research study lead to rejection of the statistical hypothesis at a given risk level, this rejection is stated as being made with a certain confidence that is given as $1 - \alpha$; namely, the confidence level, discussed in Chapter 9.

10.2 TYPICAL STATISTICAL HYPOTHESES

Although a broad spectrum of possible statistical hypotheses might be tested, only the the following will be considered in this HANDBOOK.

- Testing the hypothesis, based upon a single sample, that a population mean has not shifted from a known value the previous year. (The average amount of extra monthly income earned by teachers has not changed from that known to have been earned by all teachers in a given school district last year.)

- Testing the hypothesis that two population means are the same. (The average age of female teachers in a given school district is the same as the average age for male teachers in that district.)

- Testing the hypothesis that two population standard deviations are the same. (The amount of variation, as measured by the standard deviation, in teachers' salaries is the same in two school districts within a given state.)

- Testing the hypothesis that the linear correlation is zero. (School district size, as measured by numbers of students, cannot be used to predict school district expenditures, i.e., the correlation between the two characteristics is equal to zero.)

- Testing the hypothesis that a sample is drawn from a population with a specified proportion possessing a given characteristic. (The proportion of teachers in a school district favoring a given issue is equal to 0.50.)

- Testing the hypothesis that two population proportions are the same. (Teachers in two different school districts oppose a given issue in the same proportion.)

- The distribution of a given characteristic is the same between two or more populations. (The distribution of years of teaching experience of teachers is the same in three school districts; the distribution of responses on an attitudinal question is the same for elementary, secondary, and college teachers.)

Excellent references for more detailed hypothesis testing are Edwards (1954), Jessen (1978), Siegel (1956), and Winer (1962).

10.3 STEPS IN TESTING STATISTICAL HYPOTHESES

Although many statistical hypotheses can be tested, the research hypotheses that can be examined are far more numerous. Fortunately, once a research hypothesis has been converted into a statistical hypothesis there is a pattern to testing hypotheses. The steps usually taken are as follows:

1. A statement of the statistical hypothesis is made. This statement is frequently referred to as the null hypothesis and is represented by the symbol H_o.

2. A level of significance is selected. This is the risk in being wrong if the statistical hypothesis is to be rejected and is frequently represented by the Greek letter alpha (a). This level of significance, or risk, is related to the confidence level discussed in the previous chapter; namely, the confidence level = $1 - a$.

3. The appropriate sampling distribution for assessing the likely validity of the hypothesis is selected. (The normal, Student's "t," and chi-square have already been considered in Chapter 9. A new distribution, the F distribution, will be introduced later in this chapter.)

4. The nonrejection and rejection (sometimes referred to as "critical") regions are determined based upon the specific hypothesis and sampling plan. To illustrate, consider Exhibit 10.1 The first curve (symmetrical) is labeled to indicate what is referred to as a "two-tailed rejection (critical) region," using the normal distribution and a 0.05 level of significance (95% confidence). The second curve (asymmetrical) is labeled to indicate what is referred to as a "one-tailed rejection region," using the chi-square distribution for 10 degrees of freedom and a 0.01 level of significance (99% confidence).

5. The appropriate experimental design or survey sampling plan is implemented and the data collected.

EXHIBIT 10.1–CRITICAL (REJECTION) REGIONS AND NONREJECTION REGIONS FOR TESTING HYPOTHESES

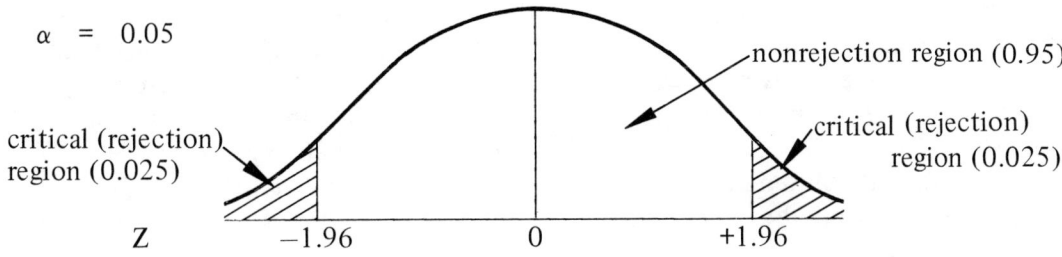

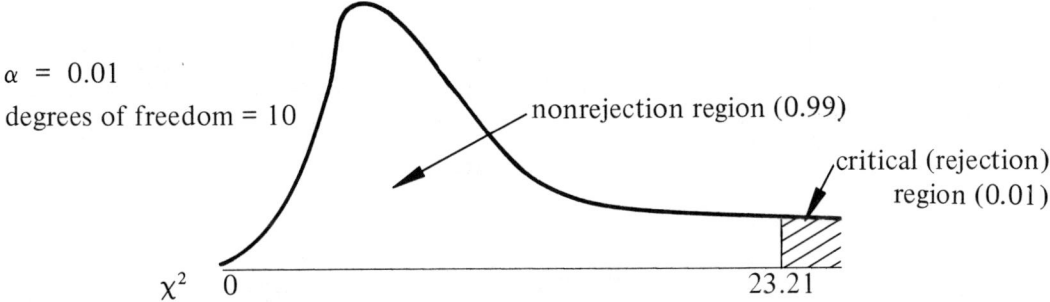

6. The necessary summary statistics (means, standard deviations, totals, proportions, correlations) are calculated, and the appropriate test statistic (such as normal, "t," chi-square, or F) is calculated under the assumption that the hypothesis, H_o, is true.

7. If the calculated test statistic falls within the rejection or critical region, the hypothesis is rejected with a confidence of $1 - \alpha$ and with an associated risk of being wrong of α. If the calculated test statistic falls within the nonrejection region, the sample results are not inconsistent with the hypothesis, H_o, at the selected level of significance. Nonrejection does not necessarily mean that H_o has been proven as being true.

One final comment is in order before considering a series of statistical hypotheses. An hypothesis can be rejected with a stated level of significance (α) or degree of confidence ($1 - \alpha$). A nonrejection of the hypothesis does not necessarily mean it is true; only that the observed sample differences are insufficiently large to make the researcher reject the hypothesis at the selected level of significance. Associated with any nonrejection of the null hypothesis is the likelihood that some other hypothesis might just as likely be true. For example, in testing the hypothesis that 50% of a population favor an issue, the sample results yielded a sample proportion of 0.54. The hypothesis, by procedures to be developed soon, is not rejected. It is conceivable that the population proportion might actually be 0.58, an hypothesis that would also not be rejected. This possibility of not rejecting the null hypothesis, when it should be rejected, is referred to as "committing a *Type II error.*" Although the topic is not pursued further in the HANDBOOK, the researcher should be aware of the possibility of committing such an error when an hypothesis is not rejected.

Conversely, the likelihood always exists that an hypothesis is rejected when it should not be. This situation is referred to as "committing a *Type I error.*" Fortunately, the analyst selects what level of Type I error is acceptable when the level of significance is identified. This value, α, is the probability of rejecting the null hypothesis when in fact it is true, i.e., the differences observed are due to sampling variation only and are not true departures from the hypothesis.

10.4 TESTING SPECIFIC STATISTICAL HYPOTHESES

A series of specific hypotheses is considered in this section. The first seven topics are presented as basic techniques. The final topic is treated more extensively to present the researcher an opportunity to test a family of hypotheses associated with the analysis of survey sampling results.

10.4.1 On a Single Population Mean

Suppose that the last complete census of teacher demographics in a large school district was conducted five years ago. The researcher believes that turnover within the system has changed and intends to measure turnover by the variable: number of years teaching within the system. The research hypothesis is that this average value has changed during the past five years. The statistical hypothesis, then, is that the mean number of years with the system has not changed. This is frequently stated symbolically as H_o: μ = some specified value.

This situation clearly calls for testing the difference between a sample mean drawn from today's population of teachers and the census value from five years ago (μ) to determine whether this difference exceeds what one might expect in random sampling. Recalling that the standard error of the sample mean is given by Formula (9.2), the appropriate test statistic becomes:

$$t_c = (\bar{X} - \mu) / S_{\bar{X}} \qquad (10.1)$$

with an associated (n − 1) degrees of freedom.

The statistical data associated with the specific sampling situation are summarized below:

The null hypothesis is that μ = 15.2 years

The 5% level of significance is selected to determine the critical regions.

The sample of 56 teachers yields the following values:

$$\bar{X} = 13.4 \text{ years}$$

$$S = 6 \text{ years}$$

$$S_{\bar{X}} = S/\sqrt{n} = 6/\sqrt{56} = 0.801 \text{ years}$$

The steps presented in Section 10.3 call for next determining the rejection and non-rejection regions based upon the level of significance and the sample size. For this example, with 55 degrees of freedom (56 − 1) and at the 5% level of significance, the appropriate tabular "t" value is seen to be (from Table H.4) $t_{0.05} = \pm 2.004$. The critical regions, associated with the rejection of the hypothesis, then are:

Reject the hypothesis for any value of the test statistic, "t_c," computed from (10.1), that exceeds ± 2.004. Stated symbolically, the hypothesis is rejected if:

$$t_c \geq + 2.004$$

or

$$t_c \leq - 2.004$$

This situation is frequently referred to as a "two-tailed test," since rejection of this hypothesis may occur if the change from 15.2 years has been either positive or negative. If the hypothesis had been stated as $\mu \geq 15.2$ years, this would be a one-tailed test, since rejection of the hypothesis can occur only when the sample mean is significantly less than the population mean hypothesized.

Based upon the above information, the calculated value of the test statistic, t_c, from Formula (10.1) is seen to be:

$$t_c = (\bar{X} - \mu) / S_{\bar{X}}$$
$$= (13.4 - 15.2) / 0.801$$
$$= -1.8 / 0.801$$
$$= -2.247$$

Since $t_c < - 2.004$, the hypothesis is rejected; and with 95% confidence it can be stated that there has been a change in the average number of years of teaching within this system. In fact, since the change is in the negative direction, it also follows that there has been a downward shift in this characteristic. If the selected level of significance had been $\alpha = 0.02$ (i.e., the 98% confidence level), the hypothesis would not have been rejected since for a rejection to occur the tabular "t" that must be exceeded in either the positive or negative direction is ± 2.396. Hence, the difference between the sample mean and the hypothesized population mean is sufficiently large to reject the hypothesis with 95% confidence, but not large enough to reject it with 98% confidence.

Consider a second example in which the average assessed property value within a school district was found to be $45,000 at the time a total reassessment occurred three years ago. To consider the possible impact of changing assessments on money available for schools locally, a sample of 30 homes was randomly selected from within the district and the newly assessed values determined. The local education association believes that there has been an upward shift in the average assessed value of property during this three-year period. It has established an acceptable risk of 0.01 and converted the research hypothesis to the following statistical hypothesis: There has been no upward change in the average assessed property value during this three-year period.

The statistical data associated with this situation is summarized below:

The null hypothesis is that $\mu \leq \$45,000$.

The 1% level of significance has been selected to determine the critical region, which is at only one end of the "t" distribution.

The sample of 30 homes yielded the following values:

$$\bar{X} = \$51,000$$
$$S = \$12,000$$
$$S_{\bar{X}} = S/\sqrt{n} = \$12,000/\sqrt{30} = \$2,191$$

Since the hypothesis calls for a one-tailed rejection and since the tabular "t" values in Table H.4 are two-tailed (i.e., half of the risk or level of significance proportions being at either end of the distribution), the appropriate column to enter would be with the risk of $\alpha = 0.02$, which, for 29 degrees of freedom (30 − 1), yields the following critical (rejection) region:

$$t_c > 2.462$$

Substituting the above values in Formula (10.1) yields the following:

$$t_c = (\bar{X} - \mu)/S_{\bar{X}}$$
$$= (\$51,000 - \$45,000)/\$2,191$$
$$= \$6,000/\$2,191$$
$$= +2.738$$

which exceeds the critical tabular "t" value of t = 2.462. Hence, with 99% confidence the hypothesis is rejected, and the association can conclude that there has been an upward shift in the average assessed value of property within the district.

10.4.2 On Two Population Means, Independent Samples

A new approach to instruction has been introduced in teaching statistics to high school juniors in a given school district. Students were randomly assigned to the teacher employing the new methods; the balance were exposed to standard instructional techniques. Assuming that other factors influencing the outcome of this study have been successfully evened out, the object is to determine whether the students exposed to the new method do better (as measured by some appropriate testing) than do juniors receiving the "usual" instruction. Although the research hypothesis is that the new method is better than the standard procedure, the statistical hypothesis is that the two methods are the same. Another way to say this is that the two samples of student scores were drawn from populations with the same mean value, or symbolically:

$$H_o : \mu_1 = \mu_2$$

In other words, the new approach to instruction is not different from the standard approach.

This situation calls for testing the significance of the difference between two sample means, where the samples are independent of each other, assuming that the null hypothesis is true, i.e., the samples came from the same population. In line with the procedures developed thus far, it becomes necessary to identify the appropriate standard error to test whether the population differences are significant. This standard error of the mean difference is given by:

$$S_{\bar{x}_1 - \bar{x}_2} = S_{po} \sqrt{n_1^{-1} + n_2^{-1}} \tag{10.2}$$

where:

$$S_{po} = \sqrt{[(n_1 - 1) S_1^2 + (n_2 - 1) S_2^2] / (n_1 + n_2 - 2)} \tag{10.3}$$

If the samples are the same size, Formula (10.3) becomes:

$$S_{po} = \sqrt{(S_1^2 + S_2^2) / 2} \tag{10.4}$$

Obviously, it is an easier formula to use. The above formulas assume sampling from a large population. If such is not the case, a finite correction factor must be applied, as indicated in Chapter 9. Such a factor tends to reduce the value of Formula (10.2).

There is a tacit assumption in calculating the pooled (S_{po}) estimate for the standard deviation (which is what Formulas (10.3) and (10.4) are): the population variances (standard deviations) are the same. This hypothesis should be tested before pooling the two sample variances to obtain S_{po}. The appropriate test of significance on two sample variances is given in the next section. If, however, the sample variances are significantly different (i.e., the two population variances are not equal), then methods other than those presented in this section are appropriate. [See U.S. Department of Commerce (1966) for the appropriate methodology.]

The test statistic for testing the hypothesis that two population means are not different is:

$$t_c = (\bar{X}_1 - \bar{X}_2) / S_{\bar{x}_1 - \bar{x}_2} \qquad (10.5)$$

with an associated $(n_1 - 1 + n_2 - 1)$ or $(n_1 + n_2 - 2)$ degrees of freedom.

The group receiving the new approach is referred to as the "experimental group," while the other group is referred to as the "control group." Summary data for these two groups, where the variable is a test score measuring achievement, are:

Group	$\bar{X}$	S	n
1: Control	74.3	4	25
2: Experimental	76.8	5	25

The level of significance has been set at $\alpha = 0.05$. Based upon the summary data, the standard error of the mean difference becomes:

$$\begin{aligned} S_{po} &= \sqrt{(S_1^2 + S_2^2)/2} \\ &= \sqrt{(4^2 + 5^2)/2} \\ &= \sqrt{41/2} = 4.528 \end{aligned}$$

and, hence:

$$\begin{aligned} S_{\bar{x}_1 - \bar{x}_2} &= S_{po}\sqrt{n_1^{-1} + n_2^{-1}} \\ &= 4.528\sqrt{25^{-1} + 25^{-1}} \\ &= 1.281 \end{aligned}$$

Based upon 48 degrees of freedom $(25 + 25 - 2)$ and the 0.05 level of significance, the critical region becomes:

$$t_c \leq -2.011 \text{ and } t_c \geq +2.011$$

While the research hypothesis really postulates a one-tailed situation, the statistical hypothesis, as stated, allows for the experimental and the control groups to differ in either direction with respect to average achievement. Substitution in the test statistic given by Formula (10.5) yields the following:

$$t_c = (\bar{X}_1 - \bar{X}_2) / S_{\bar{x}_1 - \bar{x}_2}$$
$$= (74.3 - 76.8) / 1.281$$
$$= -2.5 / 1.281$$
$$= -1.951$$

Since this calculated value for the test statistic does not exceed either critical "t" value from Table H.4, there is insufficient reason to reject the hypothesis. This does not mean that the hypothesis has been demonstrated as being correct. The t_c value, while not significant at the level stipulated before the sampling, is extremely close to the tabular value, which suggests that had the confidence level selected previous to data collection been slightly lower, the hypothesis might have been rejected. There would, of course, be a slightly increased risk (i.e., greater than 0.05).

Suppose that an education association member within a school district (District B) in a certain state felt that teachers within this district did not have as long a tenure with this district as they did in another large district (District A) in the same state. Since census data were not available, a sample of teachers from both school districts would have to be selected and the mean values examined in light of the research hypothesis. The statistical hypothesis? Average tenure in District B is greater than or equal to average tenure in District A—or symbolically:

$$H_o: \mu_B \geq \mu_A$$

indicating a one-tailed test.

While sampling within the local district was not a problem (yielding 100 teachers), sampling within the other district was difficult and led to a sample of only 45 teachers, although they were still drawn randomly. To take some action on this situation, the association member needed 99% confidence ($\alpha = 0.01$).

The results of the sampling indicate the following:

Group	$\bar{X}$	S	n
1: District A	12.5 years	4 years	45
2: District B	10.1 years	3 years	100

Since this is a one-tailed test, the critical region for the calculated t_c value is seen to be:

$$t_c > +2.35 \text{ (approximately)}$$

which is obtained from Appendix Table H.4, with a risk of 0.02 (two-tailed) and an estimated tabular "t" value of 2.35 (estimated, since 143 degrees of freedom does not appear within the table).

Since the samples are not of the same size, Formula (10.3) must be used to arrive at the pooled estimate, S_{po}, for the standard deviation (this pooling is based upon the assumption that the two population standard deviations are not different, a test that is presented in the next section):

$$\begin{aligned}
S_{po} &= \sqrt{[(n_1 - 1) S_1^2 + (n_2 - 1) S_2^2] / (n_1 + n_2 - 2)} \\
&= \sqrt{[(45 - 1) 4^2 + (100 - 1) 3^2] / (45 + 100 - 2)} \\
&= \sqrt{1595 / 143} \\
&= \sqrt{11.15} \\
&= 3.34
\end{aligned}$$

The standard error of the mean difference from Formula (10.2) becomes:

$$\begin{aligned}
S_{\bar{X}_1 - \bar{X}_2} &= S_{po} \sqrt{n_1^{-1} + n_2^{-1}} \\
&= 3.34 \sqrt{(45^{-1} + 100^{-1})} \\
&= 3.34 \sqrt{0.0322} \\
&= 0.60
\end{aligned}$$

The test statistic, then, from Formula (10.5) becomes:

$$\begin{aligned}
t_c &= (\bar{X}_1 - \bar{X}_2) / S_{\bar{X}_1 - \bar{X}_2} \\
&= (12.5 - 10.1) / 0.60 \\
&= 2.4 / 0.60 \\
&= 4.00
\end{aligned}$$

which is certainly greater than the critical value from Table H.4; namely, +2.35. For this analysis, there is better than a 99% certainty that the hypothesis is not true. Therefore, teachers in District B have an average tenure less than those in District A, with better than 99% confidence. As a matter of fact, with the calculated value of $t_c = +4$, the confidence level is considerably higher, better than 99.9%.

10.4.3 On Two Population Means, Paired (Matched) Samples

Once in a while in a research situation two samples cannot be treated as independent, yet there is an interest in comparing the differences between the mean values of a given characteristic for the two samples. Such a situation occurs when the observations on the characteristics of interest can be matched or paired between the first and the second sample. A classical example is the pretest/posttest situation in which a group of persons are given a pretest, subjected to some experimental condition, and then take a posttest. It should be clear that the observations for each AU, in all likelihood, cannot be assumed to be independent. Therefore, a modification in the procedure identified in Section 10.4.2 must be introduced to allow for possible correlations between the two sets of observations. Such a procedure is referred to as a "paired" or "matched" set. This HANDBOOK presents a simple procedure for such a situation.

Assume that the AU's for the first and second sample have been paired such that the observation for each sample can be associated with a single AU or with paired AU's; for example, pre- and posttest scores associated with the same individuals or test scores associated with matched pairs of students who have been classified as control and experimental. The approach is to perform an analysis of the mean of the differences between the observations for the first and the second paired sample values. To illustrate, consider the data in Exhibit 10.2.

Subjects were paired by a specific set of criteria, so that the subjects in Column 1 are associated with paired subjects in Column 3. For example, subjects A and K, B and L are paired subjects.

EXHIBIT 10.2—A COMPARISON OF TEST SCORES BETWEEN AN EXPERIMENTAL & CONTROL GROUP WHERE SUBJECTS HAVE BEEN MATCHED OR PAIRED

Control group		Experimental group		D_i	D_i^2
Subject	Score	Subject	Score		
(1)	(2)	(3)	(4)	(5)	(6)
A	85	K	81	−4	16
B	73	L	77	+4	16
C	56	M	63	+7	49
D	82	N	84	+2	4
E	97	O	95	−2	4
F	59	P	63	+4	16
G	53	Q	51	−2	4
H	77	R	79	+2	4
I	84	S	82	−2	4
J	91	T	97	+6	36
				15	153

The control group was subjected to a two-week refresher course using standard teaching techniques. The experimental group was exposed to the same refresher course but was given instruction via innovative procedures. Final test scores for the two groups appear in Columns 2 and 4. For example, the first paired subjects scored 85 and 81, respectively, on the test. Column 5 represents the positive (or negative) difference between the experimental and control pairs of subjects. Note that the plus and minus signs must be recorded. The final column is the square of each of these differences. If the D_i column is treated as the variable of interest, then an hypothesis might be that there is no difference between the mean values for the control and the experimental group or, stated in another way,

$$H_o: \mu_{\bar{D}} = 0$$

A possible research hypothesis might be that the experimental conditions should lead to better test scores, on the average, than for the control group. The appropriate statistical hypothesis, then, would be that the mean of the differences between the two groups is less than or equal to zero or, stated symbolically,

$$H_o: \mu_{\bar{D}} \leq 0$$

A rejection of this statistical hypothesis would lead to an acceptance, with a given probability, of the research hypothesis. This latter hypothesis is tested in the material that follows.

Adapting techniques in Section 10.4.1, the appropriate test statistic now becomes:

$$\boxed{t_c = \bar{D} / S_{\bar{D}}} \qquad (10.6)$$

where:

$$\bar{D} = \Sigma D_i / n$$

n = number of paired observations

and

$$S_{\bar{D}} = S_D / \sqrt{n.}$$

It should be recalled that

$$S_D^2 = [\Sigma D_i^2 - (\Sigma D_i)^2/n] / (n-1)$$

from Formula (5.4).

The statistical data associated with this sampling situation are as follows:

- The null hypothesis is that $\mu_{\bar{D}} \leq 0$.
- The 10% level of significance is selected for this test.
- The sample of 20 subjects yields the following values:

$$\bar{D} = 15/10 = 1.5 \text{ test score units}$$

$$S_D = \sqrt{[153 - (15)^2/10]/(10-1)}$$

$$= 3.808$$

$$S_{\bar{D}} = 3.808/\sqrt{10} = 1.20$$

Note that n represents the number of paired subjects, not the number of subjects.

Analogous to Section 10.4.1, the degrees of freedom are $(n-1)$. For these degrees of freedom and at the level of significance identified, the appropriate tabular "t" value from Appendix Table H.4 is seen to be $t_{0.10} = +1.383$. The critical region associated with the rejection of the hypothesis, then, is:

Reject the hypothesis for any value of the test statistic, "t_c", given in Formula 10.6 that exceeds +1.833. Stated symbolically, the hypothesis is rejected if:

$$t_c > +1.833$$

This situation is for a one-tailed rejection region since the interest is in whether the experimental conditions provided for a significantly better average test score than the control.

Based upon the information above, the calculated value for the test statistic from Formula 10.6 is seen to be:

$$t_c = \bar{D}/S_{\bar{D}}$$

$$= 1.5/1.20$$

$$= 1.25$$

Since t_c is less than 1.383, the hypothesis cannot be rejected. Hence, an insufficient difference exists between the paired group mean values to warrant concluding that the experimental conditions have caused a positive difference, on the average, in test scores.

10.4.4 On Two Population Standard Deviations (Variances)

The previous section indicates that a test on two sample standard deviations is necessary before running a test on the sample means to ascertain whether it was likely that the population standard deviations were the same. Such a test is also of interest in situations where the variation in the characteristic being studied is an important issue. Consider two groups of students, both taking the same subject but with different teachers. The two groups averaged 77.5 on their final examinations, but the standard deviations were quite different, being 7 and 4.3, respectively. A question that might be asked is, Assuming that the two groups came from the same population, is it likely that the sample standard deviations would be this different by chance alone in random sampling? Or, to put it another way, is it likely that the two populations from which these two groups may have been drawn could have had the same standard deviations? Any teacher would probably prefer the group with the smaller standard deviation because it suggests less variability among test scores and, hence, probably more homogeneity among the students. The approach remains similar to that used to test an hypothesis about two samples; namely, that they came from the same population. For this summary measure, the null hypothesis would be:

$$H_0: \sigma_1^2 = \sigma_2^2$$

or:

$$H_0: \sigma_1 = \sigma_2$$

Consider the first example in the previous section. Students were randomly assigned to an experimental and a control group for purposes of testing a new teaching approach for a statistics course in high school. There were 25 students in each group; and the standard deviations were, respectively, $S_2 = 5$ (experimental) and $S_1 = 4$ (control). Since the value of 5 is larger than 4, the question which must be answered is, Is one standard deviation sufficiently larger than the other to conclude that there is a low probability that the two population standard deviations could be the same?

The appropriate test statistic is:

$$\boxed{F_c = S_L^2 / S_S^2} \quad (10.7)$$

where:

$$S_L^2 > S_S^2$$

and v_1 and v_2 represent the degrees of freedom associated with the numerator ($n_L - 1$) and denominator ($n_S - 1$) variances. Tabular values for various sample size combinations (degrees of freedom associated with the two samples) and upper percentage points for the F distribution are given in Appendix Table H.6. (The symbol v represents the Greek letter "nu".)

The test statistic in (10.7), referred to as an "F test," is really a two-tailed test since the differences can be in either direction. However, because the statistic identified in Formula (10.7) calls for putting the larger variance in the numerator, a one-tailed situation has been forced. Therefore, the level of significance *for this F test only* is double the percentage value given in Table H.6. As an illustration, the above data on the statistics course and the new teaching approach are now analyzed.

The summary data for the two groups are:

$$n_1 = 25 \quad S_1^2 = 4^2 = 16$$

$$n_2 = 25 \quad S_2^2 = 5^2 = 25$$

The 10% level of significance has been selected, resulting in the use of the F distribution table indicating "upper 5% points." Since the samples are of the same size, the degrees of freedom for the numerator and the denominator are 24 each ($25 - 1$). The critical region for rejection then becomes:

$$F_c > 1.98$$

that is, the calculated test statistic based upon the two sample variances must exceed 1.98 if the hypothesis that the population variances are the same is to be rejected. In this case, the calculated test statistic becomes, from Formula (10.7):

$$F_c = S_L^2 \,/\, S_S^2$$

$$= 25 \,/\, 16$$

$$= 1.56$$

(Note that the larger of the two variances is placed in the numerator.)

Since the calculated value for F of 1.56 is less than the tabular value of 1.98, the hypothesis cannot be rejected. There is, therefore, insufficient variability in the sample variances to conclude that they could have come from populations with different variances.

A group studying retirement plans in several states believes that there is a greater amount of variability among take-home pay checks for retired teachers in one system than in another.

A sample of 25 retired teachers is selected from the area believed to have the greater variability and 30 from another. The observed standard deviations (used as the measures of variability) are, respectively, $S_1 = \$225$ and $S_2 = \$150$. The null hypothesis in this situation is:

$$H_O: \quad \sigma_1 \leq \sigma_2$$

The group studying these plans has selected the 5% level of significance as a requirement to reject this hypothesis. Since the hypothesis is that the standard deviation in the first population is less than or equal to the standard deviation in the second population, rejection can occur only if the sample standard deviation for the first group is significantly greater than that for the second group, resulting in a one-tailed test. The appropriate value of F from Table H.6, then, is read from the table indicating the "upper 5% points," resulting in a critical value for 24 (25 − 1) and 29 (30 − 1) degrees of freedom, respectively, of:

$$F_c > 1.90$$

The test statistic then becomes from Formula (10.7):

$$F_c = S_1^2 / S_2^2$$
$$= (\$225)^2 / (\$150)^2$$
$$= 2.25$$

This value exceeds the critical value of F from the table; therefore, the hypothesis is rejected. With better than 95% confidence the variability in the first population is concluded to be greater than that in the second population. This indicates a wider variability in retired teacher take-home pay checks in Group 1 as opposed to that in Group 2. This does not imply anything about the average levels of the take-home pay checks.

* * * * *

In summary, the research hypothesis is usually restated into a statistical hypothesis that excludes the research hypothesis. In other words, the statistical hypothesis is set up in such a way that its rejection usually means that the research hypothesis is true with the indicated level of confidence.

10.4.5 On a Linear Correlation or Regression

In the previous chapter an estimation procedure was described using a sample linear regression equation. For this procedure to be valid, the correlation between the two variables (years of teaching experience and contract salary in $1,000) must be significantly different from 0. Putting it another way, if the relationship between X and Y is purely random, then using a regression equation for predictive purposes makes little sense.

This section identifies a simple procedure for testing the null hypothesis that the correlation in the population is zero, indicated symbolically as:

$$H_o: \rho = 0$$

where ρ (the Greek letter *rho*) is the symbol for the population correlation coefficient.

Since "significantly different from zero" could mean either positive or negative, this becomes a two-tailed test.

The test statistic for testing the above null hypothesis is:

$$\boxed{t_c = r\sqrt{(n-2)/(1-r^2)}} \qquad (10.8)$$

where the associated degrees of freedom can be seen to be $(n-2)$.

For the example cited above, the sample size was $n = 30$ and the calculated value of $r^2 = 0.9347$ and $r = 0.9668$. Assuming that the desired level of significance is $\alpha = 0.01$, the critical value of the tabular "t" becomes:

$$t_c > +2.763 \quad \text{or} \quad t_c < -2.763$$

The calculated value of the test statistic from Formula (10.8) becomes:

$$\begin{aligned}
t_c &= r\sqrt{(n-2)/(1-r^2)} \\
&= 0.9668\sqrt{(30-2)/(1-0.9347)} \\
&= 0.9668\sqrt{428.79} \\
&= 0.9668 \times 20.71 \\
&= 20.0
\end{aligned}$$

which is clearly in the critical region, exceeding the tabular value of $t = +2.763$. It can be concluded with better than 99% confidence that a significant linear relationship exists between these two variables.

Correlations are not always as strong as the one above; and, hence, use of Formula (10.8) provides a useful means for testing the hypothesis of no correlation in the population for correlations that appear fairly small. To illustrate, suppose a sample of

25 yields a correlation coefficient of r = 0.52. Is it likely that this sample value has come from a population whose correlation is not equal to zero? The null hypothesis is again:

$$H_o: \rho = 0$$

Assuming that the level of significance is taken as α = 0.01, the appropriate critical value for "t" from Appendix Table H.4 with 23 degrees of freedom (25 − 2) becomes:

$$t_c > +2.807 \quad \text{or} \quad t_c < -2.807$$

The calculated value of the test statistic, given by Formula (10.8) is:

$$\begin{aligned} t_c &= r\sqrt{(n-2)/(1-r^2)} \\ &= 0.52\sqrt{(25-2)/(1-0.52^2)} \\ &= 0.52\sqrt{31.52} \\ &= 0.52 \times 5.614 \\ &= +2.92 \end{aligned}$$

Again, significant, but just barely. The hypothesis of no correlation is rejected with 99% confidence. However, the confidence bands used in predicting may be so sufficiently large as to be useless.

One final point relates to departure from linearity in the bivariate case. Exhibit 7.7 in Chapter 7 presented hypothetical data relating a predicting variable X to Y. For this example, certain calculations reduced the total variation in Y (i.e., $\Sigma(Y - \bar{Y})^2$) into its components; namely, that component due to the linear regression, that due to variation in Y unexplained by the best fitting nonlinear relationship, and the incremental variation in Y explained by the best nonlinear relationship over the linear relationship. For that example, these sums of squares were:

1,269.62	total variation in Y [$\Sigma(Y - \bar{Y})^2$]
920.09	variation in Y explained by the linear regression
16.00	variation in Y unexplained by the best nonlinear relationship (residual variation)
333.53	incremental variation in Y explained by the best nonlinear relationship over the linear relationship (departure from linear regression).

These values are frequently summarized in a table (referred to as an analysis of variance table) for purposes of testing two hypotheses:

1. There is no significant linear relationship
2. There is no significant departure from linearity (i.e., a nonlinear relationship does not exist).

The above four sums of squares are displayed in Exhibit 10.3. The appropriate calculations and tests are then described.

EXHIBIT 10.3–SOURCES OF VARIATION IN A BIVARIATE LINEAR AND NON-LINEAR REGRESSION ANALYSIS

Source of variation	Sum of squares	Degrees of freedom	Mean sum of squares	F
	(1)	(2)	(3)	(4)
Due to linear regression (A)	920.09	1 (1)	920.16	A/C = 920.16
Departure from linear regression (B)	333.53	6 (k-2)	55.59	B/C = 55.59
Residual (C)	16.00	16 (n-k)	1.00	....
Total variation	1,269.62	23 (n-1)	....	....

In indicating the appropriate degrees of freedom (the values in parentheses in the degrees-of-freedom column in Exhibit 10.3), n is the sample size (number of bivariate observations) and k is the number of Y means used to calculate the residual variability. Exhibit 7.8 displays the eight such Y means involved in the calculations.

The values in Column 3 of Exhibit 10.3 are obtained by dividing the values in Column 1 by the corresponding values in Column 2. The values in Column 3 now become estimates of the same population variance under the hypotheses that:

- There is no linear regression.
- There is no curvilinear regression.

The appropriate F ratios are identified in Column 4. Assuming that the 0.01 level of significance is being used, the two test procedures follow:

- *The hypothesis is that there is no linear regression* (i.e., $\rho = 0$):

  The tabular F value for 1 and 16 degrees of freedom [the degrees of freedom associated with the numerator and denominator of the F ratio in Column 4] at the 0.01 level of significance defines the critical region as:

$$F_c > 8.53$$

Since the desire is to detect the case for which the numerator estimate of a population is larger than the denominator, this is a one-tailed test.

The calculated value for F is seen from Exhibit 10.3 to be:

$$F_c = 920.16 / 1.00 = 920.16$$

Since the calculated value of F exceeds the critical value given above, the hypothesis is rejected and it is concluded with 99% confidence that a linear regression does exist.

- *The hypothesis is that there is no curvilinear regression*:

  The tabular value of F for 6 and 16 degrees of freedom at the 0.01 level of significance defines the critical region as:

$$F_c > 4.20$$

The calculated value for F is seen from Exhibit 10.2 to be:

$$F_c = 55.59 / 1.00 = 55.59$$

Since the calculated value of F exceeds the critical tabular F value given above, it is concluded with 99% confidence that the hypothesis can be rejected; and, hence, a significant curvilinear regression exists.

Exhibit 7.8 demonstrates the presence of both the linear and nonlinear relationships. The implication is that while a linear relationship is significant, a nonlinear relationship explains significantly more of the variation to be meaningful. It is possible to have a nonsignificant linear relationship with a significant curvilinear relationship. This is demonstrated in Exhibit 10.4.

10.4.6 On a Single Population Proportion

Five years ago, when a complete census was accomplished within a school district, 65% of the teachers favored a given issue. Today, the education association wants to know whether there has been a change in this percentage in either direction. The statistical hypothesis becomes:

$$H_0: \pi = 0.65$$

that is, no change has occurred during this time period.

EXHIBIT 10.4—AN ILLUSTRATION OF A SIGNIFICANT CURVILINEAR RELATIONSHIP AND A NONSIGNIFICANT LINEAR RELATIONSHIP IN THE BIVARIATE CASE

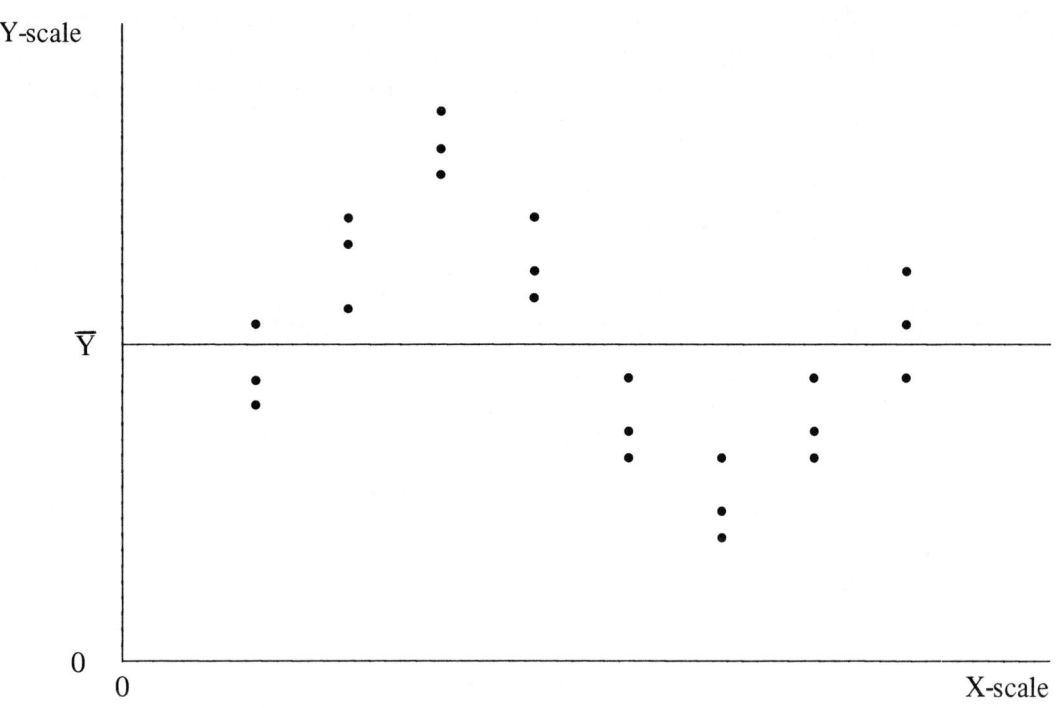

A sample of 200 teachers is to be randomly selected from this school district, and a survey instrument mailed. Included on this survey will be a question on the same issue favored five years ago by 65% of the district teachers.

The associated level of significance for testing this hypothesis has been selected as 0.05.

Since the sample proportion will be used as an estimate of the current population proportion, the statistical question is, Is the difference between the sample proportion and the hypothesized population proportion sufficiently large that it is unlikely that the sample was drawn from a population with the specific value for π? The test statistic for this situation, provided the sample size meets certain criteria (to be discussed at the end of this section), is:

$$Z_c = (p - \pi) / \sigma_p \qquad (10.9)$$

where σ_p is the standard error of a sample proportion and is given by the expression:

$$\sigma_p = \sqrt{\pi(1-\pi)/n} \qquad (10.10)$$

where it has been assumed that the population is sufficiently large to ignore the finite correction factor discussed in Chapter 9. The test statistic, given in Formula (10.9) for sufficiently large samples (say n > 100), is approximated quite well by the normal distribution.

The survey results have been tabulated and 0.59 of the teachers in the sample now favor this issue. Since the test statistic is approximately normally distributed for large samples, the appropriate critical tabular value for the 0.05 level of significance for a two-tailed test is:

$$Z_c < -1.96 \quad \text{or} \quad Z_c > +1.96$$

The standard error of the sample proportion based upon Formula (10.10) becomes:

$$\begin{aligned} \sigma_p &= \sqrt{\pi(1-\pi)/n} \\ &= \sqrt{0.65(1-0.65)/200} \\ &= \sqrt{0.2275/200} \\ &= 0.0337 \end{aligned}$$

The calculated test statistic from Formula (10.9) becomes:

$$\begin{aligned} Z_c &= (p - \pi)/\sigma_p \\ &= (0.59 - 0.65)/0.0337 \\ &= -0.06/0.0337 \\ &= -1.78 \end{aligned}$$

Since the calculated value for Z_c does not fall in the critical or rejection region ($-1.78 > -1.96$), the null hypothesis cannot be rejected. The research conclusion is that there has not been a large enough change in opinion, based upon this sample of 200, to warrant rejecting the hypothesis.

In analyzing the current situation on retention of teachers within the district, a team of citizens felt that the percentage of teachers who had been with the district for less than ten years had increased from what it was several years ago when a complete census indicated that this proportion was 0.52. An acceptable level of significance to this group is $\alpha = 0.10$. The statistical hypothesis becomes:

$$H_o: \pi \leq 0.52$$

because a rejection of this hypothesis would mean that there is better than 90% confidence that $\pi > 0.52$. Such a conclusion would support the belief of this citizens' group.

In a sample of 150 teachers, 87 had been working in the school district for less than ten years. This converts to a proportion of 87/150, or 0.58.

Since the test statistic is approximately normally distributed, the appropriate critical tabular value becomes:

$$Z_c > +1.282$$

For this situation, the standard error of the sample proportion becomes from Formula (10.10):

$$\begin{aligned}\sigma_p &= \sqrt{\pi(1-\pi)/n} \\ &= \sqrt{0.52(1-0.52)/150} \\ &= \sqrt{0.52 \times 0.48/150} \\ &= \sqrt{0.001664} \\ &= 0.041\end{aligned}$$

The calculated test statistic from Formula (10.9) becomes:

$$\begin{aligned}Z_c &= (p-\pi)/\sigma_p \\ &= (0.58 - 0.52)/0.041 \\ &= 0.06/0.041 \\ Z &= 1.463\end{aligned}$$

which exceeds the critical tabular value, resulting in a rejection of the null hypothesis with better than 90% confidence. Therefore, a significant increase over several years ago has occurred in the proportion of teachers who have been with the school district less than ten years.

With respect to the impact of sample sizes on the normal approximation, used in Formula (10.9), the following should be noted:

1. For samples with $n < 25$ the approximation is not reliable and special tables should be used [see Siegel (1956) or U.S. Department of Commerce (1966)].

2. For situations in which π is close to 0.5, the approximation is appropriate for $n > 25$.

3. When π is near 0 or 1, the approximation holds fairly well, provided $n(\pi)(1-\pi) \geq 9$.

In most situations encountered by the researcher, samples are usually of sufficient size that the approximation is acceptable.

10.4.7 On Two Population Proportions

Among the number of ballot issues that will appear in an upcoming statewide election is one whose passage might have an impact on the state education system. Of interest is how the urban/suburban voter views the issue as opposed to the small town/rural voter. A sample of 600 voters is to be selected randomly from the most recent voter registration list within the state; and interviews will be conducted on a number of issues, among which is this specific ballot measure. The object is to determine whether these two groups of voters differ in their views on the ballot measure.

The statistical hypothesis is that the proportion favoring this issue is the same in both populations of voters; namely,

$$H_0: \pi_1 = \pi_2$$

where π_1 and π_2 are the true but unknown population proportions favoring the issue for the urban/suburban and small town/rural groups, respectively. The procedure involves selecting the sample and then determining whether the observed difference between the two sample proportions exceeds what one would expect in random sampling from populations with the same values for π, at the specified level of significance.

Because of the nature of the arithmetic operations in this situation, the approach previously followed of comparing differences to the appropriate standard error is modified in the following discussion.

A level of significance of $\alpha = 0.05$ was established for this situation. The sample was selected; and the results, as they related to this specific ballot issue, were as follows:

Opinion of the issue	Urban/suburban	Small town/rural	Totals
Support	300 (0.75)	130 (0.65)	430 (0.717)
Oppose	100 (0.25)	70 (0.35)	170 (0.283)
Totals	400	200	600

Note: Numbers in parentheses are the proportions supporting and opposing the issue for urban/suburban, small town/rural, and all responses combined.

This tabular display of the survey results is referred to as a "double-entry table" and also as a "2 x 2 (two columns and two rows) contingency table." From the table it is seen that 75% of the urban/suburban sample favor the issue, while only 65% of the small town/rural sample favor it. The question at hand? Is the difference of 10% sufficiently large to warrant saying that the two samples came from populations having different proportions favoring the issue?

Before proceeding with the data analysis, the necessary symbolism and formulas are presented. The specific 2 x 2 contingency table above can be expressed in a general form by the following table:

	Column (1)	Column (2)	Row totals
Row (1)	a_{11}	a_{12}	r_1
Row (2)	a_{21}	a_{22}	r_2
Column totals	c_1	c_2	n

The entries in the body of the table (a_{11}, a_{12}, a_{21}, a_{22}) can be identified by the subscripts. The first subscript indicates the row of the entry; the second, the column. For example, a_{12} would be the number of observations in the total sample that fall in the first row and the second column. In a similar way, r_1 and r_2 represent the row totals, and c_1 and c_2 represent the column totals. The total sample size is given by n.

The appropriate test statistic to test the hypothesis that $\pi_1 = \pi_2$ is given by the following expression:

$$\chi_c^2 = n \, [|a_{11} \times a_{22} - a_{21} \times a_{12}| - \tfrac{n}{2}]^2 \, / \, (r_1 \times r_2 \times c_1 \times c_2) \tag{10.11}$$

where the absolute value signs (| |) indicate that the value of the difference is always taken as positive and the "x" indicates multiplication.

Formula (10.11) is distributed as chi-square with one degree of freedom; and the associated critical region is one-tailed, being at the right end of the curve. The larger the difference between the two sample proportions, the greater the calculated value for chi-square.

Now, on with the analysis of this example: The null hypothesis is that the two population proportions are identical. The appropriate critical tabular value for chi-square with one degree of freedom and $\alpha = 0.05$ is:

$$\chi_c^2 \geq 3.84$$

The calculated test statistic from Formula (10.11) becomes:

$$\chi_c^2 = n[|a_{11} \times a_{22} - a_{12} \times a_{21}| - \tfrac{n}{2}]^2 / (r_1 \times r_2 \times c_1 \times c_2)$$

$$= 600\left[|300 \times 70 - 100 \times 130| - \frac{600}{2}\right]^2 / (430 \times 170 \times 400 \times 200)$$

$$= 600\,(7{,}700)^2 / 5{,}848{,}000{,}000$$

$$= 6.083$$

which is significant at the 0.05 level. There is, therefore, better than 95% confidence that the populations from which these two samples were drawn had a different proportion of voters who supported this ballot measure. Urban/suburban voters appear to support the issue more strongly.

Two nationwide surveys of public school teachers, conducted five years apart, produced the following results as responses to the question, What is your highest degree?

	1976	1980	Totals
Bachelor's or less	725 (0.725)	680 (0.680)	1,405 (0.702)
Above bachelor's	275 (0.275)	320 (0.320)	595 (0.298)
Totals	1,000	1,000	2,000

Note: Numbers in parentheses are proportions in 1976, 1980, and for the combined sample with "bachelor's or less" and "above bachelor's."

The question to be examined is, Has there been a change in the academic levels of teachers in public schools, nationwide, during this five-year period?

The 0.01 level of significance is selected to provide 99% confidence in rejecting the null hypothesis; namely,

$$H_0: \pi_1 = \pi_2$$

The critical tabular value for chi-square with one degree of freedom becomes:

$$\chi_c^2 = 6.64$$

From Formula (10.11), the calculated chi-square statistic becomes:

$$X_c^2 = [|a_{11} \times a_{22} - a_{21} \times a_{12}| - \frac{n}{2}]^2 / (r_1 \times r_2 \times c_1 \times c_2)$$

$$= 2{,}000 \, [|725 \times 320 - 680 \times 275| - \frac{2{,}000}{2}]^2 / (1{,}000 \times 1{,}000 \times 1{,}405 \times 595)$$

$$= 2{,}000 \, (45{,}000 - 1{,}000)^2 / (1{,}000 \times 1{,}000 \times 1{,}405 \times 595)$$

$$= 4.631$$

Since the calculated value for chi-square ($\chi_c^2 = 4.631$) is less than the critical value of 6.64, the null hypothesis cannot be rejected. The conclusion: Differences between the two sample proportions are not great enough to conclude that there has been a change in academic levels of teachers, nationwide. However, if the 0.05 level of significance had been selected, the calculated value for chi-square (4.631) would have exceeded the tabular value for $\alpha = 0.05$ of 3.84, resulting in a rejection of the null hypothesis with 95% confidence. For this set of sample data it can be concluded with 95% confidence, but not with 99% confidence, that the samples were drawn from populations with different proportions of teachers with a bachelor's degree or less (and, hence, "above bachelor's" also).

This result points up the importance of selecting a level of significance in advance of a testing situation. The risk associated with making a false rejection should be specified in advance of sampling and conducting the analysis.

One final comment on this specific hypothesis testing situation: If samples are small such that the frequencies within any of the four tabular cells is less than five, the exact tests recommended in U.S. Department of Commerce (1966) should be employed.

10.4.8 On Analyzing Survey Sampling Results

The planning and conduct of national, state, or local surveys result in large amounts of data that can be classified in contingency tables more complex than the simple 2 x 2 tables just examined. For example, responses to attitudinal questions can be classified by sex, age, school system size, academic year, and even responses to other questions. This section identifies four ways to analyze such survey data.

Classical methodology calls for the extension of the 2 x 2 contingency approach into more complex analyses that still use the chi-square distribution through a variety of formulas that expand on Formula (10.11) in this chapter. [Most of the available references require knowledge of more advanced mathematics than is assumed for readers of this HANDBOOK. These references are given in National Education Association (1979).]

The kinds of survey data referred to in this section are given in the set of hypothetical survey results indicated in Exhibit 10.5. These data represent responses to the question, Suppose you could go back to your college days and START OVER AGAIN; in view of your present knowledge, would you become a teacher?

EXHIBIT 10.5–HYPOTHETICAL DATA ON TEACHER WILLINGNESS TO TEACH AGAIN FOR LARGE, MEDIUM, AND SMALL SCHOOL SYSTEMS FOR YEARS 1966, 1971, AND 1976[1]

		1966	1971	1976	Total
Large School Systems					
Certainly would teach	n	285	200	165	650
	%	51.8	44.4	41.2	46.4
Probably would teach	n	120	115	105	340
	%	21.8	25.6	26.2	24.3
Chances are about even	n	90	60	45	195
	%	16.4	13.3	11.2	13.9
Probably would not teach	n	40	50	50	140
	%	7.3	11.1	12.5	10.0
Certainly would not teach	n	15	25	35	75
	%	2.7	5.6	8.8	5.4
Total		550	450	400	1,400
Medium School Systems					
Certainly would teach	n	550	275	240	1,065
	%	55.0	42.3	40.0	47.3
Probably would teach	n	250	195	155	600
	%	25.0	30.0	25.8	26.7
Chances are about even	n	110	80	70	260
	%	11.0	12.3	11.7	11.6
Probably would not teach	n	65	65	90	220
	%	6.5	10.0	15.0	9.8
Certainly would not teach	n	25	35	45	105
	%	2.5	5.4	7.5	4.7
Total		1,000	650	600	2,250
Small School Systems					
Certainly would teach	n	375	200	180	755
	%	53.6	50.0	51.4	52.1
Probably would teach	n	175	105	90	370
	%	25.0	26.2	25.7	25.5
Chances are about even	n	85	50	40	175
	%	12.1	12.5	11.4	12.1
Probably would not teach	n	45	25	25	95
	%	6.4	6.2	7.1	6.6
Certainly would not teach	n	20	20	15	55
	%	2.9	5.0	4.3	3.8
Total		700	400	350	1,450

[1]The question asked was, Suppose you could go back to your college days and START OVER AGAIN; in view of your present knowledge, would you become a teacher?

These reported sample data constitute a three-way contingency table where the three classifications are years (1966, 1971, and 1976), school system size (small, medium, and large), and response to the attitudinal question (five such possibilities). This table is sometimes referred to as a "3 x 3 x 5 contingency table."

Presented in the following material are four possible research hypotheses that might be set forth and the methodology for analyzing these hypotheses. First, an explanation is given of the symbolism necessary to perform the associated testing of the statistical hypotheses.

The symbol n_{ijk} represents the number of observations in the sample for the attitude classification i, the school system classification j, and the year k.

While the use of the subscripts will vary from one analysis procedure to another, the following generally holds:

n_{ijk} represents the sample cell entry, where:

$i = 1, 2, \ldots, r$ (number of rows) (attitudes)

$j = 1, 2, \ldots, c$ (number of columns) (system size)

$k = 1, 2, \ldots, t$ (number of time periods)

The hypotheses to be examined related to proportions associated with the various classifications within the populations from which the samples have been selected. For example, π_{ij2} would represent the proportion of individuals in school district size j who would have attitude classification i for the second time period under consideration. It may be of interest to determine whether there have been any changes in these proportions in the populations being sampled. For example, can it be inferred from the sample data that for large school systems a shift in attitudes has occurred over the three-year periods under study?

While the classical techniques for analysis referred to earlier are appropriate and have gained widespread acceptance, the approach set forth in Kullback (1959) and Ku, Varner, and Kullback (1971) is felt to be more tractable in terms of its calculations. Hence, this approach will be presented for the four specific hypotheses.

In the following analyses it is assumed that the samples were drawn from the population of all public school teachers by unrestricted random sampling (i.e., each teacher in the population had an equal probability of being in the sample).

Example 1: *Testing the hypothesis that the distribution of attitudes in 1976 depends upon school system size.*

The statistical hypothesis would be that the distribution of attitudinal responses is independent of school system size (i.e., small, medium, and large school system teachers felt the same way with regard to this question in 1976). Data for 1976 for the three school system sizes (taken from Exhibit 10.5) are summarized in Exhibit 10.6.

EXHIBIT 10.6—HYPOTHETICAL DATA ON TEACHER WILLINGNESS TO TEACH AGAIN FOR LARGE, MEDIUM, AND SMALL SCHOOL SYSTEMS IN 1976

		Large	Medium	Small	Total
Certainly would teach	n	165	240	180	585
	%	41.2	40.0	51.4	43.3
Probably would teach	n	105	155	90	350
	%	26.2	25.8	25.7	25.9
Chances are about even	n	45	70	40	155
	%	11.2	11.7	11.4	11.5
Probably would not teach	n	50	90	25	165
	%	12.5	15.0	7.1	12.2
Certainly would not teach	n	35	45	15	95
	%	8.8	7.5	4.3	7.0
Totals		400	600	350	1,350

For the following calculations, the natural, or Napierian, logarithm is indicated by the symbol *ln*. (Tables of natural logarithms can be found in most standard mathematical tables.)

The appropriate methodology to test the hypothesis that attitudinal responses are independent of school system size is:

Calculate, for 1976:

$$\hat{I}(1) = \sum_i \sum_j n_{ij} \ln(n \cdot n_{ij} / n_{i \cdot} n_{\cdot j})$$

$$= 2\left[n \ln n + \sum_i \sum_j n_{ij} \ln n_{ij} - \sum_i n_{i \cdot} \ln n_{i \cdot} - \sum_j n_{\cdot j} \ln n_{\cdot j} \right]$$

where *i* represents the attitude classification, *j* represents the school system size, and:

$$n = \sum_i \sum_j n_{ij} = \sum_i n_{i \cdot} = \sum_j n_{\cdot j}$$

$$n_{i \cdot} = \sum_j n_{ij} \text{ and } n_{\cdot j} = \sum_i n_{ij}$$

$\hat{I}(1)$ is distributed as chi-square with $(r-1)(c-1)$ degrees of freedom, where *r* represents the number of attitude classifications and *c* represents the number of school system sizes.

Using data in Exhibit 10.6, the following steps are necessary to calculate the test statistic, denoted by $\hat{I}(1)$:

$$n \ln n = 1350 \ln 1350 = 9{,}730.611$$

$$\sum_i \sum_j n_{ij} \ln n_{ij} = [165 \ln 165 + 105 \ln 105 + 45 \ln 45 + \ldots + 25 \ln 25 + 15 \ln 15] = 6{,}401.609$$

$$\sum_i n_i \cdot \ln n_i \cdot = [585 \ln 585 + 350 \ln 350 + \ldots + 95 \ln 95] = 7{,}834.500$$

$$\sum_j n \cdot j \ln n \cdot j = [400 \ln 400 + 600 \ln 600 + 350 \ln 350] = 8{,}285.020$$

From these totals it follows that

$$\hat{I}(1) = 2[9{,}730.611 + 6{,}401.609 - 7{,}834.500 - 8{,}285.020]$$
$$= 2 \times 12.7$$
$$= 25.4$$

For this analysis, r (the number of rows) is 5 and c (the number of columns) is 3. Therefore, the degrees of freedom are $(5-1)(3-1)$, or 4×2 equals 8. The table value of chi-square for 8 degrees of freedom at the 0.10 level of significance is 13.362. Hence, the hypothesis is rejected with 90% confidence. As a matter of fact, the calculated value of $\hat{I}(1)$ is also significant at the 0.005 level (tabular chi-square equals 21.96), thereby increasing the confidence that the hypothesis may be rejected to 99.5%.

A review of Exhibit 10.6 indicates that attitudes for large- and medium-size school systems are fairly similar, but a significantly greater proportion who "certainly would teach" again exists in the smaller school systems.

Example 2: *Testing the hypothesis that the distribution of attitudes is different from year to year, when all size systems are combined.*

The statistical hypothesis would be that the distribution of attitudes is not different from year to year. Data for all size school systems combined for each of the three years given in Exhibit 10.5 are summarized in Exhibit 10.7.

To test the hypothesis that the distribution of attitudes for all school systems combined is not different for these three years, calculate for all school system sizes combined:

$$\hat{I}(2) = 2 \sum_i \sum_j n_{ij} \ln (n \cdot n_{ij} / n_i \cdot n \cdot j)$$
$$= 2 [n \ln n + \sum_i \sum_j n_{ij} \ln n_{ij} - \sum_i n_i \cdot \ln n_i \cdot - \sum_j n \cdot j \ln n \cdot j]$$

where i represents the attitude classification and j now represents the specific year, and:

$$n = \sum_i \sum_j n_{ij} = \sum_i n_{i\cdot} = \sum_j n_{\cdot j}$$

$$n_{i\cdot} = \sum_j n_{ij} \text{ and } n_{\cdot j} = \sum_i n_{ij}$$

$\hat{I}(2)$ is distributed as chi-square with $(r-1)(c-1)$ degrees of freedom, where r represents the number of attitude classifications and c now represents the number of years.

EXHIBIT 10.7–HYPOTHETICAL DATA ON TEACHER WILLINGNESS TO TEACH AGAIN FOR ALL SIZE SCHOOL SYSTEMS COMBINED, 1966, 1971, AND 1976

		1966	1971	1976	Totals
Certainly would teach	n	1,210	675	585	2,470
	%	53.8	45.0	43.3	48.4
Probably would teach	n	545	415	350	1,310
	%	24.2	27.7	25.9	25.7
Chances are about even	n	285	190	155	630
	%	12.7	12.7	11.5	12.4
Probably would not teach	n	150	140	165	455
	%	6.7	9.3	12.2	8.9
Certainly would not teach	n	60	80	95	235
	%	2.7	5.3	7.0	4.6
Totals		2,250	1,500	1,350	5,100

Using data in Exhibit 10.7 and the preceding formulas yields the following calculations:

$n \ln n = 5{,}100 \ln 5{,}100 = 43{,}538.7$

$\sum_i \sum_j n_{ij} \ln n_{ij} = [1{,}210 \ln 1210 + 545 \ln 545 + \ldots + 165 \ln 165 + 95 \ln 95] = 31{,}404.171$

$\sum_i n_{i\cdot} \ln n_{i\cdot} = [2{,}470 \ln 2{,}470 + 1{,}310 \ln 1310 + \ldots + 235 \ln 235] = 36{,}827.011$

$\sum_j n_{\cdot j} \ln n_{\cdot j} = 2{,}250 \ln 2{,}250 + 1{,}500 \ln 1{,}500 + 1{,}350 \ln 1{,}350 = 38{,}067.484$

From these totals, it follows that:

$\hat{I}(2) = 2[43{,}538.7 + 31{,}404.171 - 36{,}827.011 - 38{,}067.484$

$\phantom{\hat{I}(2)\ } = 2 \times 48.376$

$\phantom{\hat{I}(2)\ } = 96.752$

For this example, the number of rows is 5 and columns 3, yielding degrees of freedom of (5 − 1) (3 − 1), or 8. As in the previous example, the calculated value of $\hat{I}$ (2) far exceeds the tabular chi-square at the 0.10 level for 8 degrees of freedom (13.36). Furthermore, the hypothesis is rejected at the 0.005 level (tabular chi-square value being 21.96), or it can be concluded that the hypothesis may be rejected with better than 99.5% confidence.

Over school systems of all sizes, an unfavorable trend has developed. Those indicating a positive attitude ("certainly" and "probably" combined) toward teaching have decreased from 78.0% in 1966 to 72.7% in 1971 to 69.2% in 1976. Conversely, those exhibiting a negative attitude ("certainly" and "probably" combined) have increased from 9.4% in 1966 to 14.6% in 1971 to 19.2% in 1976. The proportion of teachers who feel that "chances are about even" that they would become a teacher again shows little change over this period.

Example 3: *Testing the hypothesis that the distributions of attitudes considering all school system sizes has changed from 1971 to 1976.*

The statistical hypothesis would be that the distributions of attitudes considering all school system sizes has not changed from 1971 to 1976.

Data on attitudes for large, medium, and small school systems for 1971 and 1976 are given in Exhibit 10.8. In addition, the sample data for 1971 and 1976 are combined in the third set of data within Exhibit 10.8.

To test the hypothesis that the distribution of attitudes over all school system sizes has not changed from 1971 to 1976, the appropriate methodology is as follows:

$$\hat{I}(3) = 2 \sum_i \sum_j \sum_k n_{ijk} \ln(n \cdot n_{ijk} / n_{\cdot \cdot k} n_{ij \cdot})$$

$$= 2 [n \ln n + \sum_i \sum_j \sum_k n_{ijk} \ln n_{ijk} - \sum_k n_{\cdot \cdot k} \ln n_{\cdot \cdot k} - \sum_i \sum_j n_{ij \cdot} \ln n_{ij \cdot})$$

where i represents the attitude classification, j represents the school system size, and k now represents the specific year.

$$n = \sum_i \sum_j \sum_k n_{ijk} = \sum_i n_{i \cdot \cdot} = \sum_j n_{\cdot j \cdot} = \sum_i \sum_j n_{ij \cdot}$$

$$n_{ij \cdot} = \sum_k n_{ijk} \qquad n_{\cdot \cdot k} = \sum_i \sum_j n_{ijk}$$

$\hat{I}(3)$ is distributed as chi-square with $(rc - 1)(t - 1)$ degrees of freedom, where r represents the number of attitude classifications, c represents the number of school system sizes, and t represents the number of years.

The computation of the appropriate sums is trickier than that in the previous two examples, which were straightforward r x c contingency tables. Additional values are given below to facilitate following the calculations.

EXHIBIT 10.8–HYPOTHETICAL DATA ON TEACHER WILLINGNESS TO TEACH AGAIN FOR LARGE, MEDIUM, AND SMALL SCHOOL DISTRICTS, 1971, 1976, AND 1971 AND 1976 COMBINED*

		Large	Medium	Small	Total
1971:					
Certainly would teach	n	200	275	200	675
	%	13.3	18.3	13.3	
Probably would teach	n	115	195	105	415
	%	7.7	13.0	7.0	
Chances are about even	n	60	80	50	190
	%	4.0	5.3	3.3	
Probably would not teach	n	50	65	25	140
	%	3.3	4.3	1.7	
Certainly would not teach	n	25	35	20	80
	%	1.7	2.3	1.3	
Total		450	650	400	1,500
1976:					
Certainly would teach	n	165	240	180	585
	%	12.2	17.8	13.3	
Probably would teach	n	105	155	90	350
	%	7.8	11.5	6.7	
Chances are about even	n	45	70	40	155
	%	3.3	5.2	3.0	
Probably would not teach	n	50	90	25	165
	%	3.7	6.7	1.9	
Certainly would not teach	n	35	45	15	95
	%	2.6	3.3	1.1	
Total		400	600	350	1,350
1971 and 1976 combined:					
Certainly would teach	n	365	515	380	1,260
	%	12.8	18.1	13.3	
Probably would teach	n	220	350	195	765
	%	7.7	12.3	6.8	
Chances are about even	n	105	150	90	345
	%	3.7	5.3	3.2	
Probably would not teach	n	100	155	50	305
	%	3.5	5.4	1.8	
Certainly would not teach	n	60	80	35	175
	%	2.1	2.8	1.2	
Total		850	1,250	750	2,850

*The percentages in the body of the tables represent the percent that the given column and row are of the total sample for the year. For example, in 1971, 13.3% (first cell entry) of the observed sample were from large school systems and "certainly would teach"; i.e., 200 ÷ 1,500 = 0.133.

Applying the formulas just given leads to the following totals:

$$n \ln n = 2{,}850 \ln 2{,}850 = 22{,}671.962$$

$$\sum_i \sum_j \sum_k n_{ijk} \ln n_{ijk} = [200 \ln 200 + 275 \ln 275 + \ldots + 165 \ln 165 + 240 \ln 240$$

$$+ \ldots + 45 \ln 45 + 15 \ln 15] = 13{,}732.172$$

$$\sum_k n_{..k} \ln n_{..k} = 1500 \ln 1500 + 1350 \ln 1350 = 20{,}700.441$$

$$\sum_i \sum_j n_{ij.} = [365 \ln 365 + 515 \ln 515 + \ldots + 80 \ln 80 + 35 \ln 35] = 15{,}695.336$$

Therefore, it follows that:

$$\hat{I}(3) = 2[22{,}671.962 + 13{,}732.172 - 20{,}700.441 - 15{,}695.336]$$

$$= 2 \times 8.357$$

$$\hat{I}(3) = 16.714$$

For this analysis, the number of rows (r) are 5, and the number of columns (c) are 3, and the number of time increments (t) are 2. The degrees of freedom are (rc − 1)(t − 1) equals (5 x 3 − 1) (2 − 1), or 14. The tabular value of chi-square for 14 degrees of freedom at the 0.10 level of significance is 21.06. Since the calculated value of $\hat{I}(3)$ of 16.714 is less than the tabular chi-square, the hypothesis may not be rejected.

The data, therefore, are not inconsistent with the hypothesis that the cell proportions for 1971 are not significantly different from those for 1976. An examination of Exhibit 10.8 supports this contention.

Example 4: *Testing the hypothesis that the attitude distribution for small school systems has not changed during the three years.*

Data for this example are given in the third table (labeled "Small School Systems") in Exhibit 10.5.

To test this hypothesis the appropriate methodology is as follows:

$$\hat{I}(4) = 2\left[n_{.j.} \ln n_{.j.} + \sum_i \sum_k n_{ijk} \ln n_{ijk} - \sum_i n_{ij.} \ln n_{ij.} - \sum_k n_{.jk} \ln n_{.jk}\right]$$

where *j* is fixed for any analysis, (i.e., a given school system size), *i* represents the attitude classification, and *k* represents the specific year.

$$n_{\cdot j \cdot} = \sum_i \sum_k n_{ijk}$$

$$n_{ij\cdot} = \sum_k n_{ijk} \qquad n_{\cdot jk} = \sum_i n_{ijk}$$

$\hat{I}(4)$ is distributed as chi-square with $(r-1)(t-1)$ degrees of freedom, where r represents the number of attitude classifications and t represents the number of years.

Applying the formulas given in the previous section, the following totals are developed:

$$n_{\cdot j \cdot} \ln n_{\cdot j \cdot} = 1{,}450 \ln 1{,}450 = 10{,}555.012$$

$$\sum_i \sum_k n_{ijk} \ln n_{ijk} = [375 \ln 375 + 200 \ln 200 + \ldots + 20 \ln 20 + 15 \ln 15] = 7{,}227.955$$

$$\sum_i n_{ij\cdot} \ln n_{ij\cdot} = [755 \ln 755 + 370 \ln 370 + \ldots + 95 \ln 95 + 55 \ln 55] = 8{,}748.027$$

$$\sum_k n_{\cdot jk} \ln n_{\cdot jk} = 700 \ln 700 + 400 \ln 400 + 350 \ln 350 = 9{,}032.619$$

From these totals, it follows that:

$$\begin{aligned}\hat{I}(4) &= 2[10{,}555.012 + 7{,}227.955 - 8{,}748.027 - 9{,}032.619]\\&= 2 \times 2.321\\&= 4.642\end{aligned}$$

For this example, r (the number of attitude classifications) equals 5 and t (the number of years) equals 3. The degrees of freedom are $(5-1)(3-1)$, or 8. The tabular chi-square for 8 degrees of freedom at the 0.10 level of significance is 13.362. Since the calculated value for $\hat{I}(4)$ of 4.642 does not exceed the tabular chi-square, the hypothesis cannot be rejected. The sample results are consistent with the belief that, for small school systems, attitudes regarding this question have not changed during the three-year period for which the samples were selected.

The broader implication of the analyses is, of course, that teachers within the small school systems do not appear to have changed their opinions over the three years in question, while teachers within the medium and large systems seem to be shifting (downward) in their willingness to teach again if they had to start all over.

In applying the above analytical techniques, as well as the available extensions to more complex hypotheses, the researcher must be sensitive to certain sampling assumptions:

- The methodology assumes that random samples of size n have been selected from some large universe(s).
- The n data points are assumed to be independent observations.

While these assumptions are not always met, the methodology presented should help the researcher gain an insight into whether observed changes in cell and margin percentages indicate real changes in the population(s) sampled.

11

MULTIVARIATE AND NONPARAMETRIC TECHNIQUES

In this final chapter on inferential statistics, several of the more useful statistical techniques are described in both the multivariate and nonparametric areas. As appropriate, references are given to which the researcher may refer for greater detail, particularly in the computational area. The novice will complete this chapter with an understanding of when these techniques are useful but not with information on how to perform actual calculations.

11.1 MULTIVARIATE TECHNIQUES

Earlier in this text the researcher was exposed to descriptive statistics associated with a single characteristic and also with two variables (linear and nonlinear regression and correlation). When more than two characteristics are of interest in a research task, a wide range of multivariate techniques can be employed. Three more are discussed in this section, several of which were briefly reviewed in Chapter 7.

11.1.1 Discriminant Analysis

Envision a situation where people must be classified politically as either liberal or conservative. Each person, known to be either liberal or conservative, has an associated set of characteristics, such as age, income, educational level, marital status and number of children, to name a few. It is important to determine which, if any, of these characteristics could conceivably be used to classify a person as either a liberal or a conservative. Putting it another way, are there some characteristics associated with individuals that can be used to discriminate between a liberal and a conservative? The process for determining whether this can be accomplished is referred to as "discriminant analysis" or "discriminatory analysis."

The statistical procedure assumes that such a distinction can be made between the individuals, if they are known to be in either one or the other of the two categories. A mathematical expression is developed that provides a basis for assigning the known individuals into either the liberal or conservative grouping. If the resulting expression (which uses some but probably not all of the characteristics) correctly classifies an acceptably large proportion of the individuals (say, 80%), the discriminant function is said to be significant and is then used to classify other persons external to the samples, as either liberal or conservative.

Other examples of the use of discriminant analysis areas follow:

- In recent studies, efforts have been made to determine whether coaching can have an impact on scores achieved on a specific standardized test. Since it was felt that it might be possible to differentiate between coached and non-coached individuals based upon certain characteristics—such as parents' income and high school quality-point index—a sample of persons from both categories was analyzed to determine whether a discriminant function could be determined that would classify an acceptable proportion of persons into the two categories.

- In an effort to mount an appropriate public relations campaign, a firm wanted to know if certain individual characteristics might be related to whether a person favored or did not favor an innovative transportation concept—a people-mover in a downtown area. A sample of persons known to favor and to oppose such a concept was selected and a series of characteristics observed for each person in the sample. The question at hand was, Which, if any, of these characteristics can be used to classify a person as favoring or opposing this transit concept? Development of such a discriminant function might provide the ability to determine in which areas a campaign might be mounted to help shift opinions.

- A series of individual characteristics was studied to determine the likelihood that a person would or would not successfully complete four years of college. A group of recent graduates was compared with a known group of persons who did not complete college. The resultant discriminant analysis provided a basis for counseling individuals on their likelihood of completing a four-year curriculum.

In each of the above examples, a simple mathematical function was calculated. Known values of the characteristics were inserted in the function and a single number, analogous to an index, obtained. Based upon the magnitude of this number, the person was classified as coached or noncoached, favoring or opposing the people-mover, and likely or not likely to complete four years of college.

An excellent discussion on discriminant analysis may be found in Bennett and Bowers (1976, pp. 95-116).

11.1.2 Factor Analysis

Factor analysis provides a methodology that allows the researcher to examine a large set of characteristics for a group of analysis units (AU's) in the hopes of identifying important underlying relationships. In a sense, factor analysis can be used by the researcher as an exploratory tool to assist in understanding how the characteristics of interest are interrelated, if at all. Factor analysis is a meaningful descriptive aid in the data reduction process.

Factor analysis can be defined as a technique used to identify an underlying set of characteristics (not measured) associated with a larger set of observed characteristics. For example, in using a battery of tests to measure characteristics of individuals, these tests (say, 15) may be measuring only five underlying characteristics plus random error. These five underlying characteristics are referred to as "factors."

A *common factor* is one associated with at least two of the observed characteristics, while a *unique factor* affects only a single observed characteristic and is presumed to include all of the independent factors unique to a given characteristic, as well as any random errors. As a research tool, factor analysis may be considered from two points of view:

- *Exploratory factor analysis*: The use of factor analysis techniques to study relationships among a set of characteristics with the intent of discovering what potential underlying factors exist to describe this larger set of characteristics. In this situation, there is no prior specification of the possible number of factors or of their names.

- *Confirmatory factor analysis*: The use of factor analysis techniques to test hypotheses regarding numbers of underlying factors and their names.

Two excellent publications on factor analysis are Kim and Mueller (1978a and 1978b), the former being more of a narrative and introductory publication. An exceptionally clear reference on factor analysis, loaded with many examples, is Fruchter (1954). Numerous other texts on factor analysis are available, but most require a higher level of acquaintance with mathematics than readers of this text are assumed to have.

Factor analysis techniques have broad applications and, thus, have been used in many areas of both theoretical and applied research. To illustrate, consider the following situations:

- In classifying prospective personnel, a large corporation uses a battery of ten tests, designed to measure such characteristics as reading ability, manual dexterity, spatial orientation, mathematical reasoning, and judgment. These tests tend to overlap and, in fact, only a few underlying factors are really being assessed by this battery of ten tests. An exploratory factor analysis is conducted to determine how many factors there are and, eventually, to pin a name on these factors.

- Fifty items are included in a specific questionnaire. To reduce the length of the instrument, responses to each are subjected to a factor analysis after the instrument is completed by a sample of 150 persons from an appropriate population. The analysis shows a high correlation among responses to specific items and a low correlation among others. Therefore, a decision is made to reduce the number of questionnaire items based upon the determination that ten common and independent factors affect 40 of the items.

- A sample of members and potential members (nonmembers) of an organization is interviewed and asked opinions on a series of items. The responses are subjected to a factor analysis. An analysis of the sample of 200 persons, whose responses are correlated over all items, yields ten factors. Although some overlap occurred among member/nonmember individuals in some factors, most members fell into a series of logical groups, and most nonmembers did likewise. The results provided a basis for approaching nonmembers about the possibility of becoming members.

- In a classic study (Thurstone and Degan, 1951) the voting records of nine U.S. Supreme Court judges were examined on 115 cases. The intent was to determine whether any grouping was evident among the nine judges and, if so, whether a name or names might be given to the groupings, such as "conservative" or "liberal."

The above examples indicate how factor analysis involves the application of techniques that can be used to identify underlying relationships among a series of characteristics of interest. These characteristics, of course, must be associated with well-defined AU's.

11.1.3 Stepwise Regression

Although it is not, strictly speaking, a multivariate technique in its own right, stepwise regression provides the researcher with the ability to examine a set of k independent characteristics (associated with a group of AU's) to determine which of them, taken in combination and at a given level of significance, provide the best prediction of some dependent characteristic. Suppose, for example, the researcher wants to predict an individual's final quality point index upon graduation from a specific four-year college using 20 possible characteristics (such as high school English average, overall high school quality point index, parents' income and sex). One approach might be to calculate the multiple regression equation using all 20 characteristics as predictors. In a generalized form the resulting regession equation might look as follows:

$$Y = a + b_1X_1 + b_2X_2 + b_3X_3 + \ldots\ldots + b_{19}X_{19} + b_{20}X_{20}$$

where the values for a and the b's are based upon fitting data by methods similar to those used for the bivariate case, discussed earlier.

Obviously, many of these characteristics will probably not contribute significantly to the prediction (that is, the error in prediction using some of the characteristics will not be significantly reduced or, to phrase it another way, the multiple coefficient of determination will not be significantly improved using some characteristics). A next step might be to ask, Which single characteristic is best? Which pair is best? Which three are best? And, when do I stop my search?

As the number of independent characteristics increases, the possible combinations of these characteristics that could be used two at a time, three at a time, and so on increase dramatically. (For example, with five independent characteristics there are ten different ways they could be examined three at a time; whereas, if there are ten independent characteristics, there are 120 different ways they could be examined three at a time.) Fortunately, with high speed computers available to the researcher, this "search" for the "best" set of characteristics can be accomplished in a fairly straightforward and logical pattern. The *SAS User's Guide* (1979) describes four procedures for arriving at the multiple regression equation, which uses only some of the independent variables in predicting the single dependent variable. These available techniques are well explained and allow the researcher to follow a logical approach (stepwise) in investigating relationships among a series of characteristics of interest. Criteria are established so that as each new characteristic is examined, a decision can be made to stop the "search" or to take another step in the process (i.e., search for another characteristic for inclusion in the regression equation). Similar information on stepwise regression is also available in two other statistical computer packages (See Appendix G).

11.2 NONPARAMETRIC TECHNIQUES

Often in research the characteristic of interest is ordinal; and, therefore, individual AU's can only be ranked or ordered. Under such conditions, if hypotheses are to be made regarding the populations from which the samples were drawn, nonparametric or distribution-free techniques apply. If the characteristic can be measured on either an interval or ratio scale, then either parametric (see Chapter 10) or nonparametric techniques may be used for inference. Nonparametric procedures require relatively larger samples to detect a departure from an hypothesis than do the corresponding parametric tests.

Discussions, with good examples, of nonparametric procedures may be found in Siegel (1956) and Marascuilo (1977). A detailed bibliography may be found in Savage (1953).

Concepts associated with four specific nonparametric techniques follow.

11.2.1 Sign Test (Paired Observations)

For this technique the AU's in two samples can be paired by some acceptable criteria. Differences between the paired values of the characteristic of interest are taken and the number of positive and negative differences noted. Intuitively, one would expect that, if the two samples came from the same population, the number of pluses and minuses should be about the same.

11.2.2 Wilcoxon Rank-Sum Test (Paired Observations)

This test is similar to the sign test but now the numerical value of the differences between the paired AU characteristics is determined and these differences ranked, regardless of whether the sign is positive or negative. If there is no difference between the two paired groups, the sum of the rankings of the + and − differences would be expected to be about the same.

11.2.3 Mann-Whitney U Test (Nonpaired Observations)

For this technique the AU's do not have to be paired to test the hypothesis that the two samples came from populations with the same distributions of the characteristic of interest. Sample AU's are ordered (ranked) from highest to lowest, regardless of which sample the AU is in. If the two samples came from the same population, one would expect to find the observations from each sample fairly evenly scattered among the combined ordered group. This test provides an ability to examine the distributions associated with the two samples.

11.2.4 Kruskal-Wallis H Test (More Than Two Samples)

For this situation more than two samples are examined to determine whether they could have come from the same or similar populations. Observations within individual samples are assigned ranks according to their positioning if all samples are combined and ranked. Rank sums are then calculated for each sample. One would expect, if there were no differences among the samples, that these sums would be approximately equal.

IV

Sample Size and Sampling Plans

Emphasis thus far in the HANDBOOK has been on underlying concepts of statistics and the survey process, procedures for calculating and interpreting various descriptive measures, and fundamental approaches to inferential statistics in estimation and hypothesis testing. Throughout, *planning before collecting data* has been emphasized as the key to a successful research endeavor. Without such planning, the results of the research too often prove worthless and incapable of providing a basis from which to generalize from sample to universe.

Part IV emphasizes sample size determination and some of the major sampling plans (designs) that can be used, particularly in surveys. The researcher should be wary of confusion and inconsistency in terminology and must understand inferential and sampling concepts, as well as how to implement the statistical aspects of a research design.

Chapter 12 deals with problems associated with sample size determinations when a simple unrestricted random sample is to be selected. Chapters 13, 14, and 15 present more complex sampling procedures, which build upon the concepts and techniques previously described.

The distinctions in sampling plans are based upon the manner in which samples are drawn. No single method of sampling is uniformly the best for all purposes and all studies. Each sample survey should have a sample design and a sample size tailored to fit the objectives, requirements, and resources of that particular study. The factors involved in making such decisions are the topic of Part IV.

12
SAMPLE SIZE DETERMINATION

Determining the appropriate sample size—consistent with research objectives, time constraints, and limited resources—is no easy task. Excellent theoretical texts address this subject. [See Mace (1974); Mendenhall, Ott, and Scheaffer (1971); and Sudman (1976). Other references are cited later.]

Chapter 12 deals only with sample size determination for the most simple cases—unrestricted random sampling to estimate proportions, means, and totals. More complex situations are covered in the final three chapters.

12.1 SOME FACTORS RELATING TO SAMPLE SIZE

Too frequently the question is asked, Is the sample large enough? Any size sample, properly selected, is big enough to say something relative to the population from which it has been selected. Instead, a more appropriate question is, Is the sample adequate for the *desired accuracy and confidence*? In essence, is the sample a quality sample? Having selected the sample by an appropriate and controlled procedure, can acceptable inferences be made?

Numerous factors affect sample size determination. They cannot be considered sequentially because a strong interrelationship exists among some of them. The experienced researcher considers each of these factors in an iterative sense and goes through the process several times before arriving at the final sample size determination.

12.1.1 The Population and Characteristics To Be Measured

The first consideration in determining the size of a sample is the population being sampled and the characteristics or variables to be measured or observed. Is it age, attitude, aptitude, or another characteristic? All important characteristics to be studied must be clearly and specifically identified.

The more *heterogeneous* the individuals in a population are with regard to a characteristic to be measured, the *larger* will be the sample required to measure that characteristic accurately; the more *homogeneous* they are, the *smaller* the sample required.

Another general factor affecting the sample size is the number of subgroups of interest in the research. For example, making estimates of average salaries for teachers as a group will require a smaller sample than will be required for males vs. females or elementary vs. secondary teachers. The more subgroupings required, the greater the total sample size.

Preliminary information about the population to be surveyed and the variation and distribution of characteristics to be measured in the population are important in determining sample size. If percentage estimates of population characteristics are to be made from sample data, the researcher needs *in advance* some idea of what the approximate sizes of the percentages are likely to be. Will the expected percentages be near 50%, or will they be nearer 10%? If they are near 50%, a larger sample will be required. If a researcher wishes to make inferences about a population mean from the sample mean, a preliminary estimate of what the standard deviation is likely to be in the population is needed.

Advance information about the population and the characteristic to be estimated is vital to efficient sample survey design. The survey should not be designed until all possible leads have been explored regarding preliminary information about the population.

Sources of advance information about populations in education include the following:

- Data published by the U.S. Department of Education, the National Education Association, state and local education agencies, state and local teachers associations, and college and university research centers.

- Results from previous studies conducted on the same or similar populations.

- Discussions with other researchers who have had experience in surveying the same or similar populations.

- Information from pilot or exploratory studies of the population. *If little is known about the population under study, an exploratory study of the population should be made, whenever feasible, before establishing a final research design, sample size, and survey instrument.* The time and resources spent in such exploratory studies usually produce major improvements in the quality of the data obtained in the final study.

Only with adequate advance information about the population and about the distribution of important characteristics in the population can the researcher make informed decisions, not only about sample size, but about sample design as well. This knowledge is needed to decide such things as, Should the survey design be a *simple* random sample, a *stratified* random sample, or a *cluster* sample? Without some advance knowledge of the population and the distribution of important characteristics, informed answers to these questions are difficult.

12.1.2 Summary Measures To Be Used

A second factor in sample size determination involves identifying which summary measures will be associated with the important population characteristics.

Will the set of data be described in terms of means, percentages, totals, or what? Sample size cannot be determined appropriately until decisions have been made about what statistics will be used for summarizing the characteristics of major interest. Many studies will include two or more types of such measures.

These decisions are important because the standard error is the essential base of all sample size formulas, and the standard errors of each estimate are different. In general, *standard errors for each statistic will be used to compute the necessary sample size for that statistic. The largest sample size from this group becomes the sample size used for the survey.*

12.1.3 Precision (Accuracy) and Confidence

A sensible goal of a survey is to obtain precise or accurate estimates of population parameters within the time and resource constraints. What constitutes *precise* data may be debatable in sample surveys. Often, the researcher can decide this only arbitrarily. Although several factors may affect the decision, the judgment of the researcher usually decides what constitutes the minimum acceptable precision (or allowable error) for data to be gathered in the survey.

The decision relating to the standards for precision, then, is the third major factor in determining sample size. This decision depends upon the answer to the following questions:

- *How much sampling error can be tolerated in the estimate?*
- *What precision is desired?*

In terms of the study requirements, is it permissible for the estimate of the population average teacher's salary to be within $200, $100, or $50 of the true value? Is it important that the sample percentage favoring a given issue be within two percentage points of the true percentage in the population, or can a sampling error as high as four or five percentage points be accepted? Responses to these questions of permissible sample errors can greatly affect the size of sample required for a survey. In general, the *smaller* the error (the better the precision), the *larger* the sample size required. For the sake of efficiency and economy, the researcher should be careful to establish an acceptable error as broad as the objectives of the study will permit. The limits established by the acceptable error or desired precision are referred to as "confidence limits," as stated earlier.

A fourth major factor in determining sample size is referred to as the "confidence level" and depends upon the answer to the following question:

- *How certain does the researcher wish to be that the calculated confidence limits, based upon the sample statistic, do in fact include the parameter being estimated?*

Is 99% confidence necessary? Or is it satisfactory to be only 95% sure? Or 90% sure? Such assurance is referred to as the "confidence level" associated with the sampling procedure that resulted in the given sample estimate of the parameter of interest. The confidence level represents the probability, or odds, that the parameter falls within the confidence limits derived from the sample data.

In surveys, there is usually no way to be 100% confident that the parameter of interest lies within the confidence limits—unless a complete census is taken. Therefore, researchers and the users of sample data must be willing to accept something less than 100% confidence that estimates made from the sample do not exceed the permissible sampling error. The researcher must decide the acceptable odds or chances in terms of the particular project requirements. Should the chances or probability be at least 19 in

20 (95%), or could they safely be only 9 in 10 (90%) that the estimate will not exceed the acceptable error? The confidence level varies from survey to survey and is usually designated as a proportion, such as 0.90 or 0.95. Three commonly used confidence levels in educational surveys are 0.90, 0.95, and 0.99. The researcher should not feel bound by convention to use one of them just because they are commonly used. *Any level may be selected, but it must be reported in the presentation of the survey results.*

Within limits, the *greater* the confidence level, the *larger* the sample size. Therefore, for the sake of efficiency and economy the researcher should select a confidence level no higher than that required to meet safely the objectives of the study.

In answering the three questions indicated above, the researcher is establishing the maximum acceptable *confidence interval* based on the sample estimate. At this point the reader might wish to review the discussion on the confidence interval concept presented in the Introduction to Part III and in Chapter 9.

12.1.4 Analyses To Be Made

How the data are to be used and presented have an important bearing on sample size determination. The following approach considers only the case of desired precision in a sample estimate of a parameter. A survey may be designed with the intent of testing various hypotheses regarding the population or populations of interest. Slightly different techniques are used in determining the appropriate sample size [consult Mace (1974) and Sudman (1976)].

12.1.5 Nonstatistical Considerations

Outside the realm of statistical concepts, several important factors can, and usually do, affect survey design and sample size. These nonstatistical considerations include such factors as the available finances, time, personnel, data processing equipment, and population listings (sampling frames).

If these considerations limit the size of the sample, the statistical precision requirements may have to be relaxed or other aspects of the study may have to be changed. For example, if the budget will permit the printing, mailing, and follow-up of only a specific number of questionnaires, this financial limitation may set a firm restriction on sample size. The tentative design and size of the sample may have to be reconsidered so that reductions can safely be made to fit the sample size restriction.

Perhaps the statistical precision could be relaxed a bit, or the confidence level could be reduced. Maybe one or two of the characteristics that require a much larger sample size than the rest could be omitted. This process of tailoring the study to meet such restrictions is always painful to the researcher interested in securing the maximum amount of data with the maximum degree of precision. Nevertheless, it frequently must be done and constitutes an important factor in determining sample size and sample design.

12.2 ESTIMATING SAMPLE SIZE FOR SPECIFIC SAMPLE STATISTICS

Although at first glance it may appear logical that the size of sample needed to provide precise estimates about population characteristics is directly related to the size of the population, it is not true. This widely held misconception of sample size requirements is the source of such comments as: "To be accurate a sample should include at least 10% of the population" or "A sample of only 2,000 teachers cannot possibly be large enough to give a true picture of the opinions of the nation's two million teachers."

The "old wives' tale" in statistics that the size of the population from which a sample is drawn determines the number of individuals needed for an "adequate" sample of that population is a mistaken idea. An examination of the formulas for computing the standard errors of various statistics (see Chapter 9) will show that the emphasis should be placed *not* on the number of individuals in the population, but rather on the *number* of individuals in the *sample*. Or, to put it another way, *the standard error of a statistic depends much more on the size of the sample than it does on the size of the population.* As a matter of fact, the only place where the size of the population (N) even enters the computations in most sample size formulas is in the correction factor for a finite population.

To determine the minimum size sample needed to estimate a given population parameter, the formula for the standard error of the statistic—which may or may not include the finite population multiplier—is generally used. All of the values in the sample size formula, except n, are usually known or are guessed at based upon experience or assumptions about the population.

When the population is small, the finite population multiplier is used and has a definite effect on the size of the standard error and the sample. As the population increases in size, the effect of the finite multiplier on the size of the standard error becomes less. This means that when the population size is very large, the finite multiplier has no effect on the size of the standard error; therefore, no increase in the size of the sample is required—above a certain point. (Appendix H tables demonstrate how little the sample size changes when the population size exceeds 25,000.)

With this general background, this section will present the procedures involved in estimating the sample size required to yield estimates with a stated degree of precision for sample proportions (or percentages), means and totals.

12.2.1 When Estimating a Proportion or Percentage

Suppose an issue of interest to educators is to be submitted to the voters in the November election, and two months before the election the proportion of registered voters who are opposed to this initiative needs to be estimated. This situation calls for the estimation of a population proportion (π). A listing of 50,000 registered voters is available for sampling. The state education association is interested in having the sample proportion (p) be within 0.05 of the true proportion, with an associated confidence of 0.90.

Since the population from which the sample is to be selected is large, the following formula may be used to estimate the required sample size:

$$n = \hat{\pi}(1 - \hat{\pi}) Z^2 / \epsilon^2 \qquad (12.1)$$

where:

- n is the estimated number of individuals necessary in the sample for the desired precision and confidence.
- $\hat{\pi}$ is the preliminary estimate of the proportion opposed to this initiative in the population.
- Z is the two-tailed value of the standardized normal deviate associated with the desired level of confidence (see Chapter 8).
- ϵ is the desired precision, acceptable error, or half of the maximum acceptable confidence interval.

Formula (12.1) requires some preliminary estimate of the value of π. This may seem unusual since the reason for sampling is to estimate π. Fortunately, the product of $\hat{\pi}(1 - \hat{\pi})$ assumes a maximum value when $\hat{\pi} = 0.50$. For any other value of $\hat{\pi}$, the product is less than 0.25. Hence, when no prior information is available for the value of $\hat{\pi}$, a safe assumption is $\hat{\pi} = 0.50$. If, on the other hand, a smaller, or larger, value for $\hat{\pi}$ can be safely assumed, the sample size will be reduced accordingly.

Formula (12.1) expresses acceptable error in *absolute* rather than *relative* terms. Suppose in the illustration cited that the analyst will accept an error of 0.05 in the sample estimate with 90% confidence. This means that if the sample proportion were found to be 0.35, the confidence limits should be no greater than 0.35 ± 0.05, or from 0.30 to 0.40.

Sometimes the acceptable error is expressed as a percentage error (relative) rather than an absolute error. The researcher must convert this relative error to an absolute error before using Formula (12.1). For example, if a 10% relative error is permissible when the true proportion is 0.30, the absolute error becomes 0.10 x 0.30 = 0.03.

Returning to the illustration given at the beginning of this section, the following values are to be substituted in Formula (12.1):

- $\hat{\pi}$ = 0.50 (the value assumed since nothing is known *a priori*).
- Z = 1.645 (the two-tailed standardized normal deviate associated with 90% confidence).
- ϵ = 0.05 (the acceptable error).

Substitution of these values in Formula (12.1) yields:

$$n = \hat{\pi}(1-\hat{\pi}) Z^2 / \epsilon^2$$
$$= 0.50 (1 - 0.50) (1.645)^2 / (0.05)^2$$
$$= (0.25)(2.706) / (0.0025)$$
$$= 0.6765 / 0.0025$$
$$= 270.6 \text{ (or a sample of 271)}$$

Hence, a sample of 271 persons from the listing of registered voters will provide a maximum error of 0.05 with 90% confidence. (Since rounding will affect the sample size, at least four significant digits should be used.)

Suppose a similar issue in another state received 65% of the votes in favor. If the researcher is willing to assume that these results provide an acceptable preliminary estimate of the proportion against the issue, the initial estimate of π becomes 0.35. (Remember the characteristic of interest is the proportion of registered voters against the issue.) Substitution in Formula (12.1) yields the following adjusted sample size:

$$n = \hat{\pi}(1-\hat{\pi}) Z^2 / \epsilon^2$$
$$= 0.35 (1 - 0.35) (1.645)^2 / (0.05)^2$$
$$= (0.35)(0.65)(2.706) / (0.0025)$$
$$= 0.6156 / 0.0025$$
$$= 246.2 \text{ (or a sample of 247)}$$

Hence, if the true value of π lies close to 0.35, a sample of 247 will provide an estimate for π with an error not exceeding 0.05 with an associated 90% confidence.

As a final illustration, suppose an estimate for π is not known and the researcher again wishes the error not to exceed 0.05 but wants an increased confidence of 95%. The only change from the first set of computations is that Z now equals 1.96. Substituting in Formula (12.1) yields the following:

$$n = \hat{\pi}(1-\hat{\pi}) Z^2 / \epsilon^2$$
$$= 0.50 (1 - 0.50) (1.96)^2 / (0.05)^2$$
$$= (0.25)(3.842) / (0.0025)$$
$$= 0.9605 / 0.0025$$
$$= 384.2 \text{ (or a sample of 385)}$$

Increasing the confidence from 90% to 95%, when the value for $\hat{\pi}$ is assumed at 0.50, raises the sample size from 271 to 385, or an increase of 114 persons. This is an excellent illustration of the need for researchers to weigh survey constraints against confidence and acceptable error. *Is the increased confidence worth the additional cost?* must be assessed within the framework of the survey objectives and available resources. The answer to this question is not statistical but practical.

These numerical examples illustrate that *the sample size increases with a requirement for increased confidence.* In addition, Formula (12.1) indicates that *as the allowable error is increased, the sample size decreases.* Both of these statements are consistent with logical dictates.

Formula (12.1) can be used in the following three situations:

- When estimating proportions in *large* populations
- When sampling *small* populations with replacement (here the person or entity in the population may be included in the sample several times, a situation rarely applicable to sample surveys in education)
- When the researcher cannot estimate the size of the population (N) to be sampled. (Although this is rare in surveys in education, it can occur. For example, it happens when registered voters who have telephones are sampled by using a random digit-dialing technique.)

The simplicity of Formula (12.1) makes it useful for illustrating the process of determining sample sizes when estimating proportions. However, since the formula does not contain a correction factor for the population size, it *overestimates* the size of the sample when sampling from small or medium-size populations. Formula (12.2) is appropriate for *estimating sample sizes when estimates for proportions are desired for any size population:*

$$n = \hat{\pi}(1-\hat{\pi}) / [(\epsilon^2 / Z^2) + \hat{\pi}(1-\hat{\pi}) / N] \qquad (12.2)$$

where:

n is the estimated number of individuals necessary in the sample for the desired precision and confidence.

$\hat{\pi}$ is the preliminary estimate of the proportion in the population.

Z is the two-tailed value of the standardized normal deviate associated with the desired level of confidence.

ϵ is the acceptable error, or half of the maximum acceptable confidence interval.

N is the number of individuals or entities in the population.

An alternative formula to (12.2), indicating the effect of the population size, is given in Formula (12.3):

$$n^{-1} = N^{-1} + \epsilon^2 \, [Z^2 \hat{\pi}(1 - \hat{\pi})]^{-1}$$ (12.3)

(Note that three terms call for computing their reciprocals.)

To illustrate the application for Formula (12.3), consider the following situation. A conference has just ended that exposed attendees to a number of new instructional techniques. Two months after the conference the sponsor wants, among other items, an estimate of the proportion of the 500 attendees who have implemented at least one of the new techniques. A confidence level of 90% and an acceptable error of 0.05 are agreed upon. These values are substituted in Formula (12.3) to arrive at the appropriate sample size for a survey. (Note that with no prior knowledge about $\hat{\pi}$, the value of 0.50 is assumed):

$$\begin{aligned} n^{-1} &= (500)^{-1} + (0.05)^2 \, [(1.645)^2 \, (0.50) \, (1 - 0.50)]^{-1} \\ &= 0.002 + (0.0025) \, [(2.706) \, (0.50) \, (0.50)]^{-1} \\ &= 0.002 + (0.0025) \cdot (0.6765)^{-1} \\ &= 0.002 + (0.0025) \, (1.478) \\ &= 0.002 + 0.00370 \\ &= 0.0057 \end{aligned}$$

or

$$n = 175.4 \text{ (or a sample of 176)}$$

This sample size of 176 for a population of 500 can be compared with the sample of 271 from the first illustration when the population is assumed to be large.

Sample size determination tables are given in Appendix H for the following conditions:

Allowable errors of 0.01, 0.02, 0.03, 0.04, and 0.05

Confidence levels of 0.90, 0.95, 0.98, and 0.99.

These tables—calculated using Formulas (12.2) and (12.3)—are based on the assumption that the true value of π is 0.50, hence providing the maximum sample sizes for the given allowable errors and confidence levels. The tables illustrate that if 1,000 attendees were at the conference, the sample size with the same allowable error and confidence level would rise to 213. The sample size relative to the population size has decreased from 35.2% (176/500) to 21.3% (213/1,000).

Situations exist in which there are more than two alternatives to items in a survey. For example, in giving an opinion on a specific issue, the respondent might have the following options: "strongly favor," "favor," "oppose," "strongly oppose." If these response categories were grouped into only two—"favor" and "oppose"—the sample size determination procedure presented above is appropriate. If, however, the confidence level and allowable errors were to apply to these four response categories *simultaneously*, other techniques are appropriate. The reader is referred to Siegel (1956) and Tortora (1978) for details.

12.2.2 When Estimating a Population Mean

Suppose a director of research of a state education association wishes to estimate the average monthly retirement income from the large population of retired teachers within the state. An acceptable error in the sample mean, as an estimate of the population mean, is $75, with an associated confidence level of 90%. Since the population from which this sample is to be selected is fairly large (in excess of 15,000 individuals), the following formula may be used to estimate the sample size:

$$n = (\hat{\sigma} Z / \epsilon)^2 \qquad (12.4)$$

where:

- n is the estimated sample size necessary for the desired precision and confidence.
- $\hat{\sigma}$ is the preliminary estimate of the population standard deviation.
- Z is the two-tailed value of the standardized normal deviate associated with the desired level of confidence.
- ϵ is the acceptable error or half of the maximum acceptable confidence interval.

The research director must specify values for $\hat{\sigma}$, Z, and ϵ in advance. In this illustration, ϵ has been set equal to $75, and the appropriate value of Z (associated with the 90% confidence level) is 1.645. Usually, the difficult value to estimate is $\hat{\sigma}$. If the results of earlier income studies are available, an estimate for σ may have been calculated and can be used. If such studies are not immediately available, the research director could use one of the sources suggested in Section 12.1.1. If two or more equally reasonable alternative estimates of the population standard deviation exist, the largest should be used to allow for the maximum sample size.

A rule of thumb is sometimes helpful in making a rough estimate of the standard deviation [See Mendenhall, Ott, and Scheaffer (1971) and U.S. Department of Commerce (1966)]. This procedure is fairly accurate if the population is large and normally distributed or tends to be symmetrical, with the largest number of items clustering in the middle of the distribution. A rough estimate of the standard deviation can be made by dividing the range (difference between largest and smallest value of the variable of interest) by six. In the above example, if no prior studies are available, the research director could estimate $\hat{\sigma}$ by assuming a largest and smallest value for monthly retirement income in the state. If the largest is $1,200 and the smallest is $600, the estimate of the population standard deviation is:

$$\hat{\sigma} = (\$1{,}200 - \$600) / 6$$
$$= \$100$$

Another method of obtaining a preliminary estimate of the standard deviation in the population is known as *step* or *sequential sampling*. In general, the technique consists of taking a preliminary sample from the population of interest and calculating the estimate of the standard deviation. On the basis of this estimate, the estimated total sample size is calculated by using Formula (12.4). Additional observations are randomly selected to bring the total sample size up to that based upon the estimate of σ from the preliminary sample. The two sets of sample data are then combined and should be of sufficient size to meet the precision and confidence requirements. This approach is used extensively in industrial quality control. Substituting the appropriate values in Formula (12.4) yields the following estimated sample size:

$$n = (\hat{\sigma} Z / \epsilon)^2$$
$$= [(\$100)(1.645) / (\$75)]^2$$
$$= [\$164.5 / \$75]^2$$
$$= (2.193)^2$$
$$= 4.8 \text{ (or a sample of 5)}$$

Assume that the acceptable error is only $25, with the confidence level and estimate of $\hat{\sigma}$ being the same. The estimate of the required sample size then becomes:

$$n = (\hat{\sigma} Z / \epsilon)^2$$
$$= [(\$100)(1.645) / (\$25)]^2$$
$$= [(\$164.5) / (\$25)]^2$$
$$= (6.58)^2$$
$$= 43.3 \text{ (or a sample of 44)}$$

These sample size estimates are highly sensitive to the variability (σ) in the population from which the sample is to be selected. Suppose, for example, the population standard deviation is estimated at $200 rather than $100. The appropriate sample size with the $25 allowable error and the 90% confidence level becomes:

$$n = (\hat{\sigma} Z / \epsilon)^2$$
$$= (\$200)(1.645) / (\$25)^2$$
$$= (\$329) / (\$25)^2$$
$$= (13.16)^2$$
$$= 173.2 \text{ (or a sample of 174)}$$

For the three examples just given, consider what happens to the estimated sample size when the confidence level is increased to 95% (Z = 1.96):

Example 1:
$$n = (\hat{\sigma} Z / \epsilon)^2$$
$$= [(\$100)(1.96) / (\$75)]^2$$
$$= [(\$196) / (\$75)]^2$$
$$= (2.613)^2$$
$$= 6.8 \text{ (or a sample size of 7, as compared with 5)}$$

Example 2:
$$n = (\hat{\sigma} Z / \epsilon)^2$$
$$= [(\$100)(1.96) / (\$25)]^2$$
$$= [(\$196) / (\$25)]^2$$
$$= (7.84)^2$$
$$= 61.5 \text{ (or a sample size of 62, as compared with 44)}$$

Example 3:
$$n = (\hat{\sigma} Z / \epsilon)^2$$
$$= [(\$200)(1.96) / (\$25)]^2$$
$$= [(\$392) / (\$25)]^2$$
$$= (15.68)^2$$
$$= 245.9 \text{ (or a sample size of 246, as compared with 174)}$$

The estimated sample size increases as both the variability in the population (σ) and the desired confidence level increase; it decreases as the allowable error increases.

Although Formula (12.4) is usually thought of in reference to large or infinite populations, it is also appropriate in two other types of situations, neither usual in sample surveys in education:

- When sampling small populations with replacement
- When the researcher cannot estimate the size of the population (N) other than knowing that it is large.

Although Formula (12.4) is simple in its use, it does not reflect the finite correction factor and, consequently, will yield an estimate of sample size larger than necessary for small and medium-size populations. Formula (12.5) is used to determine the *size of a simple random sample needed to estimate a population mean regardless of the size of the population*:

$$n = \hat{\sigma}^2 / [(\epsilon/Z)^2 + (\hat{\sigma}^2/N)] \quad (12.5)$$

where:

- n is the estimated sample size necessary for the desired precision and confidence.
- $\hat{\sigma}$ is the preliminary estimate of the population standard deviation.
- Z is the two-tailed value of the standardized normal deviate associated with the desired level of confidence.
- ϵ is the acceptable error, or half of the maximum acceptable confidence interval.
- N is the population size.

An alternative to Formula (12.5), indicating the effect of the population size, is given in Formula (12.6):

$$n^{-1} = N^{-1} + (\epsilon / \hat{\sigma} Z)^2 \quad (12.6)$$

(Note that two terms call for reciprocals, n^{-1} and N^{-1}.) This expression is analogous to Formula (12.3) for estimating proportions.

To illustrate the use of Formula (12.6), suppose a local education association is reviewing a new type of major medical insurance policy for its members and needs to know the mean age of the 2,000 teachers in the school system to within one year of the true mean age, with 95% confidence. How large a sample will be needed to yield this information? Using data from a study made a few years earlier, the standard deviation of teacher ages in the population is estimated at 7 years. Substitution of this information in Formula (12.6) yields:

$$n^{-1} = N^{-1} + (\epsilon / \hat{\sigma} Z)^2$$
$$= (2{,}000)^{-1} + [(1) / (7)(1.96)]^2$$
$$= 0.0005 + [(1) / (13.72)]^2$$
$$= 0.0005 + (0.07289)^2$$
$$= 0.0005 + 0.005313$$
$$= 0.005813$$

or:

$$n = 172.03 \text{ (or a sample size of 173)}$$

If the confidence level is relaxed to 90%, the resultant sample size becomes:

$$n^{-1} = N^{-1} + (\epsilon / \hat{\sigma} Z)^2$$
$$= (2{,}000)^{-1} + [(1) /(7)(1.645)]^2$$
$$= 0.0005 + (1 / 11.515)^2$$
$$= 0.0005 + (0.08684)^2$$
$$= 0.0005 + 0.007541 \leftarrow$$
$$= 0.008041$$

or

$$n = 124.4 \text{ (or a sample size of 125)}$$

To illustrate the utility of Formula (12.6), the first term to the right of the equals sign, N^{-1}, represents the effect of the population size in reducing the sample size. The second term in (12.6), $(\epsilon / \hat{\sigma} Z)^2$, is the reciprocal of the righthand side of Formula (12.4) and is the contribution for a very large or infinite population. In the final example, on the line indicated by the arrow, ($\leftarrow$), the reciprocal of the second term (0.007541) is the sample size for a large or infinite population; namely, n = 132.6, or a sample of 133. The combination of the two terms, 0.0005 + 0.007541, or 0.008041, provides the reciprocal of the sample size when adjusting for a finite population; namely, 125. In this case, the effect of knowing that the population is relatively small is to reduce the sample size from 134 to 125.

12.2.3 When Estimating a Population Total

The procedure for determining the size of sample needed to estimate a population total with a stated degree of accuracy and confidence is similar to that described when estimating a proportion or a mean. Suppose a state education association wants to establish a group surety bond program to cover its members who serve as school treasurers of funds earned by the senior class, dramatics club, science club, etc. Before submitting specifications to various bonding companies, certain basic information must be obtained, the most important being the total amount of money in the funds to be supervised by all such teachers in the state.

The research director can find no preliminary data on the subject. The only population list from which a sample could be selected is a list of the 1,500 schools in the state. Therefore, a pilot study of the population must be conducted to obtain a preliminary estimate of the standard deviation of the amounts contained in such school funds in the state. This pilot study indicates that the amounts fall into a fairly normal distribution and that the standard deviation is approximately $\hat{\sigma} = \$60$. Because of the clustered nature of the pilot sample, the standard deviation of the pilot study might underestimate the true standard deviation in the population. To be on the safe side, the preliminary estimate of the standard deviation is increased to $\hat{\sigma} = \$75$. The precision requirements of the estimate are set at $10,000, with a confidence of 0.95. Thus, the problem is to determine the sample size required to estimate within the required precision the total amount of money entrusted to the care of the teachers who are school treasurers.

The research director uses Formula (12.7), which can be applied to *populations of any size and gives the required sample size for estimating a total in a finite population* with a given precision:

$$n = D^2 / [1 + (D^2 / N)] \qquad (12.7)$$

where:

$$D = N Z \hat{\sigma} / \epsilon$$

and:

- n is the estimated sample size for the given precision and confidence level.
- N is the population size.
- $\hat{\sigma}$ is the preliminary estimate of the standard deviation of the variable of interest in the population.
- ϵ is the allowable error, or half of the maximum acceptable confidence interval.
- Z is the two-tailed value of the standardized normal deviate associated with the desired level of confidence.

To simplify the calculations, the value for D should be calculated first and substituted in Formula (12.7). For this illustration, D is:

$$D = NZ\hat{\sigma}/\epsilon$$
$$= (1,500)(1.96)(\$75)/(\$10,000)$$
$$= (\$220,500)/(\$10,000)$$
$$= 22.05$$

Substituting the value for D into Formula (12.7) yields:

$$n = D^2 / [1 + (D^2 / N)]$$
$$= (22.05)^2 / [1 + (22.05^2 / 1,500)]$$
$$= 486.2 / (1 + 0.3241)$$
$$= (486.2) / (1.3241)$$
$$= 367.2 \text{ (or a sample of 368)}$$

Although not widely used, an optional formula for estimating the sample size when estimating population totals is desired is:

$$\boxed{n^{-1} = N^{-1} + N^{-2}(\epsilon/Z\hat{\sigma})^2} \qquad (12.8)$$

where the symbols are as defined following Formula (12.7).

12.2.4 Effect of Subgroups on Sample Size

The number of subgroups or subcategories into which the findings of the survey are to be grouped for analysis is an extremely important factor in determining sample size. The greater the number of subcategories, the larger the total sample size needed to provide population parameter estimates for the subcategories that will meet the study's minimum precision requirements. Consider the previous example in which the local education association was seeking a new type of major medical insurance policy for its members and needed to know the mean age of teachers in the school system with a precision of ± 1 year and a confidence of 0.95. A sample of 173 from the 2,000 teachers was determined as adequate for the precision and confidence level requirements.

But suppose the mean ages for each of two subgroups—male and female teachers—were required, and approximately 1,500 female and 500 male teachers are employed by the school system. The problem now is, How many *men* are needed in the sample to meet the precision requirements of the study? because the *smallest* subgroup for which data will be analyzed is taken as the basic unit in constructing an estimate of the total sample size required.

The smallest subgroup is treated as though it were a separate population; and the size of the sample needed to estimate the mean of this subpopulation, with the stated accuracy and confidence requirements, is determined. Thus, in this example an estimate of the standard deviation of the subpopulation—judged to be $\hat{\sigma} = 5$ years—is obtained and substituted in Formula (12.6) to obtain the necessary sample size, as follows:

$$\begin{aligned} n^{-1} &= N^{-1} + [\epsilon / \hat{\sigma} Z]^2 \\ &= (500)^{-1} + [1 / (5)(1.96)]^2 \\ &= 0.002 + (0.1020)^2 \\ &= 0.002 + 0.01040 \\ &= 0.0124 \end{aligned}$$

or:

$$n = 80.6 \text{ (or a sample size of 81)}$$

A subsample of 81 males is needed to estimate with the desired accuracy and confidence the mean age for the 500 male teachers who comprise the subpopulation. The next concern is, How many teachers from the total 2,000 must be selected to be reasonably sure that about 81 males will be in the sample? To find this number, Formula (12.9) is used:

$$\boxed{n = n_s N / N_s} \qquad (12.9)$$

where:

- n is the estimated total sample size necessary to yield estimates in the smallest subpopulation with the desired precision and confidence level.
- n_s is the estimated sample size for the smallest subpopulation to yield estimates with the desired precision and confidence level.
- N is the total population size.
- N_s is the size of the smallest subpopulation of interest.

Substituting in Formula (12.9) yields:

$$\begin{aligned} n &= n_s N / N_s \\ &= (81)(2,000) / 500 \\ &= (81)(4) \\ &= 324 \end{aligned}$$

A total sample of 368 teachers is needed to assure that at least 92 will be in the smallest subgroup, i.e., the number of men needed to meet the minimum precision requirements. This approach to determining sample size when data for subgroups are to be analyzed is used only when it is *impossible* to identify and sample persons in the subpopulations separately.

If the populations of men and women could have been identified separately, the total sample size would have been reduced inasmuch as Formula (12.6) would have been used to determine both sample sizes. This, however, constitutes a stratified random sample design rather than a simple random sample design (discussed in detail in Chapter 13).

Seldom will a researcher be faced with a problem in which a simple random sample is used without wishing to make some type of subgroup analysis of the data. Therefore, the effect of subgroups, even in simple random samples, is an important determinant of sample size in nearly all studies. This is one of the important reasons for getting as much advance information about the population as possible. Information about the size and distribution of subpopulations to be sampled and analyzed is essential if the total sample size is to be large enough to yield estimates with the desired precision for these subgroups.

When the size of the total sample is established on the basis of the number of individuals needed to meet the minimum precision requirements for a given statistic in the *smallest* subgroup, estimates for similar statistics in larger subgroups will exceed the minimum precision requirements with the same degree of confidence.

12.3 ADJUSTING THE PRELIMINARY SAMPLE SIZE

Section 12.1 points out numerous factors to be considered in estimating the necessary sample size. These factors have been presented as decision points in the process of determining sample size. Decisions on these factors must be made concurrently, not sequentially. Initially, the sample size should be based upon that estimate in the sample requiring the largest sample. Specifically, if several parameters are to be estimated, which is usually the case, sample sizes should be determined for each estimate with its associated precision and confidence level. The largest sample size from among this set becomes the preliminary sample size for the survey. The researcher is now ready to subject this decision to a series of examinations and possible adjustments.

12.3.1 Adjustment for Nonresponse

Although experienced sample surveyors may wish for a 100% response to their survey instrument, most do not expect it. Nonresponse by a part of the sample raises two major problems: (a) the effect of nonresponse on sample size and (b) the possible effect of nonresponse on the nature of the findings.

In the previous discussions of sample size, the formulas have been given in terms of the sample size needed to estimate a population parameter with a stated precision and confidence. Suppose the sample size needed to estimate a mean is 150. The estimated mean and its precision can be computed only from the data actually *received* from the sample. If only 130 replies are received, the sample size in the formula used to compute the standard error will equal 130, not 150. The standard error will be larger and, in turn, the confidence interval will be larger than expected; therefore, the estimate will not meet the precision requirements.

The surveyor must anticipate what the percentage of nonresponse is likely to be and compensate for it *numerically* by increasing the sample size. Although advance information on the population is important, advance information on nonresponse is usually difficult to obtain. The best clues are usually from similar studies on similar populations. Often the researcher can do little more than guess what the response rate will be. The guess should be conservative, since it is safer to underestimate than to overestimate the expected response.

Formula (12.10) is useful in *adjusting sample size to compensate numerically for expected nonresponse*.

$$n_a = \frac{n}{P_r} \quad (12.10)$$

where:

n_a is the sample size adjusted for the expected rate of response.

n is the preliminary estimate of sample size.

P_r is the expected rate of response expressed as a proportion.

To demonstrate the use of Formula (12.10), suppose the preliminary sample size is 150 and only 90% of the survey instruments are expected to be returned. What should the adjusted sample size be so that 150 instruments will be returned? Substituting in Formula (12.10), the adjusted sample size is:

$$n_a = \frac{n}{P_r}$$
$$= \frac{150}{0.9}$$
$$= 167$$

This warning should be emphasized: *Increasing the preliminary sample size to anticipate nonresponse does not in any way take into account possible differences existing between the respondent and nonrespondent groups so far as the characteristics under study are concerned.*

Any difference between the respondent and nonrespondent groups is called the "nonresponse bias." Although this is a major problem in sample survey research, it is outside the scope of this HANDBOOK. Various methods of estimating nonresponse bias are treated in Sudman (1976).

The researcher must not assume that increasing sample size to allow for nonresponse compensates for nonresponse bias. This is decidedly *not* the case. Increasing the sample size only helps assure a sample of sufficient size to compute *arithmetically* confidence limits of estimates with the desired precision for those who respond. Such estimates may or may not contain a nonresponse bias. The only *sure* way to eliminate the possibility of nonresponse bias in sample surveys is to eliminate *nonresponse,* and keeping the sample size reasonably small and devoting sufficient resources and time to effective follow-up procedures are the best ways to increase the survey response rate. For mailed questionnaire surveys, a follow-up procedure involving five or six carefully planned follow-up communications is usually needed to achieve a high response. An up-to-date sampling frame also helps reduce nonresponse. Finally, if survey timing and costs permit, a sample of nonrespondents may provide an indication of how they differ, if at all, from the respondents.

12.3.2 Eliminating Certain Estimates

After the preliminary decision on sample size has been made and adjusted for anticipated nonresponse, the researcher usually checks this against the budget and frequently finds that the sample is too large. Sometimes additional funds may be secured to conduct the survey as desired, but more often than not the study will have to be pared to fit the existing budget. One possibility is to re-examine the characteristics and the types of estimates to be made. Some may not be as important as they appeared at first.

Another is to carefully examine the parameter estimate causing the greatest sample size requirement. If its precision so far exceeds any other that such accuracy is not crucial to the study, perhaps the estimate can be omitted from the study and one requiring a smaller sample used instead.

12.3.3 Adjusting Precision Requirements

If the estimate producing an unusually large sample size is vital to the study and cannot be omitted, the precision requirements should be re-examined. Is the stated precision actually required for this particular estimate? Could the permissible error be relaxed? Could the confidence level be reduced without much harm? Perhaps both the permissible error and the confidence level could be adjusted. Sometimes small adjustments in the precision requirements can substantially effect the sample size, especially when subgroups are involved.

12.3.4 Combining Subgroups

Perhaps the single most profitable possibility in reducing the preliminary estimate of sample size is re-examination of the smallest subgroup used in making the preliminary estimate. Is a subgroup that small vital to the study? Could it be enlarged by combining it with one or more contiguous groups? Suppose in the initial planning for a study a researcher decides to analyze teacher opinions according to the number of years of teaching experience. Five subgroups are identified with the following estimated number of teachers in each of the subpopulations:

Years of experience	Estimated number in population
1-5	2,500
6-10	2,000
11-15	1,800
16-20	1,600
21-30	1,000
31 or more	500

The key subgroup in establishing the sample size for the population is the "31 or more" group, which is estimated to have only 500 in the population. The researcher should ask, Is separate analysis of data for this subgroup vital to the study or could the "21-30" group be combined with it to form a larger subgroup consisting of "21 years or more"? If this can be done, the new subgroup, which will still be the smallest in the distribution, will have 1,500 teachers rather than 500. The combining of tentative subgroupings usually results in substantial reductions in sample size requirements.

As many subgroups as desired may be combined as long as they are contiguous. The more combining that can be done without disturbing the essential needs of the study, the more savings will accrue in terms of sample size requirements.

12.3.5 Redefining the Population To Be Surveyed

When a severe problem of sample size reduction faces the researcher, the best alternative is to redefine the population to be studied. Suppose a statewide committee on problems of instruction, jointly established by the state education association and the state department of education, considers pupil discipline one of the most serious instructional problems facing classroom teachers. Although this problem occurs at all grade levels, it seems to be particularly acute in the secondary grades. The committee secures a modest sum of money to conduct a statewide survey on problems in pupil discipline as viewed by teachers. After drawing up a preliminary survey design including separate analyses of problems in the elementary and secondary grades, the researcher is convinced that a survey of this sample size cannot be funded within the budget. Two choices are available: (a) design a survey that reports data for all teachers only and omits analysis by grade levels or (b) redefine the population to be surveyed to comprise only teachers in the secondary grades. The committee decides to redefine the population to be surveyed.

12.3.6 Changing the Sample Design

When the preliminary sample size is too large to meet time, budget, or personnel limitations, re-examining the shape of the distribution of the most important characteristic(s) used to determine sample size is a good practice. If the distribution of the characteristic in the population is skewed, a *stratified sample design* may be used and the same precision obtained with a smaller sample.

A *stratified sample design* may also be helpful in reducing sample size when the individuals in the subgroups to be analyzed can be identified separately in the population frame from which the sample is to be selected. An example of this type was mentioned in Section 12.2.4.

Should the researcher find that the distribution of the important characteristic in the population appears to fall into natural groupings, which seem to have similar distributions within each grouping, the advantages and disadvantages of using a *cluster sample design* should be considered. Such a design might provide a means of reducing the sample size. The cluster sample design is particularly helpful in reducing the costs involved in face-to-face interview surveys.

Both the stratified sample and cluster sample are more complex than the simple random design and will be described in detail in Chapters 13 and 14.

12.3.7 Change in the Type of Survey

Changing the type of survey—say, from a face-to-face interview survey to a mailed survey—should not be overlooked as a means of reducing the cost of conducting a study. Although this usually does not result in a reduction of the sample size needed to meet the same precision requirements for estimates, substantial reductions can result in the cost per survey instrument administered.

A good discussion of the pros and cons of various types of survey measuring instruments and their administration will be found in Stephan and McCarthy (1958).

12.3.8 Combining Resources

One way to meet a cost squeeze is to combine the resources for one survey with those of another survey to be administered to the same or similar population. Questions originally intended for separate survey instruments in separate samples can be combined into a single instrument and sent to a single sample. A *gain* rather than a loss in information received occurs because of the additional cross analyses that can be made with the replies to the questions. On other occasions two questionnaires may be sent to the same sample in succession; this is not a wise practice, however, and should be avoided whenever possible.

For certain types of surveys the researcher should not overlook the possibility of purchasing the services of commercial research agencies. Many excellent organizations maintain competent research staffs for surveying certain populations. A researcher can contract with one of these agencies to ask specific questions of a specific population. The costs can be reasonable, especially if time is not an important factor. Sometimes a competent commercial agency can help bring survey costs into line with budget limitations.

13

STRATIFIED SAMPLING PLANS

Stratified random sampling is a technique of sampling that draws independent unrestricted or simple random samples from each of several subgroups or strata into which the population has been divided. The subgroup or stratum limits are carefully defined, and the total population is grouped into specific strata *before* sampling. The word *strata* does not imply a hierarchy of the subgroups; it merely indicates divisions of the population. Each analysis unit (AU) or element in the population of interest must fall into only one of the strata; for example, classifying school districts into various strata according to pupil enrollment levels.

Ideally, a stratified sample is drawn when the population to be sampled can be divided into groupings or strata that are internally relatively alike (homogeneous) with regard to the major characteristics or variables under consideration and that are relatively different (heterogeneous) among the strata.

Reasons for using stratification

1. When separate subpopulation sampling frames (i.e., the listing of population AU's) require that subsamples be drawn independently.
2. When some characteristics must be treated in a *slightly* different way for different subgroups.
3. When a larger sample is not possible, and the sampling error must be reduced.
4. When simple random sampling would not yield enough members of certain subgroups to perform a planned subgroup analysis in addition to the total group analysis.
5. When one or more subgroups are scheduled for more intensive analysis bringing in additional variables or other variations.
6. When total sample size or cost restrictions must be made, and some subgroups within the population are much more costly than others to survey.

If the population does not fall into strata that are *homogeneous within* strata and *heterogeneous among* strata on *all* the important characteristics, consideration should be given to simple random, cluster, or some combination type of sampling plan before a final decision about the sampling plan is made.

13.1 PATTERNS FOR ALLOCATIONS OF SAMPLE TO STRATA

The stratified simple random sample is characterized by having several predefined subgroups or subpopulations, each with its own sampling frame. This allows the researcher to draw a sample from each subgroup and vary the sampling fraction from one subgroup to another. The particular overall pattern of sampling fractions to be used and the conditions that call for their use are important early decisions. The following two sections on the "single important variable approach" and "multi-important variable approach" will outline the process of *evaluating* a stratified simple random sampling plan in connection with specific survey problems. Defining the strata and determining the total sample size are discussed in the section on *planning the survey*.

Allocation of the sample to the various strata may be approached in two general ways: proportional and disproportional. When the same sampling rate (or proportion) is used for the elements in every stratum, the process is called "proportional allocation." If the sampling rate varies from stratum to stratum, the process is known as "disproportional allocation."

The first three reasons given for using stratification on p. 227—independent sampling frames (#1), differing forms of treatment from stratum to stratum (#2), and reducing sampling error by stratification (#3)—may be best served by *either* disproportional or proportional allocation.

The last three reasons for using stratification—subgroup precision requirements (#4), additional variables for one subgroup (#5), and variable costs per unit measured among strata (#6)—would be best served by using disproportional allocation. When variable costs are a factor, "optimum disproportional allocation" describes the most efficient distribution of the sample among strata within certain restrictions, such as total cost, maximum total sample size, or maximum sampling error permissible.

The final choice is determined by taking into account the requirements made of the data by the researcher and the requirements imposed on the sample by the budget.

13.1.1 Proportional Allocation

When the same sampling rate is used in every stratum, the process is called "proportional allocation." If N is the number of individuals in the population and n is the number of individuals in the total sample, n/N yields the proportion of individuals to be sampled from each stratum. Knowledge of the number of individuals in each stratum (N_j) is necessary. (The subscript denotes an individual stratum and can assume index values from 1 to r, which is the total *number* of *strata* in the population.)

Assume that in a population of 2,000 classroom teachers, the total sample size is to be 400. If the population is stratified by sex, there are 500 men (N_1) and 1,500 women (N_2). Exhibit 13.1 illustrates a proportional allocation solution to this problem.

EXHIBIT 13.1—PROPORTIONAL ALLOCATION OF SAMPLE SIZE TO A STRATIFIED SIMPLE RANDOM SAMPLE WITH TWO STRATA

Stratum	Population size N_j	Sampling ratio n/N	Sample size n_j
(1)	(2)	(3)	(4)
Men	500	1/5	100
Women	1,500	1/5	300
TOTAL	N = 2,000	400/2,000 = 1/5	n = 400

This allocation process is relatively easy if N, n, and N_j are known. Determination of the total sample size necessary, given certain precision requirements, will be discussed later. If the population sizes of the strata are not known or cannot be estimated very well, stratification is not feasible.

The proportional allocation process is easier than the disproportional in establishing sample ratios and computing the parameter estimates and their sampling errors. When a high-speed computer is *not* available, the advantage of the simplicity of proportional allocation often outweighs the advantages of disproportional allocation.

Stratified sampling techniques are called for when the only population sampling frame available is separated into two or more parts (Reason 1). For example, a study of undergraduates at a large university called for sampling frames of dormitory residents. The women's and the men's housing offices were willing to make resident lists available, but there was no way of combining the frames before sampling. In this example the only way to satisfy statistical requirements of unrestricted random sampling is to treat the two samples as a single stratified simple random sample.

Sometimes, the entire population cannot be treated the same with regard to some of the important variables to be studied. Variations in the forms of questions or forced choice answers may be necessary for some items. This would lead to separate analysis of these items for each subgroup, although other variables under study may not require this distinction (Reason 2). To illustrate: Questions on the use of time directed to women residents in college dormitories will differ from those directed to men residents. If somewhat different questions are to be asked regarding the use of time, sampling frames may need to be separated. Separate sampling frames require statistical treatments of the data as a *stratified* random sample.

Most discussions of stratification emphasize the distribution of the population on the most important variable. If the data are homogeneous within strata and heterogeneous among strata, a stratified simple random sample will have less sampling error than an unrestricted random sample (Reason 3). However, in educational surveys there are probably more occasions for using stratification that do *not* cause an improvement in the sampling error than occasions that do. For practical reasons, a loss of statistical efficiency may result from the more pressing need of other factors, such as studies including analyses of more than a single important variable, or the impossibility of selecting an unrestricted random sample from the sampling frame(s).

13.1.2 Disproportional Allocation

When the sampling rate varies from stratum to stratum, the process is known as "disproportional allocation." If N is the number of individuals in the population and n is the number of individuals in the sample, the overall sampling ratio is n/N. The sampling ratio for the jth stratum is n_j/N_j, where n_j is the number of individuals in the *sample* from the jth stratum and N_j is the number of individuals in the *population* from the jth stratum.

In the earlier example a *disproportional* allocation with *equal numbers* of individuals (200) in each stratum sample would be as shown in Exhibit 13.2. Although the same *number* of individuals is selected from each stratum in this example, the sampling *rates* for the strata are different because of differences in population sizes in the strata.

EXHIBIT 13.2–DISPROPORTIONAL ALLOCATION OF SAMPLE SIZE TO STRATIFIED SIMPLE RANDOM SAMPLE WITH TWO STRATA

Stratum	Population size N_j	Sample Size n_j	Sampling Ratio n_j/N_j
(1)	(2)	(3)	(4)
Men..............	$N_1 = 500$	$n_1 = 200$	$\frac{200}{500} = 2/5$
Women..........	$N_2 = 1{,}500$	$n_2 = 200$	$\frac{200}{1{,}500} = 2/15$
TOTAL..........	$N = 2{,}000$	$n = 400$	$\frac{400}{2{,}000} = 1/5$[1]

[1] Although 1/5 is the overall sample ratio, it is not a sampling ratio in the sense that this term was used in the sampling process.

The sample ratios for the strata were determined in the previous example by arbitrarily deciding to have $n_1 = n_2$ and $n = 400$. Alternative ways exist to determine the sampling rates for the separate strata; these will emerge during the following discussion.

In disproportional allocation of sample size, variations in stratum sampling rates may assume several *patterns*:

1. All strata are sampled at different nonoptimum rates.
2. Some adjacent strata have the same sampling ratio, but at least two different sampling ratios are used.
3. All strata are sampled at different rates, with the total sample size optimally allocated to satisfy certain restrictions.
4. One stratum has a sample size fixed for some specific reason, and the other strata are (a) sampled proportionately using $(n-n_1)/(N-N_1)$ as the sampling ratio for the remaining strata or (b) sampled as in Pattern 3.
5. One stratum is surveyed completely, i.e., $n_1 = N_1$, sampling ratio 1/1; other strata are (a) sampled as in Pattern 1, (b) sampled as in Pattern 3, or (c) sampled as in Pattern 4a.

If a population subgroup will not be adequately represented numerically in a simple random sample when the researcher wants to compute additional estimates for the subgroup with a desired degree of precision (Reasons 4 and 5), disproportional stratified simple random sampling is necessary. The number of individuals who should be in the subgroup is determined by the procedures described in Chapter 12. That number of individuals is established as a fixed sample size as in Pattern 4.

Disproportional sampling from strata also may be desirable when *widely* varying costs-of-measurement per individual exist in the different strata (Reason 6).

On occasion when a stratified simple random sample is planned and sample size formula from Chapter 12 are applied to pertinent subgroups because separate estimates of variables for them are of interest, *proportional* allocation of the sample may result in an unwieldy or illogical total sample size. Such a problem arose in trying to ensure that an adequate number of male teachers were present in a total sample of elementary school teachers in a city. There were 100 male teachers and 700 female teachers in the school system. Precision requirements for the *total* sample called for a sample of at least 125 teachers. Precision requirements for items related only to male teachers called for a sample of at least 50 men. Under proportional allocation procedures, the corresponding sample for the female teachers would be 350. A total sample of 400 teachers is clearly unnecessary considering that the original estimate of 125 teachers was all that was needed. The answer to this problem lies in using a *disproportional* allocation pattern.

To do this, first determine the total sample size necessary when planning optimum allocation [Formula (13.3)]. Then find the optimum sample size for female teachers [Formula (13.7)]. Combine the original estimate of 50 for the men and the new estimate for the women from Formula (13.7). The result will usually be an estimate larger than either the original estimate of 125 or the result of Formula (13.3); consequently, better than minimum precision can be expected.

The weighting of stratum values when computing estimates of parameters and their standard errors is an important point to remember when considering a *disproportional* allocation of the sample to strata. Disproportional allocation requires arithmetic weighting; this procedure can become complicated and time-consuming, especially when a high-speed computer is not available and many variables are to be computed.

In determining the arithmetic weights to be applied to each stratum, the correct weight for a stratum is N_j/N, where N_j is the number of individuals in the *population* from the jth stratum and N is the number of individuals in the total *population*. Exhibit 13.3 and its associated examples demonstrate the effect of not using weights or using incorrect

EXHIBIT 13.3–EXAMPLE OF CORRECT AND INCORRECT STRATUM WEIGHTS APPLIED TO DATA FROM HYPOTHETICAL STRATIFIED SIMPLE RANDOM SAMPLE WITH DISPROPORTIONAL ALLOCATION

Stratum	Population size N_j	Sample size n_j	Sampling ratio n_j/N_j	Stratum totals T_j^*	Estimate of stratum mean μ_j	Correct stratum weight N_j/N	Incorrect stratum weight n_j/n
(1)	(2)	(3)	(4)	(5)	(6)	(7)	(8)
1	10	2	2/10 or 0.2	30	15	0.33	0.25
2	20	6	6/20 or 0.3	120	20	0.66	0.75
Total group	N = 30	n = 8	n/N = 8/30				

*Indicated totals are for sample values.

weights based on *sample* size, n_j/n, in attempting to compute a simple unbiased estimate of the population mean.

Correctly Weighted Estimate of the Population Mean

$$\hat{\mu} = \frac{(N_1\hat{\mu}_1 + N_2\hat{\mu}_2)}{N}$$

$$= \frac{10(15) + 20(20)}{30}$$

$$= \frac{150 + 400}{30} = 18.3$$

Incorrectly Weighted Estimate of the Population Mean

$$\mu = \frac{(n_1\hat{\mu}_1 + n_2\hat{\mu}_2)}{n}$$

$$= \frac{2(15) + 6(20)}{8}$$

$$= \frac{30 + 120}{8} = 18.7$$

Weighting procedures are also important in the computation of unbiased estimates of means, proportions, and totals when the sample size has been disproportionately allocated to the strata.

Optimum allocation of the sample size is a special type of disproportional allocation that gives the most efficient distribution of the number of individuals in the sample among the various strata. The criteria for efficiency in optimum allocation are based on one or more of the following:

- The most efficient allocation of sample size when a total sample size restriction is imposed.
- The most efficient allocation of sample size when minimum standard error is desired.
- The most efficient allocation of sample size when widely varying costs of measurement exist between individuals, with or without a total cost restriction.

When the criteria have been established and the necessary information obtained, the allocation of n to the strata is made by using the appropriate formulas to be found in the latter part of this chapter. Exhibit 13.4 gives helpful guides to choosing the appropriate set of formulas for optimum allocation in specific types of sampling problems. The essential element in optimum allocation is the variance of the characteristic in the population comprising *each* stratum. Optimum allocation depends upon the known strata variances or a reasonable estimate of them.

Optimum allocation (Pattern 3) is most often used when the average cost of measuring a unit varies greatly from stratum to stratum (Reason 6); for example, in interview type surveys. Proposing to interview the deans of men at several types of colleges and universities, the survey director decided it was inefficient to interview the same proportion

215

EXHIBIT 13.4–GUIDE TO ALLOCATION PROCEDURES FOR OPTIMUM ALLOCATION PROBLEMS WITH GIVEN RESTRICTIONS USING PATTERNS 3, 4b, AND 5b[1]

Patterns	Equal average cost/item in stratum		Variable average costs/item in stratum		
	Total n restriction	Permissible error restriction	Total n restriction	Total cost restriction	Permissible error restriction
3–Optimum allocation of all strata	Use Formula (13.8) to get opt. $\bar{n}_j$.	Use Formulas (13.4) or (13.6) to get $\bar{n}$. (13.8) to get opt. n_j.	Use Formula (13.9) to get opt. $\bar{n}_j$.	Use Formula (13.10) to get $\bar{n}$. Use Formula (13.9) to get opt. $\bar{n}_j$.	Use Formula (13.11) to get $\bar{n}$. Use Formula (13.9) to get opt. $\bar{n}_j$.
4b–One stratum sample size fixed, optimum allocation of remaining strata	$n_1 = n_1$ Use Formula (13.12) to get opt. $\bar{n}_j$.	$n_1 = n_1$ Use Formulas (13.4) or (13.6) to get $\bar{n}_a$. Use Formula (13.8), using $\bar{n}_a$ for $\bar{n}$ to get opt. $\bar{n}_j$.	$n_1 = n_1$ Use Formula (13.13) to get opt. $\bar{n}_j$.	$n_1 = n_1$ Use Formula (13.10) to get $\bar{n}_a$. Use Formula (13.9), using $\bar{n}_a$ for $\bar{n}$ to get opt. $\bar{n}_j$.	$n_1 = n_1$ Use Formula (13.11) to get $\bar{n}_a$. Use Formula (13.9), using $\bar{n}_a$ for $\bar{n}$ to get opt. $\bar{n}_j$.
5b–Census of one stratum, optimum allocation of remaining strata	$n_1 = N_1$ Use Formula (13.12) to get opt. $\bar{n}_j$.	$n_1 = N_1$ Use Formulas (13.4) or (13.6) to get $\bar{n}_a$. Use Formula (13.8), using $\bar{n}_a$ for $\bar{n}$ to get opt. $\bar{n}_j$.	$n_1 = N_1$ Use Formula (13.13) to get opt. $\bar{n}_j$.	$n_1 = N_1$ Use Formula (13.10) to get $\bar{n}_a$. Use Formula (13.9), using $\bar{n}_a$ for $\bar{n}$ to get opt. $\bar{n}_j$.	$n_1 = N_1$ Use Formula (13.11) to get $\bar{n}_a$. Use Formula (13.9), using $\bar{n}_a$ for $\bar{n}$ to get opt. $\bar{n}_j$.

[1] For description of patterns, see page 230.

of deans of large state universities (widely scattered in the Midwest and Far West) as that at small private men's colleges (concentrated in New England and Middle Atlantic states). The average cost per interview had been estimated, and all that remained was to set the total sample size and apply Formula (13.8) to determine optimum allocation of the sample to the two strata. If there had been a total cost restriction on the study, Formula (13.9) would yield the total sample size required. Application of Formula (13.8) would then make the optimum allocation.

When a maximum permissible error is set (this is difficult in the deans of men study because of the financial problems of a large sample), a total n is decided upon by using Formula (13.10), and optimum allocation is again achieved with Formula (13.8).

When varying costs are known or accurately estimated, optimum sample size will tend to allocate smaller subsamples to the more expensive strata and larger subsamples to the less expensive strata.

Often this sort of optimum allocation will result in one of two situations: (a) either one stratum will be sampled at a rate that yields too small a sample for separate analysis or (b) a stratum sample size will be larger than the population of that stratum. These two cases require an alteration of the sample size of that stratum and the reallocation (optimum) of the remaining sample. The researcher who has this problem when average costs vary between strata should read the following discussion of Reasons 4 and 5 and use Exhibit 13.4 as a guide to optimum allocation procedures.

Separate analysis is often desired for one or more strata. With certain precision requirements made for the subgroup analysis, ordinary allocation through simple random sampling, proportional or optimum stratified sampling may not yield enough individuals. This problem may arise when additional variables are needed in the subgroup to satisfy separate study requirements (Reason 5) or when no additional variables are needed, but a separate analysis is required of the total sample variables (Reason 4).

Consider a case where a researcher wished to conduct an interest inventory survey in a certain school system. As a condition for granting permission to include the system's elementary school children in the survey, the superintendent requested a report on every sixth-grade child and added some questions to the questionnaire for that group. Although the researcher did not need this information, the sample design was planned to meet this restriction. Because a between-grade analysis was desired, the researcher planned a stratified simple random sample of each grade with a census of all pupils in the sixth grade. A guide to the appropriate allocation procedures for this problem, which is Pattern 5b (a census of one stratum and optimum allocation of the remaining strata), is given in Exhibit 13.4.

13.1.3 Proportional vs. Disproportional Allocation

The relative advantages and disadvantages of proportional allocation vs. disproportional allocation of total sample size to the various strata should be carefully considered as they relate to each proposed study. The major advantages and disadvantages are as follows:

Proportional allocation	*Disproportional allocation*
1. The same sampling ratio is used for each stratum. This is simple and easy to determine.	1. A different sampling ratio is used for each stratum. These ratios are sometimes complicated to determine.
2. Proportional allocation yields a self-weighting sample that requires no arithmetic weights. Sample results can be used just as tabulated to compute statistics and standard errors. The process is simple and rapid.	2. Since the sample from each stratum is disproportionate to the population contained in that stratum, the tabulated stratum data must be weighted before unbiased estimates of parameters for the total population can be computed. This is time-consuming and costly when computing estimates of many variables and when a high-speed computer is not available.
3. With certain types of populations, especially badly skewed ones, proportional allocation tends to require unwieldy and unnecessarily large sample sizes.	3. With a given sample size, optimum allocation gives the sample distribution of total sample that yields the lowest sampling error.
4. When separate analyses are to be made for certain population subgroups, proportional allocation tends to require an unnecessarily large total sample size.	4. When separate analyses are to be made for certain population subgroups, disproportional allocation permits the inclusion of the appropriate sample size from the subgroup without increasing the size of the remainder of the sample.
5. The proportional allocation of the sample does not provide for varying cost considerations among strata.	5. Optimum allocation of sample size to strata provides for cost differential considerations where the cost of surveying the population of some strata differs considerably from that of surveying other strata.

13.2 SINGLE IMPORTANT VARIABLE APPROACH TO STRATIFICATION

In almost all education surveys the researcher wants data on several variables; however, for stratification purposes it is often necessary to *assume* that only *one single* important variable exists. The strata are defined with this variable whenever possible. The following discussion assumes either that only one important variable is under consideration in the study or that all important variables are highly positively correlated with the variable used in defining the strata. Where it is possible to stratify on the basis of any one of several important variables, consideration should be given to the effect of stratification on the basis of each variable before final judgment is made.

13.2.1 When Sampling Frames Are Independent

Often the total population to be surveyed is obtainable only in two or more separate listings—perhaps even in two or more places—but a *simple random* sample of the population is desired. If numbers can be assigned to all the individuals and if a table of random numbers can be used to choose the sample, a simple random sample is possible. If, however, a systematic sampling procedure is used and one part of the population listing simply follows the one ahead, in effect, the population has been sampled by a proportionately stratified procedure. In the latter case, if stratification formulas are used in computing the statistics, smaller sampling errors will result on variables highly correlated with the stratification variable.

A corollary to this discussion is that sampling frames *must be independent* if a stratified simple random sample is to be drawn.

13.2.2 When Subgroups Must Be Treated Somewhat Differently

Discussion of this aspect of surveys, which may lead to stratification, is included in Section 13.1.1. Although some population subgroups might require a slightly different treatment necessitating stratified sampling, this is not always the case. If the question is not too involved, two or more versions may be included on all questionnaires or interview schedules with instructions to guide the respondent or interviewer to the appropriate items.

13.2.3 When Large Gains In Precision Are Made

As a goal of stratification, a gain in precision over simple random sampling is the hardest to achieve in practice. The greatest gain comes when the individuals within the strata are as much alike as possible and the strata are as different as possible with regard to *all* the important variables. The definitions of the strata often affect these factors and can either help or hinder statistical efficiency.

Some authors have said that little precision is gained from stratification in opinion or attitude studies, probably because most subgroups tend not to have extreme viewpoints and seldom will a proportion be less than 0.10 or greater than 0.90. Unless an opinion is highly skewed in a distribution, few appreciable gains will be made in precision.

Quantitative variables that approximate the ideal patterns (homogeneous within strata, heterogeneous between) are more likely to show the greatest gains in precision with use of stratification rather than simple random sampling.

13.2.4 When Subgroups Must be Adjusted for Statistical Reasons

A discussion of the adjustment of subgroups for statistical reasons was presented in Section 13.1.2.

13.2.5 When Subgroup Size Must Be Increased To Allow for More Intensive Examination Than Planned for the Total Group

As indicated in Section 13.1.2, the analysis of a subgroup on variables not included for the other subgroups calls for stratification. Unless the questions are included in all interview schedules or questionnaires and ignored on all but the ones of the specified subgroup, stratification of the population would be necessary.

If the precision requirements for the subgroup would not be met with a simple random or proportional stratified sample, a disproportional allocation of the total sample may solve the problem.

13.2.6 When Adjustments for Variable Costs Are Beneficial

A general rule of thumb to determine whether cost factors should be taken into account: If the most expensive stratum is at least three times as costly as the least expensive stratum, cost *should* be taken into account. Formula (13.9) reveals that the cost factor is a square-root function. Consequently, small differences in average costs do not make appreciable differences in the total.

Cost, as the term is used here, is the average expense required to administer survey instruments or schedules to individuals in a given stratum of the population. The total cost factor is the sum of the stratum costs required to administer a survey instrument to a given sample.

13.3 "MULTI-IMPORTANT VARIABLE" APPROACH

The efficiency of stratification is difficult to estimate when considering more than one variable; yet this is the typical condition under which stratification is employed in sample surveys in education. It is a rare study, indeed, that has only one important variable. Therefore, a discussion of the multivariable approach is necessary, although the results in terms of providing concrete answers will be meager.

No statistical formulas are available in this area, and few general guidelines exist. Consequently, a great deal of empirical judgment is needed. After the strata have been tentatively defined, each important variable must be considered separately and then an evaluation made of the overall effect. Before defining the strata, the researcher should decide what the important variables are and what the precision requirements are for *each variable.* After the strata have been defined and the necessary preliminary estimates of stratum variances are obtained for each variable, the total sample sizes necessary for measurement of each variable may be ascertained. This can be a very involved procedure.

If the largest sample size needed is not too large, given the budgetary or other resource limitations imposed on the study, it is selected as the sample size for the study. In the case of optimum allocation, the variable calling for the largest sample size should be used as the basis for allocation of the sample to the strata. When n_j (the number of individuals in a sample from a stratum) is known for all strata, the preliminary estimates of the standard error may be determined for the variables. If this allocation has increased any of the standard errors beyond the requirements established at the beginning of the study, the researcher should investigate the following possibilities: (a) increasing the total sample size, (b) increasing the size of the sample in the one or more strata with the greatest variance of the variables with an oversize standard error, or (c) reallocating the sample in the direction of the optimum allocation of the variable with the oversize standard error. Reallocation of the same total sample size will mean that the precision requirements will not be met for the variable requiring the largest sample; however, reallocation and an increase in total sample size will permit the researcher to come nearer to meeting the original precision requirements.

13.4 PLANNING THE SURVEY THAT EMPLOYS A STRATIFIED SIMPLE RANDOM SAMPLE DESIGN

The problem of designing a stratified simple random sampling plan involves a sequence of decisions that should be regarded as *circular* rather than linear. Often, the effects of each alternative cannot be foreseen when making a tentative decision; consequently, the final decision is frequently the result of a series of trials and errors.

The following discussion assumes that—

- The decision has been made to conduct a particular study.
- The population has been defined and as much preliminary information as possible about it has been gathered.
- A preliminary, but fairly firm decision, has been made to use a stratified simple random sampling technique.
- The important variables have been defined and put into question form.
- At least a tentative questionnaire has been developed.
- The estimates to be computed for important variables and the precision requirements for them have been tentatively settled. These decisions are, of course, all subject to change if some aspect or requirement of the data or if the collection and processing of the data put undue strain on other requirements or standards. The next problem facing the researcher is to define the strata.

Some stratification systems are predetermined by the availability of sampling frames or interest in certain natural subgroups. In other cases, strata must be developed to reduce the sampling error of as many important variables as possible. Usually, the *reason* for deciding upon a stratification design is the primary factor in determining the strata limits.

If stratification is being used because no unified sampling frame is available for the entire population (Reason 1), the subgroup divisions are determined essentially by the available frames. Combining small strata or dividing a large stratum may sometimes seem advisable. Combining strata can be done only if (a) the subgroups are logically related and the new subgroup fits reasonably into the entire subgroup scheme and (b) there is some way the sampling frames can be combined to draw one simple random sample from the newly combined subgroups. Division of a subgroup into two or more smaller strata requires that the individuals in each of the smaller strata be separately identifiable in the sampling frame.

When different procedures for measuring the same variable on several subgroups call for stratification (Reason 2), the subgroups are probably naturally defined. Further subdivisions may be made if desired, but the restrictions mentioned previously are still applicable. Similar situations occur when stratification is required because a special analysis is planned for one or more subgroups (Reasons 4 and 5).

Variable costs (Reason 6) also affect the number of ways to stratify a population. If benefit is to occur from optimum allocation of the sample, the greatest benefit will be gained by stratifying the population so that the average cost of each stratum is as divergent as possible from the average costs of other strata.

When stratification is selected as a means of reducing sampling error (Reason 3), the picture becomes much more complicated. The ideal stratification of population into subgroups for statistical efficiency is based on the variable in question. In terms of a single important variable, a stratification system that divides the population into categories of that important variable will probably *not* give an efficient estimate of other variables. This is because the population is divided into subgroups that are maximally homogeneous within and maximally heterogeneous between strata in terms of a *single* characteristic. Other characteristics may, and probably will, vary in different ways. The exception to this is for those variables that are highly positively correlated with the single important variable.

For example, the mean of teachers' salaries for school systems is highly positively correlated with the per pupil expenditure in the school system and is less highly correlated with the per capita income of the school system. On the other hand, average teacher salary may have little if any correlation with the average class size in the school system or with teacher opinion on a specific question.

Often, not enough preliminary information is available on a *single* most important variable for all individuals in a population to prestratify the population by that variable. For instance, a researcher interested in teachers' salaries seldom knows a teacher's salary until the teacher is asked. The researcher usually seeks another variable for which information is available and that is as highly correlated with the variable of interest as possible. In teachers' salaries, it might be size of school system, years of experience in the school system, or highest college degree held.

To give a second illustration, for a national study of teacher evaluation practices in school systems, the systems had to be stratified by the number of *teachers* employed in the system. However, the population listing of school systems had only the number of pupils enrolled in the system. Since the number of pupils in a system is highly positively correlated with the number of teachers in that system, stratification by enrollment could be expected to yield substantial gains in the study.

When more than one important variable is concerned, the best stratification is by some variable that correlates highly with the greatest number of other variables.

13.5 TOTAL SAMPLE SIZE AND STRATUM ALLOCATION

The various approaches to determining the total number of individuals necessary for a sample of a given population when using a stratified simple random sampling plan can be classified as either inductive or deductive.

- *Inductive*—In the inductive approach, the total sample size is determined by treating the strata as though they were separate populations. The appropriate sample size for each stratum is determined as described in Chapter 12 for simple random samples. These strata sample sizes are added together to determine the total sample size. Since the inductive approach builds a total sample size from the sum of the various stratum sample sizes, no special formulas apply to the entire sample size.

- *Deductive*—In the deductive approach, the total sample size is determined first, and then it is allocated to the various strata by either proportional or optimum allocation procedures. Specific formulas are available in the deductive approaches both for the determination of sample size required to meet certain precision and cost requirements and for the allocation of the total sample size to each of the various strata.

The items of information needed in deductive formulas and the symbols used to indicate the items are as follows:

N the number of individuals in the total population.

N_j the number of individuals in the population in the jth stratum.

N_j/N the true weight for the jth stratum.

r the number of strata.

e   the maximum permissible error for the statistic used as an estimate (one-half the width of the confidence interval desired precision).

$\hat{\sigma}_j$ an estimate of the standard deviation of the characteristic in the jth stratum based on Formulas (13.1) or (13.2).

Z   the relative deviation (standard score) corresponding to the level of confidence desired.

Other symbols used are as follows:

$\tilde{n}$ the preliminary estimate of the total number of individuals necessary for a sample when certain restrictions are made.

$\tilde{n}_j$ the preliminary estimate of the number of individuals necessary in a stratum for a sample when certain restrictions are made.

opt. $\tilde{n}_j$ the preliminary estimate of the number of individuals necessary for a stratum for optimum allocation of the total sample to strata when certain restrictions are made.

n_a the preliminary estimate of the total number of individuals necessary for a sample *minus* the number in the specially treated stratum (a). The remaining strata are treated as a total group with total sample size equal to n_a.

Note that the formulas dealing with the determination of total sample size and its allocation to the various strata call for either the variance (σ^2) or an estimate of the variance ($\hat{\sigma}^2$) of the specific variable for each of the strata when either proportional allocation or optimum allocation is planned. Chapter 12 discusses the problems of obtaining preliminary estimates of the variance ($\hat{\sigma}^2$) of estimated means and totals for variables and of estimated proportions when the data are attributes. These methods may be extended and applied to (a) the populations of the separate strata in stratified sampling and (b) an estimate of the variance of the variable in each stratum ($\hat{\sigma}_j^2$) obtained. In other words, the procedures discussed in Chapter 12 for randomly or systematically sampling the total population are applicable to *each* of the separate strata *considered* as separate populations.

The formula for estimating the variance (σ^2) of a population *mean* and population *total* (presented earlier) is repeated for convenience—as Formula (13.1). An estimate of the variance (σ^2) of the *proportion* or *percentage* of a population attribute is obtained by Formula (13.2). These two formulas are helpful in estimating variances for use in formulas that estimate total sample size and its allocation to specific strata.

If the characteristic is a variable (i.e., estimating *means* or *totals*), an estimate of the *variance of the characteristic* in a population is given by Formula (13.1):

$$\hat{\sigma}^2 = S^2 = \frac{\Sigma (X - \bar{X})^2}{n - 1} \qquad (13.1)$$

where:

$\hat{\sigma}^2$ is an estimate of the variance of a variable in a population.

S^2 is the variance of a variable in a sample.

> X   is any value of a variable for an analysis unit (AU).
>
> $\overline{X}$ is the arithmetic mean of the observations of a variable in a sample.
>
> n   is the number of AU's in the sample.

If the characteristic is an attribute (i.e., estimating *proportions*), an estimate of the *variance of the characteristic* in the population is found by Formula (13.2):

$$\hat{\sigma}^2 = p(1-p)/n \tag{13.2}$$

where:

> $\hat{\sigma}^2$ is an estimate of the variance of an attribute in a population.
>
> p   is the proportion of observations possessing this attribute in the sample of size n.

Formulas (13.3) through (13.6) may be appropriately applied when estimating the *total* sample size $(\tilde{n})$ required in stratified random sampling with either *proportional* or *optimum* allocation of the total sample size to the various strata. The introductions to the formulas state the conditions particularly applicable to the formula.

The total sample size necessary when estimating the mean of a characteristic or the proportion of a population possessing a characteristic when proportional allocation is planned is found as follows:

$$\tilde{n} = NZ^2 \sum_j^r N_j \hat{\sigma}_j^2 \div (N^2 e^2 + Z \sum_j^r N_j \hat{\sigma}_j^2) \tag{13.3}$$

where the symbols are as defined earlier in this chapter.

The total sample size necessary when estimating the mean of a characteristic or the proportion of a population possessing a certain characteristic when optimum allocation is planned is found as follows:

$$\tilde{n} = Z^2 (\sum_j^r N_j \hat{\sigma}_j)^2 \div (N^2 e^2 + Z^2 \sum_j^r N_j \hat{\sigma}_j^2) \tag{13.4}$$

where the symbols are as defined earlier in this chapter.

The total sample size necessary when estimating the total of a characteristic when proportional allocation is planned is found as follows:

$$\tilde{n} = N \sum_j^r N_j \hat{\sigma}_j^2 \div (e^2/Z^2 + \sum_j^r N_j \hat{\sigma}_j^2) \tag{13.5}$$

where the symbols are as defined earlier in this chapter.

The total sample size necessary when estimating the total of a characteristic when optimum allocation is planned is found as follows:

$$\tilde{n} = (\sum_j^r N_j \hat{\sigma}_j)^2 \div (e^2/Z^2 + \sum_j^r N_j \hat{\sigma}_j^2) \qquad (13.6)$$

where the symbols are as defined earlier in this chapter.

Formulas (13.7) through (13.13) may be appropriately applied in *allocating* the total sample size as determined by one of Formulas (13.3) through (13.6) to the various strata. Exhibit 13.4 provides a helpful guide to the appropriate application of Formulas (13.3) through (13.13).

The size of the sample in each stratum when using proportional allocation is found as follows:

$$\tilde{n}_j = \tilde{n} \, N_j/N \qquad (13.7)$$

where the symbols are as defined earlier in this chapter and $\tilde{n}$ is defined by Formula (13.3) or (13.5).

To estimate the optimum stratum sample sizes, sometimes it is necessary to know or estimate C and the C_j,

where:

- C is the total cost of the sample and is the aggregate of the stratum costs ($\Sigma n_j C_j$) required to administer a survey instrument or schedule to a sample.
- C_j is the average cost per unit required to administer survey instruments or schedules to individuals in the jth stratum of the population.

The total cost of a study (C) is usually fixed by the available financial resources; the problem is to allocate this total cost to the various strata in a way that will provide the smallest standard error in the estimate of the parameter. The average cost per unit in the jth stratum (C_j) must be estimated or determined from other studies or from a pilot study.

When the average cost per unit in each stratum does not vary from stratum to stratum and the total sample size is fixed, the optimum size of each stratum (Pattern 3) is found by:

$$opt. \, \tilde{n}_j = N_j \hat{\sigma}_j \tilde{n} / \sum^r N_j \hat{\sigma}_j \qquad (13.8)$$

where the symbols are as defined earlier in this chapter and $\tilde{n}$ is defined by Formulas (13.4) or (13.6).

If the average cost per unit in the most costly stratum is at least three times as costly as the least costly stratum, it may be wise to take the cost factor into account when allocating a sample among strata.

When the average cost per unit in each stratum varies widely from stratum to stratum and the total sample size is fixed, the optimum size of each stratum (Pattern 3) is found by:

$$\text{opt. } \tilde{n}_j = (\tilde{n} N_j \hat{\sigma}_j / \sqrt{C_j}) \div (\sum^r [N_j \hat{\sigma}_j / \sqrt{C_j}]) \qquad (13.9)$$

where the symbols are as defined earlier in this chapter.

When the average cost per unit in each stratum varies widely from stratum to stratum and there is a total cost restriction, the total sample size necessary is given by:

$$\tilde{n} = (C \sum^r N_j \hat{\sigma}_j / \sqrt{C_j}) \div (\sum^r N_j \hat{\sigma}_j \sqrt{C_j}) \qquad (13.10)$$

where the symbols are as defined earlier in this chapter.

When the total sample size has been determined, Formula (13.9) may be applied to allocate the sample optimally among strata.

When the average cost per unit in each stratum varies widely from stratum to stratum and a maximum permissible error is specified, the total sample size necessary is found as follows:

$$\tilde{n} = \left[\frac{\sum^r N_j \hat{\sigma}_j \sqrt{C_j}}{e^2 + \sum^r N_j \hat{\sigma}_j} \right] \times \left[\sum^r N_j \hat{\sigma}_j / \sqrt{C_j} \right] \qquad (13.11)$$

where the symbols are as defined earlier in this chapter.

When the total sample size has been determined, Formula (13.9) may be applied to allocate the sample optimally among the strata.

On occasion, an optimum sample size, as determined by the preceding formulas, will not allocate a large enough stratum sample size to allow for special analysis of one of the stratum. When this happens, the sample size necessary for that stratum can be determined by the methods described in Chapter 12 for simple random samples; this sample size can then be considered as fixed for that one stratum and Formula (13.12) applied.

If the average cost per unit in each stratum does not vary from stratum to stratum and the total sample size and the size of one of the strata are fixed, the optimum size of each of the remaining strata is found as follows:

$$\text{opt. } \widetilde{n}_j = N_j \hat{\sigma}_j \, (\widetilde{n} - n_1) \div [\overset{r}{\Sigma} N_j \hat{\sigma}_j - N_1 \hat{\sigma}_1] \qquad (13.12)$$

where the symbols are as defined earlier in this chapter and:

- N_1 is the number of individuals in the population in the fixed stratum.
- $\hat{\sigma}_1$ is the estimated standard deviation of a characteristic in the fixed stratum.
- n_1 is the number of individuals in the sample in the fixed stratum.

A comparison of results obtained after optimum allocation of all strata by Formula (13.8) and the results obtained after increasing n_1 and optimum allocation of the remaining strata by Formula (13.12) shows that the standard error will be increased if the same maximum total sample size is used. This is logical because the change in sample sizes is away from the optimum that is designed to allocate the sample to obtain minimum sampling error.

When the average cost per unit in each stratum varies widely from stratum to stratum, the total sample size is fixed, and one stratum requires a larger sample size than optimally allocated by Formula (13.9), the optimum sample sizes for the remaining strata are given by:

$$\text{opt. } \widetilde{n}_j = \left(N_j \hat{\sigma}_j / \sqrt{C_j} \right)(\widetilde{n} - n_1) \div [\, \overset{r}{\Sigma} (N_j \hat{\sigma}_j / \sqrt{C_j}) - N_1 \hat{\sigma}_1 / \sqrt{C_1} \,] \qquad (13.13)$$

where the symbols are as defined earlier in this chapter and in Formula (13.12).

If the average costs do not vary among the strata and there is a maximum permissible error restriction, or if the average costs do vary and there is a maximum cost restriction, or if there is a maximum permissible error restriction, this information must be used in determining the total sample size. When the specially treated stratum sample size is fixed (Pattern 4b) or a census of the population is planned for one stratum (Pattern 5b), the total size of the remaining sample is determined as if the special strata were not included. If the adjustment on the special stratum was an increase in size over that indicated by optimum allocation procedures and the procedures indicated in Exhibit 13.4 are followed, other than optimum results for the total sample estimates will be obtained. The deviations will be in the direction of a larger sample size and smaller sampling errors than required.

For a guide to solutions to other optimum allocation problems with given restrictions and various patterns see Exhibit 13.4.

In stratified simple random sampling *independent samples* of a specific size must be drawn from *each* stratum. In doing this three steps are needed:

- The elements or individuals in each stratum must be separately identifiable for sampling purposes.
- The sample size (n_j) for each stratum must be determined by the procedures and formula previously discussed in this section.

- Within each separate stratum, the sample from that stratum must be selected by using the techniques for simple random or systematic sampling described in Chapter 2.

In drawing the sample, it is important to label or in some way identify the stratum to which each individual selected in the sample belongs. Such identification of all individuals in the sample is needed for computing the sample statistics and the population estimate.

13.6 ESTIMATING POPULATION PARAMETERS AND THEIR STANDARD ERRORS

The necessary formulas for analyzing the distribution of characteristics obtained from stratified simple random sampling plans are presented first for a *proportional* allocation plan and then, where there are differences, for *disproportional* samples. Although some may seem complicated, they are relatively simple in logic. Basically, they are the same formulas as those used for computing the mean or some other statistic of a simple random sample, with subscripts to identify the statistic with its stratum and an appropriate set of arithmetic weights for the stratum. The formula for computing a particular statistic becomes logical when it is viewed in two parts: (a) procedures for computing the basic statistic and (b) procedures for weighting that statistic.

13.6.1 Definition of Symbols To Be Used

The following symbols are used in the formulas presented in Chapter 13:

In the total group	In a stratum	Definition
	subscript j	is the index number of a stratum.
N	N_j	is the number of individuals in the population.
	N_j/N	is the true stratum weight.
n	n_j	is the number of AU's in the sample.
r		is the number of strata in the distribution.
	subscript i	is the index number of an AU in the jth stratum.
	X_{ji}	is the value of a characteristic of the ith AU in the jth stratum.
	$\sum^{N_j} X_{ji}$	is the sum of the values of the characteristic as measured on the AU's in the jth stratum in the population.
	$\sum^{n_j} X_{ji}$	is the sum of the values of the characteristic as measured on the AU's in the jth stratum in the sample.

In the total group	In a stratum	Definition
	f_j	is the number of AU's possessing a certain characteristic in the jth stratum and may refer to either the population or the sample.
$\hat{\mu}$	$\hat{\mu}_j$	is an unbiased estimate of the arithmetic mean of the observations of a characteristic in a population.
$\bar{x}$	$\bar{x}_j$	is the arithmetic mean of the observations of a characteristic in a sample.
$\bar{x}_w$		is the weighted mean of the observations of a characteristic in a sample.
$\hat{\sigma}^2$	$\hat{\sigma}^2_j$	is an unbiased estimate of the variance of a characteristic in a population.
S^2	S^2_j	is the variance of a characteristic based on sample observations.
$\sum\limits_{}^{r} \sum\limits_{}^{n_j} (X_{ji} - \bar{X})^2$		is the sum of the squared deviations of observations of all AU's in the sample from the mean of all the observations. It can be found by: $$\Sigma\Sigma X_{ji}^2 - (\Sigma\Sigma X_{ji})^2 \div n$$
	$\sum\limits_{}^{n_j}(X_{ji} - \bar{X}_j)^2$	is the sum of the squared deviations of the sample observations of the jth stratum from the mean of the same stratum.
$\hat{T}$	$\hat{T}_j$	is an unbiased estimate of the population total or aggregate of values of the characteristic as measured for the AU's in the sample.
$\hat{\Pi}$	$\hat{\Pi}_j$	is an unbiased estimate of the proportion of AU's possessing a specified characteristic in a population.
p	p_j	is the proportion of AU's possessing a specified characteristic in a sample.
q	q_j	is the proportion of AU's not possessing a specified characteristic in the sample.
$\hat{\sigma}_{\bar{x}}$	$\hat{\sigma}_{\bar{x}_j}$	is an estimate of the standard error of the sample mean, i.e., the standard deviation of the distribution of sample means of all possible samples of size n from a given population.
$s_{\bar{x}}$	$s_{\bar{x}_j}$	is the sample standard error of the sample mean, i.e., the standard deviation of the distribution of sample means of all possible samples of size n from a given population.

In the total group	In a stratum	Definition
$1 - n/N$	$1 - n_j/N_j$	is the finite population correction factor.
S_w^2		is the pooled within-stratum variance (i.e., the weighted sum of the variances of all strata).
$\hat{\sigma}_T$	$\hat{\sigma}_{T_j}$	is an estimate of the standard error of a total, i.e., the standard deviation of the distribution of population totals or aggregates estimated from all possible samples of size n from a given population.
S_T	S_{T_j}	is the sample standard error of a sample total, i.e., the standard deviation of the distribution of population totals or aggregates estimated from all possible samples of size n from a given population.
$\hat{\sigma}_p$	$\hat{\sigma}_{p_j}$	is an estimate of the standard error of the sample proportion, i.e., the standard deviation of the distribution of sample proportions of all possible samples of size n from a given population.
S_p	S_{p_j}	is the sample standard error of the sample proportion, i.e., the standard deviation of the distribution of sample proportions of all possible samples of size n from a given population.

13.7 FORMULAS FOR STRATIFIED SIMPLE RANDOM SAMPLING–PROPORTIONAL ALLOCATION

In stratified simple random sampling with proportional allocation, the population is divided into two or more meaningful strata and simple random samples are selected from each stratum by using the *same* sampling ratio for *all* strata. In general, proportional allocation, which selects the *same proportion* of individuals from each strata, results in subsamples of *differing* sizes from each of the strata. This method of allocation of sample size to strata provides every individual in the population with the same probability of being chosen in the sample; hence, proportional allocation yields a *self-weighting* sample that requires *no* arithmetic weights. As in nonstratified sampling plans, a *systematic* sampling procedure may be substituted for the simple random sampling procedure within strata if *no systematic variation* in the sampling frame exists that correlates with the variables being measured. However, the same procedure—either simple random or systematic—should be used in *all* strata.

When these procedures have been followed in the sampling operation, the sample statistics and their standard errors are computed appropriately by Formulas (13.14) through (13.35).

An unbiased estimate of an ungrouped data mean of a stratum from a stratified simple random sample is found as follows:

$$\hat{\mu}_j = \overline{X}_j = \sum_{i}^{n_j} X_{ji} / n_j \qquad (13.14)$$

An unbiased estimate of an ungrouped data mean of a population from a stratified simple random sample drawn proportionately from each stratum is found as follows:

$$\hat{\mu} = \bar{X} = \sum_{}^{r} \sum_{}^{n_j} X_{ji} / n \tag{13.15}$$

An unbiased estimate of an ungrouped data variance of a stratum from a stratified simple random sample is found as follows:

$$\hat{\sigma}_j^2 = S_j^2 = \sum_{}^{n_j} (X_{ji} - \bar{X}_j)^2 / (n_j - 1) \tag{13.16}$$

The computational formula for Formula (13.16) is as follows:

$$\hat{\sigma}_j^2 = S_j^2 = \frac{\sum_{}^{n_j} X_{ji}^2 - \frac{[\sum_{}^{n_j} X_{ji}]^2}{n_j}}{n_j - 1} \tag{13.17}$$

An unbiased estimate of the within-stratum variance (ungrouped or grouped data) *of a population from a stratified simple random sample drawn proportionally from each stratum is found as follows:*

$$\hat{\sigma}_w^2 = S_w^2 = \sum_{}^{r} n_j S_j^2 / n \tag{13.18}$$

An estimate of the standard error of a mean of a finite stratum from a stratified simple random sample without replacement is found as follows:

$$\hat{\sigma}_{\bar{X}_j} = S_{\bar{X}_j} = \sqrt{\frac{S_j^2}{n_j}(1 - n_j/N_j)} \tag{13.19}$$

An estimate of the standard error of a mean for a very large stratum (or when sampling from a finite population with replacement) from a stratified simple random sample is found as follows:

$$\hat{\sigma}_{\bar{X}_j} = S_{\bar{X}_j} = \sqrt{S_j^2 / n_j} \tag{13.20}$$

An estimate of the standard error of a mean when sampling from a finite population without replacement using proportional stratified simple random sampling is found as follows:

$$\hat{\sigma}_{\bar{X}} = S_{\bar{X}} = \sqrt{(1 - n/N) \times (S_w^2 / n)} \qquad (13.21)$$

An estimate of the standard error of the mean when sampling from a finite population without replacement using proportional stratified simple random sampling (when strata variances are considered equal) and can, therefore, be pooled is found as follows:

$$\hat{\sigma}_{\bar{X}} = S_{\bar{X}} = \sqrt{(1 - n/N) \times (S_{po}^2 / n)} \qquad (13.22)$$

where:

$$S_{po}^2 = \sum_{}^{r} \sum_{}^{n_j} (X_{ji} - \bar{X}_j)^2 / (n - r)$$

Formula (13.22) is applicable in situations of proportional sampling from strata *only when stratum variances can be considered equal.* This judgment may be approximated by the researcher, but more objective procedures should be used for results that deserve a high degree of confidence. (See U.S. Department of Commerce, 1966.)

An unbiased estimate of the total or aggregate value of a stratum from a stratified simple random sample is found as follows:

$$\hat{T}_j = N_j \bar{X}_j \qquad (13.23)$$

An unbiased estimate of the total or aggregate value of a stratified simple random sample when drawn proportionally from each stratum is found as follows:

$$\hat{T} = N\bar{X} \qquad (13.24)$$

An estimate of the standard error of a total or aggregate value of a stratum from a stratified simple random sample is found as follows:

$$\hat{\sigma}_{\hat{T}_j} = S_{\hat{T}_j} = \sqrt{(N_j^2 S_j^2 / n_j) \div (1 - n_j / N_j)} \quad (13.25)$$

An estimate of the standard error of a total or aggregate value of a stratified simple random sample when drawn proportionately from each stratum is found as follows:

$$\hat{\sigma}_{\hat{T}} = S_{\hat{T}} = \sqrt{(N^2 S_w^2 / n) \div (1 - n/N)} \quad (13.26)$$

An unbiased estimate of the proportion of AU's possessing a certain characteristic in a stratum from a stratified simple random sample is found as follows:

$$\hat{\Pi}_j = p_j = f_j / n_j \quad (13.27)$$

An unbiased estimate of the proportion of AU's possessing a certain characteristic in a population estimated from a stratified simple random sample is found as follows:

$$\hat{\Pi} = p = \sum^r N_j p_j / N \quad (13.28)$$

An estimate of the standard error of a proportion of AU's possessing a certain characteristic in a stratum from a stratified simple random sample is found as follows:

$$\hat{\sigma}_{p_j} = S_{p_j} = \sqrt{[p_j q_j / (n_j - 1)] \div (1 - n_j / N_j)} \quad (13.29)$$

An estimate of the standard error of a proportion of AU's possessing a certain characteristic in a population from a stratified simple random sample when drawn proportionally from each stratum is found as follows:

$$\hat{\sigma}_p = S_p = \sqrt{\frac{N-n}{N} \left[\sum^r \frac{N_j^2}{N^2} \cdot \frac{p_j q_j}{(n_j - 1)} \right]} \quad (13.30)$$

13.8 FORMULAS FOR STRATIFIED SIMPLE RANDOM SAMPLING– DISPROPORTIONAL ALLOCATION

This sampling plan calls for dividing the population into two or more meaningful strata and selecting simple random samples from each stratum. The sampling ratio used for each stratum is, in general, different from one or more other strata; hence, the sample results require arithmetic weights to yield unbiased estimates of population parameters and their standard errors. The procedure used to determine the sample size or the sampling rate for each stratum may have followed any one of the several patterns, including optimum allocation, described previously in Chapter 13. The important factor is that the proportion of individuals selected in at least one stratum differs from the proportion selected in one or more other strata If a disproportional procedure of any type was used in selecting the sample, formulas appropriate for computing the sample statistics and standard errors of disproportional samples must be used. These formulas may differ from those that give estimates for a proportionally allocated sample, which were presented in the previous section. When the formula for disproportional allocation is the same as the corresponding formula for proportional allocation, it will *not* be repeated in this section. Whenever a *difference exists,* the formula appropriate for computing the sample statistic or standard error of data collected in a disproportionate random sample of a population is given here.

An unbiased estimate of the mean of a population from a stratified simple random sample drawn disproportionally from each stratum is found as follows:

$$\hat{\mu} = \bar{X}_w = \sum^r N_j \bar{X}_j \Big/ \sum^r N_j \qquad (13.31)$$

An estimate of the standard error of a mean when sampling from a finite population without replacement using disproportional stratified simple random sampling is found as follows:

$$\hat{\sigma}_{\bar{X}} = S_{\bar{X}} = \sqrt{\sum^r (N_j^2 S_j^2 / n_j)(1 - n_j/N_j) \div N^2} \qquad (13.32)$$

An unbiased estimate of a total or aggregate when sampling from a finite population without replacement using a disproportional stratified simple random sample is found as follows:

$$\hat{T} = \sum^r N_j \bar{X}_j \qquad (13.33)$$

An estimate of the standard error of a total or aggregate value of a stratified simple random sample when drawn disproportionately from each stratum is found as follows:

$$\hat{\sigma}_T = S_T = \sqrt{\sum_{j}^{r} (N_j^2 S_j^2 / n_j)(1 - n_j / N_j)} \qquad (13.34)$$

An estimate of the standard error of a proportion of AU's possessing a certain characteristic in a population from a stratified simple random sample when drawn disproportionally from each stratum is found as follows:

$$\hat{\sigma}_p = S_p = \sqrt{\Sigma N_j (N_j - n_j) p_j q_j \div \left[(n_j - 1)(N^2)\right]} \qquad (13.35)$$

14
CLUSTER SAMPLING PLANS

The smallest units into which a population can be divided are termed the elements or analysis units (AU's)—the individuals comprising the population to be sampled. In *stratified* random sampling the elements of the population are divided into groups named *strata*, and the elements within each stratum are randomly sampled as individuals. In *cluster* sampling the elements of the population are divided into groups called *clusters*, and the clusters are randomly sampled. In *stratified* sampling the sampling units are the *elements* or individuals that comprise the population, while in *cluster* sampling the sampling units are *groups* of individuals. In both cases, the ultimate sample to which the questionnaires are to be sent—or with whom the interview schedules are to be administered—is composed of the individuals or AU's of the population.

Cluster sampling can be thought of as a procedure in which the population is sampled in chunks or blocks, rather than as separate individuals. If *all* of the individuals in all the selected chunks or clusters are taken in the sample of the population, this is termed a "one-stage cluster random sampling plan." If a *sample* of the individuals in each of the selected clusters is taken as the final sample of the population, this is a "two-stage cluster random sampling plan." The term *random* is used to denote the procedure used in the selection process. If a *systematic* procedure is used, it should be so noted.

In a "two-stage cluster sampling plan," the clusters are referred to as "primary sampling units" (PSU's) or "first-stage sampling units." The individuals or elements in the selected clusters from which the second-stage sample is drawn are referred to as "secondary sampling units" (SSU's).

14.1 WHEN CLUSTER SAMPLING IS APPROPRIATE

The conditions that produce statistically *efficient* stratified sampling also make for statistically *inefficient* cluster sampling. The more alike (homogeneous) elements are within strata and the more different (heterogeneous) elements are between strata, the smaller the sampling error when a stratified sampling plan is used. In contrast, the more different the elements are within clusters and the more like each other the clusters are, the smaller the sampling error will be when a cluster sampling plan is used.

Unfortunately, in educational surveys, making heterogeneous clusters is virtually impossible, and usually the researcher has little choice but to retain the features of the clusters as they appear in the population. Frequently, the features of natural clusters may not be conducive to small sampling errors. The ideal conditions for cluster sampling are (a) wide differences among individuals in clusters and (b) clusters similar in composition, i.e., that have small differences among such cluster statistics as means, percentages, and standard deviations. The latter condition suggests that each cluster is itself a miniature representation of the total population.

Two main reasons, based on practical rather than statistical considerations, can lead to a decision to use a cluster random sampling plan in educational surveys: deficiencies in sampling frames and cost considerations.

14.1.1 Deficiencies in Sampling Frames

The most frequent use of cluster sampling designs occurs because of the lack of complete and up-to-date listings of the individuals in the population to be surveyed. Assume that a researcher wishes to survey English teachers in the nation's secondary schools. At present, no national listing of English teachers exists, and constructing such a listing in a reasonable time is virtually impossible since there are a large number of English teachers in the United States. The nearest thing to a complete listing of English teachers would be a list of secondary schools, which would provide a way of cluster sampling English teachers. A random sample of secondary schools could be selected, and then the researcher would write the principal of each and request the names of all English teachers. If a questionnaire were mailed to *all* the teachers on the lists of names received, it would be a "one-stage cluster sample." If the lists of names received were *randomly sampled,* and the researcher mailed a questionnaire only to this sample, it would be a "two-stage cluster sample" of U.S. English teachers.

The purpose of cluster sampling is not to obtain a more reliable sample in terms of the number of AU's included, nor is it to get the most reliable results per unit of cost, but to overcome fundamental *deficiencies in sampling frames.* Although cluster designs typically have larger sampling errors per AU's surveyed than do simple random designs, a cluster design often makes a survey feasible where otherwise it would be impossible. Thus, cluster sampling is sometimes necessary because a complete, up-to-date, and accessible listing of individual members of the population does not exist.

14.1.2 Cost Considerations

The second reason for using cluster sampling plans in educational surveys is to reduce costs. Seldom is this a major reason in mailed surveys because obtaining a mailed response from widely scattered persons costs the same as it would if the respondents were clustered geographically. Therefore, where cost is determined entirely by the *number* of AU's in the sample, the sample design that will produce the most reliable results for a fixed-size sample will involve no clustering of the sample at all, providing the sampling frames are available.

In interview-type studies, however, cost can be crucial because of the time and travel required to interview the persons selected for the sample. The same would be true in making an inspection survey of school faculties over a large area. Another instance in which cost factors may become important is in surveys such as those involving the administration of test instruments to samples of students in large school systems or, perhaps, in several school systems.

In the above examples cluster sampling can prove beneficial in helping to reduce survey costs or at least hold them within budgetary limits. By grouping the AU's of the population into geographic clusters before they are sampled, cluster sampling can minimize travel time, travel cost, and the number of interviewers or testers required to conduct a given survey.

14.1.3 Constraints on Balance of Chapter Discussion

Because in educational surveys cluster sampling is used mainly *to overcome deficiencies in population listings or sampling frames,* the discussion in this chapter is restricted to such conditions. Therefore, the following conditions are assumed to exist in the subsequent discussion:

- Cluster sampling has been forced upon the surveyor because a complete, up-to-date listing of the population elements is not available.
- The surveyor does have a listing of a set of clusters, such as school systems, schools, or classes, which contains all the elements in the population.
- The surveyor does *not* have discretion over the number of population AU's within the various clusters; the number is fixed for each cluster and varies from cluster to cluster.

When the researcher needs to investigate the cost of cluster sampling, extensive treatments and illustrations of cost factor relationships can be found in Mace (1964, Chapter 11) and Jessen (1978, Section 4.7).

14.2 STEPS IN CLUSTER RANDOM SAMPLING

The procedural steps in cluster random sampling for both one- and two-stage plans are given below in outline form. In cluster sampling and in the analysis of cluster sampling results, *each element in the sample must be identified with the cluster* to which it belongs. Plans must be made to record the unique association for each AU. If this is not done with the utmost care, sample results and analyses will probably be substantially influenced for the worse.

14.2.1 One-Stage

Step 1. Divide the population into clusters. The *clusters* should be as much *alike* one another in terms of the variations of individuals within the groups as is possible. There should be as much *difference* among individuals *within single clusters* as is possible. In most educational surveys no choice in cluster composition is possible, and the surveyor must use natural clusters just as they appear in the population, e.g., school systems, schools, or classes. For natural clusters of fixed size, the surveyor should consult Chapter 15 (combination sampling plans) before drawing a sample.

Step 2. Determine the sampling proportion (or the number of clusters) for use in drawing the sample. The discussions and references appearing later in this chapter will be helpful in making this decision.

Step 3. Draw a sample of clusters using a simple random procedure, when possible, or a systematic random procedure from all the clusters. Such procedures have been described earlier.

Step 4. Collect desired information from *all* elements contained in the selected clusters, being careful to note the cluster into which each AU falls.

14.2.2 Two-Stage

Step 1. Divide the population into clusters, as described in Step 1 of one-stage cluster sampling.

Step 2. Determine the sampling proportion (or number of clusters) for use in drawing a sample of clusters; all the clusters in the population are termed PSU's. The discussion and references appearing later in this chapter will be helpful in making this decision.

Step 3. Draw a sample of clusters using a simple random procedure, whenever possible, or a systematic random procedure from all the clusters or PSU's, as described earlier.

Step 4. Determine either the sampling proportion or the number of elements needed for drawing a sample of elements from each of the PSU's. All the elements contained in the PSU's are termed SSU's. The SSU's may be sampled in either of two ways, depending upon the decision of the surveyor: (a) the SSU's in all PSU's may be sampled at the *same* sampling rate or (b) the SSU's in various PSU's may be sampled at *different* rates. In self-weighting samples, the advantages of which are pointed out in Chapter 13, the SSU's in the various PSU's will be sampled at the same rate.

Step 5. Draw the sample by *consistently* employing a simple random procedure, whenever possible, or a systematic procedure for PSU's, regardless of whether the same or different sampling rates are decided upon in Step 4.

Step 6. Collect the desired information from individuals selected in the second-stage sample, being careful to note the cluster into which each AU falls.

14.3 DETERMINING SAMPLE SIZE

The base line for comparing the precision of various sampling plans is the simple random sample. Therefore, the only satisfactory approach in making comparisons of precision among various sampling plans is to see how the results of a specific plan compare with the results that a simple random sample of the population could be expected to yield. Although this sounds simple enough, in practice it is often difficult if not impossible. This is particularly true in connection with cluster sample designs since the performance of cluster sampling in relation to that of simple random sampling depends so greatly on the distribution of the AU's within the clusters.

When the clusters have *wide* distributions of individuals within them, cluster sampling can approach the precision of simple random sampling; at other times it is much less precise than simple random sampling. Thus, giving general advice on sample size requirements to the researcher faced with having to use a cluster design is difficult, especially when a population divided into natural clusters over which the researcher has no control in terms of the distribution of individuals within clusters is being sampled. In the final analysis there may be no definite answer to the problem of sample size when cluster sampling, and the researcher may be forced to make what amounts to an "educated guess."

Thus, the problem of estimating sample size in cluster samples becomes little more than speculation, especially when scant preliminary information about the population is available. In fact, some major statistical texts term it just that—speculation. Because no simple discussion of the problem is possible, the researcher faced with a cluster sampling problem should study the following references carefully before making even a tentative decision about the appropriate sample size for the study: Cochran (1963); Hansen, Hurwitz, and Madow (1953, Vols. 1 and 2); Stephan and McCarthy (1958); and Sukhatme (1958).

14.3.1 Sampling Probabilities

Although few general rules exist in regard to sample size and sample allocation when cluster sampling, discussing a few problems that arise most frequently in educational surveys may be helpful to save time in problem identification among the many possibilities discussed in the previously cited references.

When cluster sampling with clusters *unequal* in size, which is typical in educational surveys, at least three choices are available for selecting the clusters to be in the sample:

- The size of the clusters can be disregarded, and all clusters can be selected with equal *probabilities* of being included in the sample.
- The size of the clusters can be taken into consideration, and clusters can be sampled with a *probability that is proportional to their size.*
- The clusters may be stratified by size, and clusters can be selected with either equal or unequal probabilities *within* strata. (This combination sample design will be considered in Chapter 15.)

No general rule exists for determining which of these choices will yield the most precise estimates. The conditions most favorable to *probability proportional to size* (pps) estimates are those in which the cluster means are unrelated or uncorrelated with the cluster sizes. If there are substantial differences in the sizes of clusters, it is well to consider the possibility of stratifying clusters before sampling.

Selecting a sample of clusters with *equal probability* from a population of clusters is identical to the procedures for simple random sampling or systematic random sampling of individuals (Chapter 2). The clusters become the sampling units rather than the individuals.

Selecting clusters with pps is done in the following manner:

Step 1. Clusters are arranged in a random listing, such as alphabetical (shown in Exhibit 14.1, Col. 1), and the size of each cluster is recorded (Col. 2).

Step 2. Record the cumulative frequencies of school sizes in Col. 3, proceeding from School A to B to C to D.

EXHIBIT 14.1 – A HYPOTHETICAL LIST OF SCHOOLS TO BE USED AS CLUSTERS WHEN SAMPLING CLUSTERS WITH PROBABILITY PROPORTIONAL TO SIZE OF SCHOOL, AS MEASURED BY NUMBER OF CLASSROOM TEACHERS

Cluster (school)	Size N_k (number of teachers)	ΣN_k	Assigned range
(1)	(2)	(3)	(4)
A	20	20	1-20
B	15	35	21-35
C	25	60	36-60
D	10	70	61-70

Step 3. Assign the probability range for each school, starting with the first school on the list as 1 (Col. 4).

Step 4. Select a cluster by drawing a random number between 1 and 70. Suppose it is 29. Since this number falls between 21 and 35, School B is selected to be in the sample of clusters.

Step 5. Proceed as in Step 4 until the proper number of sample selections have been made. Whenever a cluster is selected more than once, it is included that many times in the sample. This will be recognized as sampling *with* replacement.

Note: Rather than sample clusters with pps, in many cluster sampling operations in education it will be simpler to stratify the clusters by size, and sample clusters with equal probability within strata (see Chapter 15).

14.3.2 Clusters Needed for Fixed Sample Size

In educational research a typical problem in cluster sampling by mail is that only a fixed maximum number of questionnaires can be handled within the survey budget. The study can be no more accurate than the maximum number of questionnaires mailed to individuals will allow. The problem in cluster sampling is, How many clusters should the researcher choose in order to yield a sample of 2,000 individuals?

Assume the sampling plan is a one-stage design where clusters are sampled with equal probability and *all* the individuals in the sample of clusters are to be sent a questionnaire. If the number of individuals in each cluster is known, then the researcher can note when 2,000 persons have been included by keeping a cumulative total of the number of individuals in the selected clusters.

If the researcher does not know the number of individuals in each cluster, the best way to estimate the number of clusters needed to yield 2,000 individuals in the ultimate sample is to divide 2,000 by the average number of individuals per cluster. If the total number of individuals in the population and the total number of clusters are known, the average number of individuals per cluster can easily be calculated. If, however, the total number of individuals in the population is not known, the average number per cluster must be estimated by a pilot study or some other method.

If the sampling plan is a *two-stage* design and the individuals in the sample of clusters are to be sampled with *equal proportions* for all clusters, the estimated number of clusters needed would be the same as that given for a one-stage sample except the number should be divided by the sampling fraction for the second stage, as shown in Formula (14.1). This formula applies when sampling unequal clusters with equal probability in the first stage and elements within all selected clusters with equal probability in the second stage.

$$\tilde{g} = (n/\bar{N}_k) \div f_2 \qquad (14.1)$$

Where:

$\tilde{g}$ is the estimated number of clusters needed to yield a sample of size n.

n   is the maximum number of individuals to be in the sample.

$\bar{N}_k$ is the average number of individuals per cluster in the population, where there are k clusters in the population.

f_2 is the sampling fraction to be used in drawing the second-stage sample.

14.3.3 Clusters Needed for Desired Precision

Perhaps the most reasonable question for the researcher to ask when faced with a cluster sample design is, How many clusters will be needed for the final sample data to be equivalent in precision to a simple random sample of the same population? A firm answer depends upon thorough knowledge of the population being sampled, the variance of specific characteristics within clusters, and the variance of the characteristics among clusters. Typically, such complete information is only known about populations that are studied repeatedly, as in a series of continuing annual or biennial studies. The researcher faced with the question of the sample size needed to yield cluster sample statistics of desired precision should consult Chapter 6 of Hansen, Hurwitz, and Madow (Vol. 1, 1953), which discusses *intraclass correlation* and *measures of homogeneity* as they relate to the relative precision of cluster sampling techniques. Next, the researcher should consult Chapters 9, 10, and 11 of Cochran (1963), followed by Chapters 6, 7, and 8 of Sukhatme (1958).

14.4 ESTIMATING POPULATION PARAMETERS AND THEIR STANDARD ERRORS

Although determining how many clusters should be selected and how many AU's should be selected from each cluster to achieve a specific degree of accuracy is difficult, some idea of the precision of the estimates, based on the sample data, is important.

This, too, is no simple matter; for if comprehensive information about the distribution of characteristics among and within clusters in the population is not known, it must be estimated from the sample. Again, Cochran (1963) and Hansen, Hurwitz, and Madow (Vols. 1 & 2, 1953) must be consulted before deciding on the most appropriate computational procedures. The techniques and formulas outlined in this section should assist the researcher in reaching a decision more quickly.

In estimating population parameters and their standard errors from cluster sample data, it is important to understand the appropriate use of a *ratio estimate* that is *slightly biased.* Up to this point, computing *unbiased* estimates of population parameters from sample data has been an almost exclusive concern. The unbiased estimate is considered the best estimate in simple random sampling and, usually, in stratified random sampling. But this is not so in cluster random sampling.

In cluster sampling, there are three ways to compute an estimate of a population mean from a cluster sample. One of these yields *unbiased* estimates of the mean, and the other two yield *biased* estimates. However, the standard errors of the latter two are generally smaller than those of the former. The three methods are as follows:

- *Mean based on estimates of totals.* To illustrate: Suppose the researcher wishes to estimate the mean salary of teachers in a population by using cluster sample data. From the sample data an estimate could be made of two totals for the population: (a) the aggregate *amount* paid to *all* teachers in the population and (b) the total *number* of teachers in the population. We can divide (a) by (b) to obtain an estimate of the mean salary of the population. Although this would be an *unbiased estimate,* it would probably have a large standard error.

- *Unweighted mean of the cluster means.* The second method would be to compute the mean salary for teachers in each cluster and to take the simple *unweighted mean* of all the cluster means. Obviously, this will give a *biased and inconsistent* estimate, but its standard error will probably be *less* than the unbiased estimate. Since this method is seldom used, it will not be discussed here.

- *Ratio-to-size estimate.* If the total salary paid to teachers in each cluster is computed, these cluster totals added, and the number of teachers in the sample divided into the totals, a third estimate of the mean of the salaries paid to teachers in the population is obtained. This is the simple arithmetic mean of the sample and in cluster sampling is termed a "ratio-to-size estimate," or simply a "ratio estimate" since it is the ratio of two random variables. One variable is the *aggregate of salaries* paid teachers in the various clusters (the numerator of the fraction) and the other is the *number* of teachers in the various clusters (the denominator of the fraction). Both of these vary randomly according to the particular clusters selected in the sample.

  This *ratio* method yields an estimate that is *biased but consistent,* and the bias decreases as the number of sample clusters increases. With a moderately large number of clusters, the bias becomes trivial and can be ignored. Most important, the standard error of this ratio estimate is usually smaller than in the other two methods. Therefore, it is the generally preferred method for computing estimates of population parameters from cluster sample data when the number of clusters is comparatively large. This applies to estimates of proportions and totals as well as to estimates of means.

Both *ratio estimate* and *unbiased estimate* formulas will be given in this section of Chapter 14. The formulas and procedures apply to one- and two-stage cluster random samples of the following types:

- *One-stage cluster random sample.* As used in this section the term means that—
  1. All the sampling is done in a single operation.
  2. The clusters vary in size.
  3. A simple random or systematic selection method is used in selecting the clusters.
  4. The clusters are selected with equal probability.
- *Two-stage cluster random sample.* As used in this section the term means that—
  1. The sampling procedure is performed in two operations.
  2. The primary sampling units (PSU's) vary in size.
  3. The PSU's are selected by a simple random or systematic sampling procedure.
  4. The PSU's are selected with equal probability.
  5. The secondary sampling units (SSU's) are selected from each of the PSU's by a simple random or systematic sampling procedure.
  6. The sampling rate by which SSU's are selected is the same for all PSU's.

14.5 DEFINITION OF SYMBOLS TO BE USED

The following symbols for the total set of AU's under consideration and for individual clusters of AU's are used in the formulas presented in the remainder of Chapter 14:

In the total group	In a cluster	Definition
Subscript k		is the index number of a cluster.
N	N_k	is the number of individuals in the population.
n	n_k	is the number of individuals in the sample.
$\bar{N}$		is the mean size of the clusters in the population, i.e., the average number of individuals per cluster in the population.
$\hat{\bar{N}}$		is an estimate of the mean size of the clusters in the population. If the mean number of individuals per cluster in the population ($\bar{N}$) is not obtainable, the mean number of individuals per cluster in the sample clusters ($\bar{n}$) can be used as an estimate ($\hat{\bar{N}}$) of $\bar{N}$.

In the total group	In a cluster	Definition
$\bar{n}$		is the mean size of the clusters in the sample, i.e., the average number of individuals per cluster in the sample clusters.
G		is the number of clusters in the population.
g		is the number of clusters randomly sampled from the G clusters in the population.
	Subscript i	is the index number of an individual (sometimes an interval) in the kth cluster.
	X_{ki}	is the value of a characteristic of the ith individual in the kth cluster.
μ	μ_k	is the arithmetic mean of the observations of a characteristic in a population.
$\hat{\mu}$	$\hat{\mu}_k$	is an unbiased estimate of the arithmetic mean of the observations of a characteristic in a population.
$\bar{X}$	$\bar{X}_k$	is the arithmetic mean of the observations of a characteristic in a sample.
$\bar{X}_w$		is the weighted mean of the observations of a characteristic in a sample.
	S_k^2	is the variance of a characteristic based on sample observations.
	$1 - n_k/N_k$	is the finite population correction factor
$1 - g/G, \dfrac{G-g}{G}$		is the finite population correction factor where g/G is the first-stage sampling fraction.
$1 - \bar{n}/\bar{N}$		is the finite population correction factor where $\bar{n}/\bar{N}$ is the second-stage sampling fraction.
$\hat{\sigma}_{\bar{X}}, S_{\bar{X}}$		is an estimate of the standard error of the sample mean, i.e., the standard deviation of the distribution of sample means of all possible samples of size n from a given population.
$\hat{\mu}', \bar{X}'$		is a biased ratio estimate of the arithmetic mean of the observations of a characteristic in a population.
$\hat{\sigma}_{\bar{X}'}, S_{\bar{X}'}$		is an estimate of the standard error of the biased estimates of the population mean.
T	T_k	is the total or aggregate of values of the characteristic as measured for the individuals in the population.

In the total group	In a cluster	Definition
$\hat{T}$	$\hat{T}_k$	is an unbiased estimate of the total or aggregate of values of the characteristic as measured for the individuals in the population.
$\hat{\sigma}_{\hat{T}}, S_{\hat{T}}$		is an estimate of the standard error of an unbiased estimate of a total, i.e., the standard deviation of the distribution of population totals or aggregates estimated from all possible samples of size n from a given population.
$\hat{T}'$		is a biased ratio estimate of the total or aggregate of values of the characteristic as measured for the individuals in the population.
$\hat{\sigma}_{\hat{T}'}, S_{\hat{T}'}$		is an estimate of the standard error of the biased ratio estimate of the population total.
	f_k	is the number of individuals possessing a certain characteristic in a cluster—for the entire cluster or for a sample.
π	π_k	is the proportion of individuals possessing a certain characteristic in the population.
$\hat{\pi}$	$\hat{\pi}_k$	is an unbiased estimate of the proportion of individuals possessing a certain characteristic in the population.
	p_k	is the proportion of individuals possessing a certain characteristic in a sample.
$\hat{\sigma}_p, S_p$		is an estimate of the standard error of the sample proportion, i.e., the standard deviation of the distribution of sample proportions of all possible samples of size n from a given population.
$\hat{\pi}', P'$		is a biased estimate of the proportion of individuals possessing a certain characteristic in a population.
$\hat{\sigma}_{P'}, S_{P'}$		is an estimate of the standard error of the biased estimate of a population proportion.

14.6 FORMULAS FOR A SINGLE-STAGE CLUSTER SAMPLE, WITH CLUSTERS VARYING IN SIZE AND SELECTED WITH EQUAL PROBABILITY

The mean value of a characteristic in a cluster (k) when the data are ungrouped is found as follows:

$$\mu_k = \sum^{N_k} X_{ki}/N_k \tag{14.2}$$

An unbiased (weighted) estimate of a population mean of the observations of a characteristic is found as follows:

$$\hat{\mu} = \bar{X}_w = \frac{G}{gN} \cdot \sum^{g} \sum^{N_k} X_{ki} \tag{14.3}$$

An estimate of the standard error of the unbiased estimate of the population mean is found as follows:

$$\hat{\sigma}_{\bar{X}_w} = S_{\bar{X}_w} = \sqrt{\frac{G(G-g)}{g(g-1)N^2} \sum^{g} (T_k - \bar{N}\bar{X}_w)^2} \tag{14.4}$$

The biased ratio estimate of the population mean of the observations of a characteristic is found as follows:

$$\hat{\mu}' = \bar{X}' = \sum^{g} \sum^{N_k} X_{ki}/n \tag{14.5}$$

(Note that this is the simple arithmetic mean of the sample observations.)

An estimate of the standard error of the biased ratio estimate of the population mean given in Formula (14.5) is found as follows:

$$\hat{\sigma}_{\bar{X}'} = S_{\bar{X}'} = \sqrt{\frac{G(G-g)}{g(g-1)N^2} \sum^{g} (T_k - N_k \bar{X}')^2} \tag{14.6}$$

The total or aggregate value of the observations of a characteristic in a cluster is found as follows:

$$T_k = \sum^{N_k} X_{ki} \tag{14.7}$$

An unbiased estimate of the population total or aggregate value of the observations of a characteristic is found as follows:

$$\hat{T} = \frac{G}{g} \sum_{}^{g} T_k \qquad (14.8)$$

An estimate of the standard error of the unbiased estimate of the total is found by either Formula (14.9) or Formula (14.10):

$$\hat{\sigma}_{\hat{T}} = S_{\hat{T}} = \sqrt{\frac{G(G-g)}{g(g-1)} \sum_{}^{g} (T_k - \bar{N}\bar{X}_w)^2} \qquad (14.9)$$

$$\hat{\sigma}_{\hat{T}} = S_{\hat{T}} = NS_{\bar{X}_w} \qquad (14.10)$$

When there is little variation of cluster means ($\bar{X}_k$) and large variation of cluster sizes (N_k), a biased *ratio estimate* is preferred to the unbiased estimate because it usually has a smaller standard error.

A biased ratio estimate of the population total or aggregate value of the observations of a characteristic is found as follows:

$$\hat{T}' = N\bar{X}' \qquad (14.11)$$

An estimate of the standard error of the biased ratio estimate of the population total is found by either Formula (14.12) or Formula (14.13):

$$\hat{\sigma}_{\hat{T}'} = S_{\hat{T}'} = \sqrt{\frac{G(G-g)}{g(g-1)} \sum_{}^{g} (T_k - N_k \bar{X}')^2} \qquad (14.12)$$

$$\hat{\sigma}_{\hat{T}'} = S_{\hat{T}'} = NS_{\bar{X}'} \qquad (14.13)$$

The proportion of individuals possessing a characteristic in a cluster (k) is found as follows:

$$\pi_k = f_k/N_k \qquad (14.14)$$

Both the aggregate or frequency (the numerator) and the number or base of a proportion (the denominator) will vary from sample to sample in cluster sampling with unequal size clusters. Therefore, an estimate of a population proportion from cluster sample data is a ratio of two random variables and subject to the conditions previously described for *ratio estimates* of a mean. Such estimates will be biased but consistent, and the bias will decrease as the sample size increases. For all practical purposes, the extent of this bias is negligible for percentages based on cluster sample data.

A biased ratio estimate of the proportion of individuals in a population possessing a certain characteristic is found as follows:

$$\hat{\pi}' = p' = \sum_{}^{g} f_k / \sum_{}^{g} N_k \qquad (14.15)$$

An approximate estimate of the standard error of the biased estimate of the population proportion is found as follows:

$$\hat{\sigma}_{p'} = S_{p'} \sim \sqrt{\frac{G(G-g)}{g(g-1)N^2} \sum_{}^{g}(f_k - N_k p')^2} \qquad (14.16)$$

14.7 FORMULAS FOR A TWO-STAGE CLUSTER SAMPLE, WITH CLUSTERS VARYING IN SIZE, THE FIRST STAGE SELECTED WITH EQUAL PROBABILITY, AND A CONSTANT SECOND-STAGE SAMPLING FRACTION (SELF-WEIGHTING)

An unbiased estimate of the mean of a cluster (k) when the data are ungrouped is found as follows:

$$\hat{\mu}_k = \overline{X}_k = \frac{1}{n_k} \sum_{}^{n_k} X_{ki} \qquad (14.17)$$

The sample variance of a cluster (k) is found as follows:

$$S_k^2 = \frac{\sum_{}^{n_k} (X_{ki} - \overline{X}_k)^2}{n_k - 1} \qquad (14.18)$$

A computational formula equivalent to Formula (14.18) when data are ungrouped is as follows:

$$S_k^2 = \frac{\sum\limits^{n_k} X_{ki}^2 - \frac{(\sum\limits^{n_k} X_{kj})^2}{n_k}}{n_k - 1} \qquad (14.19)$$

An unbiased estimate of the population mean is found as follows:

$$\hat{\mu} = \bar{X} = \sum\limits^{g} \sum\limits^{N_k} X_{ki} / n \qquad (14.20)$$

An estimate of the standard error of the unbiased estimate of the population mean is found as follows:

$$\hat{\sigma}_{\bar{X}} = S_{\bar{X}} = \sqrt{\frac{G(G-g)}{gN^2} \cdot \frac{\sum\limits^{g}(N_k\bar{X}_k - \bar{N}\bar{X})^2}{g-1} + \frac{Gg(\bar{N}-\bar{n})}{nN^2} \sum\limits^{g} N_k S_k^2} \qquad (14.21)$$

Although the estimate of the population mean is unbiased, it is not the most efficient. A biased *ratio estimate,* which is available (see Formula 14.22), usually has a smaller sampling error. The bias is negligible when n becomes large; this makes the *ratio estimate preferable in survey work.* For an explanation of ratio estimates see the discussion at the beginning of this section.

The ratio estimate of the population mean given by Formula (14.22) is identical to that of the unbiased estimate of the population mean given by Formula (14.20). This condition exists only in the case of an unbiased estimate of the population mean obtained from a self-weighting sample. Although the unbiased estimate and the biased ratio estimate of the population mean are the same, the *estimates of their variances are different.* For this reason the researcher must be particularly careful to apply Formulas (14.21) and (14.23) appropriately.

A biased ratio estimate of the population mean is found as follows:

$$\hat{\mu}' = \bar{X}' = \sum\limits^{g} \sum\limits^{N_k} X_{ki}/n \qquad (14.22)$$

An estimate of the standard error of the biased ratio estimate of the population mean is found as follows:

$$\hat{\sigma}_{\bar{X}'} = S_{\bar{X}'} = \sqrt{\frac{G(G-g)}{g(g-1)N^2} \sum^g N_k^2 (\bar{X}_k - \bar{X}')^2 + \frac{G(\bar{N}-\bar{n})}{nN^2} \sum^g N_k S_k^2} \qquad (14.23)$$

An unbiased estimate of the population total for a cluster (k) is found as follows:

$$\hat{T}_k = N_k \bar{X}_k \qquad (14.24)$$

An unbiased estimate of the population total is found as follows:

$$\hat{T} = N\bar{X} = \sum^g \hat{T}_k \qquad (14.25)$$

An estimate of the standard error of the unbiased estimate of a population total is found either by Formula (14.26) or Formula (14.27):

$$\hat{\sigma}_{\hat{T}} = S_{\hat{T}} = \sqrt{\frac{G(G-g)}{g(g-1)} \sum^g (N_k \bar{X}_k - \bar{N}_k \bar{X})^2 + \frac{Gg(\bar{N}-\bar{n})}{n} \sum^g N_k S_k^2} \qquad (14.26)$$

$$\hat{\sigma}_{\hat{T}} = S_{\hat{T}} = NS_{\bar{X}} \qquad (14.27)$$

A biased ratio estimate of the population total is found as follows:

$$\hat{T}' = N\bar{X}' \qquad (14.28)$$

An approximate estimate of the standard error of the biased ratio estimate of the population total is found either by Formula (14.29) or Formula (14.30):

$$\hat{\sigma}_{\hat{T}'} = S_{\hat{T}'} \sim \sqrt{\frac{G(G-g)}{g(g-1)} \sum N_k^2 (\bar{X}_k - \bar{X}')^2 + \frac{G(\bar{N}-\bar{n})}{n} \sum^g N_k S_k^2} \qquad (14.29)$$

$$\hat{\sigma}_{\hat{T}'} = S_{\hat{T}'} \sim NS_{\bar{X}} \qquad (14.30)$$

An unbiased estimate of the population proportion of individuals possessing a certain characteristic in a cluster (k) is found as follows:

$$\hat{\pi}_k = p_k = f_k/n_k \tag{14.31}$$

In two-stage cluster sampling both the aggregate or frequency (the numerator) and the number or base of a proportion (the denominator) will vary from sample to sample when sampling with unequal size clusters. Therefore, an estimate of a population proportion from such data is a ratio of two random variables and subject to the conditions as previously described for *ratio estimates* of a mean. Such estimates will be biased but consistent, and the bias will decrease as the sample size increases. Practically, the extent of this bias is negligible in most sample surveys in education.

A biased estimate of the population proportion of individuals possessing a certain characteristic is found as follows:

$$\hat{\pi}' = p' = \frac{\sum\limits^{g} f_k}{\sum\limits^{g} n_k} \tag{14.32}$$

An approximate estimate of the standard error of the biased estimate of the population proportion is found as follows:

$$\hat{\sigma}_{p'} = S_{p'} \sim \sqrt{\frac{G(G-g)}{gN^2} \frac{\sum\limits^{g} N_k^2 (p_k-p')^2}{g-1} + \frac{G(\bar{N}-\bar{n})}{nN^2} \sum\limits^{g} N_k \frac{n_k p_k (1-p_k)}{n_k-1}} \tag{14.33}$$

14.8 SUMMARY

In cluster random sampling the elements of the population are divided into groups called *clusters,* and a sample of clusters is selected randomly. When all the elements in the selected clusters are included in the sample of the population, it is a *one-stage cluster random sampling plan.* When a *sample* of the elements in each of the selected clusters is chosen to be in the final sample of the population, it is a *two-stage cluster random sampling plan.*

The ideal conditions for cluster sampling are (a) wide differences among elements in clusters and (b) clusters similar in composition from cluster to cluster. The latter condition suggests that each cluster is itself a miniature representation of the total population.

Two nonstatistical reasons can lead to the use of a cluster sampling plan in educational surveys: (a) deficiencies in sampling frames and (b) cost considerations. Because cluster sampling is used mainly in educational surveys to overcome deficiencies in population listings or the sampling frames, the discussion in this chapter has been limited to such conditions. There is no simple solution to most cluster sampling problems; therefore, the researcher considering a cluster sampling design should study the suggested references carefully.

15

COMBINATION SAMPLING PLANS

The principles of stratifying and clustering can be combined in various ways to form a sample design adapted to the needs and requirements of a specific survey. The combinations presented in this chapter by no means exhaust the possibilities; they are merely indicative of the types that can be useful.

Most of the combination sample designs used in education surveys result from efforts to overcome basic deficiencies in sampling frames or to optimize survey cost and sample variation. Chapter 14 points out that the conditions that produce *efficient* stratified sampling produce *inefficient* cluster sampling. Combination sample designs offer the researcher the possibility of combining these counteracting effects to achieve a balance between them. Some common types of combinations used in educational surveys are discussed in this chapter.

15.1 STRATIFIED ONE-STAGE CLUSTER

The more homogeneous elements are within strata and the more heterogeneous elements are among strata, the better will be the results when a stratified sampling plan is used. The reverse is true when a cluster sampling plan is used.

An educational surveyor usually has no control over the heterogeneity of the elements within clusters and, therefore, has no alternative but to retain the clusters just as they appear in the population. Typically, the elements in educational surveys are relatively homogeneous within the clusters for the characteristics being surveyed.

The sampling variation resulting from homogeneity of elements within clusters may be reduced by stratifying the clusters into an appropriate number of strata, in which the clusters are relatively alike within strata and different between strata, and then sampling the clusters within these strata. This combination of sample designs is termed "stratified cluster random sampling." If all elements in the selected clusters are included in the survey, it is termed a "stratified one-stage cluster random sample." If the elements of the selected clusters are sampled, it is a "stratified two-stage cluster random sample."

The following are the steps in *stratified one-stage cluster* random sampling:

Step 1. Group the clusters containing the total population elements into an appropriate number of strata, established on the basis of one of the characteristics under study or a characteristic highly positively correlated with the characteristics under study. The clusters within a stratum should be as nearly alike as possible, and the clusters within the stratum should differ as much as possible from the clusters in other strata.

Step 2. Determine the number of clusters to be drawn from each stratum. (See Chapters 13 and 14.) Clusters may be sampled *from the strata* either proportionately or disproportionately as fits the needs of the particular study. In general, sampling within strata with probability proportional to size of cluster will tend to reduce the size of the variance.

Step 3. Draw a sample of clusters from each stratum by a random or systematic procedure. (See Chapter 2.)

Step 4. Collect desired information from *all* individuals contained in selected clusters.

Exhibit 15.1 gives an example of the data needed in preparing to conduct a stratified one-stage cluster random sample of English teachers in the United States. The sampling frame is a listing of secondary schools stratified by the number of pupils enrolled. This is an example of a practical problem in which combination sampling designs are helpful. The elements in the population are teachers, but the only available characteristic for stratifying clusters is enrollment. Since the number of pupils and the number of teachers have a high positive correlation, the amount of sampling variability among teachers can be reduced by stratifying clusters by the number of pupils. This is acceptable procedure so long as the characteristics under study have a high positive correlation with this factor.

EXHIBIT 15.1—DATA NEEDED FOR A STRATIFIED, DISPROPORTIONATE ONE-STAGE CLUSTER RANDOM SAMPLE OF ENGLISH TEACHERS IN WHICH THE SAMPLING FRAME IS A LISTING OF SECONDARY SCHOOLS IN THE UNITED STATES STRATIFIED BY THE NUMBER OF PUPILS ENROLLED

Stratified population clusters (Secondary schools)			Number of schools in sample	Sampling rate for selecting schools	Expected number of English teachers in sample schools[b]
Stratum number	Stratum size (enrollment)	Number in population[a]			
(1)	(2)	(3)	(4)	(5)	(6)
1	3,000-6,099	98	25	1:4	926
2	1,000-2,999	2,738	50	1:55	741
3	300-999	8,532	50	1:171	241
4	1-299	12,846	100	1:129	112
Total		24,214	225		2,020

[a] Actual number of secondary schools contained in NEA Research's card deck listing for 1958-59.

[b] Based on the total enrollment in the sampled schools in each stratum divided by 135, the estimated average number of students taught by one English teacher.

In Exhibit 15.1 the resulting stratified cluster sample of 2,020 elements was selected disproportionately from the four strata. Therefore, it is *not* a self-weighting sample; and data for each strata must be appropriately weighted to yield unbiased estimates of the population parameters.

Usually, in education surveys when stratified sampling designs are combined with one-stage cluster sample designs, the clusters will be selected from the strata at disproportionate sampling rates. This approach usually reduces the sampling variation in this type of combination sampling plan.

15.2 STRATIFIED, DISPROPORTIONATE TWO-STAGE CLUSTER WITH EQUAL SAMPLING RATES IN SECOND STAGE

If the researcher chooses *a sample* of the English teachers in the selected secondary schools, it would be a *stratified, disproportionate two-stage cluster sample.* The teachers (SSU's: secondary sampling units) may be selected from the sample of schools (PSU's: primary sampling units) selected in the first stage in two ways:

- At the *same* sampling rate in each of the sample schools in all strata—the resulting sample of teachers being a *stratified, disproportionate two-stage cluster sample selected with equal sampling rates in the second stage.*
- At sampling rates *differing* from stratum to stratum—the resulting sample of teachers being a *stratified, disproportionate two-stage cluster sample selected with unequal sampling rates in the second stage.*

Since the *schools* were originally selected with sampling rates differing from stratum to stratum (stratified disproportionate sampling), the latter type of sample (unequal rates) can be designed to yield *self-weighting* estimates of population parameters, but the former type of sample (equal rates) cannot be so designed. If disproportionate stratified sampling is used in selecting the PSU's in the first stage and all PSU's are sampled at the *same* sampling rate in the second stage, the resulting sample of SSU's will require weighting to yield unbiased estimates of population parameters. For this reason most educational surveyors try to avoid this type of two-stage sample.

15.3 STRATIFIED, DISPROPORTIONATE TWO-STAGE CLUSTER SAMPLE WITH UNEQUAL SAMPLING RATE IN SECOND STAGE

Self-weighting two-stage samples have decided advantages and, therefore, are the most commonly used types of two-stage samples. They are preferred because the actual sample data yield either unbiased estimates or slightly biased but consistent estimates of population parameters without complicated sets of stratum and cluster weights. This is desirable even when a high speed computer is available for processing sample data. The discussion of *stratified, disproportionate two-stage cluster samples selected with unequal sampling rates in the second stage* will be restricted here to the *self-weighting* type sample.

Many complex problems are involved in stratified two-stage cluster sampling because within-stratum and among-stratum variances and within-cluster and among-cluster variances all affect the parameter estimates obtained from sample data. Therefore, precise sample size determination in such samples is difficult; and *there is no substitute for adequate preliminary information* regarding the nature of the population to be surveyed and the expected variances to be encountered. Even with considerable preliminary information, sample size determination is sometimes little more than speculation; and, frequently, *preliminary* sample size estimates are based on the *assumption* that the two-stage procedure will yield data equivalent to those of a simple random sample. Although such *assumptions* usually have little, if any, basis in fact, the researcher sometimes has no alternative from which to start in making a preliminary estimate of sample size because adequate information about the population to be surveyed is not available. Under such conditions, this preliminary estimate of sample size becomes only the assumed *starting point* from which the researcher attempts to construct a more realistic estimate of the sample size needed to meet the precision requirements of the survey.

The steps in making a *self-weighting stratified, disproportionate two-stage cluster sample* are as follows:

Step 1. Determine (at least tentatively) what the total size of the ultimate sample (of SSU's) should be in terms of the total number of population elements. (See Chapter 12 for the principles of sample size determination.)

Step 2. Obtain the overall sampling rate or sampling fraction by dividing the sample size determined in Step 1 into the total number of elements in the population. For example, the sampling rate can be expressed as 1:1,000, or as 1/1,000, or as 0.001. Thus, each element in the population should have an overall chance of 1 in 1,000 of being included in the sample.

Step 3. Group the PSU's containing the total population of SSU's into an appropriate number of strata, as described in Step 1 of stratified one-stage cluster sampling.

Step 4. Determine the number of PSU's (or the sampling rate) to be used to select clusters from each of the strata. (See Step 2 of stratified one-stage cluster sampling.)

Step 5. Obtain the sampling rate for selecting PSU's in each stratum by dividing the number of PSU's to be selected in each stratum by the total number of PSU's in the population in that stratum.

Step 6. Draw a sample of PSU's at the appropriate sampling rates from each stratum by either a simple random or systematic procedure, as described in Chapter 2.

Step 7. Determine the self-weighting sampling rate for sampling SSU's within PSU's in each stratum by dividing the overall sampling rate established in Step 1 by the rate with which PSU's were selected from that stratum as determined in Step 5. For example, if the overall sampling rate for the survey is 1/1,000 and if PSU's in Stratum A were sampled in the first stage at the rate of 1/10, the self-weighting sampling rate to use for sampling SSU's within PSU's drawn from Stratum A is 1/100. Repeat this process for each stratum.

Step 8. Draw either a simple random or systematic sample of SSU's from each of the PSU's selected in the first stage by using the appropriate self-weighting sampling ratio for that stratum as determined in Step 7.

Step 9. Collect desired information from the sample of population elements (SSU's) selected in the second stage (Step 8), *being careful to note the cluster into which each analysis unit falls.*

When PSU's are selected from within strata by using probability proportional to size of cluster in the nine-step procedure outlined above, slight modifications must be made so that SSU's are selected from each PSU to yield a self-weighting sample. Because each PSU selected with probability proportional to size within a stratum has its individual probability of being selected, that specific probability must be considered in determining the sampling rate for selecting SSU's from that particular PSU in the second stage. This procedure is necessary if a self-weighting sample is to be obtained.

Exhibit 15.2, which gives approximate data used in selecting the national sample for NEA Research's 1980 Teacher Opinion Poll, illustrates a stratified two-stage systematic self-weighting sample of the approximately 2,024,000 classroom teachers in the United States obtained by the nine-step procedure described above. The total sample size was established at 2,025 teachers. Thus, the overall sampling rate for teachers was 1:1,000.

The number of school systems to be selected within the various strata is indicated in Column 4 of Exhibit 15.2. Consequently, the sampling rates for PSU's from each stratum are the rates shown in Column 5. To obtain the self-weighting sampling rate for selecting teachers from each of the selected systems, the overall sampling rate of 1/1,000 was divided by the sampling rate used in sampling systems from that stratum in the first stage (Column 5). These second-stage sampling rates are shown in Column 7. Sampling at this rate should yield the expected number of teachers (SSU's) shown in Column 8. (The actual sample size of 2,165 was slightly larger than that expected, due primarily to the variability within stratum of numbers of teachers in the clusters.) Thus, when the sampling rate for selecting the PSU's from a stratum in the first stage (Column 5) is multiplied by the sampling rate for the SSU's in the second stage (Column 7), the combined probability for selecting teachers from that stratum is the same as the combined probability of selecting teachers from every other stratum (Column 9). The sample of teachers, therefore, yields self-weighting estimates of population parameters.

A modification of this two-stage procedure is to select systems within strata *in the first stage* with probability proportionate to size or estimated size of the school system and *in the second stage* to select teachers within these systems with appropriate sampling rates to yield a self-weighting sample. This procedure has the advantage of reducing the standard errors of the population parameters estimated from the sample.

Formula (15.1), which should be used to make the sample self-weighting when the PSU's have been selected from within strata by using probability proportional to size or estimated size of PSU, determines the number of individuals to be selected from each cluster chosen in the first stage of the sample:

EXHIBIT 15.2.—DATA USED IN SELECTING A SELF-WEIGHTING STRATIFIED DISPROPORTIONATE TWO-STAGE CLUSTER SAMPLE OF CLASSROOM TEACHERS BY USING A LISTING OF PUBLIC SCHOOL SYSTEMS IN THE UNITED STATES STRATIFIED BY THE NUMBER OF PUPILS ENROLLED, 1979-80

System stratum	Stratum limits (enrollment)	Total number of systems	Number of systems in sample	Sampling rate for systems (1st stage)	Estimated number of teachers in population	Sampling rate for teachers (2nd stage) (1,000 ÷ Col. 5)	Expected number of teachers in sample	Probability of selecting a particular teacher
(1)	(2)	(3)	(4)	(5)	(6)	(7)	(8)	(9)
1	100,000 & over	22	22	1:1	207,000	1:1,000	207	.001
2	50,000-99,999	47	27	1:1.7	134,000	1:588	131	.001
3	25,000-49,999	118	34	1:3.5	170,000	1:286	171	.001
4	12,000-24,999	347	42	1:8.3	254,000	1:120	256	.001
5	6,000-11,999	926	51	1:18.2	358,000	1:54.9	359	.001
6	3,000- 5,999	1,856	45	1:41.2	364,000	1:24.3	363	.001
7	1,200- 2,999	3,475	42	1:82.7	336,000	1:12.1	336	.001
8	300- 1,199	4,836	34	1:142.2	169,000	1:7.0	170	.001
9	1- 299	4,004	32[a]	1:125.1	32,000	1:8.0[a]	32[a]	.001
Total		15,631	339	—	2,024,000	—	2,025	.001

Source:

NEA Research: Data used in 1980 Nationwide Teacher Opinion Poll, February 1980.

[a] The teachers in the many small school systems selected in the first stage from the stratum were combined as if in a single system and the appropriate number of teachers was selected by use of random numbers.

$$n_{jk} = \frac{N_{jk}(n_j/N_j)}{g_j p_{jk}} \qquad (15.1)$$

where

- n_{jk} is the number of individuals to be selected from the kth cluster in the jth stratum.

- g_j is the number of clusters randomly sampled (with replacement) from the G_j clusters in the jth stratum.

- p_{jk} is the probability that the kth cluster in the jth stratum was selected in the sample.

- N_j is the number of individuals in the population in the jth stratum.

- n_j is the number of individuals in the sample in the jth stratum.

- N_{jk} is the number of individuals in the population in the kth cluster in the jth stratum.

15.4 STRATIFIED THREE-STAGE CLUSTER

In educational research it may be necessary to use a stratified three-stage cluster sample design and even more stages in certain surveys. Estimating the sampling variability in such samples is a complicated problem. In general, such complex designs should be used only as a last resort.

An example of a three-stage design is that used in the study of the status of school health education in the United States (Sliepcevich, 1964). The first national study of its kind made in this field, it was *exploratory* and had as one of its purposes to provide a broad preliminary view as revealed by testing a sample of public school students. Since staff, time, and budget were limited, a three-stage sample design was necessary. The first stage was a stratified systematic sample of school systems; the second stage, a random sample of the sixth-, ninth-, and twelfth-grade classes in each selected school system; and the third stage, a random sample of the students in each selected class stratified by sex. Note that *stratification* was used in *all three stages*. (See Exhibit 15.3.)

Unless a great deal is known about the population being surveyed, with samples this complex, accurately estimating the amount of sampling variation inherent in the design and, consequently, the size of the standard errors associated with the parameter estimates is almost impossible. For this reason the results of such complex samples should be examined carefully, and conclusions should be drawn with caution. The report of the study specifically states such limitations and precautions.

EXHIBIT 15.3—THREE-STAGE CLUSTER SAMPLE IN WHICH STRATIFICATION IS USED IN ALL THREE STAGES

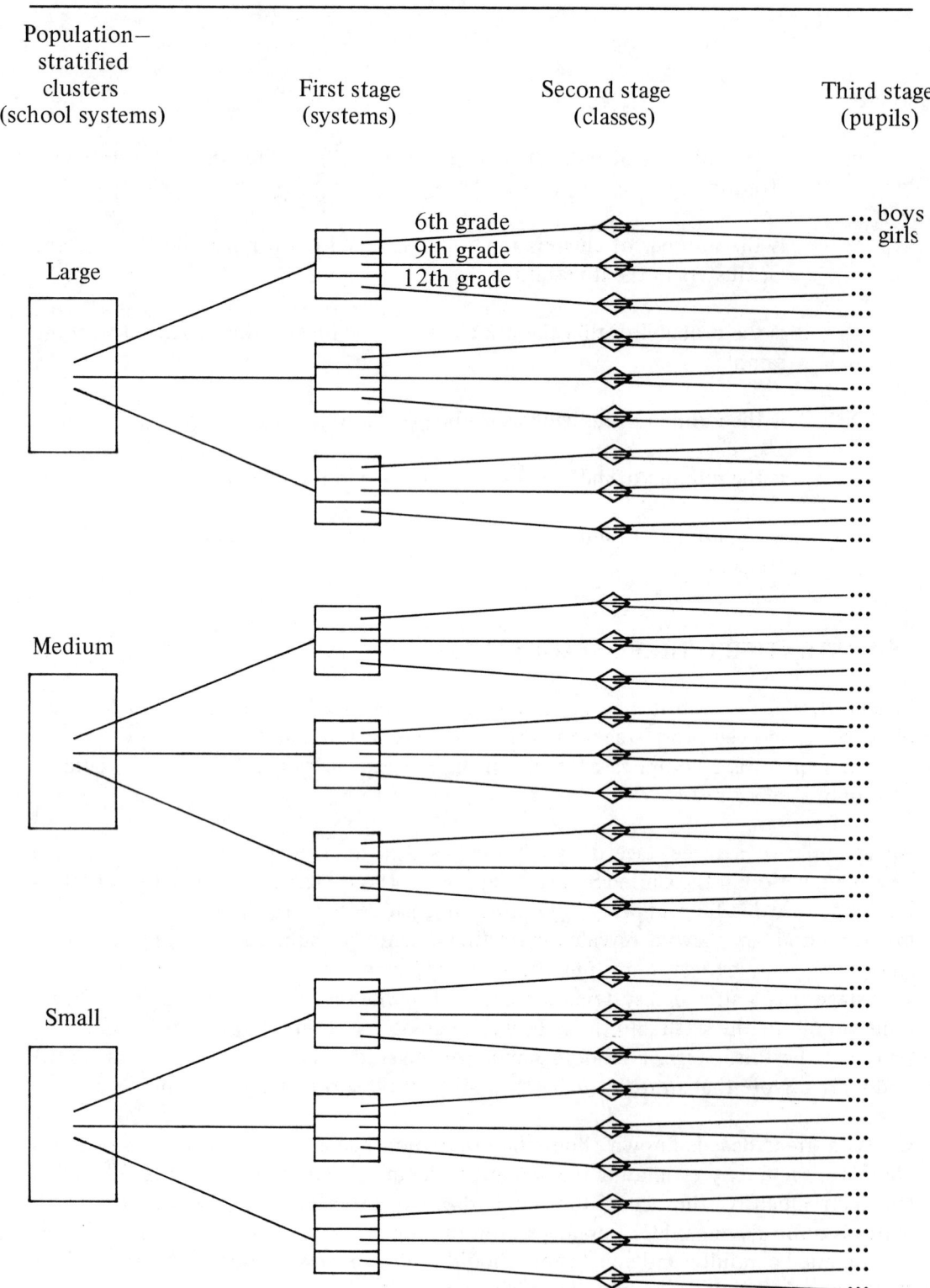

15.5 COMMENTS ON PARAMETER ESTIMATES AND THEIR STANDARD ERRORS

Since there are many potential combinations of stratified and cluster sampling designs, it is possible only to illustrate how calculations of parameter estimates and their standard errors are computed from such sample data. Although some of the formulas appear complicated, they are relatively simple in logic. Basically, they are the same formulas as those used for computing the mean or some other statistic of a simple random sample with subscripts to identify the statistic with its cluster and stratum, plus an appropriate set of arithmetic weights for the cluster and stratum. The logic for computing a particular statistic becomes evident when the formula is viewed in two parts: (a) procedures for computing the basic statistic and (b) procedures for weighting that statistic.

Before using these formulas, the researcher should review the introductions to the sections on "Estimating Population Parameters and Their Standard Errors" in Chapters 13 and 14 (particularly the latter) because ratio estimates are especially important in combination sampling. *Ratio estimates* obtained from combination sampling usually have smaller standard errors than unbiased estimates and, therefore, *are usually preferred.*

This section contains only selected *examples* of how population parameter estimates may be computed for certain combination sample designs. In general, these formulas are the component parts, or modules, which may be fitted together logically to construct the appropriate procedure for computing estimates of population parameters for combination sample data.

Before venturing far with the problems of computing such estimates, the survey researcher should consult such statistical texts as Sudman (1976); Hansen, Hurwitz, and Madow (Vols. 1 and 2, 1953); Stephan and McCarthy (1958); and Sukhatme (1958) and, in addition, would be well advised to consult a statistician with experience in this field.

15.6 DEFINITIONS OF SYMBOLS TO BE USED

The following symbols are used in the formulas presented in the remainder of this chapter.

In the total group	In a stratum	In a cluster	Definition
Subscript j			is the index number of a stratum.
	Subscript k		is the index number of a cluster.
		Subscript i	is the index number of an individual in the kth cluster of the jth stratum.
		X_{jki}	is the value of a characteristic of the ith individual in the kth cluster in the jth stratum.
N	N_j	N_{jk}	is the number of individuals in the population.

In the total group	In a stratum	In a cluster	Definition
n	n_j	n_{jk}	is the number of individuals in the sample.
	$\bar{N}_j$		is the mean size of the clusters in the population, i.e., the average number of individuals per cluster in the population of the jth stratum.
	$\hat{\bar{N}}_j$		is an estimate of the mean size of the clusters in the population. If the mean number of individuals per cluster in the population (N_j) is not obtainable, the mean number of individuals per cluster in the sample clusters ($\bar{n}_j$) can be used as an estimate ($\bar{N}_j$) of $\bar{N}_j$.
	$\bar{n}_j$		is the mean size of the sample clusters in the jth stratum.
r			is the number of strata in the total population.
	G_j		is the number of clusters in the population in a stratum.
	g_j		is the number of clusters randomly sampled from the G_j clusters in the population in a stratum.
μ	μ_j	μ_{jk}	is the arithmetic mean of a characteristic of the analysis units in a population.
$\hat{\mu}$	$\hat{\mu}_j$	$\hat{\mu}_{jk}$	is an unbiased estimate of the arithmetic mean of a characteristic of the analysis units in a population.
$\bar{X}$	$\bar{X}_j$	$\bar{X}_{jk}$	is the arithmetic mean of a characteristic of the analysis units based on sample observations.
$\bar{X}_w$	$\bar{X}_{wj}$		is the weighted mean of a specific characteristic in a sample.

In the total group	In a stratum	In a cluster	Definition
		S^2_{jk}	is the variance of a characteristic based on sample observations.
	$1 - g_j / G_j$	$1 - n_{jk}/N_{jk}$	is the finite population correction factor.
$\hat{\sigma}_{\overline{X}}$	$\hat{\sigma}_{\overline{X}_j}$		is an estimate of the standard error of the sample mean, i.e., the standard deviation of the distribution of sample means of all possible samples of size n from a given population.
$S_{\overline{X}}$	$S_{\overline{X}_j}$		is the sample standard error of the sample mean, i.e., the standard deviation of the distribution of sample means of all possible samples of size n from a given population.
$\hat{\mu}', \overline{X}'$	$\mu'_j, \overline{X}'_j$		is a biased ratio estimate of the arithmetic mean of a characteristic in a population.
$\sigma_{\overline{X}}', S_{\overline{X}}'$	$\hat{\sigma}_{\overline{X}_j}', S_{\overline{X}_j}'$		is an estimate of the standard error of the biased estimates of the population mean.
T	T_j	T_{jk}	is the total or aggregate of values of the characteristic for the individuals in the population.
$\hat{T}$	$\hat{T}_j$	$\hat{T}_{jk}$	is an unbiased estimate of the total or aggregate of values of the characteristic for the individuals in the population.
$\hat{\sigma}_{\hat{T}}, S_{\hat{T}}$	$\sigma_{\hat{T}_j}, S_{\hat{T}_j}$	$\hat{\sigma}_{\hat{T}_{jk}}, S_{\hat{T}_{jk}}$	is an unbiased estimate of the standard error of a total, i.e., the standard deviation of the distribution of population totals or aggregates estimated from all possible samples of size n from a given population.
$\hat{T}'$	$\hat{T}'_j$		is a biased ratio estimate of the total or aggregate of values of the characteristic for the individuals in the population.

In the total group	In a stratum	In a cluster	Definition
$\hat{\sigma}_{\hat{T}'}$, $S_{\hat{T}'}$	$\hat{\sigma}_{\hat{T}'_j}$, $S_{\hat{T}'_j}$		is an estimate of the standard error of the biased ratio estimate of the total or aggregate of values of the characteristics for the individuals in the population.
		f_{jk}	is the number of individuals possessing a specified characteristic in the kth cluster in the jth stratum for the entire cluster or for a sample.
π	π_j	π_{jk}	is the population proportion of individuals possessing a specified characteristic.
$\hat{\pi}$	$\hat{\pi}_j$	$\hat{\pi}_{jk}$	is an unbiased estimate of the population proportion of individuals possessing a specified characteristic.
p	p_j	p_{jk}	is the proportion of individuals possessing a specified characteristic in a sample.
$\hat{\sigma}_p$	$\hat{\sigma}_{p_j}$		is an estimate of the standard error of an unbiased estimate of the population proportion based upon the sample proportion, i.e., the standard deviation of the distribution of sample proportions of all possible samples of size n from a given population.
S_p	S_{p_j}		is the sample standard error of the sample proportion, i.e., the standard deviation of the distribution of sample proportions of all possible samples of size n from a given population.
$\hat{\pi}'$, p'	$\hat{\pi}'_j$, p'_j		is a biased ratio estimate of the proportion of individuals possessing a specified characteristic.

In the total group	In a stratum	In a cluster	Definition
$\hat{\sigma}_{p'}, S_{p'}$	$\hat{\sigma}_{p'_j}, S_{p'_j}$		is an estimate of the standard error of the biased ratio estimate of a population proportion.

15.7 FORMULAS FOR STRATIFIED ONE-STAGE CLUSTER SAMPLE WITH CLUSTERS VARYING IN SIZE AND DRAWN DISPROPORTIONATELY FROM STRATA

The mean value of a characteristic in a cluster (k) in the jth stratum when the data are ungrouped is found as follows:

$$\mu_{jk} = \sum^{N_{jk}} X_{jki} / N_{jk} \tag{15.2}$$

An unbiased estimate of a population mean of the observations of a characteristic in the jth stratum is found as follows:

$$\hat{\mu}_j = \overline{X}_{w_j} = \frac{G_j}{g_j N_j} \sum^{g_j} \sum^{N_{jk}} X_{ki} \tag{15.3}$$

An estimate of the standard error of the unbiased estimate of the jth stratum population mean is found as follows:

$$\hat{\sigma}_{\overline{X}_{w_j}} = S_{\overline{X}_{w_j}} = \sqrt{\frac{G_j(G_j - g_j)}{g_j(g_j - 1)N_j^2} \sum^{g_j} (T_{jk} - \overline{N}_j \overline{X}_{w_j})^2} \tag{15.4}$$

An unbiased estimate of the entire population mean of a characteristic of a stratified population is found as follows:

$$\hat{\mu} = \overline{X}_w = \sum \frac{N_j}{N} \overline{X}_{w_j} \tag{15.5}$$

An estimate of the standard error of the unbiased estimate of the entire population mean of a stratified population is found as follows:

$$\hat{\sigma}_{\overline{X}_w} = S_{\overline{X}_w} = \sqrt{\sum_{}^{r} \frac{N_j^2}{N^2} S_{\overline{X}_{w_j}}^2} \qquad (15.6)$$

(NOTE: For a description of *ratio estimates* see Chapter 14.)

The biased ratio estimate of the population mean of the observations of a characteristic for a stratum is found as follows:

$$\mu_j' = \overline{X}_j' = \frac{\sum^{g_j} \sum^{N_{jk}} X_{jki}}{n_j} \qquad (15.7)$$

An estimate of the standard error of the biased ratio estimate of the jth stratum population mean is found as follows:

$$\hat{\sigma}_{\overline{X}_j'} = S_{\overline{X}_j'} = \sqrt{\frac{G_j(G_j - g_j)}{g_j(g_j - 1)N_j^2} \sum^{g_j} (T_{jk} - N_{jk}\overline{X}_j')^2} \qquad (15.8)$$

The biased ratio estimate of the entire population mean of a characteristic of a stratified population is found as follows:

$$\hat{\mu}' = \overline{X}' = \sum^{r} \frac{N_j}{N} \overline{X}_j' \qquad (15.9)$$

An estimate of the standard error of the biased ratio estimate of the entire population mean of a stratified population is found as follows:

$$\hat{\sigma}_{\overline{X}'} = S_{\overline{X}'} = \sqrt{\sum^{r} \frac{N_j^2}{N^2} S_{\overline{X}_j'}^2} \qquad (15.10)$$

The total or aggregate value of the observations of a characteristic in a cluster (k) in the jth stratum is found as follows:

$$T_{jk} = \sum^{N_{jk}} X_{jki} \qquad (15.11)$$

An unbiased estimate of the population total or aggregate value of the observations of a characteristic in a stratum (j) is found as follows:

$$\hat{T}_j = \frac{G_j}{g_j} \sum^{g_j} T_{jk} \qquad (15.12)$$

An estimate of the standard error of the unbiased estimate of a stratum population total or aggregate value is found as follows:

$$\hat{\sigma}_{\hat{T}_j} = S_{\hat{T}_j} = \sqrt{\frac{G_j(G_j - g_j)}{g_j(g_j - 1)} \sum^{g_j} (T_{jk} - \bar{N}_j \bar{X}_{w_j})^2} \qquad (15.13)$$

An unbiased estimate of the population total or aggregate value of the observations of a characteristic (X) in the entire population is found as follows:

$$\hat{T} = N\bar{X}_w \qquad (15.14)$$

An estimate of the standard error of the unbiased estimate of the population total of the entire population is found as follows:

$$\hat{\sigma}_{\hat{T}} = S_{\hat{T}} = \sqrt{N^2 S^2_{\bar{X}_w}} \qquad (15.15)$$

(NOTE: For a description of *ratio estimates* see Chapter 14.)

A biased ratio estimate of the population total or aggregate value of the observations of a characteristic in a stratum (j) is found as follows:

$$\hat{T}'_j = N_j \bar{X}'_j \qquad (15.16)$$

An estimate of the standard error of the biased ratio estimate of the stratum population total is found as follows:

$$\hat{\sigma}_{\hat{T}'_j} = S_{\hat{T}'_j} = \sqrt{\frac{G_j(G_j - g_j)}{g_j(g_j - 1)} \sum_{}^{g_j} (T_{jk} - N_{jk}\overline{X}'_j)^2} \qquad (15.17)$$

A biased ratio estimate of the population total for the entire group is found as follows:

$$\hat{T}' = N\overline{X}' \qquad (15.18)$$

An estimate of the standard error of the biased ratio estimate of the population total for the entire group is found as follows:

$$\hat{\sigma}_{\hat{T}'} = S_{\hat{T}'} = \sqrt{N^2 S^2_{\overline{X}'}} \qquad (15.19)$$

The proportion of individuals possessing a characteristic in a cluster (k) is found as follows:

$$\pi_{jk} = \frac{f_{jk}}{N_{jk}} \qquad (15.20)$$

(NOTE: For a description of *ratio estimates* see Chapter 14.)

A biased ratio estimate of the population proportion of individuals possessing a certain characteristic in a stratum (j) is found as follows:

$$\hat{\pi}'_j = p'_j = \sum_{}^{g_j} f_{jk} / \sum_{}^{g_j} N_{jk} \qquad (15.21)$$

An approximate estimate of the standard error of the biased ratio estimate of the stratum (j) population proportion is found as follows:

$$\hat{\sigma}_{p'_j} = S_{p'_j} = \sqrt{\frac{G_j(G_j - g_j)}{g_j(g_j - 1)N_j^2} \sum_{}^{g_j} (f_{jk} - N_{jk}p'_j)^2} \qquad (15.22)$$

A biased ratio estimate of the entire population proportion of individuals possessing a certain characteristic in a stratified population is found as follows:

$$\hat{\pi}' = p' = \sum^r \frac{N_j}{N} p_j'$$ (15.23)

An approximate estimate of the standard error of a biased ratio estimate of the population proportion of a stratified population is found as follows:

$$\hat{\sigma}_{p'} = S_{p'} = \sqrt{\sum^r \frac{N_j^2}{N^2} S_{p_j'}^2}$$ (15.24)

15.8 FORMULAS FOR DISPROPORTIONATE, STRATIFIED TWO-STAGE CLUSTER RANDOM SAMPLE, WITH CLUSTERS VARYING IN SIZE AND DRAWN WITH EQUAL PROBABILITIES FROM STRATA IN THE FIRST STAGE, CLUSTERS SAMPLED AT A CONSTANT SELF-WEIGHTING RATE WITHIN EACH STRATUM IN THE SECOND STAGE

An unbiased estimate of the mean of a cluster (k) in the jth stratum when the data are ungrouped is found as follows:

$$\hat{\mu}_{jk} = \overline{X}_{jk} = \frac{1}{n_{jk}} \sum^{n_{jk}} X_{jki}$$ (15.25)

The sample variance of a cluster (k) from the jth stratum is found as follows:

$$S_{jk}^2 = \frac{\sum^{n_{jk}} (X_{jki} - \overline{X}_{jk})^2}{n_{jk} - 1}$$ (15.26)

The computational formula for Formula (15.26) when data are ungrouped is as follows:

$$S_{jk}^2 = \frac{\sum^{n_{jk}} X_{jki}^2 - \frac{(\sum^{n_{jk}} X_{jki})^2}{n_{jk}}}{n_{jk} - 1}$$ (15.27)

An unbiased estimate of the population mean of the jth stratum is found as follows:

$$\hat{\mu}_j = \bar{X}_j = \frac{1}{n_j} \sum^{g_j} \sum^{n_{jk}} X_{jki} \quad (15.28)$$

An estimate of the standard error of the population mean of the jth stratum is found as follows:

$$\hat{\sigma}_{\bar{X}_j} = S_{\bar{X}_j} = \sqrt{\frac{G_j(G_j - g_j)}{g_j N_j^2} \frac{\sum^{g_j}(N_{jk}\bar{X}_{jk} - \bar{N}_j\bar{X}_j)^2}{(g_j - 1)} + \frac{G_j g_j (\bar{N}_j - \bar{n}_j)}{n_j N_j^2} \sum^{g_j} N_{jk} S_{jk}^2} \quad (15.29)$$

An unbiased estimate of the population mean of the total group is found as follows:

$$\hat{\mu} = \bar{X} = \frac{1}{n} \sum^{r} \sum^{g_j} \sum^{n_{jk}} X_{jki} \quad (15.30)$$

An estimate of standard error of the unbiased estimate of the population mean is found as follows:

$$\hat{\sigma}_{\bar{X}} = S_{\bar{X}} = \sqrt{\sum^{r} \frac{N_j^2}{N^2} S_{\bar{X}_j}^2} \quad (15.31)$$

(NOTE: For description of *ratio estimates* see Chapter 14.)

A biased ratio estimate of the population mean of a stratum is found as follows:

$$\hat{\mu}_j' = \bar{X}_j' = \frac{1}{n_j} \sum^{g_j} \sum^{n_{jk}} X_{jki} \quad (15.32)$$

An estimate of the standard error of the biased ratio estimate of the population mean of a stratum is found as follows:

$$\hat{\sigma}_{\bar{X}_j'} = S_{\bar{X}_j'} \sqrt{\frac{G_j(G_j - g_j)}{g_j(g_j - 1) N_j^2} \sum^{g_j} N_{jk}^2 (\bar{X}_{jk} - \bar{X}_j')^2 + \frac{G_j(\bar{N}_j - n_j)}{n_j N_j^2} \sum^{g_j} N_{jk} S_{jk}^2} \quad (15.33)$$

A biased ratio estimate of the population mean of a stratified population is found as follows:

$$\hat{\mu}' = \bar{X}' = \frac{1}{n} \sum^{r} \sum^{g_j} \sum^{n_{jk}} X_{jki} \qquad (15.34)$$

An estimate of the standard error of the biased ratio estimate of the population mean of a stratified population is found as follows:

$$\hat{\sigma}_{\bar{X}'} = S_{\bar{X}'} = \sqrt{\sum^{r} \frac{N_j^2}{N^2} S_{\bar{X}'_j}^2} \qquad (15.35)$$

An estimate of the population total for a cluster in the jth stratum when data are ungrouped is found as follows:

$$\hat{T}_{jk} = N_{jk} \bar{X}_{jk} \qquad (15.36)$$

An unbiased estimate of the population total in a stratum is found as follows:

$$\hat{T}_j = N_j \bar{X}_j \qquad (15.37)$$

An estimate of the standard error of the unbiased estimate of a population total in the jth stratum is found as follows:

$$\hat{\sigma}_{\hat{T}_j} = S_{\hat{T}_j} = \sqrt{\frac{G_j(G_j - g_j)}{g_j(g_j - 1)} \sum^{g_j} (N_{jk}\bar{X}_{jk} - \bar{N}_j\bar{X}_j)^2 + \frac{G_j g_j (\bar{N}_j - \bar{n}_j)}{n_j} \sum^{g_j} N_{jk} S_{jk}^2} \qquad (15.38)$$

An unbiased estimate of the entire population total or aggregate value of a characteristic in a stratified population is found as follows:

$$\hat{T} = \Sigma N_j \bar{X}_j \qquad (15.39)$$

271

An estimate of the standard error of the unbiased estimate of the entire population total in a stratified population in each stratum is found as follows:

$$\hat{\sigma}_{\hat{T}} = S_{\hat{T}} = \sqrt{\sum_{j}^{r} N_j^2 S_{\bar{X}_j}^2} \qquad (15.40)$$

(NOTE: For a description of *ratio estimates* see Chapter 14.)

A biased ratio estimate of the population total in the jth stratum is found as follows:

$$\hat{T}_j' = N_j \bar{X}_j' \qquad (15.41)$$

An approximate estimate of the standard error of the biased ratio estimate of the population total in the jth stratum is found as follows:

$$\hat{\sigma}_{\hat{T}_j'} = S_{\hat{T}_j'} = \sqrt{\frac{G_j(G_j - g_j)}{g_j(g_j - 1)} \sum_{jk}^{g_j} N_{jk}^2 (\bar{X}_{jk} - \bar{X}_j')^2 + \frac{G_j(\bar{N}_j - \bar{n}_j)}{n_j} \sum_{}^{g_j} N_{jk} S_{jk}^2} \qquad (15.42)$$

A biased ratio estimate of the entire population total or aggregate value of a characteristic in a stratified population is found as follows:

$$\hat{T}' = \sum_{}^{r} N_j \bar{X}_j' \qquad (15.43)$$

An estimate of the standard error of the biased ratio estimate of the entire population total for a stratified population is found as follows:

$$\hat{\sigma}_{\hat{T}'} = S_{\hat{T}'} = \sqrt{\sum_{j}^{r} N_j^2 S_{\bar{X}_j}^2} \qquad (15.44)$$

An estimate of the population proportion of individuals possessing a certain characteristic in a cluster in the jth stratum is found as follows:

$$\hat{\pi}_{jk} = p_{jk} = \frac{f_{jk}}{n_{jk}} \qquad (15.45)$$

(NOTE: For a description of *ratio estimates* see Chapter 14.)

A biased ratio estimate of the population proportion of individuals possessing a certain characteristic in a stratum is found as follows:

$$\hat{\pi}'_j = p'_j = \sum_{}^{g_j} f_{jk} / \sum_{}^{g_j} n_{jk} \qquad (15.46)$$

An approximation of the standard error of the biased ratio estimate of the population proportion of a stratum is found as follows:

$$\hat{\sigma}_{p'_j} = S_{p'_j} = \sqrt{\frac{G_j(G_j - g_j)}{g_j(g_j - 1)N_j^2} \sum_{}^{g_j} N_{jk}^2 (p_{jk} - p'_j) + \frac{G_j(\bar{N}_j - \bar{n}_j)}{n_j N_j} \sum_{}^{g_j} N_{jk} n_{jk} \frac{p_{jk}(1 - p_{jk})}{n_{jk} - 1}}$$

$$(15.47)$$

A biased ratio estimate of the population proportion of individuals possessing a certain characteristic in the total group is found as follows:

$$\hat{\pi}' = p' = \frac{1}{n} \sum^r \sum^{g_j} f_{jk} \qquad (15.48)$$

An approximation of the standard error of the biased ratio estimate of the population proportion in the total group is found as follows:

$$\hat{\sigma}_{p'} = S_{p'} = \sqrt{\sum^r \frac{N_j^2}{N^2} S_{p_j}^2} \qquad (15.49)$$

15.9 SUMMARY

The principles of stratified and cluster random sampling can be combined in various ways to meet specific survey needs. Combination sample designs offer the researcher the possibility of achieving a balance between the two counteracting effects of stratifying and clustering. Some common types of combination sample designs used in educational surveys have been discussed in Chapter 15.

Special formulas are needed for computing estimates of population parameters and their standard errors from combination sample data. This chapter has presented examples of some of these. Before a researcher ventures far in using a combination sample design in connection with a specific survey, the references cited in this text should be studied and an experienced statistician consulted.

APPENDIXES

GLOSSARY

Analysis unit (AU): the object or entity on which a measurement or observation is to be made. For example, the AU might be a public school teacher, a school district, a registered voter, etc.

Arithmetic mean: the arithmetic average of all the observations in a set of observations.

Attribute: a characteristic of an analysis unit that is clearly present or absent, or that contains more than two possible categories into which each analysis unit can be assigned. For example, a teacher is either male or female, retired or active, an NEA member or not an NEA member. In a survey, an individual might be asked to select from among the following categories (attributes): strongly favor, favor, indifferent, oppose, strongly oppose.

Average: a general term for any central tendency measure; the most commonly used measures are the mean, median, and mode.

Average deviation: the average of the absolute differences of the observations from some central point, usually the arithmetic mean.

Characteristic: something that can be used to differentiate between analysis units. A characteristic may be either quantitative (a variable) or qualitative (an attribute). For a teacher, age is a variable and sex is an attribute.

Class interval: the range within classes or groups of a frequency distribution; a band of values assumed to be equally distributed or concentrated for purposes of computation or graphing.

Cluster sampling: a method of sampling in which each sampling unit is a collection, or cluster, of analysis units. For example, high schools represent logical clusters of teachers.

Coefficient of correlation: an index number measuring the degree of linear relationship between two variables, i.e., the tendency for values of one variable to change systematically with changes in values of a second variable; no relationship = 0.00, a perfect relationship = + 1.00 or − 1.00.

Coefficient of determination: the proportion of the total variation in one variable that is explained by another variable in a linear sense.

Coefficient of variation: ratio of the standard deviation to the arithmetic mean.

Continuous variable: a variable capable, actually or theoretically, of assuming any value within a range of values—as opposed to a discrete variable, which may take only whole-number values; test scores are treated as being continuous although they are less obvious examples than time, distance, weight, etc.

Cumulative frequency distribution: a listing of the various values that individual analysis units may assume, ordered from high to low or from low to high, coupled with the frequency of occurrence of observations having a value "less than" or "greater than" the particular value.

Data: in a survey or an experiment, the set of characteristics associated with each analysis unit. For example, associated with a teacher may be salary, age, years of teaching experience, etc.

Data element: the specific value of a characteristic based upon measurement or observation.

Discrete variable: a variable that may assume only a fixed set of values, e.g., number of pupils in a classroom.

Discriminant analysis: a statistical procedure for identifying, which—among a set of characteristics associated with analysis units—can serve to assign each analysis unit to a specific population (e.g., persons likely to complete four years of college and persons not likely to complete four years of college).

Factor analysis: any of several complex statistical procedures for analyzing the interrelationships among a set of tests (or other variables) for the purpose of identifying the factors, preferably few in number, that cause the interrelationships; widely used in efforts to understand the organization of intelligence, personality, and the like.

Frequency: the number of occurrences or members of a group falling into a specified class. For example, 15 male and 40 female teachers in a given school.

Frequency distribution: a listing of the various values that individual analysis units may assume, usually ordered, coupled with the frequency of their occurrence in the sample or population.

Frequency polygon: a type of graph used commonly to portray a distribution of a given variable.

Histogram: a plot of a frequency distribution in the form of a rectangle whose bases are equal to the cell interval sizes and whose areas are proportional to the cell frequencies.

Hypothesis: a tentative assumption or belief made in order to test or examine its logic. The null hypothesis is usually that which is being tested, such as "male and female teachers have the same average salary after ten years of teaching."

Interquartile range: the range for the variable of interest (e.g., teachers' salaries) that includes the middle 50% of the observations.

Mean: most widely used measure of central tendency; equals the sum of scores divided by the number of cases. (Note: there are others—geometric, harmonic.)

Mean deviation: the average of the absolute differences of the observations from the arithmetic mean.

Median: the central or middle member of a set of observations that have been ranked.

Mode: the value that occurs most often in a set of observations.

Nonparametric: pertaining to procedures used in statistical inference to test hypotheses about population distributions; does not involve testing hypotheses about specific parameters.

Normal distribution: a frequency distribution represented graphically as a symmetrical, bell-shaped curve, in which the mean, median, and mode are equal; it extends infinitely far in both positive and negative directions and possesses a known probability distribution.

Parameter: a summary or descriptive measure (e.g., mean or standard deviation) for a population or universe: i.e., a parameter is to a population as a statistic is to a sample.

Parametric: pertaining to procedures used in statistical inference to estimate parameters or to test hypotheses about parameters.

Percentile (P): any of the 99 points along the scale of score values that divide a distribution into 100 groups of equal frequency: e.g., P_{73} is that point below which fall 73 percent of the cases in a distribution.

Population: the entire group or set of analysis units in which the researcher has an interest (universe).

Probable error: 0.6745 times the standard deviation; within one probable error of the mean in a normal distribution will fall 50% of the observations.

Quartile: any of the three points that divide a frequency distribution into four groups of equal frequency. The first quartile (Q_1) equals the twenty-fifth percentile (P_{25}); $Q_2 = P_{50}$ = median; and $Q_3 = P_{75}$.

Random sampling: a method of selecting an observation from a population in such a manner that each observation has a known probability of being in the sample, usually taken as equally likely.

Range: the interval between the largest and smallest observations in a set of data.

Regression equation: a numerical expression that can be used to predict the value of one variable based upon a specific value of another variable. The line from the equation may be linear or nonlinear: e.g., predicting a teacher's salary based upon the number of years of teaching experience.

Relative frequency: the actual frequency expressed as a proportion of the total population or total sample size.

Reliability: consistency or stability of a test or other measuring instrument; necessary for, but not sufficient for, validity. Commonly expressed as a reliability coefficient or a standard error of measurement.

Rho: term and symbol used to denote a Spearman rank-difference correlation coefficient.

Sample: a group or set of observations selected from a larger set, referred to as a "population" or "universe." For example, a group of four teachers selected from a given high school would constitute a sample from that school. Note that "sample" does not necessarily connote "goodness" or representativeness.

Sampling frame: a listing of all analysis units of interest. The population of interest.

Standard deviation: a measure of variation used to describe how a set of observations varies about its arithmetic mean. Specifically, it is the square root of the average of the squared deviations from the arithmetic mean.

Standard error of estimate: a measure of the accuracy with which one variable can be predicted from another variable using a regression equation. It is a measure of the variability around the regression line.

Standard error of the mean: a measure of the accuracy of the sample arithmetic mean as an estimate of the population arithmetic mean. The standard deviation of all possible sample means taken about the population mean.

Standard score: any of several derived scores based on the number of standard deviations between a specified raw score and the mean of the distribution.

Statistic: a summary measure computed for a sample, such as the arithmetic mean, the median, the standard deviation, etc. An estimate in a sample of the corresponding parameter in the population.

Statistically significant; statistical significance: sample results that deviate from a hypothesis and are greater than can be explained by random variation or chance alone are called statistically significant.

Stratification: classification of the analysis units of interest into a logical set of mutually exclusive categories. For example, classifying school systems (the analysis unit) in the United States according to enrollment (the strata).

Systematic sampling: a method of selecting a sample by taking an observation at fixed intervals from the sampling frame. For example, if every tenth teacher were taken from a school district, this would be a systematic sample. The first observation must be taken at random within the first interval of the frame.

T-score: a standard score having a mean of 50 and a standard deviation of 10.

Type I error: rejecting a null hypothesis when it is true.

Type II error: not rejecting a null hypothesis when it is false.

Validity: the extent to which a test does the job desired of it; the evidence may be either empirical or logical.

Variability or variation: a general term relating to the amount of scatter or dispersion there is among a set of observations.

Variable: (1) any trait or characteristic that may change with the analysis unit. (2) more strictly, any representation of such a trait or characteristic that is capable of assuming different values: e.g., a test score is a variable.

Variance: a statistic, equal to the square of the standard deviation (SD^2); widely used in research.

Z-score: the basic standard score; widely used in test-related research; $Z = (X - \overline{X})/S$, where X = raw score, $\overline{X}$ = mean score, and S = standard deviation.

B

REFERENCES

American Society for Quality Control, Statistics Technical Committee. *Glossary and Tables for Statistical Quality Control.* Milwaukee, Wis.: the Society, 1973.

Andrews, F. M., and others. *A Guide for Selecting Statistical Techniques for Analyzing Social Science Data.* Ann Arbor, Mich.: University of Michigan, 1976.

Bennett, Spencer, and Bowers, David. *An Introduction to Multivariate Techniques for Social and Behavioural Sciences.* London, England: MacMillan Press, Ltd., 1976. 156 pp.

Cochran, William G. *Sampling Techniques.* Second edition. New York: John Wiley & Sons, 1963. 413 pp.

Dixon, W. J., and Massey, F. J. *Introduction to Statistical Analysis.* New York: McGraw-Hill Book Co., 1951. 370 pp.

Edwards, Allen L. *Experimental Design in Psychological Research.* Third edition. New York: Holt, Rinehart and Winston, 1968. 455 pp.

Edwards, Allen L. *Statistical Methods for the Behavioral Sciences.* New York: Rinehart & Co., 1954. 542 pp.

Fruchter, Benjamin. *Introduction to Factor Analysis.* New York: D. Van Nostrand Co., 1954. 280 pp.

Guilford, J. P., and Fruchter, Benjamin. *Fundamental Statistics in Psychology and Education.* Fifth edition. New York: McGraw-Hill Book Co., 1973. 546 pp.

Hansen M. H.; Hurwitz, W. N.; and Madow, W. G. *Sample Survey Methods and Theory: Vol. I, Methods and Applications.* New York: John Wiley & Sons, 1953. 638 pp.

Hansen, M. H.; Hurwitz, W. N.; and Madow, W. G. *Sample Survey Methods and Theory: Vol. II, Theory.* New York: John Wiley & Sons, 1953. 332 pp.

Hildebrand, David K.; Laing, James D.; and Rosenthal, Howard. *Analysis of Ordinal Data.* Sage University Paper series on Quantitative Applications in the Social Sciences, 07-008. Beverly Hills, Calif., and London, England: Sage Publications, 1977. 79 pp.

Iversen, Gudmund R., and Norpoth, Helmut. *Analysis of Variance.* Sage University Paper series on Quantitative Applications in the Social Sciences, 07-001. Beverly Hills, Calif., and London, England: Sage Publications, 1976. 95 pp.

Jessen, Raymond J. *Statistical Survey Techniques.* New York: John Wiley & Sons, 1978. 520 pp.

Kim, Jae-On, and Mueller, Charles W. *Introduction to Factor Analysis: What It Is and How To Do It.* Sage University Paper series on Quantitative Applications in the Social Sciences, 07-013. Beverly Hills, Calif., and London, England: Sage Publications, 1978a. 79 pp.

Kim, Jae-On, and Mueller, Charles W. *Factor Analysis: Statistical Methods and Practical Issues.* Sage University Paper series on Quantitative Applications in the Social Sciences, 07-014. Beverly Hills, Calif., and London, England: Sage Publications, 1978b. 88 pp.

Ku, H.H.; Varner, R.N.; and Kullback, S. "On the Analysis of Multidimensional Contingency Tables." *Journal of the American Statistical Association* 66:55-64; March 1971.

Kullback, S. *Information Theory and Statistics.* New York: John Wiley & Sons, 1959.

Lyman, Howard B. *Test Scores and What They Mean.* Third edition. Englewood Cliffs, N.J.: Prentice-Hall, 1978. 190 pp.

Mace, Arthur E. *Sample-Size Determination.* Huntington, N.Y: Robert E. Krieger Publishing Co., 1974. 226 pp.

Marascuilo, Leonard A., and McSweeney, Maryellen. *Nonparametric and Distribution-Free Methods for the Social Sciences.* Monterey, Calif.: Brooks/Cole Publishing Co., 1977. 556 pp.

Mayer, Martin. "Sampling the Samplers." *Esquire Magazine* 54:186-97; November 1970.

Mendenhall, William, and Ramey, Madelaine. *Statistics for Psychology.* North Scituate, Mass.: Duxbury Press, 1973. 413 pp.

Mendenhall, W.; Ott, L.; and Scheaffer, R. L. *Elementary Survey Sampling.* Belmont, Calif.: Wadsworth Publishing Co., 1971. 247 pp.

National Education Association. *Analysis Methodology for Testing Significance of Changes in Sampled Frequencies.* NEA Research Memo. Washington, D.C.: the Association, November 1979. 19 pp.

Nie, N., and others. *Statistical Package for the Social Sciences.* Second edition. New York: McGraw-Hill Book Co., 1970.

Parten, Mildred. *Surveys, Polls, and Samples: Practical Procedures.* New York: Harper and Brothers, 1950. 624 pp.

Reynolds, H. T. *Analysis of Nominal Data.* Sage University Paper series on Quantitative Applications in the Social Sciences, 07-007. Beverly Hills, Calif.: and London, England: Sage Publications, 1977. 82 pp.

SAS Institute. *SAS User's Guide.* Raleigh, N.C.: the Institute, 1979.

Savage, I. R. "Bibliography of Nonparametric Statistics and Related Topics." *Journal of the American Statistical Association* 48:844-906; 1953.

Siegel, S. *Nonparametric Statistics.* New York: McGraw-Hill Book Co., 1956. 312 pp.

Sliepcevich, Elena M. *Summary Report of a Nationwide Study of Health Instruction in the Public Schools.* (Sponsored by the Samuel Bronfman Foundation.) Washington, D.C.: School Health Education Study, 1964. 74 pp.

Slonim, M. J. *Sampling.* New York: Simon and Schuster, 1960. 144 pp.

Stephan, F. Frederick, and McCarthy, Philip J. *Sampling Opinions: An Analysis of Survey Procedures.* New York: John Wiley & Sons, 1958. 451 pp.

Sudman, S. *Applied Sampling.* New York: Academic Press, 1976. 249 pp.

Sukhatme, P. V. *Sampling Theory of Surveys with Applications.* Ames: Iowa State College Press, 1954 (reprinted 1958). 491 pp.

Thurstone, L.L., and Degan, J. W., "A Factorial Study of the Supreme Court." *Psychometric Lab.* Report No. 64. Chicago, Ill.: University of Chicago, 1951. 7 pp.

Tortora, R. D. "A Note on Sample Size Estimation for Multinomial Populations." *The American Statistician* 32:100-102; August 1978.

U.S. Department of Commerce, National Bureau of Standards (Mary G. Natrella, author). *Experimental Statistics.* Handbook 91. Washington, D.C.: Government Printing Office, October 1966.

U.S. Department of the Interior, Office of Education. *National Survey of the Education of Teachers.* Bulletin 1933. No. 10. Vol. I-IV. Washington, D.C.: Government Printing Office, 1935.

University of California. *BMDP Biomedical Computer Programs, P-Series, 1977.* Berkeley, Calif.: University of California Press, 1977.

Williams, B. *A Sampler on Sampling.* New York: John Wiley & Sons, 1978.

Winer, B. *Statistical Principles in Experimental Design.* McGraw-Hill Book Co., 1962. 672 pp.

ARITHMETIC OPERATIONS

Since statistics involves the collection, processing, and analysis of numerical values, the researcher must understand basic arithmetic operations and associated symbolism. The following material, which by no means is exhaustive, should be sufficient to allow for the use of all formulas contained within this text.

The following arithmetic operations and formulas will consider two measures or variables: namely, teachers' salaries and years of tenure within a school district. Define X_i and Y_i, respectively, as the salary in $1,000 and years of tenure for a given teacher, referred to as the "i^{th} teacher." Define n as the number of teachers for whom salary and years of tenure are being examined. For five teachers these data can be presented as follows:

Teacher	Salary in $1,000	Years of tenure
A	$12.5	2
B	14.2	4
C	15.0	7
D	16.4	8
E	17.9	9

Teacher A, for example, earns $12,500 per year and has been in the teaching profession for two years. Because there are five teachers, n equals 5. Frequently, a computational expression in statistics requires that the individual values of the variable of interest be added. This procedure is represented by the Greek letter *sigma*: Σ (note that this is a capital *sigma*). To indicate the process of adding up all five teachers' salaries, the appropriate expression becomes:

$$\sum_{1}^{5} X_i = 76.0$$

The "1" below and the "5" above the Σ symbol indicate that the addition is from teacher #1 to teacher #5. The expression to the left of the equal sign is frequently written as ΣX, where it is understood that the addition consists of all the values of the variable of interest.

Still another required computation is to square the individual values and to add them up. This, for the five teachers' salaries, would be given by:

$$\sum_{1}^{5} X_i^2 = 1{,}172.26$$

where the expression to the left of the equal sign is frequently written as ΣX^2. The general expression to add up all n values of interest, then, is seen to be:

$$\sum_{1}^{n} X_i = \Sigma X$$

Similar to the calculations for average salary, the corresponding sums for years of tenure are seen to be:

$$\sum_{1}^{5} Y_i = 30 \quad \sum_{1}^{5} Y_i^2 = 214$$

The arithmetic mean, or average salary, is found to be:

$$\overline{X} = 76.0 / 5 = 15.2$$

In many statistical operations, the arithmetic mean is subtracted from each of the individual observations or, symbolically, $(X - \overline{X})$. This difference of $(X - \overline{X})$ is frequently represented as "x," or small X. Since a number of operations are accomplished using "x," data for the five teachers' salaries are repeated in the following table:

Teacher	X	X^2	x	x^2	|x|
	(1)	(2)	(3)	(4)	(5)
A	12.5	156.25	−2.7	7.29	2.7
B	14.2	201.64	−1.0	1.00	1.0
C	15.0	225.00	−0.2	0.04	0.2
D	16.4	268.96	1.2	1.44	1.2
E	17.9	320.41	2.7	7.29	2.7
	76.0	1,172.26	0.0	17.06	7.8

The five column totals are defined as follows:

- Column 1 − ΣX: addition of the individual salaries.
- Column 2 − ΣX^2: squaring of the individual salaries and then the addition of these five squared salaries.
- Column 3 − Σx: subtraction of the arithmetic mean from each of the five salaries and then the addition of these differences. (Note: The result will always be equal to zero when the mean is subtracted.)

Column 4 — Σx^2: squaring of the individual values in Column 3, followed by the addition of these squared values.

Column 5 — $\Sigma |x|$: the two vertical lines around the "x" are referred to as "absolute value" indicators and call for treating the differences in Column 3 as positive values. Once these positive differences have been obtained, the expression calls for the addition of these differences.

Note that $(\Sigma X)^2 = (76.0)^2 = 5,776$ is not the same as $\Sigma X^2 = 1,172.26$.

Some research problems involve more than one variable. The summation notation can be extended to cover any number of variables. The five teachers' salaries and corresponding years of tenure are given in the following table:

Teacher	X	Y	XY	x	y	y^2	xy
	(1)	(2)	(3)	(4)	(5)	(6)	(7)
A	12.5	2	25.0	−2.7	−4	16	10.8
B	14.2	4	56.8	−1.0	−2	4	2.0
C	15.0	7	105.0	−0.2	1	1	−0.2
D	16.4	8	131.2	1.2	2	4	2.4
E	17.9	9	161.1	2.7	3	9	8.1
	76.0	30	479.1	0.0	0	34	23.1

Columns 2, 5, and 6 contain information on the Y variable similar to that just presented for X, namely, $\Sigma Y = 30$, $\Sigma y = 0$, and $\Sigma y^2 = 34$. The two new columns are as follows:

Column 3 — ΣXY: for each teacher the salary is multiplied by years of tenure [Column 1 times Column 2 entries] and the results added.

Column 7 — Σxy: for each teacher the entry in Column 4 is multiplied by the entry in Column 5 and the results totaled. [Note: For teacher C, −0.2 times 1 is a negative quantity. If the signs in Columns 4 and 5 are the same, the product in Column 7 is positive; if the signs differ, the product is negative.]

Note that $\Sigma XY = 479.1$ is not the same as $[\Sigma X][\Sigma Y] = (76.0)(30) = 2280$.

The following example summarizes all of the symbols presented in this section. Five pupils from a given high school graduate at the same time and have completed their freshman year at the same junior college. The X variable is the high school average grade at the time of graduation and the Y variable is the grade point index for the freshman year, where the grade of A equals 4.0.

Pupil	X	Y	X²	Y²	XY
A	72	2.4	5,184	5.76	172.8
B	80	2.7	6,400	7.29	216.0
C	85	3.1	7,225	9.61	263.5
D	89	3.0	7,921	9.00	267.0
E	96	3.8	9,216	14.44	364.8
	422	15.0	35,946	46.1	1,284.1

Pupil	x	y	x²	y²	xy	|x|	|y|
A	−12.4	−0.6	153.76	0.36	7.44	12.4	0.6
B	− 4.4	−0.3	19.36	0.09	1.32	4.4	0.3
C	0.6	0.1	0.36	0.01	0.06	0.6	0.1
D	4.6	0.0	21.16	0.00	0.00	4.6	0.0
E	11.6	0.8	134.56	0.64	9.28	11.6	0.8
	0	0	329.2	1.1	18.1	33.6	1.8

The appropriate summations are seen to be:

$$\Sigma X = 422 \qquad \Sigma X^2 = 35,946 \qquad \Sigma XY = 1,284.1$$
$$\Sigma Y = 15.0 \qquad \Sigma Y^2 = 46.1 \qquad \Sigma x = \Sigma y = 0$$
$$\Sigma x^2 = 329.2 \qquad \Sigma y^2 = 1.1 \qquad \Sigma xy = 18.1$$
$$\Sigma |x| = 33.6 \qquad \Sigma |y| = 1.8 \qquad n = 5$$

Note also that:

$$[\Sigma X][\Sigma Y] = (422)(15.0) = 6,330$$
$$[\Sigma X]^2 = (422)^2 = 178,084$$
$$[\Sigma Y]^2 = (15.0)^2 = 225.0$$

$$\bar{X} = \frac{\Sigma X}{n} = \frac{422}{5} = 84.4$$

$$\bar{Y} = \frac{\Sigma Y}{n} = \frac{15.0}{5} = 3.0$$

When reading any statistical reference, the researcher should always check the symbolism to be certain either that it is consistent with that presented in this section or that it is easily understood.

D

ELEMENTARY PROBABILITY

Samples for use in survey studies may be selected in a number of ways, and several were described in Chapter 2 of this text. There are yet other sampling procedures, such as judgment selection, purposive selection, incidental selection, haphazard selection, and selection by volunteers. Under the right conditions any of these sampling methods will yield reasonably accurate estimates of parameters in the population sampled, but seldom can the researcher be sure that conditions are right. There is virtually no way of knowing how accurate such estimates are, short of taking a census of the whole population. Even if a census were made to verify an estimate made under one set of conditions, it is no guarantee of similar success under different circumstances.

The only type of sample selection with mathematical properties that will permit calculation of the precision, or confidence limits, of sample estimates is *probability sampling*. A probability sample is one selected in accordance with a probability model for which it is possible to state in advance of selecting the sample (a) the probability that any given population analysis unit will be included in the sample and (b) the relationship of this probability to the probabilities for all other population elements.

A *probability model* is a sampling plan or sampling design in which specific probabilities are assigned for choosing population elements to be included in the sample. In their complexity, probability models may vary from simple random sample to complicated multistage sample designs. The complexity of the design does not destroy its usefulness as a probability model; it only complicates the procedures for selecting the sample and, subsequently, for analyzing data obtained from the sample. On the other hand, the simplest design cannot serve as a probability model unless the probability by which the population elements are to be selected can be stated specifically.

Some Aspects of Probability

Probability is generally the ratio of the number of ways in which an event can succeed (or fail) to the number of ways in which it can occur. Suppose there are 1,000 slips of paper in a bowl, numbered 1 through 1,000. What is the probability that the slip numbered 863 will be selected on the first draw? If the slips are well shuffled so that chance is the only factor affecting the selection, the probability is 1 in 1,000, 1:1,000, or 1/1,000.

Instead of slips of paper, suppose 250 blue beads, 250 red beads, and 500 white beads are placed in a bowl. What is the probability of drawing a blue bead on the first try? The probability would be 250 to 1,000, or 1/4. The numerator of the ratio, then, is the number of outcomes favorable to a specific event and the denominator is the number of possible outcomes.

Every probability may also be expressed as a proportion, usually a decimal with the base (or total) of 1.0. Thus, the probability of drawing slip number 863 from the 1,000 slips of paper in the bowl would be 1 in 1,000, 1/1,000, or 0.001. The probability of drawing a blue bead from the bowl of 1,000 beads is 250 in 1,000, 1/4, or 0.250. In statistics, the most common way of expressing probabilities is as a decimal proportion.

Multiplication Rule

From the previous example of the 250 blue, 250 red, and 500 white beads in a bowl, it was observed that the probability of drawing a blue bead on a single draw was 1 in 4, or 0.250, since only one-fourth of the beads are favorable to this outcome. The probability of drawing a red bead is, likewise, 1 in 4. But the probability of drawing a white bead is 1 in 2 since one-half of all the beads are favorable to this outcome.

Suppose two draws are made; the first bead is replaced after being drawn. What is the probability that the first bead will be blue and the second bead will be white? The probability of event B (blue) followed by event W (white) is the product of the two probabilities:

$$(1/4) \cdot (1/2) = 1/8$$

or

$$(0.25) \cdot (0.50) = 0.125$$

Since the probability of drawing a white bead in no way depends on the outcome of the first draw, events B and W are *independent*. *If two or more events are independent, the probability that they will all occur is the product of their separate probabilities.* This statement of the relationships of probabilities is the multiplication rule. Notice that here each bead was replaced after each draw so that the probabilities remain the same on each successive draw, regardless of what happened on the previous drawings. This is also an example of random sampling *with replacement*.

Addition Rule

What is the probability that on a single draw the bead will be either a blue or a white bead? *The probability that one of a number of mutually exclusive events (those that cannot occur at the same time) will occur is the sum of the probabilities that the separate events will occur.* This statement of relationships of probabilities is the *rule of addition*. Applying this rule to the example, the probability of either event B or event W occurring would be:

$$1/4 + 1/2 = 3/4$$
$$0.25 + 0.50 = 0.75$$

Conditional Probability

Rather than replace the bead after each draw, suppose the sampling procedure is modified by placing each bead selected in a separate bowl. (This is an example of random sampling *without replacement*.) On the first draw the probabilities of selecting a blue, red, or white bead remain the same as before. But the probabilities on the second draw have changed slightly because there is one less bead of the same color. On the third draw the probabilities are different from either the first or the second. The probabilities on each successive draw are affected by the prior events that have taken place. This relationship is referred to as "conditional probability," sometimes called "dependent probability." When the probability of an event is changed by the occurrence or nonoccurrence of another event, the two events are not independent. *If two events are not independent, the probability that both events will occur is the product of the probability of the first and the probability of the second, if the first has occurred.*

If we make three selections from the bowl of beads without replacement, what is the probability that the first three will be blue, red, and white? The probability of drawing a blue bead on the first draw would be the same as before, 250/1,000, or 0.250. The probability of drawing a red bead on the second draw would be 250/999, or 0.2503, since there is one less bead in the bowl. The probability of drawing a white bead on the third draw would be 500/998, or 0.5010 since there are two less beads in the bowl. The conditional probability of drawing a white bead if one blue and one red bead have already been drawn is 0.5010. The probability of selecting blue, red, and white, on the first three draws without replacement is:

$$(0.250)(0.2503)(0.5010) = 0.0314$$

In statistical notations when a confidence level of 0.95 is specified, this is actually a probability of 0.95, or 95 in 100, or 19 in 20 chances that a certain event will occur. Similarly, when the 0.90 level of confidence is specified, this is actually a probability of 0.90, or that a certain event should happen 90 times in 100 (9 in 10 chances).

Combinations and Permutations

Sample surveys are drawn from populations that contain some specific (finite) number of N units. The number of separate and distinct samples of size n that can be drawn from the total population of N units is equal to the number of *combinations* of N units taken n at a time. Formula D.1 is useful in *determining the total possible combinations*.

$$_NC_n = \frac{N!}{n!(N-n)!} \tag{D.1}$$

where:

$_NC_n$ is the number of combinations of N units taken n at a time.

N is the population size.

n is the sample size.

N! (read N factorial) is the product of all the integers from N to 1, e.g., if N = 4, N! is equal to $(4)(3)(2)(1) = 24$.

n! is the product of all the integers from n to 1 (0! is defined as 1)

(N−n)! is the product of all the integers from (N−n) to 1.

To illustrate the concept of combinations and the use of Formula (D.1), suppose a small school contained only five teachers: A, B, C, D, E. How many *different* samples (combinations) of size three would it be possible to draw from this population? Substituting in Formula (D.1) yields:

$$_NC_n = \frac{N!}{n!(N-n)!} = \frac{5!}{3!(5-3)!}$$

$$_5C_3 = \frac{(5)(4)(3)(2)(1)}{(3)(2)(1)(2)(1)}$$

$$= \frac{120}{12}$$

$$= 10 \text{ combinations}$$

Thus, it is possible to have ten different samples or combinations from these five teachers chosen three at a time. This assumes (a) that no teacher appears more than once in a single sample, (b) that the order of selection does not matter and (c) that teachers chosen either in order ABC or CBA would constitute a single combination. The ten samples or combinations are:

ABC ABD ABE ACD ACE
ADE BCD BCE BDE CDE

If the researcher wants to know the total number of different *arrangements* of the five teachers if samples of size three are drawn, Formula (D.2) should be used. This gives the total number of *permutations* possible. The difference between combinations and permutations is that in combinations the order of the objects or selections is of no importance. Selections ABC, BAC, and CBA are considered as the same combination. In permutations, the order or arrangement of selections or objects is important, ABC, BAC, and CBA are considered three different permutations. *The formula for the number of permutations* is:

$$_NP_n = \frac{N!}{(N-n)!} \qquad (D.2)$$

where N!, N, n, and (N−n)! are defined following Formula (D.1) and $_NP_n$ is the number of permutations of N units taken n at a time.

Substituting in Formula (D.2), the number of permutations for the previous example of the population of five teachers with samples of size three would be:

$$_NP_n = \frac{N!}{(N-n)!} = \frac{5!}{(5-3)!}$$

$$_5P_3 = \frac{(5)(4)(3)(2)(1)}{(2)(1)}$$

$$= \frac{120}{2}$$

$$= 60$$

Thus, there are 60 possible permutations of five things taken three at a time, but only ten combinations.

E

INDEX TO DESCRIPTIVE FORMULAS

This Appendix provides an alphabetical listing for the descriptive formulas that appear in this Handbook and cites page and formula number.

Arithmetic mean — p. 27

$$\text{arithmetic mean} = \Sigma X / n \qquad (4.1)$$

where

- X = the value of an individual observation (characteristic)
- Σ = the symbol that means "to add up" or "to sum" what follows the symbol
- ΣX = the indication that individual values of the variable are to be added or summed
- n = the number of observations or AU's

Average deviation from the mean — p. 41

$$A.D. = \Sigma |X - \bar{X}| / n$$
$$= \Sigma |x| / n \qquad (5.1)$$

where n is the sample size and "x" is defined as an individual deviation from the arithmetic mean, or $x = (X - \bar{X})$. The same formula applies for a population with $\bar{X}$ being replaced by μ and n by N.

Coefficient of Concordance — p. 89 ff.

$$W = 12s / k^2 n (n^2 - 1) \qquad (7.14)$$

where

- $s = \Sigma R_j^2 - (\Sigma R_j)^2 / n$
- ΣR_j = sum of the ranks for each analysis unit across the classifications
- k = the number of classifications
- n = the number of AU's

Correlation, linear — p. 60 ff.

$$r = S_{xy} \div (S_x \cdot S_y) \qquad (7.1)$$

or

$$r^2 = A \div (B \times C) \qquad (7.2)$$

where

$$A = [n\Sigma XY - (\Sigma X)(\Sigma Y)]^2 \qquad (7.3)$$
$$B = [n\Sigma X^2 - (\Sigma X)^2] \qquad (7.4)$$
$$C = [n\Sigma Y^2 - (\Sigma Y)^2] \qquad (7.5)$$

Mean, arithmetic — p. 27

$$\text{arithmetic mean} = \Sigma X / n \qquad (4.1)$$

where

X = the value of an individual observation (characteristic)
Σ = the symbol that means "to add up" or "to sum" what follows the symbol
ΣX = the indication that individual values of the variable are to be added or summed
n = the number of observations or AU's

Mean deviation — p. 41

$$A.D. = \Sigma |X - \bar{X}| / n$$
$$= \Sigma |x| / n \qquad (5.1)$$

where n is the sample size and "x" is defined as an individual deviation from the arithmetic mean, or $x = (X - \bar{X})$. The same formula applies for a population with $\bar{X}$ being replaced by μ and n by N.

Proportion, population — p. 52

$$\pi = f / N \qquad (6.1)$$

where

π = the symbol representing the population proportion possessing a specific characteristic
f = the frequency of analysis units (number of such AU's) possessing the given level of the characteristic
N = the total number of AU's in the population

Proportion, sample — p. 52

$$p = f / n \tag{6.2}$$

where

- p = the symbol representing the sample proportion possessing a specific characteristic
- f = the frequency of analysis units possessing the given level of the characteristic
- n = the sample size

Regression, Both Variables Subject to Errors in Measurement — p. 71 ff.

The slope of the regression line is estimated by dividing the n plotted points into three groups from the lowest to the highest values of X. Each of the extreme groups (call the lowest values of X, Group 1; the highest values, Group 3) should have an equal number of points, as near to n/3 as possible. The estimate for the slope of the line is given as:

$$b = (\bar{Y}_3 - \bar{Y}_1) / (\bar{X}_3 - \bar{X}_1)$$

where

- $\bar{Y}_3$ = average Y value for Group 3
- $\bar{Y}_1$ = average Y value for Group 1
- $\bar{X}_3$ = average X value for Group 3
- $\bar{X}_1$ = average X value for Group 1

The Y intercept is given by the same formula as previously used:

$$a = \bar{Y} - b\bar{X}$$

Regression, One Variable Subject to Errors in Measurement — p. 64 ff.

$$Y' = a + bX + e \tag{7.7}$$

where

$$b = S_{xy} / S_x^2 \tag{7.8}$$

or

$$b = \sqrt{A \div B}$$

where A and B are as defined for correlation in Formulas (7.3) and (7.4),

$$a = \overline{Y} - b\overline{X} \qquad (7.9)$$

and

e = the amount by which an individual observed value of Y, for a given value of X, deviates from the regression line value, namely, Y'.

Spearman Rank Order Correlation Coefficient — p. 88 ff.

$$r_s = 1 - 6(\Sigma d^2) / n(n^2 - 1) \qquad (7.13)$$

where

d = the difference between the two ranked values associated with each individual analysis unit

n = number of analysis units

Standard deviation, population — pp. 43, 45

$$\sigma = \sqrt{\Sigma(X - \mu)^2 / N}$$
$$= \sqrt{\Sigma x^2 / N} \qquad (5.2)$$

μ = the population arithmetic mean
N = the population size
Σ = the summation sign
$\sqrt{}$ = the square root sign
x = (X - μ)

or

$$\sigma = \sqrt{[\Sigma X^2 - (\Sigma X)^2 / N] / N} \qquad (5.6)$$

or

$$\sigma = \sqrt{[N\Sigma X^2 - (\Sigma X)^2] / N^2} \qquad (5.7)$$

Standard deviation, sample — pp. 43, 44

$$S = \sqrt{\Sigma(X - \bar{X})^2 / (n - 1)}$$
$$S = \sqrt{\Sigma x^2 / (n - 1)} \qquad (5.3)$$

where

$\bar{X}$ = the sample arithmetic mean
n = the sample size
Σ = the summation sign
$\sqrt{}$ = the square root sign
x = $(X - \bar{X})$

or

$$S = \sqrt{[\Sigma X^2 - (\Sigma X)^2 / n] / (n - 1)} \qquad (5.4)$$

or

$$S = \sqrt{[n\Sigma X^2 - (\Sigma X)^2] / n(n - 1)} \qquad (5.5)$$

T-score, conversion to raw score — p. 57

$$X = \mu + \sigma(T - 50) / 10 \qquad (6.7)$$

T-score, population – p. 56

$$T = 50 + 10Z$$
$$= 50 + 10(X - \mu)/\sigma \qquad (6.5)$$

where

μ = the population arithmetic mean

σ = the population standard deviation

X = the original value, or raw score, for the variable of interest

T = the new positional measure with its mean of 50 and its standard deviation of ten

T-score, sample – p. 56

$$T = 50 + 10(X - \overline{X})/S \qquad (6.6)$$

where

X = the original variable of interest

$\overline{X}$ = the sample arithmetic mean

S = the sample standard deviation

T = The T-score associated with the given value for X

Z-score, population – p. 54

$$Z = (X - \mu)/\sigma \qquad (6.3)$$

where

X = the individual value of the characteristic (e.g., an individual teacher's age)

μ = the arithmetic mean for the population (the average age for all teachers within the district)

σ = the standard deviation within this same population

Z-score, sample — p. 55

$$Z = (X - \bar{X}) / S \qquad (6.4)$$

where

    X = the individual value of the characteristic
    $\bar{X}$ = the sample arithmetic mean
    S = the sample standard deviation

APPROPRIATE STATISTICAL METHODOLOGIES

Most persons who have been exposed to a single course in elementary statistics tend to walk away confused and overawed by all of the material, particularly if mathematical derivations are emphasized. This text has, on the other hand, emphasized applications and interpretations. Still, the researcher will be confronted with the standard questions: For my research project, which technique or techniques are appropriate? Which descriptive statistics should I use? Which inferential procedures are right for my research efforts? Unfortunately, there usually is no single "right" way to proceed.

An excellent document released by the University of Michigan Survey Research Center —Andrews et al. (1976)—leads the researcher through a series of questions, the answers to which lead to a specific branch and either another question or the appropriate technique in response to the questions. For example, the first question is, How many variables does the problem involve? Available answers are one, two, or more than two variables. The answer to this question determines the appropriate branch for the researcher to pursue. The document is quite detailed and presents numerous techniques along with excellent references.

Rather than repeat the entire process of the Michigan report, an abbreviated approach follows, based upon only the materials found in this text. This appendix, along with Appendix E, will provide the researcher with a starting point for identifying appropriate methodologies.

The following material examines one-characteristic and two-characteristics situations only.

F.1 A SINGLE CHARACTERISTIC

Exhibit F.1 identifies possible appropriate descriptive measures, depending upon whether the characteristic is nominal, ordinal, interval, or ratio.

Exhibit F.2 summarizes possible inferential procedures available when dealing with a single characteristic.

EXHIBIT F.1 – POSSIBLE DESCRIPTIVE MEASURES BASED UPON THE SCALE OF MEASUREMENT[a]

Scale of measurement	Descriptive measures of:		
	Central tendency	Variation	Position
Nominal	mode (31)	—	proportions (52)
Ordinal	median (28)	interquartile range (36)	percentiles (50) proportions (52)
Interval/Ratio	mean (27), median (26) mode (31)	range (36) interquartile range (36) average deviation (40) standard deviation (43)	percentiles (50) standard scores (54)

[a] Items in parentheses indicate the starting page for discussion in this text.

EXHIBIT F.2 – POSSIBLE INFERENTIAL TECHNIQUES WHEN DEALING WITH A SINGLE CHARACTERISTIC[a]

Scale of measurement	Possible inferential techniques
Nominal & ordinal	Confidence intervals for a proportion or a percentage (132) Testing hypotheses on a single proportion (162) Testing hypotheses on two proportions (166)
Interval & Ratio	Confidence intervals for a sample mean (128) Confidence intervals for a total (130) Confidence intervals for a variance or standard deviation (137) Testing hypotheses on a single sample mean (146) Testing hypotheses on two population means (149) Testing hypotheses on two population variances or standard deviations (156)

[a] Inferential procedures for each of the above techniques are initiated on the indicated pages of this text.

F.2 TWO CHARACTERISTICS

In addition to the descriptive measures for single characteristics indicated in Exhibit F.1, the introduction of a second characteristic provides an additional set of measures of association. These new measures of association are given in Exhibit 7.17 and are repeated here as Exhibit F.3.

EXHIBIT F.3 – GUIDE FOR CHOICE OF MEASURES OF ASSOCIATION, TWO CHARACTERISTICS[a]

Characteristics	Measures of association
Both interval or ratio	Pearson's r (60) Correlation ratio[b]
Both ordinal	Spearman's rho (88) Kendall's tau[c]
One nominal or ordinal and dichotomous; one interval or ratio	Biserial coefficient[b] Point biserial coefficient[b]
Both nominal and/or ordinal and both dichotomous	Phi coefficient[c] Tetrachoric correlation coefficient[c] Contingency coefficient[c]
Both nominal and/or ordinal and two or more categories	Contingency coefficient[c]

[a] If no reference is cited, methodology and calculations are presented in this text, beginning on page indicated in parentheses.

[b] Edwards (1954)

[c] Siegel (1956)

In addition to the inferential techniques for single characteristics given in Exhibit F.2, several additional techniques are presented in Exhibit F.4 when a second characteristic is introduced.

EXHIBIT F.4 – POSSIBLE INFERENTIAL TECHNIQUES WHEN DEALING WITH TWO CHARACTERISTICS[a]

Characteristics	Possible inferential techniques
Both nominal or ordinal	Testing hypotheses of independence in a two-way contingency table (166)
Both interval or ratio	Finding confidence intervals in bivariate linear regression (134) Testing hypotheses on linear correlation or regression (158)

[a] Items in parentheses indicate the starting page for discussion of the given procedure in this text.

G

COMPUTERIZED STATISTICAL PROGRAMS

The speed and versatility of today's computers have made possible the use of highly complicated statistical procedures by almost any researcher, provided access is available to such a computer system. In recent years, the technology of the large-scale computer system has been adapted and is now available in small, virtually pocket-size, hand calculators. This appendix references several more widely used statistical programs (packages) that are available on most large-scale computer systems and also identifies two small hand calculators that are currently the best available for statistical analyses.

1. STATISTICAL PROGRAMS

At the present time (the reader should note the date of this text because of possible additions to the list which follows), the following are the more widely utilized statistical programs:

- *BMDP Biomedical Computer Programs.* P-Series. University of California Press, Berkeley, California 1977.

- Nie, N.; Hull, C.; Jenkins, J.; Steinbrenner, K.; and, Bent, D. *SPSS, Statistical Package for the Social Sciences.* Second edition. McGraw-Hill Book Co., New York, New York, 1970.

- *SAS User's Guide.* 1979 edition. SAS Institute, Inc., P.O. Box 10066, Raleigh, North Carolina 27605.

Other programs are available but are not in as wide usage as the above. The researcher is cautioned, in using any of these available statistical packages, to be certain that all up-to-date system modifications and enhancements are available. Most service bureaus, which make computer time available for a fee, keep their systems well maintained.

2. SMALL ELECTRONIC CALCULATORS

The market has been flooded during recent years with a range of special-purpose, small hand calculators. Two of them are particularly noteworthy in terms of their specific applications to statistical analyses:

- S-61 (Commodore): This is perhaps the finest small statistical calculator available today. In addition to the operations and functions available on the TI-55 (see below), the S-61 also has in its repertoire of available routines the following: combinations, permutations, a random number generator, the "t" distribution, the F distribution, the normal distribution, chi-square, the Poisson distribution, the hypergeometric distribution, the binomial distribution, the "goodness of fit" test, the "t" test for two independent samples, the "t" test for paired samples, and processing of grouped data. There are eight memory banks available for storage and utilization.

- TI-55 (Texas Instruments): This small calculator allows for direct calculations associated with the arithmetic mean, variance, standard deviation, linear regression, and trend-line analysis. In addition, for repetitive calculations, the instrument is programmable. Standard functions such as squares, square roots, reciprocals, logarithms and trigonometric operations are also available. Ten memory banks are available to the user.

The TI-55 is currently under $50 and the S-61 is under $80. Both are useful for the individual who has frequent requirements to summarize and analyze data but does not have access to a large-scale computer system with statistical packages, such as those indicated above.

STATISTICAL TABLES

Table H.1 — 20,000 Random Digits
Table H.2 — Proportions of Areas Under the Normal Curve Between the Mean and Z-Scores from 0.00 to 3.09
Table H.3 — Selected Standard Scores (Z-Scores) Associated with Proportions of Areas Under the Normal Curve for Proportions from 0.05 to 0.499
Table H.4 — Student's "t" Distribution
Table H.5 — Chi-Square Distribution
Table H.6 — The F Distribution (Upper Percentage Points)
Table H.7 — Appropriate Sizes of Simple Random Samples for Specific Permissible Errors Expressed as Absolute Proportions When the True Proportion in the Population is 0.50 and the Confidence Level is 90, 95, 98, or 99 Percent

TABLE H.1 – 20,000 RANDOM DIGITS

9986	0901	9814	4143	1389	1945	6092	8906	1522	3776
0466	2111	0581	6968	6685	3885	6782	4085	7779	7433
9797	7113	8912	1398	6446	5340	1749	0490	7124	0239
0039	8086	7155	1590	7039	2480	6350	9402	4925	5352
8728	1168	2577	2733	2514	7371	3754	5076	3430	6931
7744	9536	6226	5253	5138	5362	7019	2552	7618	7342
0453	5639	3371	7030	0179	9521	1692	5108	2926	2745
1094	4435	7270	0521	1575	4296	1552	7091	0432	6186
5645	0291	3989	9875	3894	3655	0957	3470	5285	1935
6554	7276	4779	7169	8914	1866	1254	6412	3752	2259
7998	9528	5905	9651	2274	1167	0412	0465	6181	4395
2807	0424	8528	9589	7830	8635	9889	9598	8450	0323
6767	4132	9804	1121	9071	5529	3643	8869	5918	3400
3638	5773	2091	8436	1936	7208	6931	9725	9922	9884
6756	6541	9367	5881	7781	7628	2031	9234	5540	1843
9300	3706	6962	6415	1686	0148	5183	9765	6831	3525
7648	8596	6051	4304	7988	9926	9453	5266	8251	9289
4717	6189	4714	4908	9854	9139	8000	0003	3860	5001
3897	1632	2479	0474	1354	3027	5291	8347	5936	0120
8235	7303	6213	6871	8835	6856	6285	4334	0505	2805
4108	8352	0294	5465	2465	1596	2120	1232	0957	5122
5655	8035	6861	2506	9402	3693	1293	3210	9439	1521
4944	1421	0092	0152	1804	5116	4743	5525	3100	6979
5433	0767	5134	5689	4130	2223	7828	0335	4226	3723
3090	1332	6455	9137	1256	7272	1615	2800	7957	6053
1273	6274	6904	6883	6521	4320	3454	5185	5450	9006
4930	1750	9959	2985	3194	9637	6410	4630	3984	6030
6648	8040	9556	9792	6231	3379	4854	2323	5616	1123
0256	2289	1276	1261	9102	3796	0732	4611	5884	8613
0223	7648	8964	4870	7963	0054	0413	2552	6576	2668
1615	7473	4991	0587	2964	0322	6154	2305	3121	5356
6691	6853	4312	4731	0262	7958	3904	7338	0715	3926
0519	7935	1588	9599	3045	4900	5241	2598	0598	9744
7546	6068	9684	1139	7540	6645	6023	0235	8728	6870
0732	5320	2740	2790	5037	6123	0597	5672	8561	0460
3343	0059	5254	6659	1673	9700	1122	1902	4277	4884
1639	3222	1143	8864	9517	8555	3885	3302	9824	2198
7876	9208	5706	2783	3025	7817	9915	4949	8758	8642
6013	2234	9360	2375	7266	1772	5580	8182	4049	7303
1418	6389	9913	2097	5498	4568	3958	0078	2934	1639
7439	5811	8884	5907	2660	9465	9376	3776	6601	5798
8944	3978	1260	5263	0248	1420	5923	1653	0309	4738
7300	3847	1380	8134	5482	3000	6956	8778	7295	1827
8857	1677	2332	6987	9258	0275	6414	9488	2537	9213
6571	9615	8443	4660	8016	5381	9785	7742	9583	4284
4711	2041	4701	6622	5023	2497	8007	7927	2302	9979
7635	5000	3655	5949	4347	6761	9447	1281	5061	8554
8201	0763	9252	6971	9126	1561	5274	5873	9008	5378
2077	2486	7671	3776	4728	0045	9636	3961	3401	4400
3001	5328	0269	9500	4121	8370	7890	7702	8409	0006

TABLE H.1 – 20,000 RANDOM DIGITS (Continued)

3460	3547	2095	9623	1763	8706	1915	3454	9389	5436
9504	9300	8316	7002	0612	4399	6248	4286	0199	5747
2589	9966	1490	6086	6136	1408	6969	5355	4298	2107
9574	4472	4386	1941	1374	3101	5124	8810	6643	2964
2717	3218	4352	6827	1402	3746	7171	9128	0702	8206
5496	5320	3655	5902	9780	6381	5189	2258	9643	4261
3849	6086	5454	1432	9364	5294	5326	9567	8505	3217
9043	0436	4906	9577	5414	4513	0830	6004	1655	2302
8348	1946	5379	3484	1297	8535	3088	7046	1261	2704
3800	3574	0712	6321	1060	1489	9839	4732	4381	8771
9899	0489	6592	3557	0073	6344	3741	3439	2374	4472
9461	6039	4778	8149	7466	7771	7116	9297	5053	0293
8975	4382	0708	4235	7088	9014	6188	0130	0408	3784
9499	0685	7548	6203	3696	6335	4120	7649	9066	4821
7260	6117	9569	8292	4095	1409	4974	1712	0238	1524
5478	7916	1716	3489	3644	8683	2679	6897	6372	8860
8359	7369	6460	7122	4599	2014	1593	7041	2356	9177
9083	0505	8966	1370	1029	7871	4803	7442	2519	8543
3816	0702	2285	2499	8263	6413	6648	0429	0238	9316
3907	1027	0682	2449	9307	3706	2286	1060	9561	6654
4424	7729	9307	6798	8681	3299	4884	2621	3656	3625
9525	1066	0438	8482	9171	0849	7601	0253	8782	5677
3568	9005	9312	1791	7337	7016	5795	6122	6016	4778
9610	3005	9108	0862	4116	8877	2433	6686	2786	6186
2921	9214	4073	9074	6996	8479	2974	3794	0061	3050
5757	9819	9175	2373	6805	1181	8366	1733	3217	1766
3177	8940	7873	2129	8131	0041	6986	4832	6305	3344
9329	0882	2134	4489	6922	9437	8973	7278	3770	3181
8791	9776	8407	1612	4446	3507	0505	3119	7502	5224
3211	9888	0740	8875	6851	6429	4939	7604	3947	3833
9367	3276	1320	9226	6406	1341	5225	2111	5156	2175
9097	7200	6495	8033	8367	2520	7738	2797	7394	4498
8568	3036	7224	8545	7893	4236	4529	1511	2821	5860
9149	7723	0974	4738	5043	1515	0054	3920	5604	7649
7989	1628	9794	0053	8183	6756	8272	3992	9191	6993
5244	0910	6841	0465	9373	3987	4360	5876	9460	5960
8183	8837	7494	7234	9170	7486	1767	1929	9750	7828
9973	9466	5790	6897	0032	1301	2441	7220	3248	8926
3874	7047	5817	0132	9226	0909	2779	6007	4183	1340
3923	6845	9114	4507	2702	8350	5890	2556	7631	1320
3507	9021	3649	2071	4627	8890	5872	0908	6042	0022
9765	2741	7769	8981	7850	4518	6073	3439	5393	3626
2765	7264	5442	5515	6657	1743	2650	5207	7943	5368
8876	0747	1047	8902	6177	2561	7862	1460	7938	8418
1243	3349	3812	1339	9698	2220	5786	4488	8538	8023
4037	1418	3814	7954	1149	5090	9661	8316	5911	7471
2515	8032	7311	1925	5016	4018	5755	8224	2313	1600
8834	8348	8562	7501	5549	3461	5226	6560	3914	3078
7254	5725	0634	8959	5704	7508	4241	8201	1061	7863
2831	2210	8886	0447	9851	9588	7059	8696	1622	7113

TABLE H.1—20,000 RANDOM DIGITS (Continued)

7944	5182	5265	4113	1057	4557	6827	8002	7156	7187
7631	7599	6230	7146	5659	5804	6714	4487	2610	2051
6270	1709	3968	1873	5717	7567	0088	0100	1362	4164
7909	2079	2418	1382	6518	4813	4997	8319	8460	9585
5806	4358	6137	1822	0390	9102	1698	4280	7173	9470
3138	1123	0084	4650	3221	6300	4260	1064	1668	0189
6134	7433	6546	5734	8469	0967	9040	4927	5283	5789
7083	6536	1642	8522	9263	4849	8217	5017	2987	7437
0941	2690	6669	6083	9799	3505	6019	0703	8147	2583
0057	9882	7765	4684	4216	0013	7514	3142	5911	4104
1799	0441	7199	6463	8773	0521	5079	6303	7557	5458
6914	1645	0019	6609	3656	7396	4753	5733	0124	0783
0082	4641	0692	7448	4185	3598	8714	3301	6988	3177
6240	4508	2196	4060	5257	5473	1319	5474	0200	9869
8675	6683	9760	1713	1309	5291	6717	4280	5025	0115
1536	2136	6561	1553	5601	7018	9165	4029	6723	2194
9071	7132	6968	9840	0110	6003	2643	9826	7341	8065
5458	4922	3029	9741	2284	5514	1597	4971	2267	1184
4835	9782	1990	4424	4181	9718	8095	2512	4539	7511
9570	5751	5042	9128	0879	1755	8386	7806	8416	9402
4740	5007	8320	8010	4716	6892	5538	4911	7265	2127
4595	5097	4194	4368	0951	7196	3909	6296	7945	8723
3191	7680	7622	2321	2760	9926	5756	7818	0912	2478
4897	6334	2071	6055	5292	5330	7048	1826	0246	8530
1851	6106	2590	0810	1626	0686	2133	3698	3274	1167
9231	1355	2356	7864	6298	7932	3288	6271	1085	4417
2205	5139	4607	2263	2168	1556	5542	4033	9815	0768
3111	2725	4603	9277	5513	5596	3193	2033	0844	5148
6126	6262	6529	1053	8780	4229	9378	3528	9229	2845
6300	0938	2525	3979	5849	1895	8356	1767	0319	5008
7009	0070	8758	9974	0047	1460	4305	1827	7171	8093
2382	8657	7587	2435	7562	7293	1462	6056	3063	5960
5517	9037	4960	7400	0632	4552	2906	0523	3153	0095
1742	8477	2354	8347	4545	5595	3085	7586	1680	8428
4235	7036	5737	9205	1239	5379	6856	2202	0730	1316
7144	1972	7438	3371	7183	7164	7698	8840	5644	5046
4746	3442	3734	5983	4323	6217	8659	9457	0597	3658
0181	9725	6694	9000	8148	5885	4086	0491	9739	8319
9625	2959	0465	8999	2687	9037	0968	4931	5227	6377
4437	5411	0316	7928	0016	1131	7633	5025	3429	0900
9665	4240	8594	0135	6585	6235	2369	8039	6493	4267
9477	1514	1177	0709	4471	7607	8213	5224	9498	2514
8131	1780	0505	2987	8821	9495	9443	2636	6681	8900
9995	9817	1843	0937	2095	5966	8219	3553	1230	7603
6916	7163	7171	7917	0160	0270	1887	1124	7484	1872
4353	9696	2827	9286	7374	7693	0316	9606	9510	6873
7485	1063	1978	7801	6895	1264	1063	4268	1576	4756
8458	6022	7882	8130	0971	5371	6187	7167	6820	1888
1431	8953	4508	4242	5781	4152	0856	4552	0521	0216
1762	1092	6304	0274	4581	1785	7217	8590	4836	5110

TABLE H.1 — 20,000 RANDOM DIGITS (Continued)

1428	8628	8536	0504	1430	1318	1739	4559	5913	9747
6879	4788	3165	7380	0687	7218	5270	5688	5021	9365
0052	3641	6447	6671	5308	3635	5208	5955	9436	6022
6344	9465	9640	1723	0853	5635	3760	8827	1188	5106
8804	6508	8913	5927	9288	4477	5015	9343	4555	1735
1870	8827	7423	4308	7863	6429	3330	1770	3638	6007
8530	9881	8529	9036	6655	5539	2774	8286	2852	6251
4032	2537	7388	7478	2112	4165	7685	4130	4219	3653
3534	3254	7958	0692	8291	8485	0041	4479	4022	3353
8303	4180	3709	3937	8362	0536	6199	1462	6540	9537
3699	2402	8786	0379	6582	5708	8317	0377	3730	5535
3578	6250	6369	4168	6000	6227	2645	3260	0060	5423
1289	4809	1596	0662	2192	7072	1359	6582	1479	3551
2000	9410	8644	2937	8917	3601	8508	3398	0343	3896
9199	5149	0961	3133	8613	8082	9650	6869	0812	0706
7694	6255	1426	8627	7579	5453	6662	1150	6164	6439
0883	6906	5477	1568	7721	9191	4793	1611	2445	7063
1814	8449	7181	6112	4559	3266	7390	1300	1915	5736
4954	8853	0706	6449	0900	2004	9442	4594	8931	6706
4242	8485	9201	6707	1341	9794	4387	4542	7462	3351
4177	4484	7333	9342	0932	8485	6293	5301	1864	0620
9475	8028	8861	1344	1720	4443	8217	2239	5207	1879
2724	5365	6942	4950	8183	1826	6618	8405	3828	0287
8074	9672	6045	2338	5379	2884	2653	7177	9806	1993
1682	4198	0117	1747	6356	2884	2492	4592	6388	9174
3726	4991	5627	3344	6572	4793	8191	2828	9842	6177
1433	2328	2522	2307	7105	2061	5018	5234	1336	7072
7902	4568	7181	4064	5103	1664	8201	7887	8918	7016
5561	3768	3651	1304	2925	5031	8141	3026	2047	9457
0498	2078	4300	8964	4737	7150	2773	6829	7780	6373
5741	6774	5287	8622	4599	2489	3375	0632	9106	4912
5688	9004	9660	7737	6757	3965	4186	0416	0741	6542
3457	5137	0606	7455	4581	4878	1374	9636	5475	6211
4335	8121	3643	2947	2948	0465	6006	1253	7565	9297
1482	2334	1770	7568	4395	5803	5531	1522	1360	7848
9044	1923	8135	6277	4982	2341	0927	1713	1837	5023
1290	9057	9984	3443	7786	5147	6531	8074	1434	8388
2398	9984	6598	2213	5145	9369	7522	3662	4229	8693
5486	7871	5913	6866	4247	8175	7158	2756	5460	1314
5842	5977	0517	0438	7320	5923	0576	8503	8216	0691
5723	8360	3349	7209	7553	4670	9865	5261	6834	8501
0199	0387	0676	2427	0082	0696	0363	8009	4493	1402
3596	5117	5657	9258	9186	7137	5247	9075	6339	2452
9913	7998	0559	2952	8914	9252	0666	5635	5532	6809
1589	0897	1530	4686	2632	7229	7888	7850	6449	5721
4680	8173	1840	0418	3590	9286	1060	1096	3129	4376
1464	5094	4644	4787	6664	8521	6461	0201	0828	7902
7081	4617	5102	9670	6404	7271	6149	8754	0736	9587
5618	1281	7572	0425	5867	0616	5461	0792	8081	3670
0692	8084	5921	1110	9211	2992	7576	9594	7049	2127

TABLE H.1 – 20,000 RANDOM DIGITS (Continued)

5913	0253	1717	5094	1714	7179	5552	9107	3770	2407
5907	1977	1989	7424	5624	8723	5846	5880	8541	6679
3843	5484	8925	1468	4099	9793	9417	0710	6591	8090
4789	6951	7772	1175	4197	5347	3523	8226	3806	2717
1993	8658	1798	0911	9176	0843	9541	3495	1826	2900
9512	4620	4952	3946	1315	7448	2410	0585	5718	3826
1826	0238	0601	4438	5850	0202	6598	2645	8531	7723
2981	9638	4014	6423	6960	4481	5963	3143	5541	9779
5137	4909	9348	4291	6794	3454	3072	8036	0008	4132
5650	0598	9742	2199	1418	0160	4883	0782	7070	5060
5509	1354	9473	3286	3282	9985	1646	3240	9923	5611
0022	1865	1600	2728	8463	5057	0537	2888	1897	0153
3497	4068	2490	3875	9109	1556	3895	9753	7969	3835
9861	4322	3291	0794	0678	2749	5797	1223	0487	8833
1504	5615	0063	6644	5027	2763	1492	9347	5610	9497
3752	1475	6271	6792	8536	4898	3058	9372	6505	1773
1695	5779	5875	3386	4343	2280	6933	4397	6540	6951
6289	3876	2233	3494	5724	1908	4094	8739	0663	9277
4973	7923	0412	8464	7828	4400	0899	5687	2233	5901
9915	2209	3760	2475	2913	6744	0388	0278	6417	6190
4393	2862	6346	1674	6058	1088	7947	7691	5473	8022
4344	1059	1427	7220	2509	2699	4515	8273	4450	4925
2348	3950	4262	5489	3616	3727	6679	9002	7635	8987
3341	2900	9919	8511	5455	9438	8269	3417	7366	4346
0513	2070	9734	1584	1186	3991	2650	4486	9601	6180
7200	6526	8898	8834	6956	0654	3003	7376	7619	8838
0571	0517	0456	3541	2132	4475	5574	5335	4756	5386
0784	6400	0669	9752	4884	7722	2422	2732	5083	9073
3906	9255	0882	1945	7269	6753	7914	3535	4765	5078
3487	4128	7086	2069	3625	3525	6200	0071	4052	8537
3484	3567	2626	8370	8130	2498	2446	0348	1221	1830
8074	1451	1652	1039	5953	8538	8810	4875	6320	7014
1406	2138	7432	6401	7330	4994	9651	8659	6707	2337
6938	9886	4033	6646	0440	5344	0037	5919	3441	9076
8738	8642	7714	6720	7441	4426	3126	9842	2899	2271
1954	2885	9722	0184	2682	6618	3265	5777	7010	6109
8854	4662	4225	1903	0139	5978	4523	6691	1260	3018
4595	9243	7482	5327	3252	3843	9167	6943	9709	8076
2347	2784	1560	4623	6908	7303	4347	9680	5504	6342
6456	5443	0618	2859	4634	9614	2319	0081	3904	9282
1882	3589	8104	4374	9510	3015	6351	2393	5285	3845
1901	0150	0184	4145	7603	4784	2402	1084	9587	0390
9962	0634	9719	6620	1351	5879	2940	6304	5088	6093
0922	6968	9365	4987	5732	1648	1013	6628	9934	4094
7251	4511	5990	1265	3104	5268	6988	4596	5495	8579
4906	6551	0952	1731	9615	2889	2724	2385	7728	2868
6334	8025	8301	0763	7444	5877	2779	6244	8081	1058
7615	2192	4422	0209	1837	9172	7100	9341	3633	7387
0985	3520	1445	6618	6943	7260	0076	6033	6641	5023
9433	9666	3548	2957	4941	4090	7735	0488	0153	0234

TABLE H.1—20,000 RANDOM DIGITS (Continued)

9497	3899	4988	1584	1197	3030	0464	5655	1547	4168
4145	8166	9814	8568	9651	9137	5312	5991	0952	3983
7634	7327	1403	6156	4680	5851	4537	5665	4565	0957
3124	3458	4903	1616	9431	6169	2396	8374	5624	9338
4081	9797	3473	5016	8174	5208	3968	8557	8297	4175
7265	1414	1381	3695	5956	7457	1581	9291	7733	9744
4122	1675	2794	8339	4045	5974	0222	6005	5109	8295
0921	5648	0750	5489	9709	4807	4340	2156	7874	5094
8730	5653	0338	8900	4296	7324	6003	2702	6984	5911
2807	6996	5785	0442	4564	9793	2468	8092	8619	0483
7409	2316	0060	7291	1082	3251	4874	6214	5106	6797
6586	7470	7850	1288	1816	4988	7419	0405	2334	5983
4604	4327	2384	7215	5330	6430	2023	2459	3228	4632
5722	9145	8739	8551	2338	1977	3986	8047	0621	3860
2019	5271	0264	9064	2341	5555	3235	1815	0307	9077
9821	5684	1026	3856	0494	2233	0554	6404	6956	5918
1317	4542	5384	6003	0954	5278	7082	6172	1535	5849
2644	7392	6395	0865	7989	9740	0897	5278	0302	3819
5982	6003	9227	9490	3746	7796	2247	7769	7535	5196
4597	6933	7129	9054	3495	4783	6499	7914	5463	0949
4619	1139	5469	2907	2283	3780	8591	8070	9072	7514
9324	5081	5194	3106	2378	9946	0923	4216	3712	7081
2971	1634	3672	6019	9048	5627	7531	0799	0541	6787
7528	5239	2982	4704	6432	6992	3874	9668	5826	7709
9343	9962	7352	2410	7816	5109	2919	5380	2714	4287
1784	9062	1069	4324	6349	6415	8925	2924	4476	1498
8608	7706	8271	3685	7170	5980	5040	5547	7267	2690
4575	8243	2137	4559	4475	3880	6641	7597	3157	1931
2441	6641	8914	1386	1504	7464	7788	2933	6483	2689
6576	5367	9861	7063	2513	8991	0626	5133	1433	0702
1136	9361	9055	7029	2772	2417	0526	9144	2246	7758
0370	2808	3735	5430	3148	3201	2634	8234	3099	9586
8456	8149	4178	5456	1189	4420	8039	7662	8030	8562
9631	0530	6323	0255	9942	0314	3068	9586	0427	0846
6085	4950	3757	5073	0697	4050	1700	8152	3429	8604
3854	2846	0318	3090	0492	1895	6593	8641	3293	6286
5308	9277	0575	0563	2593	4808	1405	4219	2107	9748
5703	9401	7386	8540	0269	7337	2793	9114	5199	8469
8108	7606	6018	1490	9668	6440	1536	7505	5648	0389
8761	4909	0810	5370	1948	2495	4295	3559	8791	9873
7950	7699	3958	2448	1478	1550	3848	0525	6626	7150
2622	9923	0583	7962	4214	7873	3552	2560	3582	0288
5237	4501	4871	3001	2626	3511	8744	3932	5736	0535
0941	5038	9070	5902	1651	4944	2460	8700	4236	3299
2824	8245	9359	7943	4676	3218	9999	0232	4440	2418
4222	5828	9965	3063	5841	4582	3479	4775	1327	1361
1314	1056	2977	6649	8213	2024	8077	2288	7344	4104
6138	0977	2732	1839	7250	1072	6052	0038	7459	5196
4162	6858	4419	2891	6020	4724	6681	2383	4100	8486
9396	3958	1165	2284	9681	6207	7094	0382	3366	7241

TABLE H.1—20,000 RANDOM DIGITS (Continued)

3971	5334	7159	6064	1481	0891	5376	0202	8304	7828
3272	6356	7738	8702	4698	0642	4878	5192	3472	0397
1416	9160	3971	1943	4260	1919	8756	0410	1639	2915
1669	0944	2035	1067	3676	7870	1169	7233	7342	6940
8070	1847	5259	9001	7262	1673	7485	2519	5669	5430
5907	7117	8720	2343	9498	8476	0651	9007	8768	5663
7518	3022	4776	2031	3240	1547	4956	0464	1888	9867
7970	1749	7496	4334	3658	4133	2728	1179	8106	1120
0433	6317	1028	2509	3699	2204	0034	5469	3860	5780
9153	2104	1728	9604	7610	9316	0143	7312	9248	6816
9309	2377	0667	0098	9891	8438	7112	0188	1399	6774
3130	2085	3191	9748	4279	3719	5401	8022	2570	0613
6802	5596	3288	9192	4212	9524	8066	5294	8949	3502
1583	4057	4387	5328	5998	0004	0175	6972	1765	8808
3523	4747	0465	1575	0655	9336	5188	4393	5195	8768
5989	0704	6971	1920	2462	0778	7041	3635	6397	9252
2028	4315	5882	8721	7575	8367	9122	8957	6639	4737
7910	1719	1457	7237	8253	7482	7691	2607	9050	7261
5901	5174	9933	1415	9665	0191	3694	9752	1937	2392
9260	9657	1589	6723	4967	2633	2499	4650	4328	4898
4935	9517	3472	4239	8309	6383	8256	9360	3681	5017
3294	8012	9850	9181	3157	6192	5231	0259	1965	0237
1405	9219	2992	7658	5571	7537	7582	1386	3457	4496
1705	8477	6846	0987	6518	3545	8489	4908	3485	9163
8274	7844	5979	2257	2546	6306	2188	5284	5928	1294
5268	1607	4340	9815	6623	3276	3738	8471	2233	3158
7846	4995	5105	3728	1107	6394	4606	5748	9688	9904
7366	0196	5715	9347	3166	9948	1861	2342	0211	3909
0886	3147	5146	1737	5848	7286	6551	2432	8201	9200
9564	7417	1646	2158	1401	4356	4143	0295	9805	1077
9878	6064	6484	7767	6224	3436	9696	8859	4271	3577
3765	3256	4827	9732	2343	8873	5368	2694	0677	0058
6495	4240	0814	4302	4027	4747	6316	6775	9362	4688
1234	1194	7712	4854	7445	5294	6099	2242	6303	1625
3231	9358	9790	3236	4743	4683	9485	6473	4058	3127
5754	3808	1905	7906	8191	5072	8832	2614	9486	6362
2961	5883	6716	8023	5946	3739	9397	2836	3934	3478
7810	0770	8280	1754	8276	1812	4239	2385	0680	8744
5969	1518	1666	9257	1329	4678	9715	5339	6882	5316
9275	4575	0011	7780	8352	6287	6004	5037	3599	8554
3018	2818	8803	9512	3445	0995	0344	7656	5067	1324
3434	8797	0091	9680	1836	0861	5702	4345	8687	9286
0692	8477	8033	0473	4891	1253	5537	0371	4484	4186
0960	4119	8886	7927	7579	6239	4817	0993	8538	2494
7596	1079	3718	4512	5148	0157	5090	7978	3396	5267
4548	3206	8978	4395	1967	7185	4123	5065	5936	9763
6284	4087	6634	2524	8092	0371	3385	8221	6596	7250
6761	8551	1053	2468	2783	3982	8013	1635	0455	3896
9349	9186	7383	8074	6006	1277	1286	7524	3660	1839
8194	1840	9783	3720	4411	7415	7262	1286	7580	5247

TABLE H.1 – 20,000 RANDOM DIGITS (Continued)

7455	8970	0420	2555	0865	6652	0299	5740	6271	8489
2410	3545	4563	8845	9625	2157	4344	5394	6893	7611
4107	1012	6459	6730	3951	7087	3976	5265	9703	4982
9004	7430	9257	0408	7910	8682	1932	7641	0060	2561
1168	3087	7034	4105	6950	7049	1802	7761	2040	7604
3649	4911	5258	1091	3049	8495	9631	8712	0783	2581
0813	4479	5869	6433	1436	6219	7670	4833	8467	0339
5920	7740	3122	3380	6407	4450	1005	0281	0428	7246
2036	7062	3307	6108	1191	7274	3065	9035	9846	6569
6300	7402	8762	8967	0776	8940	8728	6633	0878	1348
1200	3239	1354	4904	7591	2615	0441	3151	7672	6840
0683	7690	9441	7308	6622	3649	3383	6640	3407	6343
8919	5854	3282	2306	2229	3009	1501	8475	3420	3986
8344	9979	9835	3186	7659	9142	7365	4896	1809	2835
4938	4203	0666	4996	7969	3127	7920	7871	0982	8359
1047	4923	1736	8094	4329	9113	3537	1767	5748	4596
3740	3188	5291	0549	4196	2356	1272	0733	0624	3625
3385	5236	6509	4608	0428	5134	3384	9036	9708	1902
6020	4244	8739	3440	6483	3487	4041	1834	5239	1587
5833	3381	6948	2401	6439	6439	9682	8590	3373	7636
4261	8995	2485	5561	4524	8986	9900	1750	7280	3519
8274	1043	3527	6067	4927	3449	1539	7203	0228	3383
1028	7994	0213	8188	0994	9437	8544	2973	7353	2296
6982	1705	9810	6171	6694	9009	4094	0259	2945	2516
7104	5836	3596	3194	7276	8513	2347	6188	8131	9301
9752	4243	7510	4305	5006	9037	8640	3029	0100	5819
6974	2184	3020	3962	6144	7809	4172	5949	2198	6218
1048	2939	7293	4134	3747	5017	5971	7197	7385	5866
8221	0634	3277	0178	0182	8998	5324	2940	1929	6811
3653	9567	3421	6153	1399	9721	8560	4347	6176	3242
7510	2868	3923	6415	0865	3555	8767	8665	6296	0485
6051	5603	6800	4034	1538	3546	9082	7063	6346	1520
4444	0240	7540	3367	8876	4063	5784	5788	0594	0803
4837	2849	9002	8463	5847	9264	9021	6919	2289	1494
0588	5666	6733	2588	7899	3206	7060	5893	5598	9550
7655	3769	2602	0812	6991	9259	1160	5588	5769	7439
9415	0498	2066	0583	8309	2569	7279	0453	3870	8118
9018	0939	9174	4967	6372	5396	7874	5556	6170	8127
1720	6421	7113	7014	3089	3716	6904	3254	6926	0353
0780	4041	0212	0201	5666	9068	8947	8515	8386	8144
9176	6038	3658	7576	5303	8330	7730	4888	5418	6669
3156	8560	9590	1308	7447	3950	7842	6120	3671	8174
6068	2994	3185	7744	5056	9906	1231	7700	4022	8728
1089	3289	8592	9052	4497	9635	5264	2875	2930	0689
2269	5793	8178	1291	6710	8107	1091	3704	2341	9016
4874	2683	7991	6627	7182	9788	5787	6454	9535	7265
1154	8018	0300	9500	9861	7527	9783	5174	4859	0306
6395	6236	0373	3998	8115	5882	8075	2221	4361	1696
3526	2425	1357	4267	7183	8831	6892	3874	1220	4292
7025	9722	7300	3557	9141	9612	7521	1170	0793	2354

TABLE H.1—20,000 RANDOM DIGITS (Continued)

1949	0405	3601	7045	0248	3413	5101	1398	4038	1149
0548	0734	2487	8989	3663	3561	4900	5595	8304	5925
8998	3855	9937	2538	3542	3146	7085	9129	6878	6840
8449	4937	6388	0849	2255	9304	0705	7140	2888	9172
4157	5137	9819	9200	5848	2404	5228	1823	9312	8879
1381	0714	2687	1749	7681	8514	8702	7528	2708	8399
2209	5826	7941	1735	0631	1882	1404	9292	5135	1811
2969	3841	0868	2335	0246	4776	9473	9294	1750	3471
5639	7726	4797	9717	9694	2153	6096	3792	5722	7339
4656	3710	4605	6110	3922	8573	6402	4953	1307	7761
3110	3280	2941	7711	5391	7892	3789	7025	2855	7927
7247	3205	5682	5868	9086	2570	1275	4267	4244	1073
9126	5013	4176	5429	9336	7583	3147	1746	9910	3279
4105	4882	5482	1953	9319	8370	5554	2621	1043	7872
6442	4779	0868	6416	4273	6919	9863	9359	5670	7930
7105	9143	6581	6169	6387	7558	0033	8999	5189	8831
4552	2951	4799	2267	1707	5454	2412	2518	5729	2513
9740	9652	0661	1980	1693	3877	0188	6475	8456	5444
6049	2224	7444	5565	2302	6873	6498	3927	9530	0782
0505	7105	0307	9080	7901	7621	4591	7022	2329	1485
4587	6272	1598	7883	0750	0589	0654	2049	0880	2012
3143	4074	6183	2943	5706	0795	7847	3146	9480	7439
0651	6579	9523	9717	6327	1337	8406	3570	0260	0095
0169	4034	2783	1354	7771	6553	9609	6499	0405	5979
7935	2718	1124	4920	2906	0721	2605	7072	1245	6308
3236	6778	0781	0885	5390	6888	2562	8577	8967	8579
5112	9373	1954	4006	1181	8323	4648	6141	5519	3622
5839	5771	0761	9822	2338	1175	0190	2042	5450	7824
7656	7130	0409	0529	4327	9710	5197	2349	3646	2433
6741	0607	5217	1247	0397	5097	2087	9409	3548	4507
5252	9561	0352	6163	4307	4574	7847	7373	8221	6304
9357	6050	8992	8436	9733	9218	3716	1422	3925	2092
1494	6341	3286	2313	2725	4389	3161	4701	2826	6939
6430	3593	0492	1062	4340	4143	3052	0575	8265	2273
7735	1964	2677	1741	0946	3730	5745	3103	7127	4983
9565	4711	3299	4719	4690	4436	4398	8552	0952	7415
5979	5003	7307	4143	1752	1490	4261	8070	4617	3948
0225	0198	9078	7071	3389	9870	9410	8837	1660	8411
7571	1243	2761	5881	6639	2844	3293	2844	6060	4381
1195	4507	1413	3612	2981	3859	0780	0183	3073	7735
5234	1157	8413	4641	7361	7765	4227	2900	5950	0903
4868	7433	9008	3126	4068	7948	8992	8906	7776	7062
1433	6311	7247	4115	7320	7648	8035	4239	3771	2260
1008	2369	7307	1077	0316	2921	6612	3968	6231	9885
7831	9427	2537	7869	7282	6156	7091	0440	2307	2965
4190	0961	6004	7950	3218	2381	6432	8744	2244	6768
5133	1040	3067	5486	0641	4874	5091	1117	3112	3462
5918	5811	8683	4537	3538	7782	9936	3918	7278	9305
7703	5753	4220	9440	7269	5385	2407	9115	9780	6646
6955	6614	5937	4493	5871	1829	7780	2074	3807	0361

TABLE H.1—20,000 RANDOM DIGITS (Continued)

5423	2041	6872	3535	0532	9264	0013	6846	2895	4809
9676	8023	0312	9123	8690	4076	3476	6796	1724	2239
1770	6798	1405	7225	2233	9204	2205	4974	4932	8808
6874	0323	4510	0290	6589	9016	9679	7658	4505	6793
7246	6277	1604	3295	4736	8779	9745	6985	6783	0144
9033	7408	9016	0488	1123	9533	7872	7234	4733	4218
5505	7273	9934	5037	9826	6555	5128	3652	1714	3383
0818	9841	7504	1380	3194	4092	8850	8207	3083	9597
7232	8470	6087	3316	8196	7123	9027	7468	1608	8118
1913	9128	0648	5472	6079	8096	4087	3263	2937	2294
5010	4242	3548	0627	3000	1079	6017	0989	8048	7003
4791	8810	0932	4327	2439	1300	8157	2884	4170	6703
1324	5372	4070	8632	7333	1067	6782	4917	4400	3653
1056	9794	0930	9710	2060	6418	2843	9545	1187	2809
7957	3335	1069	9927	1588	0690	1606	2827	0477	7621
3273	3262	1336	3233	8345	6982	7520	5020	5630	2075
5274	2824	4208	5985	7329	8543	4562	4393	0723	2501
4116	3179	5723	8351	3958	1519	6981	3903	8105	9096
6068	1395	7250	7580	8220	8179	7845	4909	4932	9977
5278	1839	4767	6759	8473	4671	1692	3768	1374	4334
4804	5650	0511	8116	6876	3182	1319	3439	4599	0414
8123	8005	0850	8929	5585	8942	3245	9189	7733	0585
0285	4253	7843	0347	1850	3237	9467	4267	4176	8705
5446	6372	6757	7537	7757	3117	4214	2740	8065	8322
6865	0600	9741	4867	7646	1828	2864	7976	4468	4314
7711	9314	3962	5275	5774	2749	7475	4124	6734	0130
4240	6663	9779	4140	6118	0738	3104	6342	7030	0936
8620	7614	2249	4619	2028	7233	4310	7807	2524	9791
5091	4626	7531	0960	8651	0422	4060	2857	5464	9044
9730	2857	8092	6242	9285	1452	7403	3561	0929	6771
3904	5355	7781	5812	7958	4593	6917	6187	0246	2222
2743	7407	0075	2738	8929	4881	6540	5881	0603	3664
9333	2342	0922	1368	5574	4615	2449	3714	3149	2155
8023	4257	1781	5661	2842	9013	6083	4242	5141	3042
4081	6272	8610	8004	3092	2363	3329	2423	8757	0415
1465	4672	4886	7625	2400	8713	7637	2426	6135	7591
2523	0618	3557	3602	3115	1321	2153	7698	5543	8678
2432	0456	0972	0284	1396	3364	2955	1007	7140	8895
4432	6155	8209	3648	8390	1082	1482	8903	6203	9328
2609	3073	1615	5132	9295	7541	2522	3661	8861	7426
1302	5367	3368	2715	9238	5100	1723	9131	5301	4247
5670	6206	9407	6844	1679	0037	0032	1781	2761	6950
7898	0848	2309	1587	9595	5380	4838	1668	2429	6811
2027	1430	6013	3002	6134	5327	7069	5040	1533	8070
3504	2141	6996	4548	8764	3195	4192	7186	1252	6704
4417	9338	5017	9282	8433	4974	7186	9124	6843	4260
0003	4071	7633	1362	1410	1120	0309	7151	2364	6618
5541	3506	7903	5166	9061	9683	9998	4515	1174	7105
2080	8981	7294	5633	7345	1939	7012	5465	7240	9009
5786	4696	4555	5230	0501	2937	7048	2978	6010	7378

TABLE H.2—PROPORTIONS OF AREAS UNDER THE NORMAL CURVE BETWEEN THE MEAN AND Z-SCORES FROM 0.00 TO 3.09

This is a double-entry table and requires locating the proper row and column before reading an entry from the table. The entries in the body of the table represent the proportion of the total area under the normal curve lying between the mean and the specific Z-Score. For example, the area corresponding to a Z-Score (standard score) of 1.35 is seen to be 0.41149. The area in the body of the table and the corresponding Z-Score are illustrated, for this example, in the normal distribution below. All other proportions are read in the same manner.

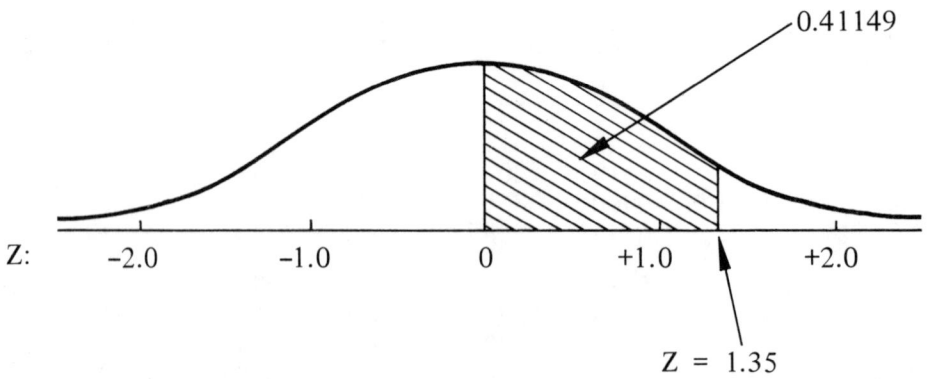

Due to the symmetry of the normal distribution, the tabular values also apply to standard scores in the negative direction.

TABLE H.2–PROPORTIONS OF AREAS UNDER THE NORMAL CURVE BETWEEN THE MEAN AND Z-SCORES FROM 0.00 TO 3.09

Z	.00	.01	.02	.03	.04	.05	.06	.07	.08	.09
0.0	.00000	.00399	.00798	.01197	.01595	.01994	.02392	.02790	.03188	.03586
0.1	.03983	.04380	.04776	.05172	.05567	.05962	.06356	.06749	.07142	.07535
0.2	.07926	.08317	.08706	.09095	.09483	.09871	.10257	.10642	.11026	.11409
0.3	.11791	.12172	.12552	.12930	.13307	.13683	.14058	.14431	.14803	.15173
0.4	.15542	.15910	.16276	.16640	.17003	.17364	.17724	.18082	.18439	.18793
0.5	.19146	.19497	.19847	.20194	.20540	.20884	.21226	.21566	.21904	.22240
0.6	.22575	.22907	.23237	.23565	.23891	.24215	.24537	.24857	.25175	.25490
0.7	.25804	.26115	.26424	.26730	.27035	.27337	.27637	.27935	.28230	.28524
0.8	.28814	.29103	.29389	.29673	.29955	.30234	.30511	.30785	.31057	.31327
0.9	.31594	.31859	.32121	.32381	.32639	.32894	.33147	.33398	.33646	.33891
1.0	.34134	.34375	.34614	.34850	.35083	.35314	.35543	.35769	.35993	.36214
1.1	.36433	.36650	.36864	.37076	.37286	.37493	.37698	.37900	.38100	.38298
1.2	.38493	.38686	.38877	.39065	.39251	.39435	.39617	.39796	.39973	.40147
1.3	.40320	.40490	.40658	.40824	.40988	.41149	.41309	.41466	.41621	.41774
1.4	.41924	.42073	.42220	.42364	.42507	.42647	.42786	.42922	.43056	.43189
1.5	.43319	.43448	.43574	.43699	.43822	.43943	.44062	.44179	.44295	.44408
1.6	.44520	.44630	.44738	.44845	.44950	.45053	.45154	.45254	.45352	.45449
1.7	.45543	.45637	.45728	.45818	.45907	.45994	.46080	.46164	.46246	.46327
1.8	.46407	.46485	.46562	.46638	.46712	.46784	.46856	.46926	.46995	.47062
1.9	.47128	.47193	.47257	.47320	.47381	.47441	.47500	.47558	.47615	.47670
2.0	.47725	.47778	.47831	.47882	.47932	.47982	.48030	.48077	.48124	.48169
2.1	.48214	.48257	.48300	.48341	.48382	.48422	.48461	.48500	.48537	.48574
2.2	.48610	.48645	.48679	.48713	.48745	.48778	.48809	.48840	.48870	.48899
2.3	.48928	.48956	.48983	.49010	.49036	.49061	.49086	.49111	.49134	.49158
2.4	.49180	.49202	.49224	.49245	.49266	.49286	.49305	.49324	.49343	.49361
2.5	.49379	.49396	.49413	.49430	.49446	.49461	.49477	.49492	.49506	.49520
2.6	.49534	.49547	.49560	.49573	.49585	.49598	.49609	.49621	.49632	.49643
2.7	.49653	.49664	.49674	.49683	.49693	.49702	.49711	.49720	.49728	.49736
2.8	.49745	.49752	.49760	.49767	.49774	.49781	.49788	.49795	.49801	.49807
2.9	.49813	.49819	.49825	.49831	.49836	.49841	.49846	.49851	.49856	.49861
3.0	.49865	.49869	.49874	.49878	.49882	.49886	.49889	.49893	.49897	.49900

TABLE H.3—SELECTED STANDARD SCORES (Z-SCORES) ASSOCIATED WITH PROPORTIONS OF AREAS UNDER THE NORMAL CURVE FOR PROPORTIONS FROM 0.05 TO 0.499.

Z-Score	Proportion Area From Mean To Z-Score
.126	.05
.253	.10
.385	.15
.524	.20
.6745	.25
.842	.30
1.036	.35
1.282	.40
1.645	.45
1.960	.475
2.326	.49
2.576	.495
3.090	.499

In the table above, the Z-Scores corresponding to specific proportions can be determined without unnecessary interpolation in Table H.2. The proportion of the total area under the normal curve from the mean to the given Z-Score is found in the righthand column of the table and the associated Z-Score on the same row in the lefthand column of the table. The specific relationships under a normal curve for a desired proportion of 0.30 are indicated in the curve below with the associated Z-Score being 0.842.

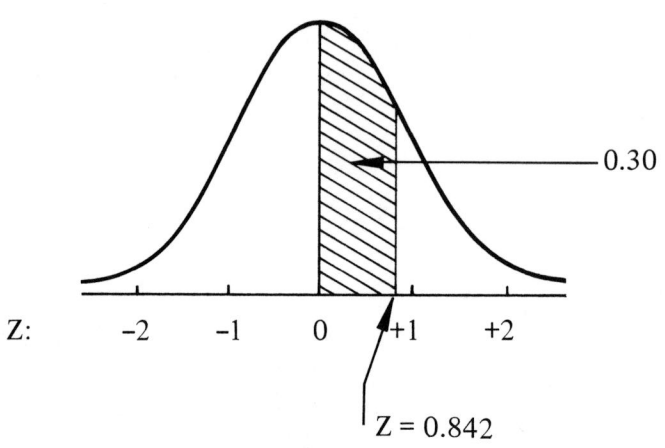

TABLE H.4—STUDENT'S "t" DISTRIBUTION

This table is a double-entry table and requires determining the degrees of freedom (df) and then selecting the appropriate tabular "t" value depending upon the confidence level or risk (level of significance). The "t" values in the body of the table are two-tailed values and are associated with the area included on both sides of the mean (the confidence level) and areas excluded on both sides of the mean (the risk or level of significance).

To illustrate, if the degrees of freedom are 15 and the desired confidence level is 0.95, the appropriate tabular "t" value is seen to be 2.132. This relationship is illustrated in the distribution below.

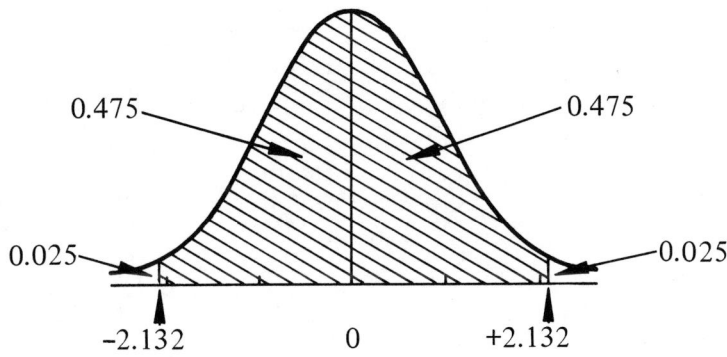

If only one tail of the "t" distribution is involved in the estimation process or in the hypothesis testing situation, then the level of significance and associated risk would be one-half of the proportion on the "risk; level of significance" row.

TABLE H.4 – STUDENT'S "t" DISTRIBUTION

Confidence level:	0.80	0.90	0.95	0.98	0.99
Risk; level of significance:	0.20	0.10	0.05	0.02	0.01
Degrees of freedom					
1	3.078	6.314	12.706	31.821	63.657
2	1.886	2.920	4.303	6.965	9.925
3	1.638	2.353	3.182	4.541	5.841
4	1.533	2.132	2.776	3.747	4.604
5	1.476	2.015	2.571	3.365	4.032
6	1.440	1.943	2.447	3.143	3.707
7	1.415	1.895	2.365	2.998	3.500
8	1.397	1.860	2.306	2.897	3.355
9	1.383	1.833	2.262	2.821	3.250
10	1.372	1.813	2.228	2.764	3.169
11	1.363	1.796	2.201	2.718	3.106
12	1.356	1.782	2.179	2.681	3.055
13	1.350	1.771	2.160	2.650	3.012
14	1.345	1.761	2.145	2.625	2.977
15	1.341	1.753	[2.132]	2.603	2.947
16	1.337	1.746	2.120	2.584	2.921
17	1.333	1.740	2.110	2.567	2.898
18	1.330	1.734	2.101	2.552	2.878
19	1.328	1.729	2.093	2.540	2.861
20	1.325	1.725	2.086	2.528	2.845
21	1.323	1.721	2.080	2.518	2.831
22	1.321	1.717	2.074	2.508	2.819
23	1.320	1.714	2.069	2.500	2.807
24	1.318	1.711	2.064	2.492	2.797
25	1.316	1.708	2.060	2.485	2.787
26	1.315	1.706	2.056	2.479	2.779
27	1.314	1.703	2.052	2.473	2.771
28	1.313	1.701	2.048	2.467	2.763
29	1.311	1.699	2.045	2.462	2.756
30	1.310	1.697	2.042	2.457	2.750
35	1.306	1.690	2.030	2.438	2.724
40	1.303	1.684	2.021	2.423	2.705
45	1.301	1.679	2.014	2.412	2.690
50	1.299	1.676	2.009	2.403	2.678
55	1.297	1.673	2.004	2.396	2.668
60	1.296	1.671	2.000	2.390	2.660
70	1.294	1.667	1.994	2.381	2.648
80	1.292	1.664	1.990	2.374	2.639
90	1.291	1.662	1.987	2.369	2.632
100	1.290	1.660	1.984	2.364	2.626
Normal	1.282	1.645	1.960	2.326	2.576

TABLE H.5—CHI-SQUARE DISTRIBUTION

This table is also a double-entry table and requires knowledge of both the degrees of freedom (df) and the desired chi-square percentile. The chi-square (χ^2) values in the body of the table correspond to only one tail of the chi-square distribution, which is an asymmetrical distribution.

To illustrate, for 20 degrees of freedom the 95th percentile point is found to be $\chi^2 = 31.41$. This point also excludes the upper 5% of the chi-square distribution for 20 degrees of freedom and is illustrated in the figure below.

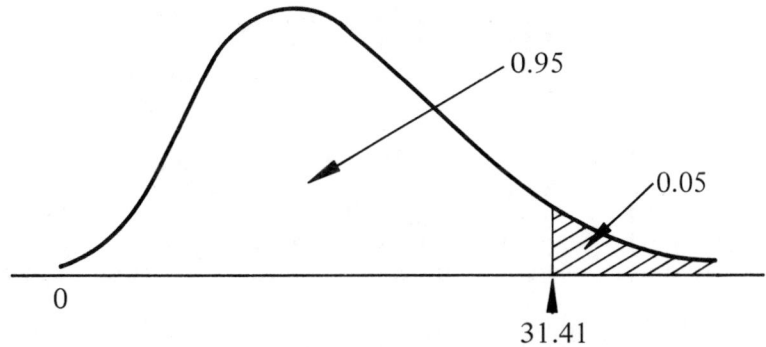

To illustrate, suppose in hypothesis testing a two-tailed test is to be conducted with the level of significance being 5%. This would exclude 2.5% of the distribution on each end of the curve. For 30 degrees of freedom, the two chi-square values would be: $\chi^2_{0.025} = 16.79$ and $\chi^2_{0.975} = 46.98$. These areas are illustrated in the figure below.

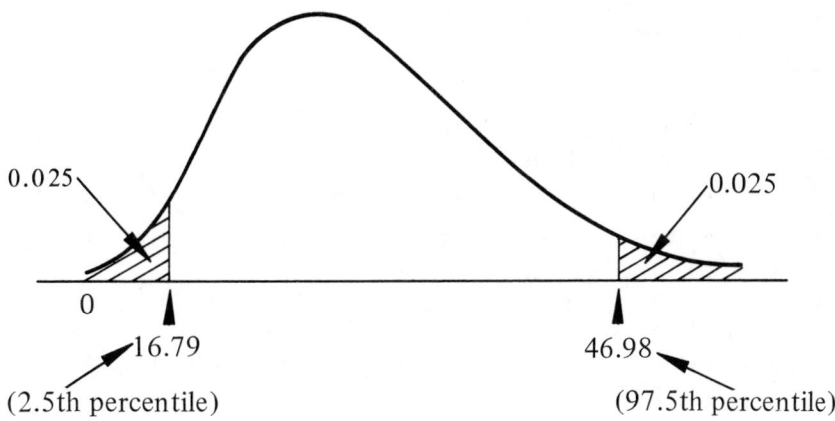

TABLE H.5–CHI-SQUARE DISTRIBUTION

df	\.005	\.010	\.025	\.050	\.100	\.900	\.950	\.975	\.990	\.995
					Percentiles					
1	.00	.00	.00	.00	.02	2.71	3.84	5.02	6.64	7.88
2	.01	.02	.05	.10	.21	4.61	5.99	7.38	9.21	10.60
3	.07	.12	.22	.35	.58	6.25	7.82	9.35	11.35	12.84
4	.21	.30	.48	.71	1.06	7.78	9.49	11.14	13.28	14.86
5	.41	.55	.83	1.15	1.61	9.24	11.07	12.83	15.09	16.75
6	.68	.87	1.24	1.64	2.20	10.65	12.59	14.45	16.81	18.55
7	.99	1.24	1.69	2.17	2.83	12.02	14.07	16.01	18.48	20.28
8	1.34	1.65	2.18	2.73	3.49	13.36	15.51	17.54	20.09	21.96
9	1.74	2.09	2.70	3.33	4.17	14.68	16.92	19.02	21.67	23.59
10	2.16	2.56	3.25	3.94	4.87	15.99	18.31	20.48	23.21	25.19
11	2.60	3.05	3.82	4.58	5.58	17.28	19.68	21.92	24.73	26.76
12	3.07	3.57	4.40	5.23	6.30	18.55	21.03	23.34	26.22	28.30
13	3.57	4.11	5.01	5.89	7.04	19.81	22.36	24.74	27.69	29.82
14	4.08	4.66	5.63	6.57	7.79	21.06	23.69	26.12	29.14	31.32
15	4.60	5.23	6.26	7.26	8.55	22.31	25.00	27.49	30.58	32.80
16	5.14	5.81	6.91	7.96	9.31	23.54	26.30	28.85	32.00	34.27
17	5.70	6.41	7.56	8.67	10.09	24.77	27.59	30.19	33.41	35.72
18	6.27	7.02	8.23	9.39	10.87	25.99	28.87	31.53	34.81	37.16
19	6.84	7.63	8.91	10.12	11.65	27.20	30.14	32.85	36.19	38.58
20	7.43	8.26	9.59	10.85	12.44	28.41	31.41	34.17	37.57	40.00
21	8.03	8.90	10.28	11.59	13.24	29.62	32.67	35.48	38.93	41.40
22	8.64	9.54	10.98	12.34	14.04	30.81	33.92	36.78	40.29	42.80
23	9.26	10.20	11.69	13.09	14.85	32.01	35.17	38.08	41.64	44.18
24	9.89	10.86	12.40	13.85	15.66	33.20	36.42	39.36	42.98	45.56
25	10.52	11.52	13.12	14.61	16.47	34.38	37.65	40.65	44.31	46.93
26	11.16	12.20	13.84	15.38	17.29	35.56	38.89	41.92	45.64	48.29
27	11.81	12.88	14.57	16.15	18.11	36.74	40.11	43.19	46.96	49.65
28	12.46	13.57	15.31	16.93	18.94	37.92	41.34	44.46	48.28	50.99
29	13.12	14.26	16.05	17.71	19.77	39.09	42.56	45.72	49.59	52.34
30	13.79	14.95	16.79	18.49	20.60	40.26	43.77	46.98	50.89	53.67
31	14.46	15.66	17.54	19.28	21.43	41.42	44.99	48.23	52.19	55.00
32	15.13	16.36	18.29	20.07	22.27	42.59	46.19	49.48	53.49	56.33
33	15.82	17.07	19.05	20.87	23.11	43.75	47.40	50.73	54.78	57.65
34	16.50	17.79	19.81	21.66	23.95	44.90	48.60	51.97	56.06	58.96
35	17.19	18.51	20.57	22.47	24.80	46.06	49.80	53.20	57.34	60.28
36	17.89	19.23	21.34	23.27	25.64	47.21	51.00	54.44	58.62	61.58
37	18.59	19.96	22.11	24.08	26.49	48.36	52.19	55.67	59.89	62.88
38	19.29	20.69	22.88	24.88	27.34	49.51	53.38	56.90	61.16	64.18
39	20.00	21.43	23.65	25.70	28.20	50.66	54.57	58.12	62.43	65.48
40	20.71	22.16	24.43	26.51	29.05	51.81	55.76	59.34	63.69	66.77

TABLE H.5–CHI-SQUARE DISTRIBUTION (Continued)

df					Percentiles					
	.005	.010	.025	.050	.100	.900	.950	.975	.990	.995
41	21.42	22.91	25.22	27.33	29.91	52.95	56.94	60.56	64.95	68.05
42	22.14	23.65	26.00	28.14	30.77	54.09	58.12	61.78	66.21	69.34
43	22.86	24.40	26.79	28.97	31.63	55.23	59.30	62.99	67.46	70.62
44	23.58	25.15	27.58	29.79	32.49	56.37	60.48	64.20	68.71	71.89
45	24.31	25.90	28.37	30.61	33.35	57.51	61.66	65.41	69.96	73.17
46	25.04	26.66	29.16	31.44	34.22	58.64	62.83	66.62	71.20	74.44
47	25.78	27.42	29.96	32.27	35.08	59.77	64.00	67.82	72.44	75.70
48	26.51	28.18	30.76	33.10	35.95	60.91	65.17	69.02	73.68	76.97
49	27.25	28.94	31.56	33.93	36.82	62.04	66.34	70.22	74.92	78.23
50	27.99	29.71	32.36	34.76	37.69	63.17	67.51	71.42	76.15	79.49
51	28.74	30.48	33.16	35.60	38.56	64.30	68.67	72.62	77.39	80.75
52	29.48	31.25	33.97	36.44	39.43	65.42	69.83	73.81	78.62	82.00
53	30.23	32.02	34.78	37.28	40.31	66.55	70.99	75.00	79.84	83.25
54	30.98	32.79	35.59	38.12	41.18	67.67	72.15	76.19	81.07	84.50
55	31.74	33.57	36.40	38.96	42.06	68.80	73.31	77.38	82.29	85.75
56	32.49	34.35	37.21	39.80	42.94	69.92	74.47	78.57	83.51	86.99
57	33.25	35.13	38.03	40.65	43.82	71.04	75.62	79.75	84.73	88.24
58	34.01	35.91	38.84	41.49	44.70	72.16	76.78	80.94	85.95	89.48
59	34.77	36.70	39.66	42.34	45.58	73.28	77.93	82.12	87.17	90.72
60	35.53	37.49	40.48	43.19	46.46	74.40	79.08	83.30	88.38	91.95
61	36.30	38.27	41.30	44.04	47.34	75.51	80.23	84.48	89.59	93.19
62	37.07	39.06	42.13	44.89	48.23	76.63	81.38	85.65	90.80	94.42
63	37.84	39.86	42.95	45.74	49.11	77.75	82.53	86.83	92.01	95.65
64	38.61	40.65	43.78	46.60	50.00	78.86	83.68	88.00	93.22	96.88
65	39.38	41.44	44.60	47.45	50.88	79.97	84.82	89.18	94.42	98.11
66	40.16	42.24	45.43	48.31	51.77	81.09	85.97	90.35	95.63	99.33
67	40.94	43.04	46.26	49.16	52.66	82.20	87.11	91.52	96.83	100.55
68	41.71	43.84	47.09	50.02	53.55	83.31	88.25	92.69	98.03	101.78
69	42.49	44.64	47.92	50.88	54.44	84.42	89.39	93.86	99.23	103.00
70	43.28	45.44	48.76	51.74	55.33	85.53	90.53	95.02	100.43	104.22
71	44.06	46.25	49.59	52.60	56.22	86.64	91.67	96.19	101.62	105.43
72	44.84	47.05	50.43	53.46	57.11	87.74	92.81	97.35	102.82	106.65
73	45.63	47.86	51.27	54.33	58.01	88.85	93.95	98.52	104.01	107.86
74	46.42	48.67	52.10	55.19	58.90	89.96	95.08	99.68	105.20	109.07
75	47.21	49.48	52.94	56.05	59.80	91.06	96.22	100.84	106.39	110.29
76	48.00	50.29	53.78	56.92	60.69	92.17	97.35	102.00	107.58	111.50
77	48.79	51.10	54.62	57.79	61.59	93.27	98.48	103.16	108.77	112.70
78	49.58	51.91	55.47	58.65	62.48	94.37	99.62	104.32	109.96	113.91
79	50.38	52.73	56.31	59.52	63.38	95.48	100.75	105.47	111.14	115.12
80	51.17	53.54	57.15	60.39	64.28	96.58	101.88	106.63	112.33	116.32
81	51.97	54.36	58.00	61.26	65.18	97.68	103.01	107.78	113.51	117.52
82	52.77	55.17	58.85	62.13	66.08	98.78	104.14	108.94	114.70	118.73
83	53.57	55.99	59.69	63.00	66.98	99.88	105.27	110.09	115.88	119.93
84	54.37	56.81	60.54	63.88	67.88	100.98	106.40	111.24	117.06	121.13
85	55.17	57.63	61.39	64.75	68.78	102.08	107.52	112.39	118.24	122.33
86	55.97	58.46	62.24	65.62	69.68	103.18	108.65	113.54	119.41	123.52
87	56.78	59.28	63.09	66.50	70.58	104.28	109.77	114.69	120.59	124.72
88	57.58	60.10	63.94	67.37	71.48	105.37	110.90	115.84	121.77	125.91
89	58.39	60.93	64.79	68.25	72.39	106.47	112.02	116.99	122.94	127.11
90	59.20	61.75	65.65	69.13	73.29	107.57	113.15	118.14	124.12	128.30

TABLE H.5—CHI-SQUARE DISTRIBUTION (Continued)

df	Percentiles									
	.005	.010	.025	.050	.100	.900	.950	.975	.990	.995
91	60.01	62.58	66.50	70.00	74.20	108.66	114.27	119.28	125.29	129.49
92	60.82	63.41	67.36	70.88	75.10	109.76	115.39	120.43	126.46	130.68
93	61.63	64.24	68.21	71.76	76.01	110.85	116.51	121.57	127.63	131.87
94	62.44	65.07	69.07	72.64	76.91	111.94	117.63	122.72	128.80	133.06
95	63.25	65.90	69.93	73.52	77.82	113.04	118.75	123.86	129.97	134.25
96	64.06	66.73	70.78	74.40	78.73	114.13	119.87	125.00	131.14	135.43
97	64.88	67.56	71.64	75.28	79.63	115.22	120.99	126.14	132.31	136.62
98	65.69	68.40	72.50	76.16	80.54	116.32	122.11	127.28	133.48	137.80
99	66.51	69.23	73.36	77.05	81.45	117.41	123.23	128.42	134.64	138.99
100	67.33	70.07	74.22	77.93	82.36	118.50	124.34	129.56	135.81	140.17

For values of chi-square with degrees of freedom greater than 100, a good approximation is given by:

$$\chi^2_{df, p} = \tfrac{1}{2} [Z_p + \sqrt{2 \times df - 1}]^2,$$

where Z_p is the appropriate normal Z-score associated with the specific percentile desired. For example, $Z_{.025} = -1.96$ and $Z_{.975} = +1.96$.

TABLE H.6—The F Distribution (Upper Percentage Points)

The F distribution, like the chi-square distribution, is asymmetrical.

It is also a double-entry table, requiring the degrees of freedom associated with the numerator of the ratio (top of the fraction) and the denominator of the ratio (bottom of the fraction). These degrees of freedom are indicated in the Tables, respectively, as ν_1 and ν_2 (nu-sub-1 and nu-sub-2).

To illustrate, consider a situation in which there are 15 degrees of freedom associated with the numerator ($\nu_1 = 15$) and 10 degrees of freedom associated with the denominator ($\nu_2 = 10$) and the level of significance is 0.01. The table labeled "Percentage Points of the F Distribution: Upper 1% Points" is entered for the column headed $\nu_1 = 15$ and the row labeled $\nu_2 = 10$. The entry in the body of the table is seen to be 4.56. Appropriate values associated with this situation appear in the figure below.

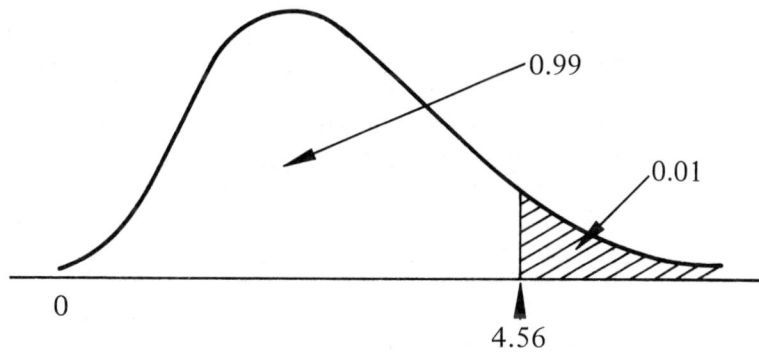

As a second illustration, suppose the numerator degrees of freedom are 8 ($\nu_1 = 8$) and the denominator degrees of freedom are 6 ($\nu_2 = 6$). at the 5% level of significance, the appropriate tabular F value is found in the third table in this series to be F = 4.15. These relationships are indicated in the figure below.

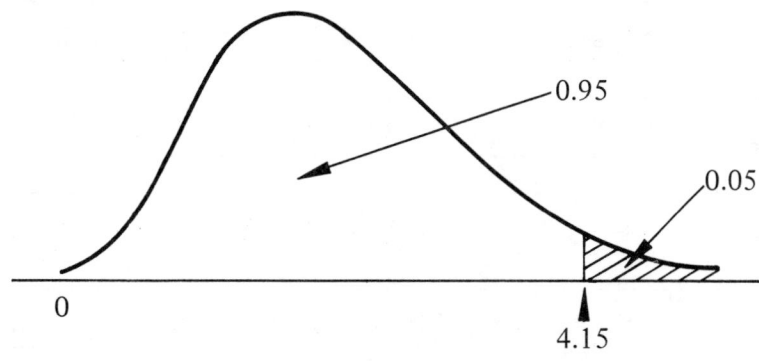

TABLE H.6 – THE F DISTRIBUTION (UPPER PERCENTAGE POINTS)

Percentage points of the F Distribution: upper 25% points

v_2 \ v_1	1	2	3	4	5	6	7	8	9	10	12	15	20	24	30	40	60	120	∞
1	5.83	7.50	8.20	8.58	8.82	8.98	9.10	9.19	9.26	9.32	9.41	9.49	9.58	9.63	9.67	9.71	9.76	9.80	9.85
2	2.57	3.00	3.15	3.23	3.28	3.31	3.34	3.35	3.37	3.38	3.39	3.41	3.43	3.43	3.44	3.45	3.46	3.47	3.48
3	2.02	2.28	2.36	2.39	2.41	2.42	2.43	2.44	2.44	2.44	2.45	2.46	2.46	2.46	2.47	2.47	2.47	2.47	2.47
4	1.81	2.00	2.05	2.06	2.07	2.08	2.08	2.08	2.08	2.08	2.08	2.08	2.08	2.08	2.08	2.08	2.08	2.08	2.08
5	1.69	1.85	1.88	1.89	1.89	1.89	1.89	1.89	1.89	1.89	1.89	1.89	1.88	1.88	1.88	1.88	1.87	1.87	1.87
6	1.62	1.76	1.78	1.79	1.79	1.78	1.78	1.78	1.77	1.77	1.77	1.76	1.76	1.75	1.75	1.75	1.74	1.74	1.74
7	1.57	1.70	1.72	1.72	1.71	1.71	1.70	1.70	1.69	1.69	1.68	1.68	1.67	1.66	1.66	1.66	1.65	1.65	1.65
8	1.54	1.66	1.67	1.66	1.66	1.65	1.64	1.64	1.63	1.63	1.62	1.62	1.61	1.60	1.60	1.59	1.59	1.58	1.58
9	1.51	1.62	1.63	1.63	1.62	1.61	1.60	1.60	1.59	1.59	1.58	1.57	1.56	1.56	1.55	1.54	1.54	1.53	1.53
10	1.49	1.60	1.60	1.59	1.59	1.58	1.57	1.56	1.56	1.55	1.54	1.53	1.52	1.52	1.51	1.51	1.50	1.49	1.48
11	1.47	1.58	1.58	1.57	1.56	1.55	1.54	1.53	1.53	1.52	1.51	1.50	1.49	1.49	1.48	1.47	1.47	1.46	1.45
12	1.46	1.56	1.56	1.55	1.54	1.53	1.52	1.51	1.51	1.50	1.49	1.48	1.47	1.46	1.45	1.45	1.44	1.43	1.42
13	1.45	1.55	1.55	1.53	1.52	1.51	1.50	1.49	1.49	1.48	1.47	1.46	1.45	1.44	1.43	1.42	1.42	1.41	1.40
14	1.44	1.53	1.53	1.52	1.51	1.50	1.49	1.48	1.47	1.46	1.45	1.44	1.43	1.42	1.41	1.41	1.40	1.39	1.38
15	1.43	1.52	1.52	1.51	1.49	1.48	1.47	1.46	1.46	1.45	1.44	1.43	1.41	1.41	1.40	1.39	1.38	1.37	1.36
16	1.42	1.51	1.51	1.50	1.48	1.47	1.46	1.45	1.44	1.44	1.43	1.41	1.40	1.39	1.38	1.37	1.36	1.35	1.34
17	1.42	1.51	1.50	1.49	1.47	1.46	1.45	1.44	1.43	1.43	1.41	1.40	1.39	1.38	1.37	1.36	1.35	1.34	1.33
18	1.41	1.50	1.49	1.48	1.46	1.45	1.44	1.43	1.42	1.42	1.40	1.39	1.38	1.37	1.36	1.35	1.34	1.33	1.32
19	1.41	1.49	1.49	1.47	1.46	1.44	1.43	1.42	1.41	1.41	1.40	1.38	1.37	1.36	1.35	1.34	1.33	1.32	1.30
20	1.40	1.49	1.48	1.47	1.45	1.44	1.43	1.42	1.41	1.40	1.39	1.37	1.36	1.35	1.34	1.33	1.32	1.31	1.29
21	1.40	1.48	1.48	1.46	1.44	1.43	1.42	1.41	1.40	1.39	1.38	1.37	1.35	1.34	1.33	1.32	1.31	1.30	1.28
22	1.40	1.48	1.47	1.45	1.44	1.42	1.41	1.40	1.39	1.39	1.37	1.36	1.34	1.33	1.32	1.31	1.30	1.29	1.28
23	1.39	1.47	1.47	1.45	1.43	1.42	1.41	1.40	1.39	1.38	1.37	1.35	1.34	1.33	1.32	1.31	1.30	1.28	1.27
24	1.39	1.47	1.46	1.44	1.43	1.41	1.40	1.39	1.38	1.38	1.36	1.35	1.33	1.32	1.31	1.30	1.29	1.28	1.26
25	1.39	1.47	1.46	1.44	1.42	1.41	1.40	1.39	1.38	1.37	1.36	1.34	1.33	1.32	1.31	1.29	1.28	1.27	1.25
26	1.38	1.46	1.45	1.44	1.42	1.41	1.39	1.38	1.37	1.37	1.35	1.34	1.32	1.31	1.30	1.29	1.28	1.26	1.25
27	1.38	1.46	1.45	1.43	1.42	1.40	1.39	1.38	1.37	1.36	1.35	1.33	1.32	1.31	1.30	1.28	1.27	1.26	1.24
28	1.38	1.46	1.45	1.43	1.41	1.40	1.39	1.38	1.37	1.36	1.34	1.33	1.31	1.30	1.29	1.28	1.27	1.25	1.24
29	1.38	1.45	1.45	1.43	1.41	1.40	1.38	1.37	1.36	1.35	1.34	1.32	1.31	1.30	1.29	1.27	1.26	1.25	1.23
30	1.38	1.45	1.44	1.42	1.41	1.39	1.38	1.37	1.36	1.35	1.34	1.32	1.30	1.29	1.28	1.27	1.26	1.24	1.23
40	1.36	1.44	1.42	1.40	1.39	1.37	1.36	1.35	1.34	1.33	1.31	1.30	1.28	1.26	1.25	1.24	1.22	1.21	1.19
60	1.35	1.42	1.41	1.38	1.37	1.35	1.33	1.32	1.31	1.30	1.29	1.27	1.25	1.24	1.22	1.21	1.19	1.17	1.15
120	1.34	1.40	1.39	1.37	1.35	1.33	1.31	1.30	1.29	1.28	1.26	1.24	1.22	1.21	1.19	1.18	1.16	1.13	1.10
∞	1.32	1.39	1.37	1.35	1.33	1.31	1.29	1.28	1.27	1.25	1.24	1.22	1.19	1.18	1.16	1.14	1.12	1.08	1.00

TABLE H.6—THE F DISTRIBUTION (UPPER PERCENTAGE POINTS) (Continued)

Percentage points of the F Distribution: upper 10% points

v_2 \ v_1	1	2	3	4	5	6	7	8	9	10	12	15	20	24	30	40	60	120	∞
1	39.86	49.50	53.59	55.83	57.24	58.20	58.91	59.44	59.86	60.19	60.71	61.22	61.74	62.00	62.26	62.53	62.79	63.06	63.33
2	8.53	9.00	9.16	9.24	9.29	9.33	9.35	9.37	9.38	9.39	9.41	9.42	9.44	9.45	9.46	9.47	9.47	9.48	9.49
3	5.54	5.46	5.39	5.34	5.31	5.28	5.27	5.25	5.24	5.23	5.22	5.20	5.18	5.18	5.17	5.16	5.15	5.14	5.13
4	4.54	4.32	4.19	4.11	4.05	4.01	3.98	3.95	3.94	3.92	3.90	3.87	3.84	3.84	3.82	3.80	3.79	3.78	3.76
5	4.06	3.78	3.62	3.52	3.45	3.40	3.37	3.34	3.32	3.30	3.27	3.24	3.21	3.19	3.17	3.16	3.14	3.12	3.10
6	3.78	3.46	3.29	3.18	3.11	3.05	3.01	2.98	2.96	2.94	2.90	2.87	2.84	2.82	2.80	2.78	2.76	2.74	2.72
7	3.59	3.26	3.07	2.96	2.88	2.83	2.78	2.75	2.72	2.70	2.67	2.63	2.59	2.58	2.56	2.54	2.51	2.49	2.47
8	3.46	3.11	2.92	2.81	2.73	2.67	2.62	2.59	2.56	2.54	2.50	2.46	2.42	2.40	2.38	2.36	2.34	2.32	2.29
9	3.36	3.01	2.81	2.69	2.61	2.55	2.51	2.47	2.44	2.42	2.38	2.34	2.30	2.28	2.25	2.23	2.21	2.18	2.16
10	3.29	2.92	2.73	2.61	2.52	2.46	2.41	2.38	2.35	2.32	2.28	2.24	2.20	2.18	2.16	2.13	2.11	2.08	2.06
11	3.23	2.86	2.66	2.54	2.45	2.39	2.34	2.30	2.27	2.25	2.21	2.17	2.12	2.10	2.08	2.05	2.03	2.00	1.97
12	3.18	2.81	2.61	2.48	2.39	2.33	2.28	2.24	2.21	2.19	2.15	2.10	2.06	2.04	2.01	1.99	1.96	1.93	1.90
13	3.14	2.76	2.56	2.43	2.35	2.28	2.23	2.20	2.16	2.14	2.10	2.05	2.01	1.98	1.96	1.93	1.90	1.88	1.85
14	3.10	2.73	2.52	2.39	2.31	2.24	2.19	2.15	2.12	2.10	2.05	2.01	1.96	1.94	1.91	1.89	1.86	1.83	1.80
15	3.07	2.70	2.49	2.36	2.27	2.21	2.16	2.12	2.09	2.06	2.02	1.97	1.92	1.90	1.87	1.85	1.82	1.79	1.76
16	3.05	2.67	2.46	2.33	2.24	2.18	2.13	2.09	2.06	2.03	1.99	1.94	1.89	1.87	1.84	1.81	1.78	1.75	1.72
17	3.03	2.64	2.44	2.31	2.22	2.15	2.10	2.06	2.03	2.00	1.96	1.91	1.86	1.84	1.81	1.78	1.75	1.72	1.69
18	3.01	2.62	2.42	2.29	2.20	2.13	2.08	2.04	2.00	1.98	1.93	1.89	1.84	1.81	1.78	1.75	1.72	1.69	1.66
19	2.99	2.61	2.40	2.27	2.18	2.11	2.06	2.02	1.98	1.96	1.91	1.86	1.81	1.79	1.76	1.73	1.70	1.67	1.63
20	2.97	2.59	2.38	2.25	2.16	2.09	2.04	2.00	1.96	1.94	1.89	1.84	1.79	1.77	1.74	1.71	1.68	1.64	1.61
21	2.96	2.57	2.36	2.23	2.14	2.08	2.02	1.98	1.95	1.92	1.87	1.83	1.78	1.75	1.72	1.69	1.66	1.62	1.59
22	2.95	2.56	2.35	2.22	2.13	2.06	2.01	1.97	1.93	1.90	1.86	1.81	1.76	1.73	1.70	1.67	1.64	1.60	1.57
23	2.94	2.55	2.34	2.21	2.11	2.05	1.99	1.95	1.92	1.89	1.84	1.80	1.74	1.72	1.69	1.66	1.62	1.59	1.55
24	2.93	2.54	2.33	2.19	2.10	2.04	1.98	1.94	1.91	1.88	1.83	1.78	1.73	1.70	1.67	1.64	1.61	1.57	1.53
25	2.92	2.53	2.32	2.18	2.09	2.02	1.97	1.93	1.89	1.87	1.82	1.77	1.72	1.69	1.66	1.63	1.59	1.56	1.52
26	2.91	2.52	2.31	2.17	2.08	2.01	1.96	1.92	1.88	1.86	1.81	1.76	1.71	1.68	1.65	1.61	1.58	1.54	1.50
27	2.90	2.51	2.30	2.17	2.07	2.00	1.95	1.91	1.87	1.85	1.80	1.75	1.70	1.67	1.64	1.60	1.57	1.53	1.49
28	2.89	2.50	2.29	2.16	2.06	2.00	1.94	1.90	1.87	1.84	1.79	1.74	1.69	1.66	1.63	1.59	1.56	1.52	1.48
29	2.89	2.50	2.28	2.15	2.06	1.99	1.93	1.89	1.86	1.83	1.78	1.73	1.68	1.65	1.62	1.58	1.55	1.51	1.47
30	2.88	2.49	2.28	2.14	2.05	1.98	1.93	1.88	1.85	1.82	1.77	1.72	1.67	1.64	1.61	1.57	1.54	1.50	1.46
40	2.84	2.44	2.23	2.09	2.00	1.93	1.87	1.83	1.79	1.76	1.71	1.66	1.61	1.57	1.54	1.51	1.47	1.42	1.38
60	2.79	2.39	2.18	2.04	1.95	1.87	1.82	1.77	1.74	1.71	1.66	1.60	1.54	1.51	1.48	1.44	1.40	1.35	1.29
120	2.75	2.35	2.13	1.99	1.90	1.82	1.77	1.72	1.68	1.65	1.60	1.55	1.48	1.45	1.41	1.37	1.32	1.26	1.19
∞	2.71	2.30	2.08	1.94	1.85	1.77	1.72	1.67	1.63	1.60	1.55	1.49	1.42	1.38	1.34	1.30	1.24	1.17	1.00

TABLE H.6—THE F DISTRIBUTION (UPPER PERCENTAGE POINTS) (Continued)

Percentage points of the F Distribution: upper 5% points

v_2 \ v_1	1	2	3	4	5	6	7	8	9	10	12	15	20	24	30	40	60	120	∞
1	161.4	199.5	215.7	224.6	230.2	234.0	236.8	238.9	240.5	241.9	243.9	245.9	248.0	249.1	250.1	251.1	252.2	253.3	254.3
2	18.51	19.00	19.16	19.25	19.30	19.33	19.35	19.37	19.38	19.40	19.41	19.43	19.45	19.45	19.46	19.47	19.48	19.49	19.50
3	10.13	9.55	9.28	9.12	9.01	8.94	8.89	8.85	8.81	8.79	8.74	8.70	8.66	8.64	8.62	8.59	8.57	8.55	8.53
4	7.71	6.94	6.59	6.39	6.26	6.16	6.09	6.04	6.00	5.96	5.91	5.86	5.80	5.77	5.75	5.72	5.69	5.66	5.63
5	6.61	5.79	5.41	5.19	5.05	4.95	4.88	4.82	4.77	4.74	4.68	4.62	4.56	4.53	4.50	4.46	4.43	4.40	4.36
6	5.99	5.14	4.76	4.53	4.39	4.28	4.21	4.15	4.10	4.06	4.00	3.94	3.87	3.84	3.81	3.77	3.74	3.70	3.67
7	5.59	4.74	4.35	4.12	3.97	3.87	3.79	3.73	3.68	3.64	3.57	3.51	3.44	3.41	3.38	3.34	3.30	3.27	3.23
8	5.32	4.46	4.07	3.84	3.69	3.58	3.50	3.44	3.39	3.35	3.28	3.22	3.15	3.12	3.08	3.04	3.01	2.97	2.93
9	5.12	4.26	3.86	3.63	3.48	3.37	3.29	3.23	3.18	3.14	3.07	3.01	2.94	2.90	2.86	2.83	2.79	2.75	2.71
10	4.96	4.10	3.71	3.48	3.33	3.22	3.14	3.07	3.02	2.98	2.91	2.85	2.77	2.74	2.70	2.66	2.62	2.58	2.54
11	4.84	3.98	3.59	3.36	3.20	3.09	3.01	2.95	2.90	2.85	2.79	2.72	2.65	2.61	2.57	2.53	2.49	2.45	2.40
12	4.75	3.89	3.49	3.26	3.11	3.00	2.91	2.85	2.80	2.75	2.69	2.62	2.54	2.51	2.47	2.43	2.38	2.34	2.30
13	4.67	3.81	3.41	3.18	3.03	2.92	2.83	2.77	2.71	2.67	2.60	2.53	2.46	2.42	2.38	2.34	2.30	2.25	2.21
14	4.60	3.74	3.34	3.11	2.96	2.85	2.76	2.70	2.65	2.60	2.53	2.46	2.39	2.35	2.31	2.27	2.22	2.18	2.13
15	4.54	3.68	3.29	3.06	2.90	2.79	2.71	2.64	2.59	2.54	2.48	2.40	2.33	2.29	2.25	2.20	2.16	2.11	2.07
16	4.49	3.63	3.24	3.01	2.85	2.74	2.66	2.59	2.54	2.49	2.42	2.35	2.28	2.24	2.19	2.15	2.11	2.06	2.01
17	4.45	3.59	3.20	2.96	2.81	2.70	2.61	2.55	2.49	2.45	2.38	2.31	2.23	2.19	2.15	2.10	2.06	2.01	1.96
18	4.41	3.55	3.16	2.93	2.77	2.66	2.58	2.51	2.46	2.41	2.34	2.27	2.19	2.15	2.11	2.06	2.02	1.97	1.92
19	4.38	3.52	3.13	2.90	2.74	2.63	2.54	2.48	2.42	2.38	2.31	2.23	2.16	2.11	2.07	2.03	1.98	1.93	1.88
20	4.35	3.49	3.10	2.87	2.71	2.60	2.51	2.45	2.39	2.35	2.28	2.20	2.12	2.08	2.04	1.99	1.95	1.90	1.84
21	4.32	3.47	3.07	2.84	2.68	2.57	2.49	2.42	2.37	2.32	2.25	2.18	2.10	2.05	2.01	1.96	1.92	1.87	1.81
22	4.30	3.44	3.05	2.82	2.66	2.55	2.46	2.40	2.34	2.30	2.23	2.15	2.07	2.03	1.98	1.94	1.89	1.84	1.78
23	4.28	3.42	3.03	2.80	2.64	2.53	2.44	2.37	2.32	2.27	2.20	2.13	2.05	2.01	1.96	1.91	1.86	1.81	1.76
24	4.26	3.40	3.01	2.78	2.62	2.51	2.42	2.36	2.30	2.25	2.18	2.11	2.03	1.98	1.94	1.89	1.84	1.79	1.73
25	4.24	3.39	2.99	2.76	2.60	2.49	2.40	2.34	2.28	2.24	2.16	2.09	2.01	1.96	1.92	1.87	1.82	1.77	1.71
26	4.23	3.37	2.98	2.74	2.59	2.47	2.39	2.32	2.27	2.22	2.15	2.07	1.99	1.95	1.90	1.85	1.80	1.75	1.69
27	4.21	3.35	2.96	2.73	2.57	2.46	2.37	2.31	2.25	2.20	2.13	2.06	1.97	1.93	1.88	1.84	1.79	1.73	1.67
28	4.20	3.34	2.95	2.71	2.56	2.45	2.36	2.29	2.24	2.19	2.12	2.04	1.96	1.91	1.87	1.82	1.77	1.71	1.65
29	4.18	3.33	2.93	2.70	2.55	2.43	2.35	2.28	2.22	2.18	2.10	2.03	1.94	1.90	1.85	1.81	1.75	1.70	1.64
30	4.17	3.32	2.92	2.69	2.53	2.42	2.33	2.27	2.21	2.16	2.09	2.01	1.93	1.89	1.84	1.79	1.74	1.68	1.62
40	4.08	3.23	2.84	2.61	2.45	2.34	2.25	2.18	2.12	2.08	2.00	1.92	1.84	1.79	1.74	1.69	1.64	1.58	1.51
60	4.00	3.15	2.76	2.53	2.37	2.25	2.17	2.10	2.04	1.99	1.92	1.84	1.75	1.70	1.65	1.59	1.53	1.47	1.39
120	3.92	3.07	2.68	2.45	2.29	2.17	2.09	2.02	1.96	1.91	1.83	1.75	1.66	1.61	1.55	1.50	1.43	1.35	1.25
∞	3.84	3.00	2.60	2.37	2.21	2.10	2.01	1.94	1.88	1.83	1.75	1.67	1.57	1.52	1.46	1.39	1.32	1.22	1.00

TABLE H.6—THE F DISTRIBUTION (UPPER PERCENTAGE POINTS) (Continued)

Percentage points of the F distribution: upper 1% points

v_2 \ v_1	1	2	3	4	5	6	7	8	9	10	12	15	20	24	30	40	60	120	∞
1	4052	4999.50	5403	5625	5764	5859	5928	5982	6022	6056	6106	6157	6209	6235	6261	6287	6313	6339	6366
2	98.50	99.00	99.17	99.25	99.30	99.33	99.36	99.37	99.39	99.40	99.42	99.43	99.45	99.46	99.47	99.47	99.48	99.49	99.50
3	34.12	30.82	29.46	28.71	28.24	27.91	27.67	27.49	27.35	27.23	27.05	26.87	26.69	26.60	26.50	26.41	26.32	26.22	26.13
4	21.20	18.00	16.69	15.98	15.52	15.21	14.98	14.80	14.66	14.55	14.37	14.20	14.02	13.93	13.84	13.75	13.65	13.56	13.46
5	16.26	13.27	12.06	11.39	10.97	10.67	10.46	10.29	10.16	10.05	9.89	9.72	9.55	9.47	9.38	9.29	9.20	9.11	9.02
6	13.75	10.92	9.78	9.15	8.75	8.47	8.26	8.10	7.98	7.87	7.72	7.56	7.40	7.31	7.23	7.14	7.06	6.97	6.88
7	12.25	9.55	8.45	7.85	7.46	7.19	6.99	6.84	6.72	6.62	6.47	6.31	6.16	6.07	5.99	5.91	5.82	5.74	5.65
8	11.26	8.65	7.59	7.01	6.63	6.37	6.18	6.03	5.91	5.81	5.67	5.52	5.36	5.28	5.20	5.12	5.03	4.95	4.86
9	10.56	8.02	6.99	6.42	6.06	5.80	5.61	5.47	5.35	5.26	5.11	4.96	4.81	4.73	4.65	4.57	4.48	4.40	4.31
10	10.04	7.56	6.55	5.99	5.64	5.39	5.20	5.06	4.94	4.85	4.71	4.56	4.41	4.33	4.25	4.17	4.08	4.00	3.91
11	9.65	7.21	6.22	5.67	5.32	5.07	4.89	4.74	4.63	4.54	4.40	4.25	4.10	4.02	3.94	3.86	3.78	3.69	3.60
12	9.33	6.93	5.95	5.41	5.06	4.82	4.64	4.50	4.39	4.30	4.16	4.01	3.86	3.78	3.70	3.62	3.54	3.45	3.36
13	9.07	6.70	5.74	5.21	4.86	4.62	4.44	4.30	4.19	4.10	3.96	3.82	3.66	3.59	3.51	3.43	3.34	3.25	3.17
14	8.86	6.51	5.56	5.04	4.69	4.46	4.28	4.14	4.03	3.94	3.80	3.66	3.51	3.43	3.35	3.27	3.18	3.09	3.00
15	8.68	6.36	5.42	4.89	4.56	4.32	4.14	4.00	3.89	3.80	3.67	3.52	3.37	3.29	3.21	3.13	3.05	2.96	2.87
16	8.53	6.23	5.29	4.77	4.44	4.20	4.03	3.89	3.78	3.69	3.55	3.41	3.26	3.18	3.10	3.02	2.93	2.84	2.75
17	8.40	6.11	5.18	4.67	4.34	4.10	3.93	3.79	3.68	3.59	3.46	3.31	3.16	3.08	3.00	2.92	2.83	2.75	2.65
18	8.29	6.01	5.09	4.58	4.25	4.01	3.84	3.71	3.60	3.51	3.37	3.23	3.08	3.00	2.92	2.84	2.75	2.66	2.57
19	8.18	5.93	5.01	4.50	4.17	3.94	3.77	3.63	3.52	3.43	3.30	3.15	3.00	2.92	2.84	2.76	2.67	2.58	2.49
20	8.10	5.85	4.94	4.43	4.10	3.87	3.70	3.56	3.46	3.37	3.23	3.09	2.94	2.86	2.78	2.69	2.61	2.52	2.42
21	8.02	5.78	4.87	4.37	4.04	3.81	3.64	3.51	3.40	3.31	3.17	3.03	2.88	2.80	2.72	2.64	2.55	2.46	2.36
22	7.95	5.72	4.82	4.31	3.99	3.76	3.59	3.45	3.35	3.26	3.12	2.98	2.83	2.75	2.67	2.58	2.50	2.40	2.31
23	7.88	5.66	4.76	4.26	3.94	3.71	3.54	3.41	3.30	3.21	3.07	2.93	2.78	2.70	2.62	2.54	2.45	2.35	2.26
24	7.82	5.61	4.72	4.22	3.90	3.67	3.50	3.36	3.26	3.17	3.03	2.89	2.74	2.66	2.58	2.49	2.40	2.31	2.21
25	7.77	5.57	4.68	4.18	3.85	3.63	3.46	3.32	3.22	3.13	2.99	2.85	2.70	2.62	2.54	2.45	2.36	2.27	2.17
26	7.72	5.53	4.64	4.14	3.82	3.59	3.42	3.29	3.18	3.09	2.96	2.81	2.66	2.58	2.50	2.42	2.33	2.23	2.13
27	7.68	5.49	4.60	4.11	3.78	3.56	3.39	3.26	3.15	3.06	2.93	2.78	2.63	2.55	2.47	2.38	2.29	2.20	2.10
28	7.64	5.45	4.57	4.07	3.75	3.53	3.36	3.23	3.12	3.03	2.90	2.75	2.60	2.52	2.44	2.35	2.26	2.17	2.06
29	7.60	5.42	4.54	4.04	3.73	3.50	3.33	3.20	3.09	3.00	2.87	2.73	2.57	2.49	2.41	2.33	2.23	2.14	2.03
30	7.56	5.39	4.51	4.02	3.70	3.47	3.30	3.17	3.07	2.98	2.84	2.70	2.55	2.47	2.39	2.30	2.21	2.11	2.01
40	7.31	5.18	4.31	3.83	3.51	3.29	3.12	2.99	2.89	2.80	2.66	2.52	2.37	2.29	2.20	2.11	2.03	1.92	1.80
60	7.08	4.98	4.13	3.65	3.34	3.12	2.95	2.82	2.72	2.63	2.50	2.35	2.20	2.12	2.03	1.94	1.84	1.73	1.60
120	6.85	4.79	3.95	3.48	3.17	2.96	2.79	2.66	2.56	2.47	2.34	2.19	2.03	1.95	1.86	1.76	1.66	1.53	1.38
∞	6.63	4.61	3.78	3.32	3.02	2.80	2.64	2.51	2.41	2.32	2.18	2.04	1.88	1.79	1.59	1.59	1.47	1.32	1.00

TABLE H.6—THE F DISTRIBUTION (UPPER PERCENTAGE POINTS) (Continued)

Percentage points of the F distribution: upper 0.1% points

v_2 \ v_1	1	2	3	4	5	6	7	8	9	10	12	15	20	24	30	40	60	120	∞
1	4053*	5000*	5404*	5625*	5764*	5859*	5929*	5981*	6023*	6056*	6107*	6158*	6209*	6235*	6261*	6287*	6313*	6340*	6366*
2	998.5	999.0	999.2	999.2	999.3	999.3	999.4	999.4	999.4	999.4	999.4	999.4	999.4	999.5	999.5	999.5	999.5	999.5	999.5
3	167.0	148.5	141.1	137.1	134.6	132.8	131.6	130.6	129.9	129.2	128.3	127.4	126.4	125.9	125.4	125.0	124.5	124.0	123.5
4	74.14	61.25	56.18	53.44	51.71	50.53	49.66	49.00	48.47	48.05	47.41	46.76	46.10	45.77	45.43	45.09	44.75	44.40	44.05
5	47.18	37.12	33.20	31.09	29.75	28.84	28.16	27.64	27.24	26.92	26.42	25.91	25.39	25.14	24.87	24.60	24.33	24.06	23.79
6	35.51	27.00	23.70	21.92	20.81	20.03	19.46	19.03	18.69	18.41	17.99	17.56	17.12	16.89	16.67	16.44	16.21	15.99	15.75
7	29.25	21.69	18.77	17.19	16.21	15.52	15.02	14.63	14.33	14.08	13.71	13.32	12.93	12.73	12.53	12.33	12.12	11.91	11.70
8	25.42	18.49	15.83	14.39	13.49	12.86	12.40	12.04	11.77	11.54	11.19	10.84	10.48	10.30	10.11	9.92	9.73	9.53	9.33
9	22.86	16.39	13.90	12.56	11.71	11.13	10.70	10.37	10.11	9.89	9.57	9.24	8.90	8.72	8.55	8.37	8.19	8.00	7.81
10	21.04	14.91	12.55	11.28	10.48	9.92	9.52	9.20	8.96	8.75	8.45	8.13	7.80	7.64	7.47	7.30	7.12	6.94	6.76
11	19.69	13.81	11.56	10.35	9.58	9.05	8.66	8.35	8.12	7.92	7.63	7.32	7.01	6.85	6.68	6.52	6.35	6.17	6.00
12	18.64	12.97	10.80	9.63	8.89	8.38	8.00	7.71	7.48	7.29	7.00	6.71	6.40	6.25	6.09	5.93	5.76	5.59	5.42
13	17.81	12.31	10.21	9.07	8.35	7.86	7.49	7.21	6.98	6.80	6.52	6.23	5.93	5.78	5.63	5.47	5.30	5.14	4.97
14	17.14	11.78	9.73	8.62	7.92	7.43	7.08	6.80	6.58	6.40	6.13	5.85	5.56	5.41	5.25	5.10	4.94	4.77	4.60
15	16.59	11.34	9.34	8.25	7.57	7.09	6.74	6.47	6.26	6.08	5.81	5.54	5.25	5.10	4.95	4.80	4.64	4.47	4.31
16	16.12	10.97	9.00	7.94	7.27	6.81	6.46	6.19	5.98	5.81	5.55	5.27	4.99	4.85	4.70	4.54	4.39	4.23	4.06
17	15.72	10.66	8.73	7.68	7.02	6.56	6.22	5.96	5.75	5.58	5.32	5.05	4.78	4.63	4.48	4.33	4.18	4.02	3.85
18	15.38	10.39	8.49	7.46	6.81	6.35	6.02	5.76	5.56	5.39	5.13	4.87	4.59	4.45	4.30	4.15	4.00	3.84	3.67
19	15.08	10.16	8.28	7.26	6.62	6.18	5.85	5.59	5.39	5.22	4.97	4.70	4.43	4.29	4.14	3.99	3.84	3.68	3.51
20	14.82	9.95	8.10	7.10	6.46	6.02	5.69	5.44	5.24	5.08	4.82	4.56	4.29	4.15	4.00	3.86	3.70	3.54	3.38
21	14.59	9.77	7.94	6.95	6.32	5.88	5.56	5.31	5.11	4.95	4.70	4.44	4.17	4.03	3.88	3.74	3.58	3.42	3.26
22	14.38	9.61	7.80	6.81	6.19	5.76	5.44	5.19	4.99	4.83	4.58	4.33	4.06	3.92	3.78	3.63	3.48	3.32	3.15
23	14.19	9.47	7.67	6.69	6.08	5.65	5.33	5.09	4.89	4.73	4.48	4.23	3.96	3.82	3.68	3.53	3.38	3.22	3.05
24	14.03	9.34	7.55	6.59	5.98	5.55	5.23	4.99	4.80	4.64	4.39	4.14	3.87	3.74	3.59	3.45	3.29	3.14	2.97
25	13.88	9.22	7.45	6.49	5.88	5.46	5.15	4.91	4.71	4.56	4.31	4.06	3.79	3.66	3.52	3.37	3.22	3.06	2.89
26	13.74	9.12	7.36	6.41	5.80	5.38	5.07	4.83	4.64	4.48	4.24	3.99	3.72	3.59	3.44	3.30	3.15	2.99	2.82
27	13.61	9.02	7.27	6.33	5.73	5.31	5.00	4.76	4.57	4.41	4.17	3.92	3.66	3.52	3.38	3.23	3.08	2.92	2.75
28	13.50	8.93	7.19	6.25	5.66	5.24	4.93	4.69	4.50	4.35	4.11	3.86	3.60	3.46	3.32	3.18	3.02	2.86	2.69
29	13.39	8.85	7.12	6.19	5.59	5.18	4.87	4.64	4.45	4.29	4.05	3.80	3.54	3.41	3.27	3.12	2.97	2.81	2.64
30	13.29	8.77	7.05	6.12	5.53	5.12	4.82	4.58	4.39	4.24	4.00	3.75	3.49	3.36	3.22	3.07	2.92	2.76	2.59
40	12.61	8.25	6.60	5.70	5.13	4.73	4.44	4.21	4.02	3.87	3.64	3.40	3.15	3.01	2.87	2.73	2.57	2.41	2.23
60	11.97	7.76	6.17	5.31	4.76	4.37	4.09	3.87	3.69	3.54	3.31	3.08	2.83	2.69	2.55	2.41	2.25	2.08	1.89
120	11.38	7.32	5.79	4.95	4.42	4.04	3.77	3.55	3.38	3.24	3.02	2.78	2.53	2.40	2.26	2.11	1.95	1.76	1.54
∞	10.83	6.91	5.42	4.62	4.10	3.74	3.47	3.27	3.10	2.96	2.74	2.51	2.27	2.13	1.99	1.84	1.66	1.45	1.00

*Multiply these entries by 100.

TABLE H.7 – APPROPRIATE SIZES OF SIMPLE RANDOM SAMPLES FOR SPECIFIC PERMISSIBLE ERRORS EXPRESSED AS ABSOLUTE PROPORTIONS WHEN THE TRUE PROPORTION IN THE POPULATION IS 0.50 AND THE CONFIDENCE LEVEL IS 90 PERCENT

POPULATION SIZE	SAMPLE SIZE FOR PERMISSIBLE ERROR (PROPORTION)				
	0.05	0.04	0.03	0.02	0.01
100	73	81	88	94	99
200	115	136	158	179	194
300	142	175	214	255	287
400	161	206	261	323	378
500	176	229	300	386	466
600	186	248	334	443	551
700	195	264	362	495	634
800	202	277	388	543	715
900	208	288	410	587	794
1,000	213	297	429	628	871
2,000	238	349	546	916	1,544
3,000	248	371	601	1,082	2,078
4,000	253	382	633	1,189	2,514
5,000	257	390	653	1,264	2,875
6,000	259	395	668	1,319	3,180
7,000	261	399	679	1,362	3,440
8,000	262	402	687	1,396	3,665
9,000	263	404	694	1,424	3,862
10,000	263	406	699	1,447	4,035
15,000	266	411	716	1,520	4,662
20,000	267	414	724	1,559	5,055
25,000	268	416	730	1,584	5,324
30,000	268	417	733	1,601	5,520
40,000	269	418	738	1,623	5,786
50,000	269	419	741	1,636	5,959
75,000	270	420	744	1,654	6,205
100,000	270	421	746	1,663	6,336
500,000	270	422	751	1,686	6,675
1,000,000	271	423	751	1,688	6,720
2,000,000	271	423	751	1,690	6,742

TABLE H.7 – APPROPRIATE SIZES OF SIMPLE RANDOM SAMPLES FOR SPECIFIC PERMISSIBLE ERRORS EXPRESSED AS ABSOLUTE PROPORTIONS WHEN THE TRUE PROPORTION IN THE POPULATION IS 0.50 AND THE CONFIDENCE LEVEL IS 95 PERCENT

POPULATION SIZE	SAMPLE SIZE FOR PERMISSIBLE ERROR (PROPORTION)				
	0.05	0.04	0.03	0.02	0.01
100	79	86	91	96	99
200	132	150	168	185	196
300	168	200	234	267	291
400	196	240	291	343	384
500	217	273	340	414	475
600	234	300	384	480	565
700	248	323	423	542	652
800	260	343	457	600	738
900	269	360	488	655	823
1,000	278	375	516	706	906
2,000	322	462	696	1,091	1,655
3,000	341	500	787	1,334	2,286
4,000	350	522	842	1,500	2,824
5,000	357	536	879	1,622	3,288
6,000	361	546	906	1,715	3,693
7,000	364	553	926	1,788	4,049
8,000	367	558	942	1,847	4,364
9,000	368	563	954	1,895	4,646
10,000	370	566	964	1,936	4,899
15,000	375	577	996	2,070	5,855
20,000	377	583	1,013	2,144	6,488
25,000	378	586	1,023	2,191	6,938
30,000	379	588	1,030	2,223	7,275
40,000	381	591	1,039	2,265	7,745
50,000	381	593	1,045	2,291	8,056
75,000	382	595	1,052	2,327	8,514
100,000	383	597	1,056	2,345	8,762
500,000	384	600	1,065	2,390	9,423
1,000,000	384	600	1,066	2,395	9,513
2,000,000	384	600	1,067	2,398	9,558

TABLE H.7—APPROPRIATE SIZES OF SIMPLE RANDOM SAMPLES FOR SPECIFIC PERMISSIBLE ERRORS EXPRESSED AS ABSOLUTE PROPORTIONS WHEN THE TRUE PROPORTION IN THE POPULATION IS 0.50 AND THE CONFIDENCE LEVEL IS 98 PERCENT

POPULATION SIZE	SAMPLE SIZE FOR PERMISSIBLE ERROR (PROPORTION)				
	0.05	0.04	0.03	0.02	0.01
100	84	89	94	97	99
200	146	162	177	189	197
300	193	221	250	276	293
400	230	272	316	358	389
500	260	314	375	436	482
600	284	351	429	510	575
700	305	383	478	580	666
800	323	411	522	647	755
900	338	436	563	711	844
1,000	351	458	600	772	931
2,000	426	594	858	1,257	1,742
3,000	458	660	1,001	1,590	2,455
4,000	477	698	1,092	1,832	3,087
5,000	488	723	1,156	2,017	3,650
6,000	496	741	1,202	2,163	4,156
7,000	502	754	1,237	2,280	4,613
8,000	507	765	1,265	2,377	5,027
9,000	510	773	1,288	2,458	5,404
10,000	513	779	1,307	2,527	5,749
15,000	522	800	1,366	2,759	7,112
20,000	527	811	1,398	2,892	8,069
25,000	530	818	1,418	2,979	8,777
30,000	531	822	1,431	3,039	9,323
40,000	534	828	1,448	3,118	10,108
50,000	535	831	1,459	3,167	10,646
75,000	537	836	1,473	3,236	11,459
100,000	538	838	1,481	3,271	11,914
500,000	540	844	1,498	3,359	13,169
1,000,000	541	845	1,501	3,370	13,345
2,000,000	541	845	1,502	3,376	13,435

TABLE H.7–APPROPRIATE SIZES OF SIMPLE RANDOM SAMPLES FOR SPECIFIC PERMISSIBLE ERRORS EXPRESSED AS ABSOLUTE PROPORTIONS WHEN THE TRUE PROPORTION IN THE POPULATION IS 0.50 AND THE CONFIDENCE LEVEL IS 99 PERCENT

POPULATION SIZE	SAMPLE SIZE FOR PERMISSIBLE ERROR (PROPORTION)				
	0.05	0.04	0.03	0.02	0.01
100	87	91	95	98	99
200	154	168	180	191	198
300	207	233	258	280	295
400	250	289	329	365	391
500	285	337	393	446	485
600	315	380	453	524	579
700	341	418	507	599	672
800	363	452	558	671	763
900	382	482	605	740	854
1,000	399	509	648	806	943
2,000	498	683	959	1,349	1,785
3,000	543	771	1,142	1,741	2,541
4,000	569	823	1,262	2,036	3,223
5,000	586	859	1,347	2,267	3,842
6,000	597	884	1,410	2,452	4,406
7,000	606	903	1,459	2,604	4,923
8,000	613	918	1,498	2,731	5,397
9,000	618	930	1,530	2,839	5,835
10,000	622	939	1,556	2,932	6,239
15,000	635	970	1,642	3,249	7,877
20,000	642	986	1,688	3,435	9,068
25,000	646	996	1,717	3,557	9,972
30,000	649	1,002	1,737	3,644	10,682
40,000	653	1,011	1,762	3,758	11,726
50,000	655	1,016	1,778	3,830	12,456
75,000	658	1,023	1,799	3,930	13,585
100,000	659	1,026	1,810	3,982	14,229
500,000	663	1,035	1,837	4,113	16,057
1,000,000	663	1,036	1,840	4,130	16,319
2,000,000	663	1,036	1,842	4,139	16,453

INDEX

A

Absolute value, 41, 167
Analysis of variance, 161 – 162
Analysis unit, 5, 12
Area sampling (*see* Sampling area)
Arithmetic mean, 6, 27, 28, 31, 33, 34, 40, 41, 42, 43, 47, 48, 55, 56, 101
Attribute, 5, 12
Average deviation, 6, 40 – 42, 46, 47, 48, 49

B

Bar chart, 24
Bar diagrams, 23
Bias, 116, 122
    nonresponse, 205 – 206
Bimodal, 31
Biserial correlation (*see* Correlation, biserial)

C

Centile, 51
Central-limit theorem, 112, 124, 126
Central tendency, 28, 34, 40
Characteristic of interest, 5, 12
Chi-square distribution (*see* Distribution, chi-square)
Chi-square test statistic (*see* Test statistic, chi-square)
Class frequency, 50
Class interval, 50
Cluster sampling, (*see* Sampling, cluster)
Coefficient of concordance (*see* Correlation, coefficient of concordance)
Coefficient of determination, 59, 60, 61, 72, 75
Coefficient of multiple determination, 86, 182
Common factor, 180
Confidence interval, 121, 123 – 140
    arithmetic mean, 128 – 130
    bivariate linear regression, 134 – 137
    proportion or percentage, 132 – 134
    total or aggregate, 130 – 132
    variance or standard deviation, 137 – 140
Confidence level, 123 – 140, 189
Confidence limits, 123 – 140, 189
Contingency coefficient, 93
Contingency table, 18, 167 – 169, 171
Continuous variable, 12, 14, 15
Control group, 150
Correlation, 101
    biserial, 92
    coefficient of concordance, 89 – 90

>   Kendall tau, 89
>   Linear, 58 – 63, 65, 68, 78 – 92
>   multiple, 86
>   partial, 87
>   phi coefficient, 93
>   point biserial, 92
>   Spearman rank, 88 – 89
>   test for significance of, 158 – 162
>   tetrachoric coefficient, 93

Correlation ratio, 78
Covariance, 60, 101
Critical region, 144 – 178
Cumulative proportion, 29
Cumulative proportion distribution, 18, 19, 22, 29, 30, 38, 50
Cumulative relative frequency, 50
Cumulative relative frequency distribution, 17
Curvilinearity, 81

D

Decile, 50, 51
Degrees of freedon, 121 – 122, 144 – 178
Delta mode, 31
DeMoivre-LaPlace distribution (*see* Distribution, normal)
Dependent variable, 59
Deviation
>   average, 6
>   standard, 6

Dichotomous, 92, 94
Discrete variable, 12, 14, 15
Discriminant analysis, 179, 180
Disproportional Allocation, 211
Distribution
>   chi-square, 93, 138, 144
>   DeMoivre-LaPlace (*see* normal)
>   F, 144
>   frequency, 17, 27, 52, 111, 113 – 116
>   Gaussian (*see* normal)
>   normal, 96, 101 – 111, 125 – 126
>   sampling, 111 – 121, 144
>   Student's t, 124 – 130, 144, 317

Double-entry table (*see* Contingency table)

E

Experimental design, 11
Experimental group, 150
Explained variation (*see* Variation, explained)

F

F distribution (*see* Distribution, F)
F test statistic (*see* Test statistic, F)
Factor analysis, 86, 180 – 181
Finite multiplier (*see* Finite population correction factor)
Finite population correction factor, 118, 119, 124, 129, 149, 164
First-order partial correlation, 87
Frequency, 17
Frequency distribution (*see* Distribution, frequency)
Frequency histogram (*see* Histogram)
Frequency polygon, 18, 19, 20

G

Gaussian distribution (*see* Distribution, normal)
Grouped data, 27, 29, 31

H

Harmonic mean, 27
Histogram, 18, 19, 21, 31, 32
Hypotheses testing, 141 – 143 (*see* Statistical hypotheses)

I

Incremental variation, 77
Independent variable, 59, 121
Inference, 6
Interquartile range, 36 – 40, 42, 49, 107
Interval scale (*see* Measurement scales, interval)

K

Kendall's coefficient of concordance (*see* Correlation, coefficient of concordance)
Kendall tau correlation (*see* Correlation, Kendall tau)
Kruskal-Wallis H Test (*see* Nonparametric techniques, Kruskal-Wallis H Test)

L

Level of confidence (*see* Confidence level)
Level of significance (α), 143 – 178
Levels of measurement (*see* Measurement scales)
Linear correlation (*see* Correlation, linear)
Linear regression (*see* Regression, linear)

M

Mann-Whitney U Test (*see* Nonparametric techniques, Mann-Whitney U Test)
Massive sample survey, 8
Matrix, 18
Mean (*see* Arithmetic mean)
Mean deviation (*see* Average deviation)
Meaningful zero point, 14
Measurement error, 71
Measurement scales
    interval, 12 – 15, 28, 34, 46, 52, 88
    nominal, 12 – 15, 28, 34, 52, 93, 94
    ordinal, 12 – 15, 52, 88, 93, 94
    ratio, 12 – 15, 28, 34, 43, 46, 52, 88, 94
Measures of association
    correlation
        biserial, 92
        coefficient of concordance, 89 – 90
        Kendall tau, 89
        linear, 58 – 63, 65, 68, 78 – 94
        multiple, 86
        partial, 87
        phi coefficient, 93
        point biserial, 92
        Spearman rank, 88
        tetrachoric coefficient, 93
    regression
        linear, 58 – 60, 63 – 85, 87 – 88
        multiple, 87
Measures of central tendency
    arithmetic mean (*see* Arithmetic mean)
    median (*see* Median)
    mode (*see* Mode)
Measures of dispersion (*see* Measures of variation)
Measures of variation
    average deviation, 40 – 42
    interquartile range, 36 – 40
    range, 36
    standard deviation, 43 – 46
    variance, 43, 44, 101
Median, 6, 27, 28 – 31, 33, 34, 37, 40, 50, 51, 101
Modal class, 31
Mode, 6, 27, 28, 31, 33, 34, 101
Multiple coefficient of determination (*see* Coefficient of multiple determination)
Multiple correlation (*see* Correlation, multiple)
Multiple regression (*see* Regression, multiple)
Multivariate techniques
    discriminant analysis 179, 180
    factor analysis 86, 180 – 181
    multiple correlation (*see* Correlation, multiple)
    multiple regression (*see* Regression, multiple)
    partial correlation (*see* Correlation, partial)
    stepwise regression (*see* Regression, stepwise)
Mutually exclusive, 13

N

Nonresponse bias, 6
Normal distribution (*see* Distribution, normal)
Nominal scale (*see* Measurement scales, nominal)
Nonrejection region (*see* Critical region)
Nonresponse to surveys, 196, 202
Nonparametric techniques, 182
    Kruskal-Wallis H Test, 183
    Mann-Whitney U Test, 183
    Sign Test, 183
    Wilcoxon Rank-Sum Test, 183
Null hypothesis, 141 − 178

O

Ogive, 19, 38
One-tailed, 105
Optimum allocation, 214
Ordinal scale (*see* Measurement scales, ordinal)

P

Parameter, 6, 100 − 101
Partial correlation
    First-order partial, 87
    Second-order partial, 87
Pearson product-moment correlation coefficient (*see* Correlation)
Percentage (*see* Proportion)
Percentile, 50 − 52, 107
Phi coefficient (*see* Correlation, phi coefficient)
Pie charts, 23
Pie diagram, 24
Point biserial correlation (*see* Correlation, point biserial)
Pooled estimate for the standard deviation, 149 − 152
Population, 5
Precision, 189 − 190, 205, 206, 218, 241
Prediction equation, 59
Primary sampling area, 10
Primary sampling unit, 10
Population parameter (*see* Parameter)
Probability sampling (*see* Sampling, probability)
Proportion, 4, 52 − 54, 101, 117, 132 − 134
Proportional allocation, 210 − 211
Proportion distribution, 29

Q

Quadratic mean, 27
Quartile, 36, 37, 50, 51, 52
Quartile point (*see* Quartile)
Quota sampling (*see* Sampling, quota)

R

Random digits, 98
Random sample, 7
Range, 36, 40, 42, 49
Ratio estimate, 242
Ratio scale (*see* Measurement scales, ratio)
Raw data, 27
Raw score, 56, 57
Regression,
    linear, 58 – 60, 63 – 85, 87 – 88
    multiple, 87
    stepwise, 181, 182
    test for significance of, 158 – 162
Regression line, 59
Rejection region (*see* Critical region)
Relative frequency, 50, 52
Relative frequency distribution 18
Research hypotheses, 141 – 143, 158
Residual variation (*see* Variation, unexplained)

S

Sample, 5
Sample fraction, 119
Sample size adjustment, 204 – 208
Sample size determination
    effect of subgroups, 202 – 204
    when estimating a population mean, 196 – 201
    when estimating a population total, 201 – 202
    when estimating a proportion or percentage, 191 – 196
Sample statistic (*see* Statistic)
Sampling
    area, 10
    cluster, 7, 208, 235, 252
    combination, 253 – 273
    probability, 10
    quota, 9
    simple random, 7, 97, 100
    step or sequential, 197
    stratified random, 7, 9, 207, 208, 209, 234
    systematic, 7
    unrestricted random (*see* simple random)
Sampling distribution (*see* Distribution, sampling)
Sampling error (*see* Sampling variability)
Sampling fraction (*see* Sample fraction)
Sampling frame, 7, 99, 236
Sampling variability, 111 – 121, 123, 143, 146
Sampling variation (*see* Sampling variability)
Scales of measurement (*see* Measurement scales)
Scatter (*see* Measures of variation)
Second-order partial correlations, 87

Sign Test (*see* Nonparametric techniques, Sign Test)
Significance level (*see* Level of Significance)
Simple random sampling (*see* Sampling, simple random)
Skew, 34, 40
Skewness, 37, 39
Slope of a regression line, 71
Spearman rank correlation (*see* Correlation, Spearman rank)
Spearman rho (*see* Correlation, Spearman rank)
Standard deviation, 6, 43 – 46, 47, 48, 49, 54, 55, 56, 57, 101, 102, 111
Standard deviation of the sampling distribution (*see* Standard error of the mean)
Standard error
    for a proportion or percentage, 132 – 134, 163, 165
    for the mean in bivariate linear regression, 134 – 137
    in sample size determination, 188
    of the mean, 111 – 121, 123 – 130
    of the total, 130
Standard scores
    T-score, 56 – 57
    Z-score, 54 – 55, 102 – 111
Statistic, 6, 100 – 101
Statistical bias (*see* Bias)
Statistical hypotheses, 141 – 146, 158
    on a linear correlation or regression, 158 – 162
    on a single population mean, 146 – 148
    on a single population proportion, 162 – 166
    on analyzing survey sampling results, 169 – 178
    on two population means, 149 – 156
    on two population proportions, 166 – 169
    on two population standard deviations (variances), 156 – 158
Step or sequential sampling (*see* Sampling, step or sequential)
Stratified random sampling (*see* Sampling, stratified random)
Straw poll, 8
Student's t distribution (*see* Distribution, Student's t)
Summary measure, 6, 40, 54
Survey design, 10
Symmetry, 37, 39
Systematic sampling (*see* Sampling, systematic)

T

T-score (*see* Standard scores, T-score)
t distribution (*see* Distribution, Student's t)
t test statistic (*see* Test statistic, t)
Test statistic
    chi-square, 145, 167 – 178
    F, 145 – 158
    t, 145 – 148, 159 – 160
    Z, 145, 163 – 166
Tetrachoric coefficient (*see* Correlation, tetrachoric coefficient)
Tilde, 29
Total range (*see* Range)
Total variation (*see* Variation, total)
Two-Tailed, 104, 106
Type I error, 146
Type II error, 146

U

Unbiased estimate
    of the population mean, 116
    of the population standard deviation, 122
    of the population variance, 122
Unexplained variation (*see* Variation, unexplained)
Unimodal, 31
Unique factor, 180
Unit of analysis (*see* Analysis unit)
Universe, 5
Unrestricted random sampling (*see* Sampling, simple random)

V

Variable, 5, 12, 17
Variance, 43, 44, 101
Variation
    explained, 75, 78
    residual (*see* unexplained)
    sampling (*see* Sampling variability)
    total, 75 – 78
    unexplained, 75 – 78

W

Wilcoxon Rank-Sum Test (*see* Nonparametric techniques, Wilcoxon Rank-Sum Test)

Y

Y-intercept, 64, 71

Z

Z-score (*see* Standard scores, Z-score)
Z test statistic (*see* Test statistic, Z)